神無
KANNA

著 桐嶋たける

Translation – Christine Schilling
Adaptation – Brynne Chandler
Production Assistant – Suzy Wells
Editorial Assistant – Mallory Reaves
Lettering & Retouch – James Dashiell
Production Manager – James Dashiell
Editor – Brynne Chandler

A Go! Comi manga

Published by Go! Media Entertainment, LLC

Kanna Volume 4
© TAKERU KIRISHIMA 2005
First published in 2005 by Media Works Inc., Tokyo, Japan.
English translation rights arranged with Media Works Inc.

Visit us online at www.gocomi.com
e-mail: info@gocomi.com

ISBN 978-1-933617-67-1

First printed in June 2008

1 2 3 4 5 6 7 8 9

Manufactured in the United States of America.

STORY AND ART BY

TAKERU KIRISHIMA

Volume 4

go!comi

Concerning Honorifics

At Go! Comi, we do our best to ensure that our translations read seamlessly in English while respecting the original Japanese language and culture. To this end, the original honorifics (the suffixes found at the end of characters' names) remain intact. In Japan, where politeness and formality are more integrated into every aspect of the language, honorifics give a better understanding of character relationships. They can be used to indicate both respect and affection. Whether a person addresses someone by first name or last name also indicates how close their relationship is.

Here are some of the honorifics you might encounter in reading this book:

-san: This is the most common and neutral of honorifics. The polite way to address someone you're not on close terms with is to use "-san." It's kind of like Mr. or Ms., except you can use "-san" with first names as easily as family names.

-chan: Used for friendly familiarity, mostly applied towards young girls. "-chan" also carries a connotation of cuteness with it, so it is frequently used with nick-names towards both boys and girls (such as "Na-chan" for "Natsu").

-kun: Like "-chan," it's an informal suffix for friends and classmates, only "-kun" is usually associated with boys. It can also be used in a professional environment by someone addressing a subordinate.

-sama: Indicates a great deal of respect or admiration.

Sempai: In school, "sempai" is used to refer to an upperclassman or club leader. It can also be used in the workplace by a new employee to address a mentor or staff member with seniority.

Sensei: Teachers, doctors, writers or any master of a trade are referred to as "sensei." When addressing a manga creator, the polite thing to do is attach "-sensei" to the manga-ka's name (as in Kirishima-sensei).

Onii: This is the more casual term for an older brother. Usually you'll see it with an honorific attached, such as "onii-chan."

Onee: The casual term for older sister, it's used like "onii" with honorifics.

[blank]: Not using an honorific when addressing someone indicates that the speaker has permission to speak intimately with the other person. This relationship is usually reserved for close friends and family.

Volume.

4

目
次

KANNA

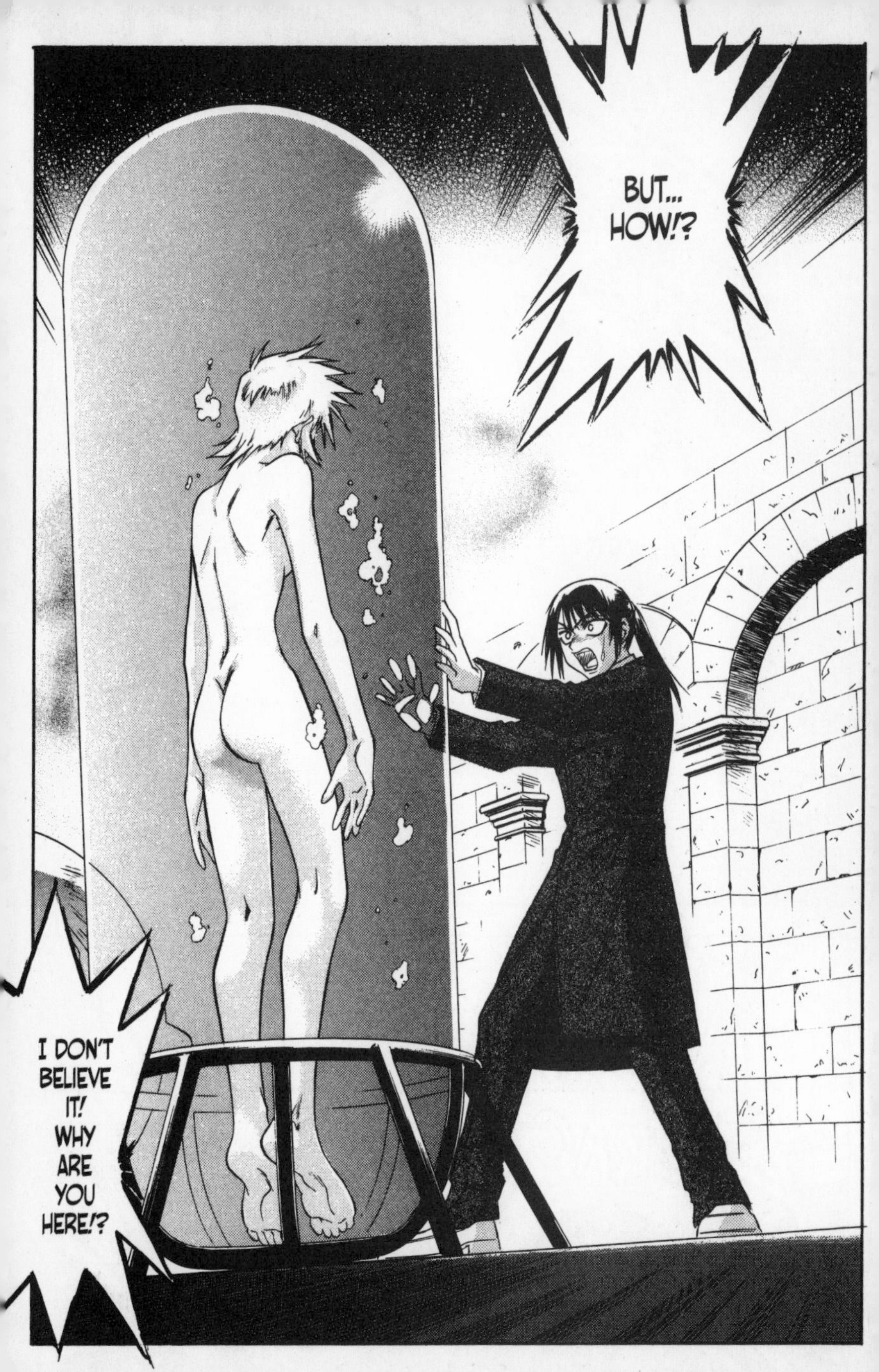
BUT... HOW!?
I DON'T BELIEVE IT! WHY ARE YOU HERE!?

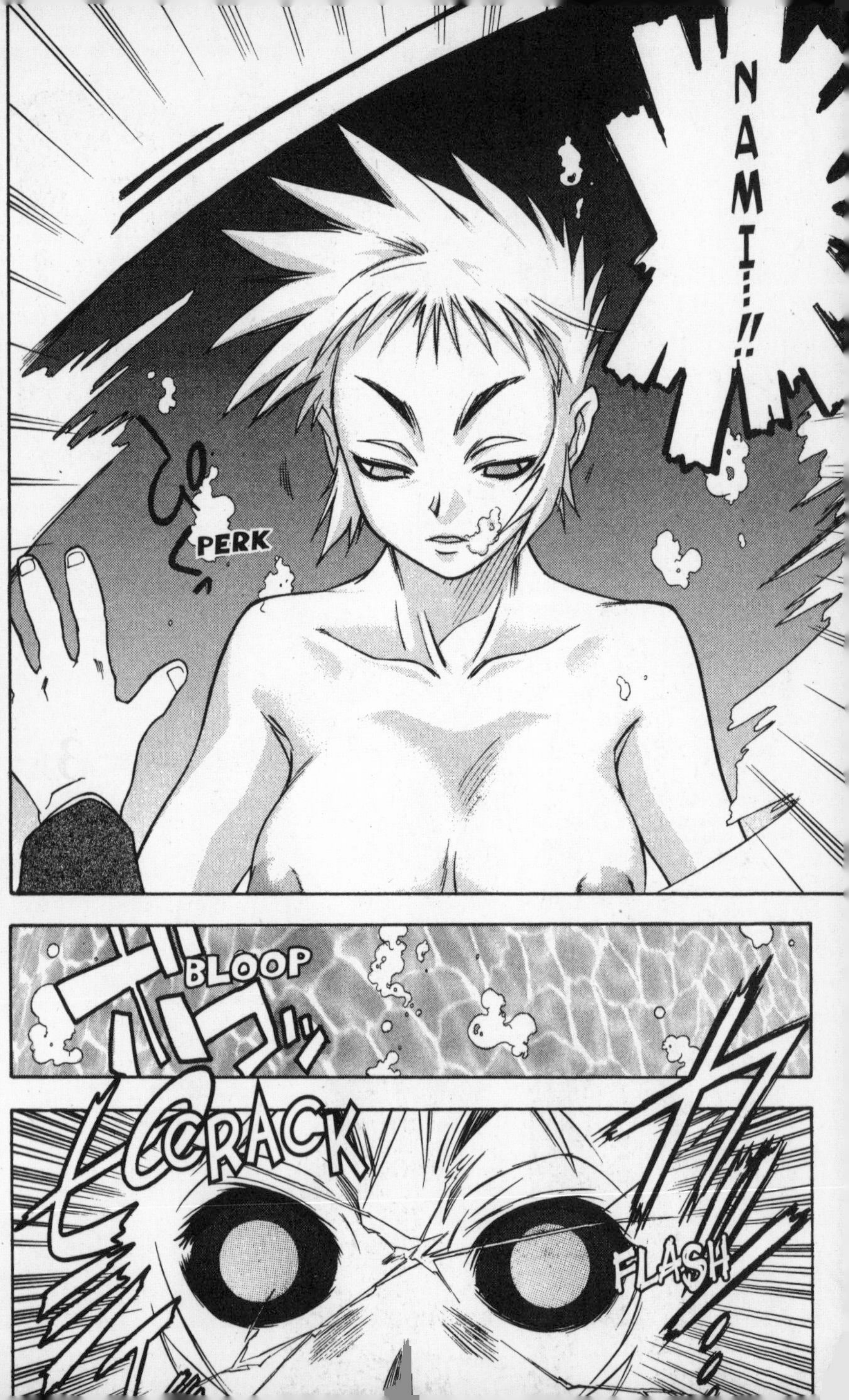
NAMI...!!
PERK
BLOOP
CRACK
FLASH

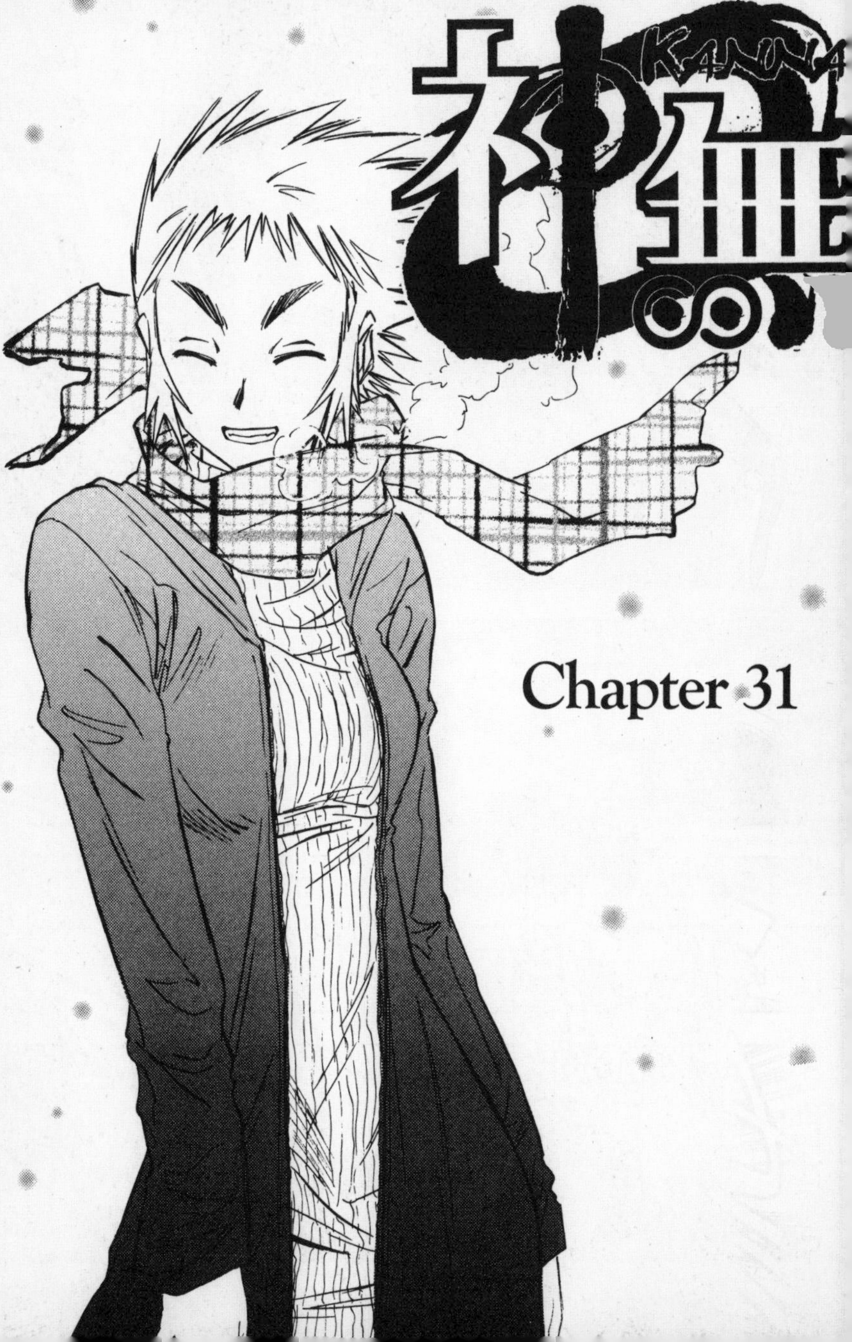
神無
KANNA

Chapter 31

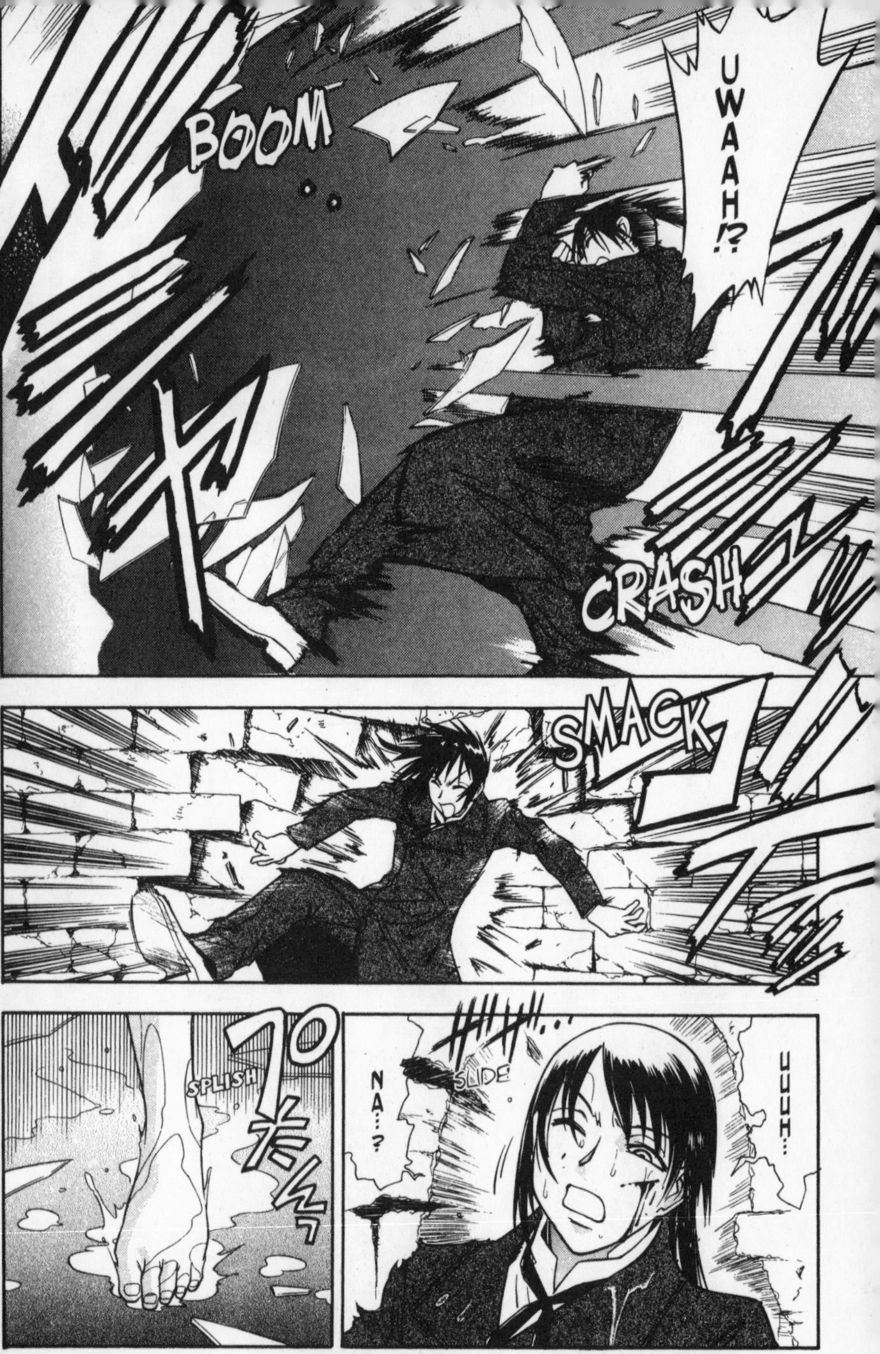
UWAAH!?
BOOM
CRASH
SMACK
UUUH...
SLIDE
NA...?
SPLISH

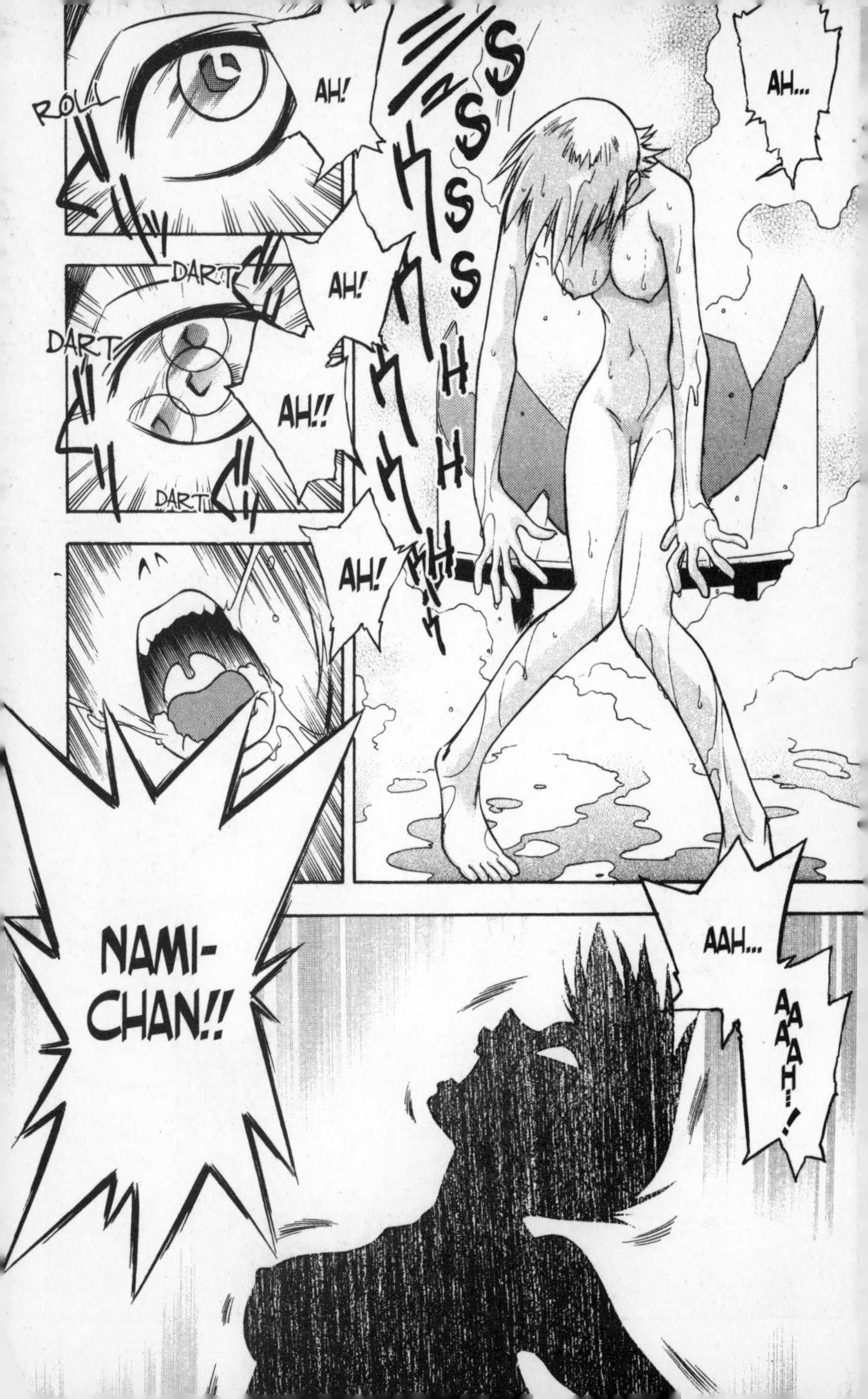
AH...
SSSSHHH
ROLL
AH!
DART
AH!
DART
AH!!
DART
AH!
AAH...
AAAAH!!
NAMI-
CHAN!!

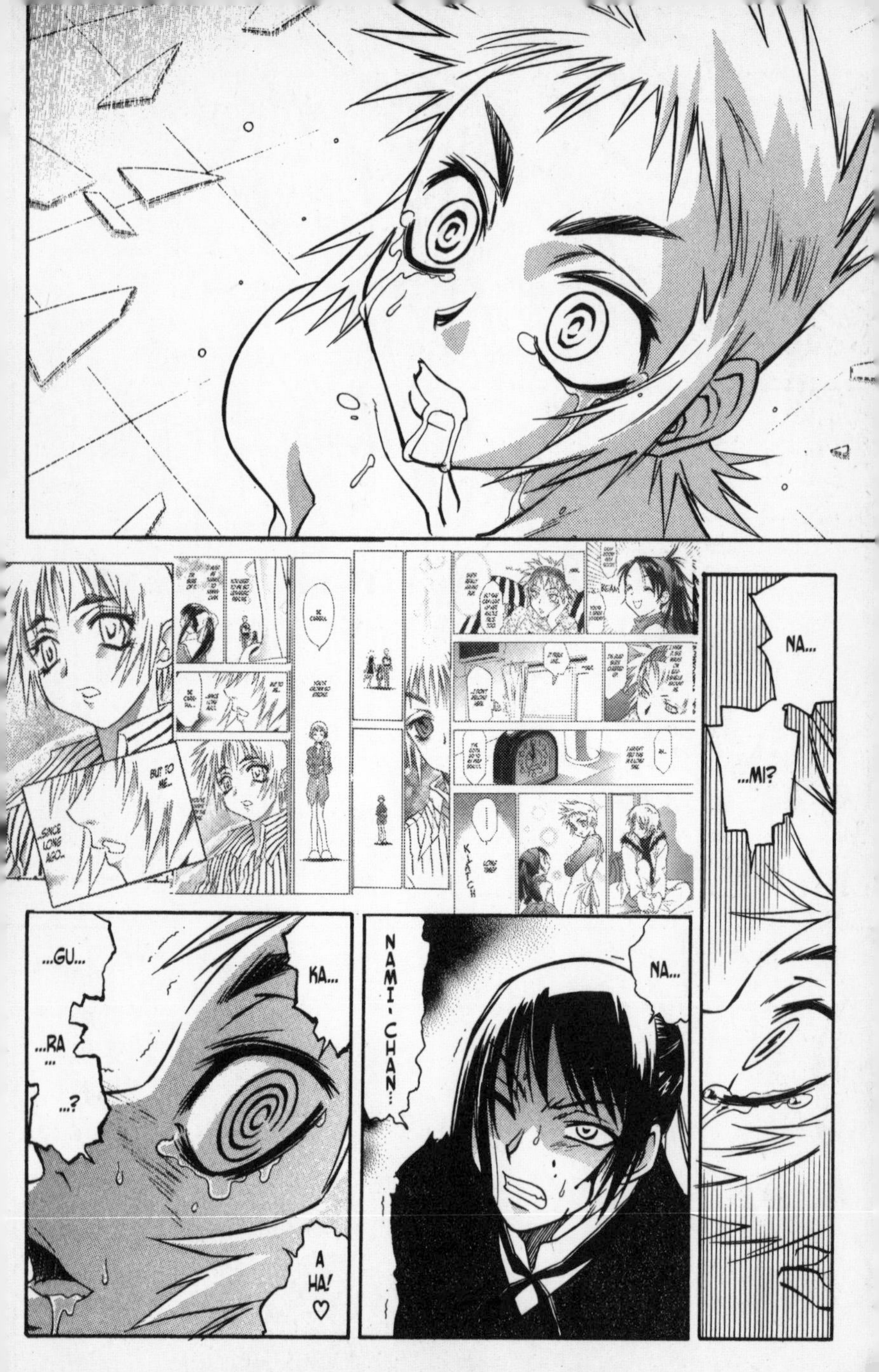
NA...
...MI?
BUT TO ME...
...SINCE LONG AGO...
NA...
NAMI-CHAN...
KA...
...GU...
...RA...
...?
A HA! ♥

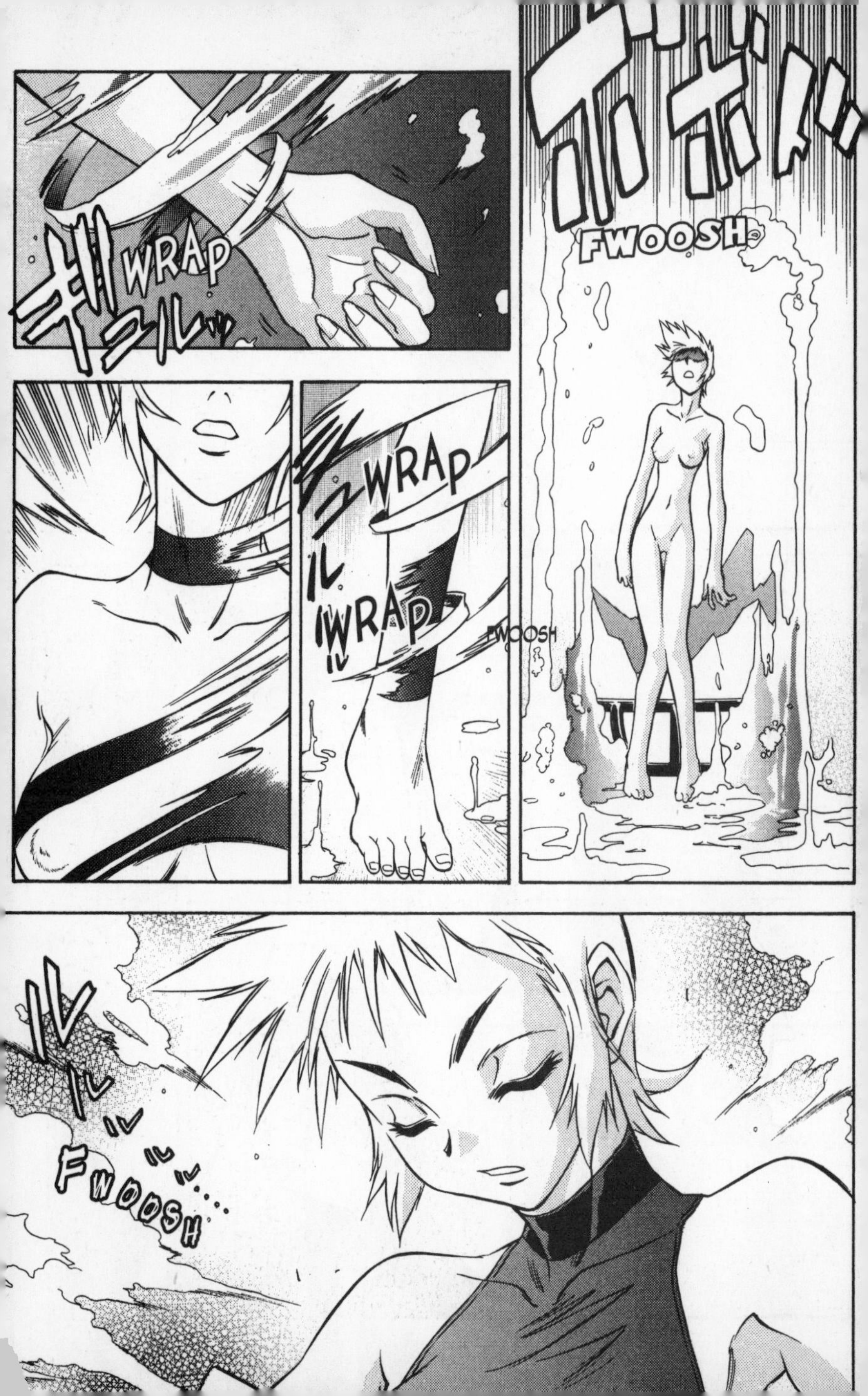
FWOOSH
FWOOSH
WRAP
WRAP
WRAP
FWOOSH

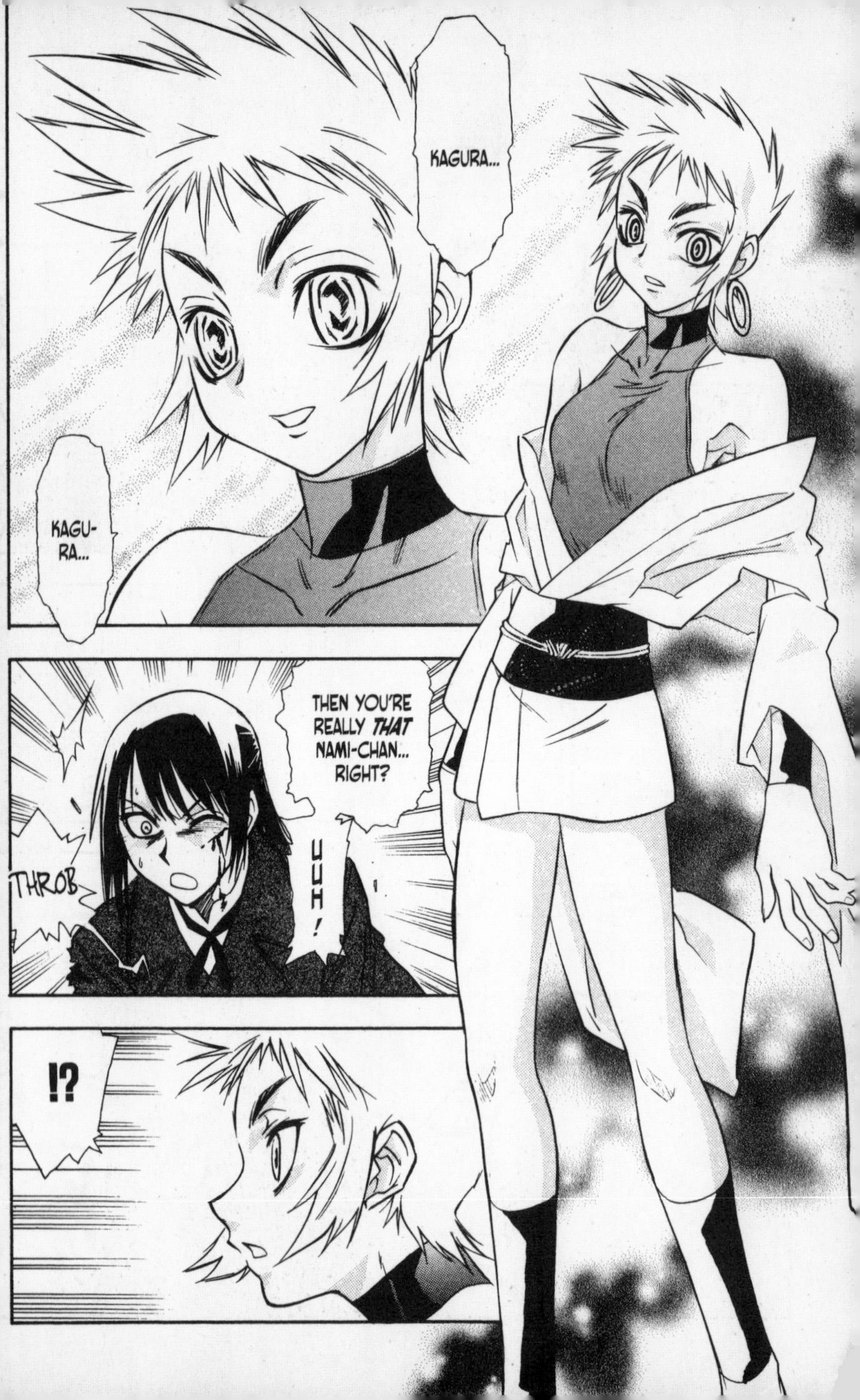
KAGURA...
KAGU-RA...
THEN YOU'RE REALLY *THAT* NAMI-CHAN... RIGHT?
UUH!
THROB
!?

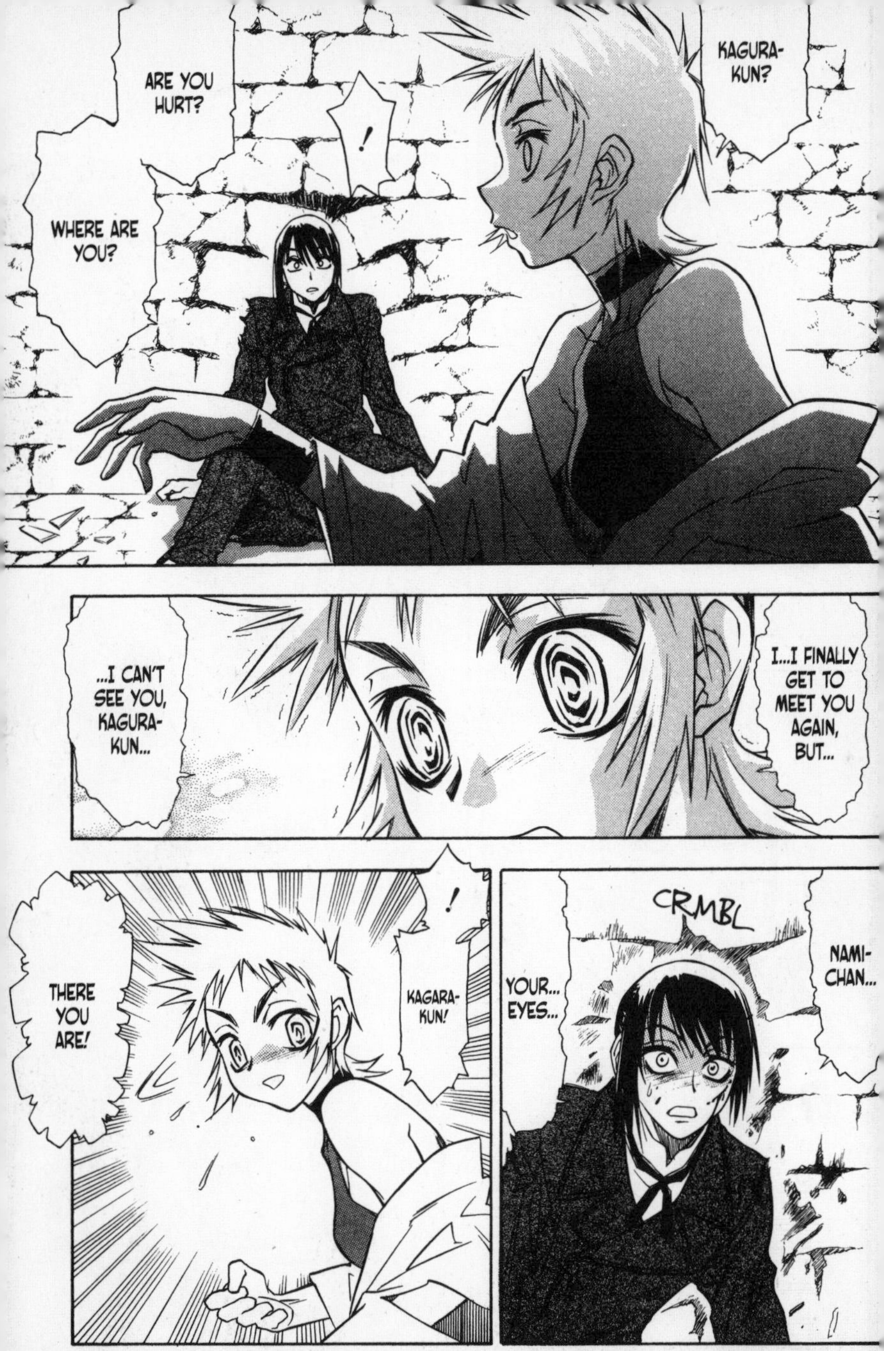

KAGURA-KUN?
ARE YOU HURT?
!
WHERE ARE YOU?
I...I FINALLY GET TO MEET YOU AGAIN, BUT...
...I CAN'T SEE YOU, KAGURA-KUN...
NAMI-CHAN...
CRMBL
YOUR... EYES...
!
KAGARA-KUN!
THERE YOU ARE!

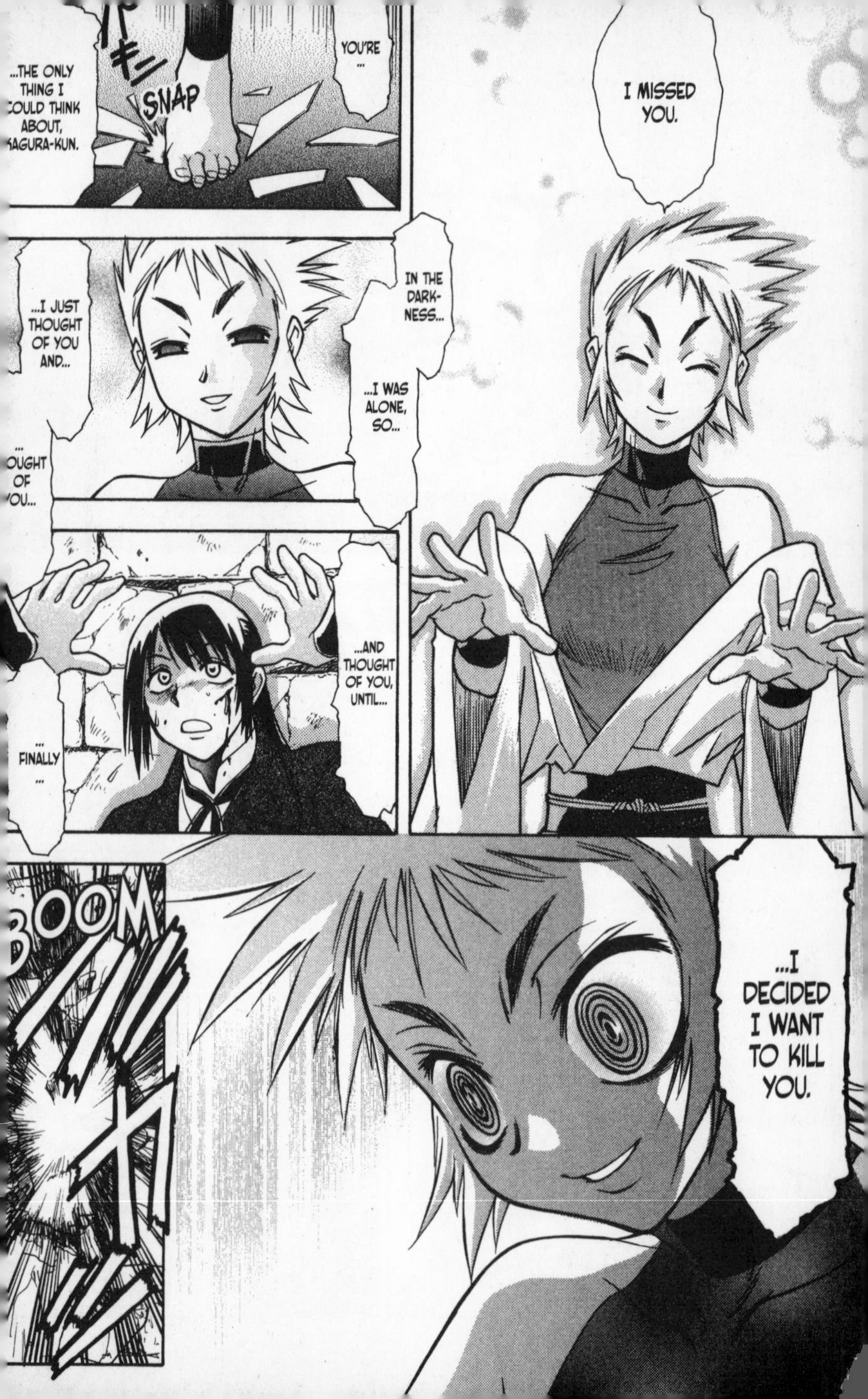
I MISSED YOU.
YOU'RE ...
SNAP
...THE ONLY THING I COULD THINK ABOUT, KAGURA-KUN.
IN THE DARK-NESS...
...I WAS ALONE, SO...
...I JUST THOUGHT OF YOU AND...
... OUGHT OF YOU...
...AND THOUGHT OF YOU, UNTIL...
... FINALLY ...
...I DECIDED I WANT TO KILL YOU.
BOOM

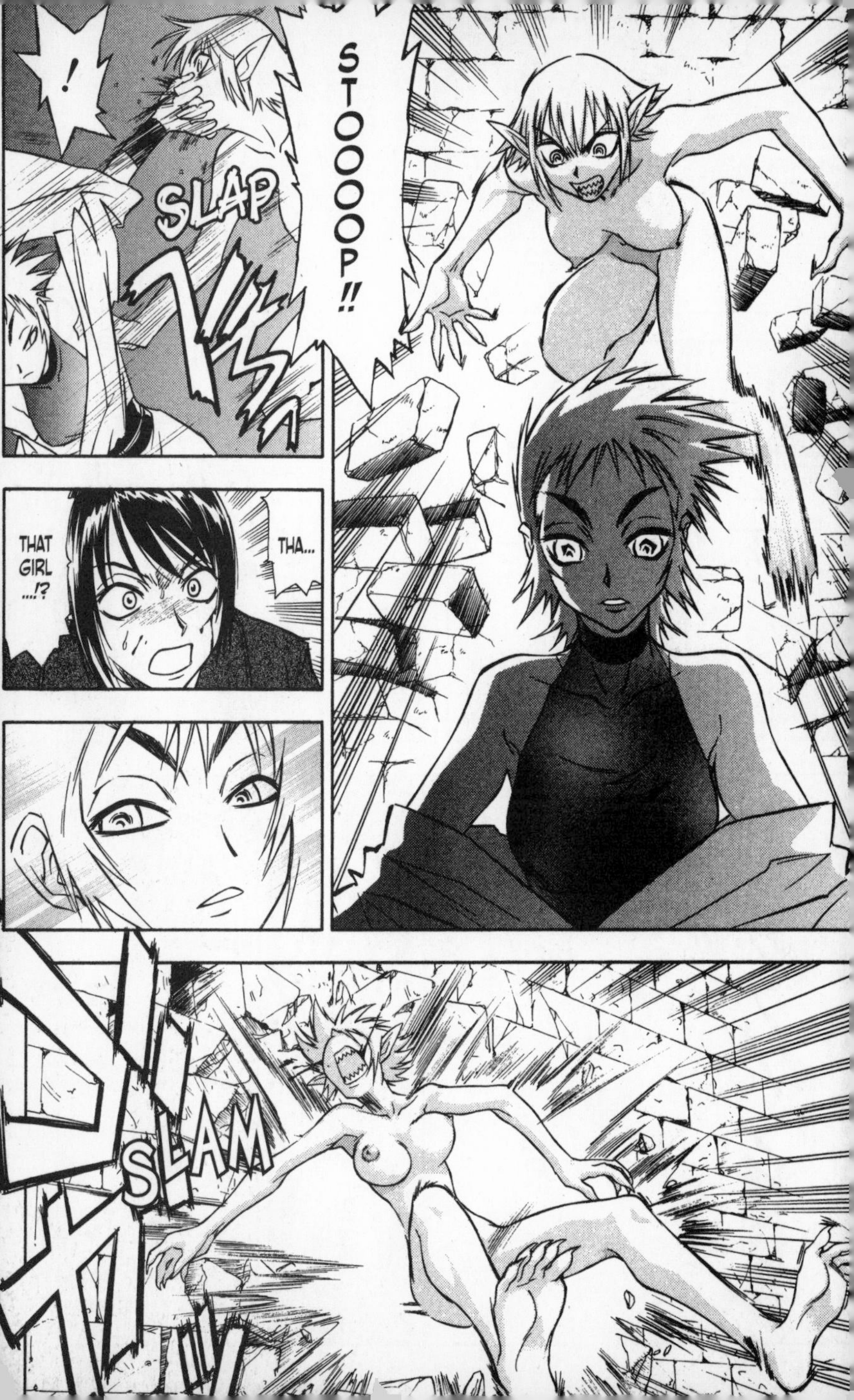
STOOOOP!!
!
SLAP
THA...
THAT GIRL ...!?
SLAM

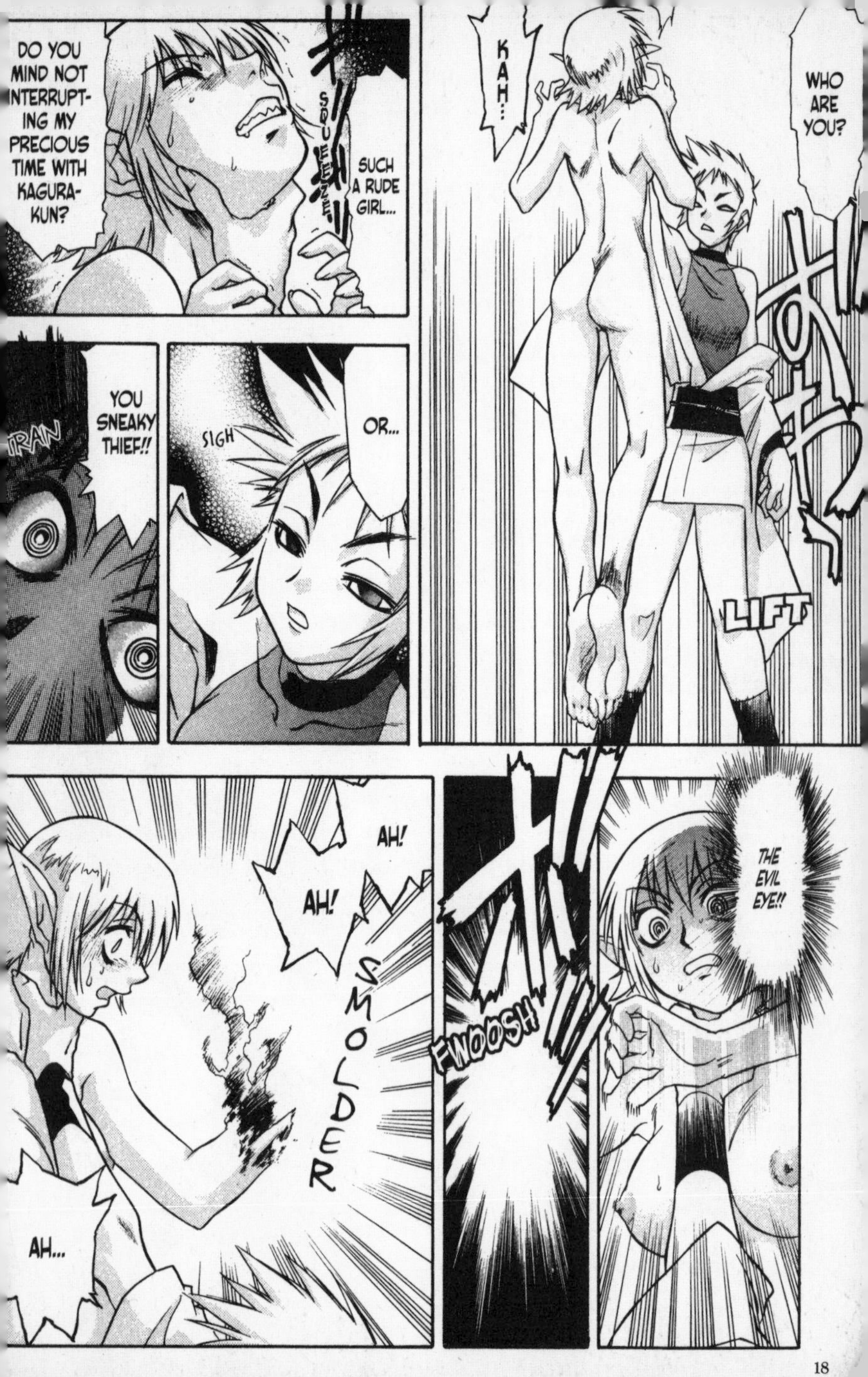
WHO ARE YOU?
KAH...
LIFT
SUCH A RUDE GIRL...
SQUEEZE
DO YOU MIND NOT INTERRUPTING MY PRECIOUS TIME WITH KAGURA-KUN?
OR...
SIGH
YOU SNEAKY THIEF!!
TRAN
THE EVIL EYE!!
FWOOSH
AH!
AH!
SMOLDER
AH...

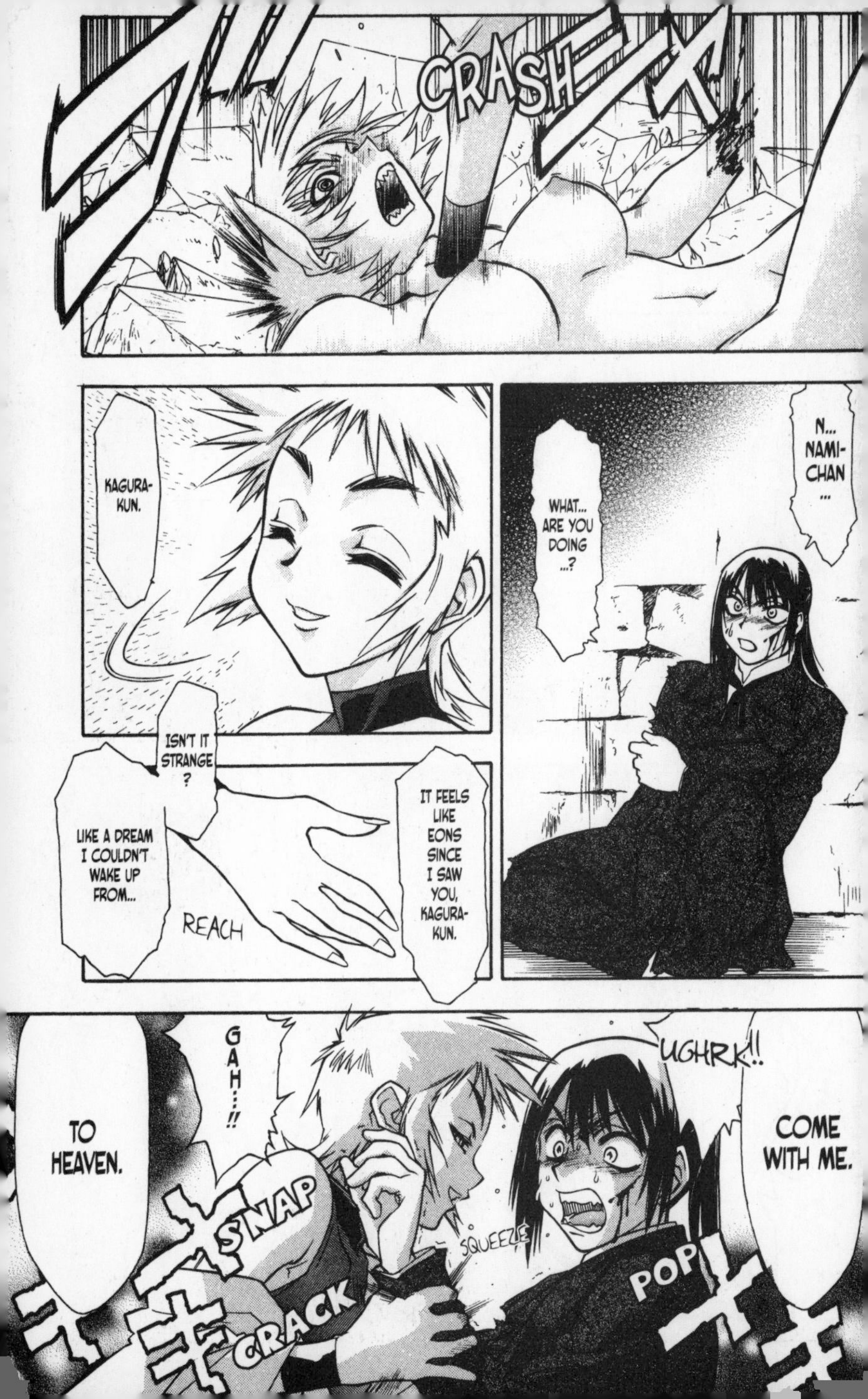
CRASH
N... NAMI-CHAN ...
WHAT... ARE YOU DOING ...?
KAGURA-KUN.
IT FEELS LIKE EONS SINCE I SAW YOU, KAGURA-KUN.
ISN'T IT STRANGE?
LIKE A DREAM I COULDN'T WAKE UP FROM...
REACH
UGHRK!!
COME WITH ME.
GAH...!!
TO HEAVEN.
POP
SQUEEZE
SNAP
CRACK

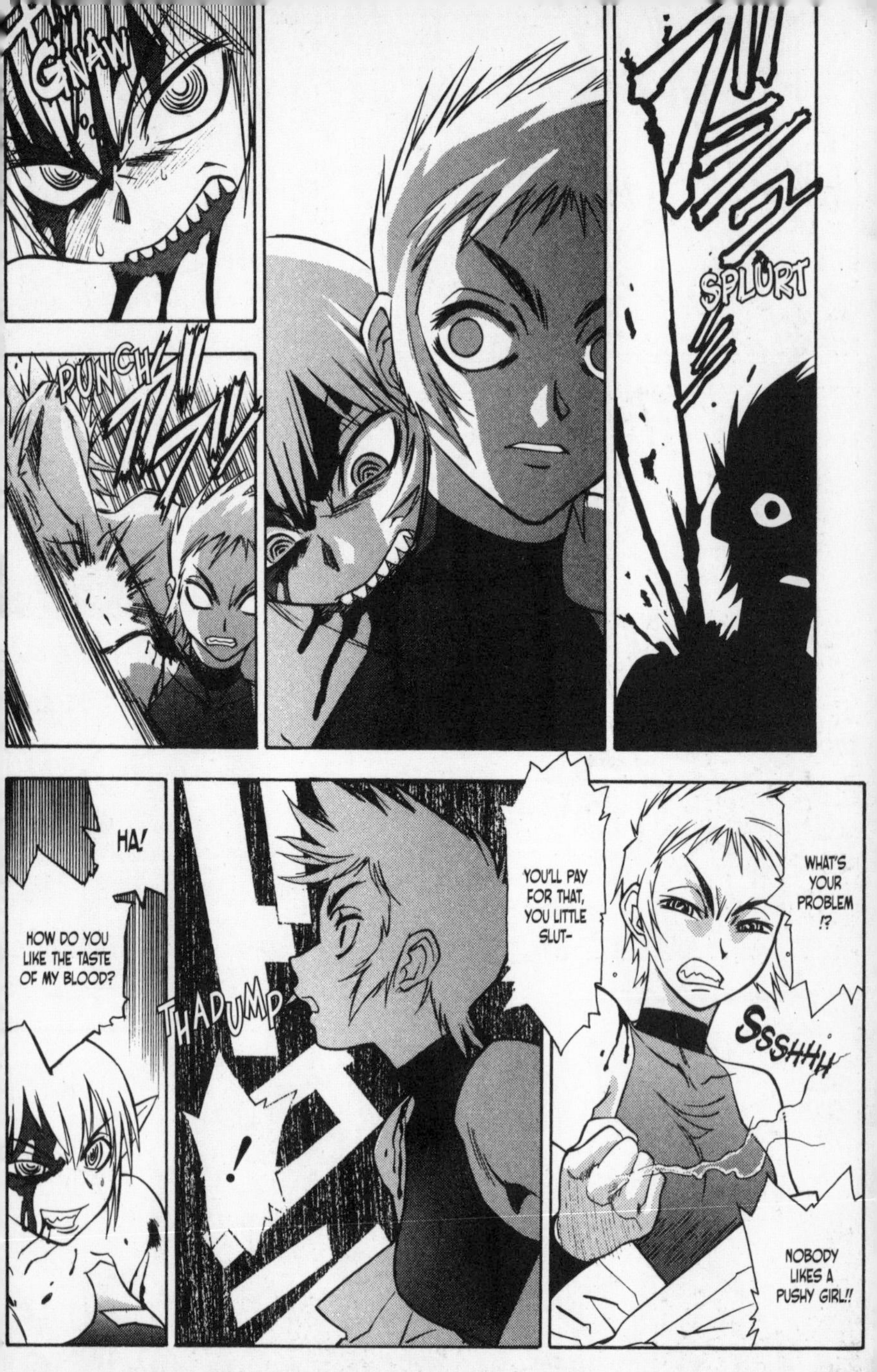
SPLURT
GNAW
PUNCH
YOU'LL PAY FOR THAT, YOU LITTLE SLUT-
WHAT'S YOUR PROBLEM !?
SSSHHH
NOBODY LIKES A PUSHY GIRL!!
THADUMP
!
HA!
HOW DO YOU LIKE THE TASTE OF MY BLOOD?

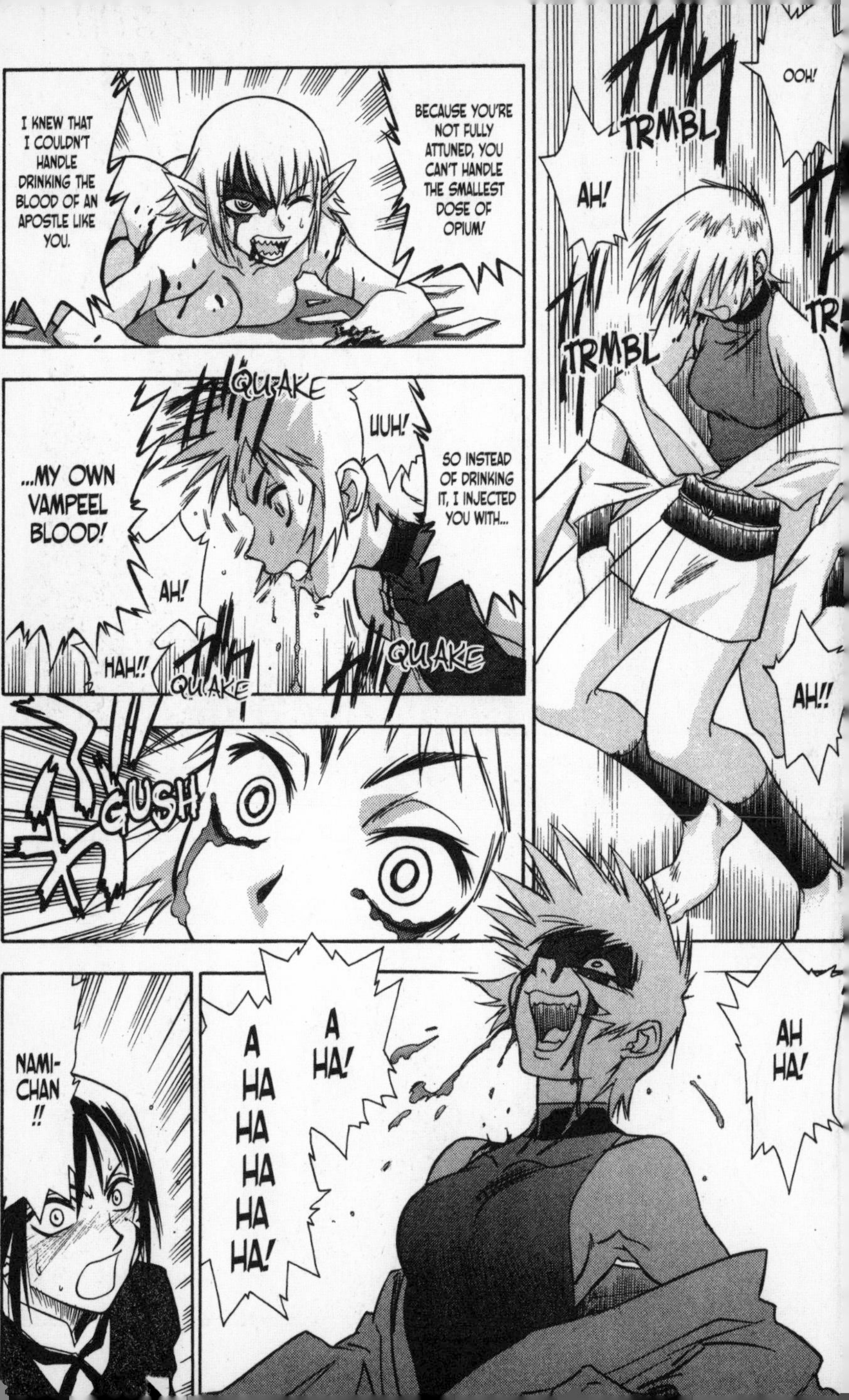
OOH!
TRMBL
AH!
TRMBL
TR
AH!!
BECAUSE YOU'RE NOT FULLY ATTUNED, YOU CAN'T HANDLE THE SMALLEST DOSE OF OPIUM!
I KNEW THAT I COULDN'T HANDLE DRINKING THE BLOOD OF AN APOSTLE LIKE YOU.
QUAKE
UUH!
SO INSTEAD OF DRINKING IT, I INJECTED YOU WITH...
...MY OWN VAMPEEL BLOOD!
AH!
QUAKE
HAH!!
QUAKE
GUSH
AH HA!
A HA!
A HA HA HA HA HA HA!
NAMI-CHAN!!

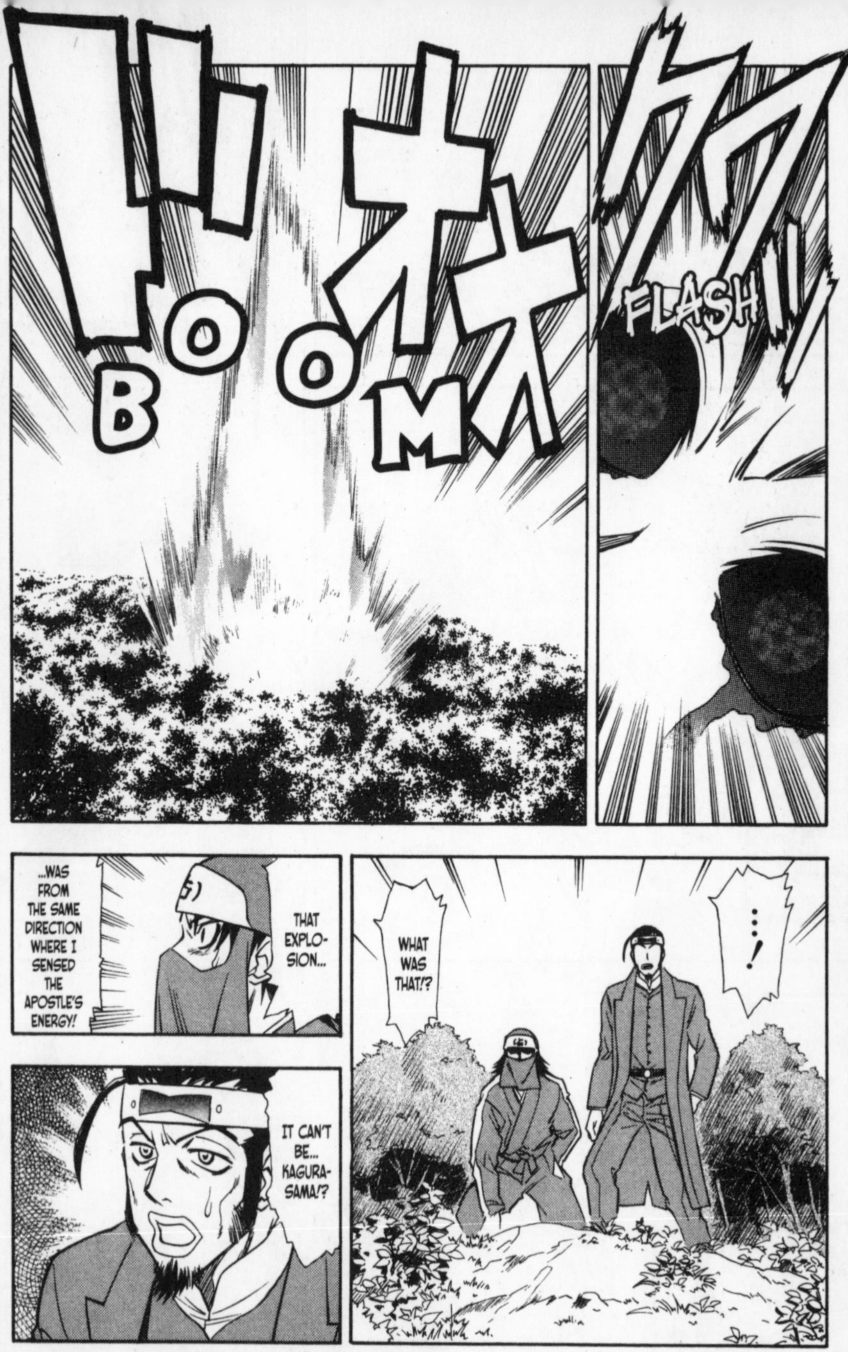
FLASH
BOOM
...!
WHAT WAS THAT!?
THAT EXPLOSION...
...WAS FROM THE SAME DIRECTION WHERE I SENSED THE APOSTLE'S ENERGY!
IT CAN'T BE... KAGURA-SAMA!?

神無 KANNA

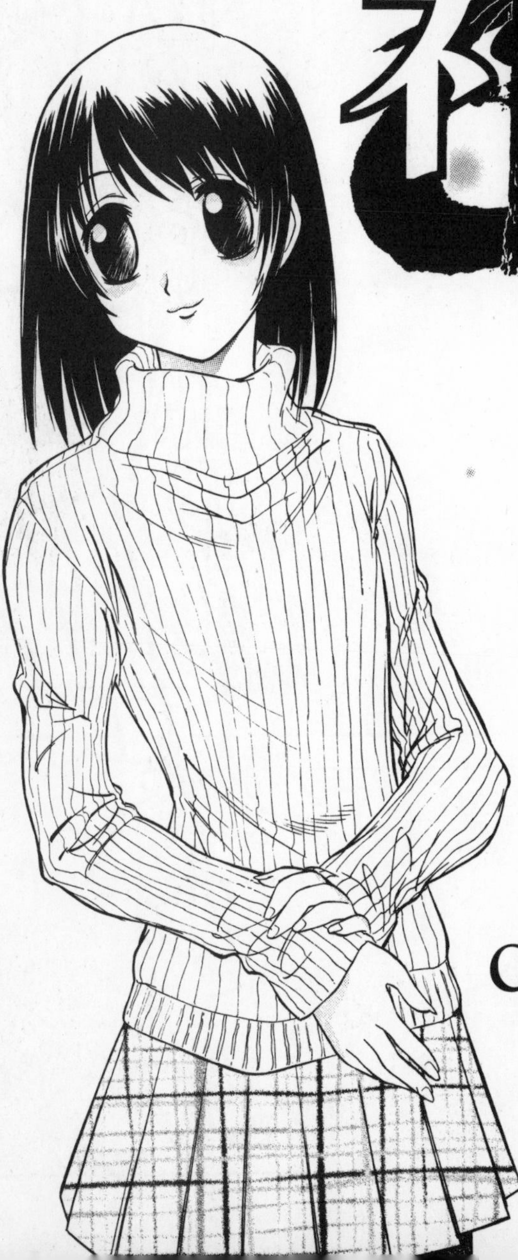

Chapter 32

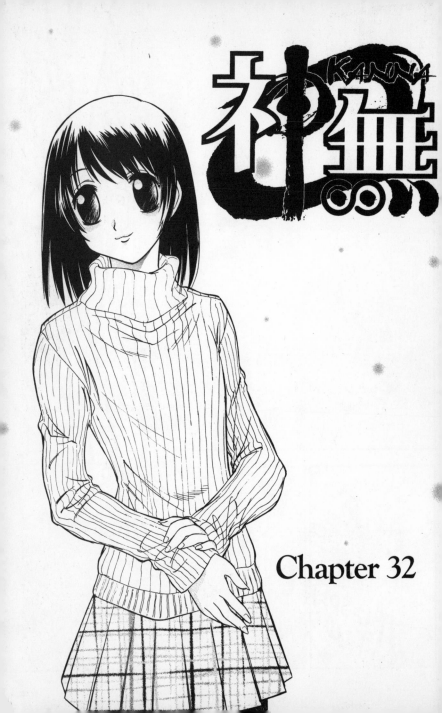

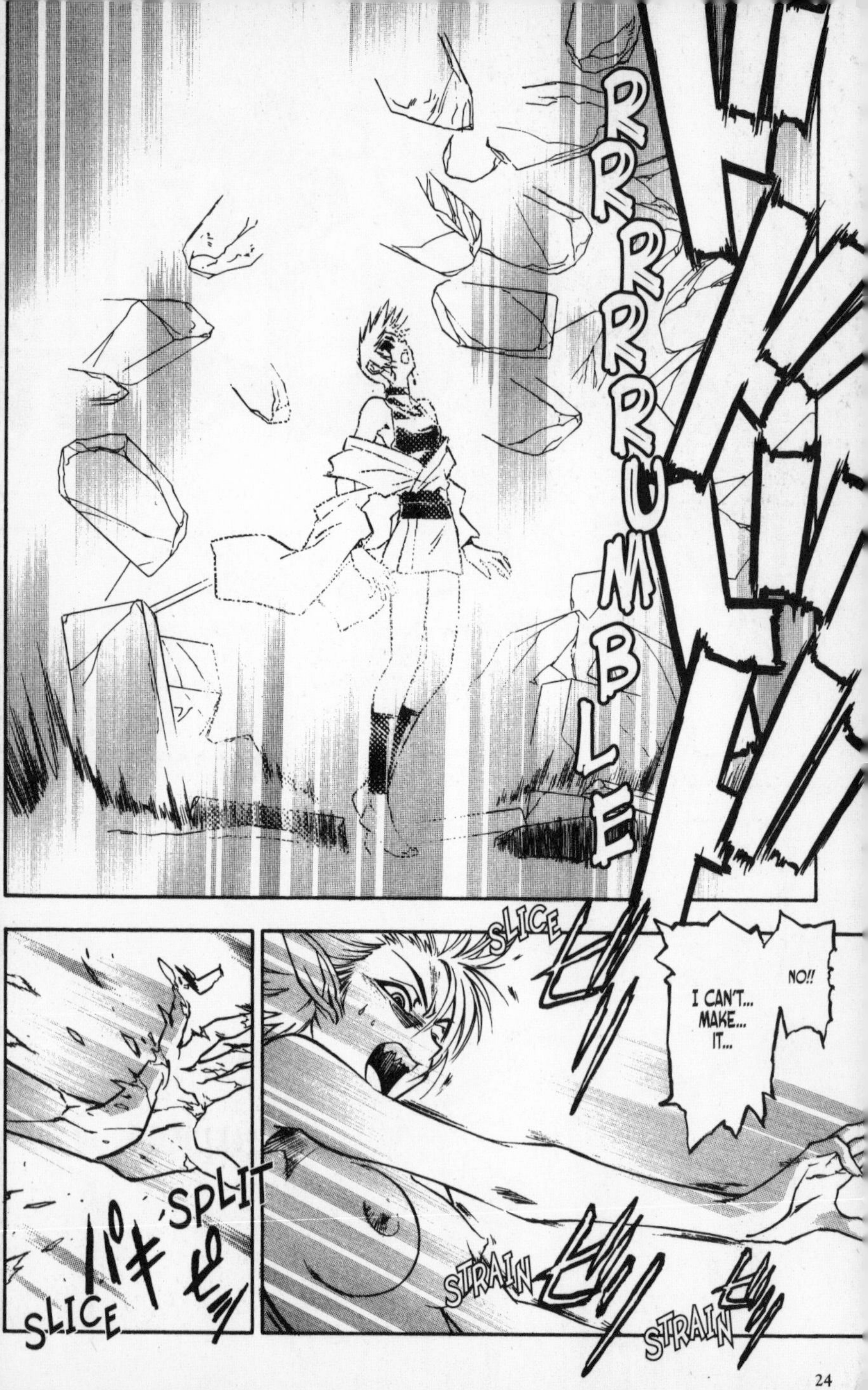
RRRRRUMBLE
NO!!
I CAN'T... MAKE... IT...
SLICE
STRAIN
STRAIN
SPLIT
パキ
SLICE

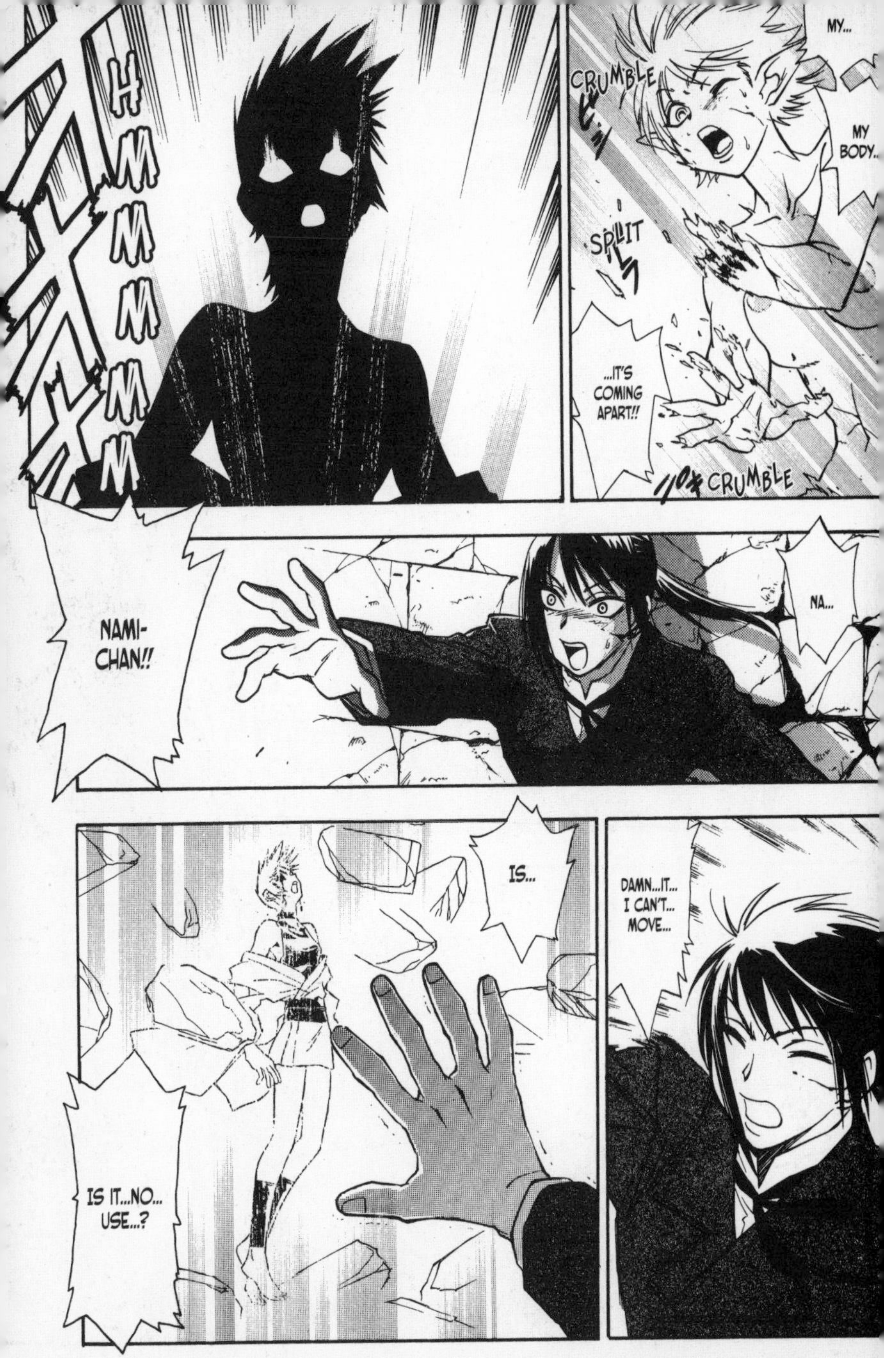
MY...
MY BODY...
CRUMBLE
SPLIT
...IT'S COMING APART!!
CRUMBLE
HMMMMMM
NA...
NAMI-CHAN!!
DAMN...IT... I CAN'T... MOVE...
IS...
IS IT...NO... USE...?

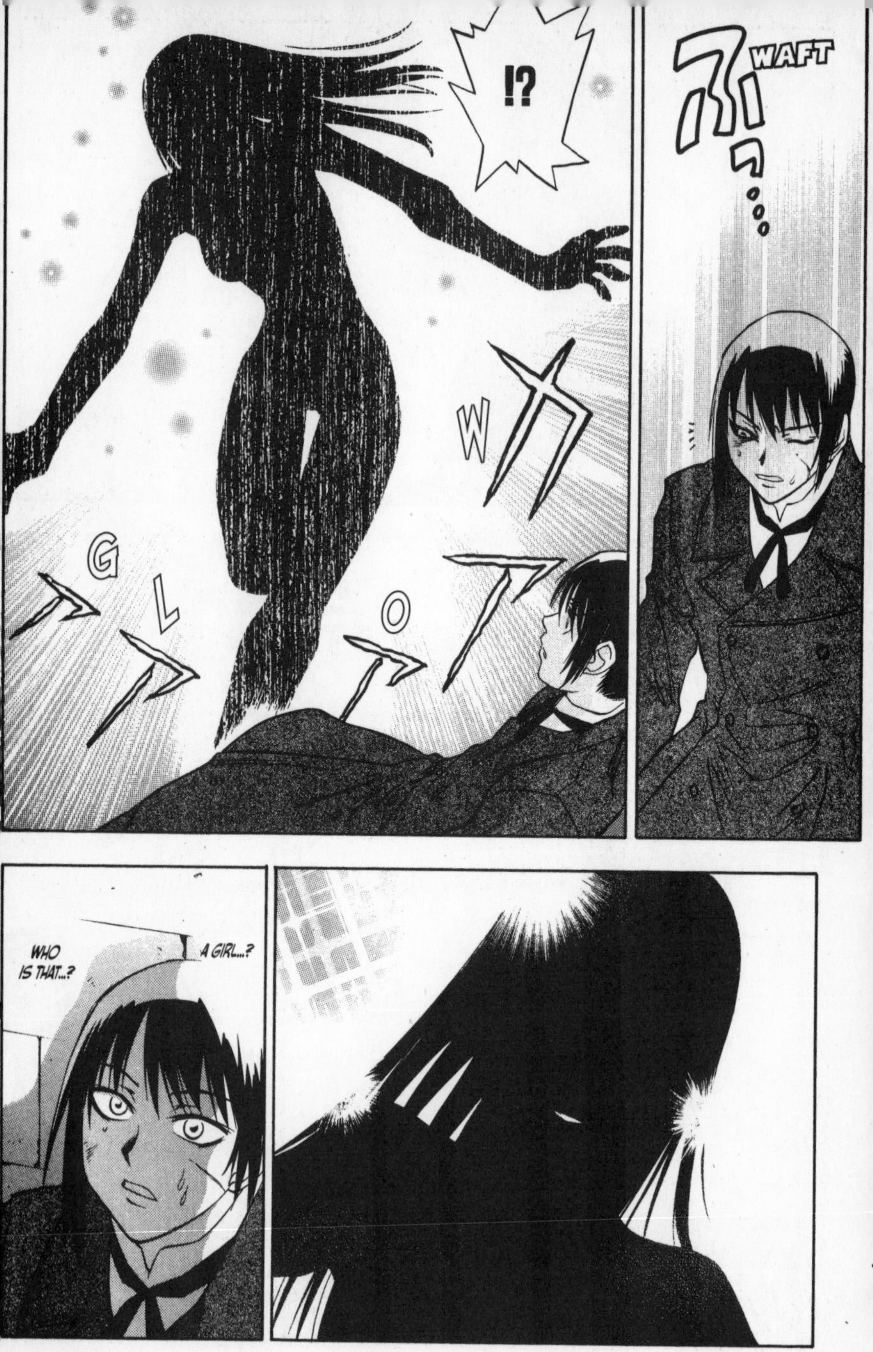
WAFT
!?
GLOW
A GIRL...?
WHO IS THAT...?

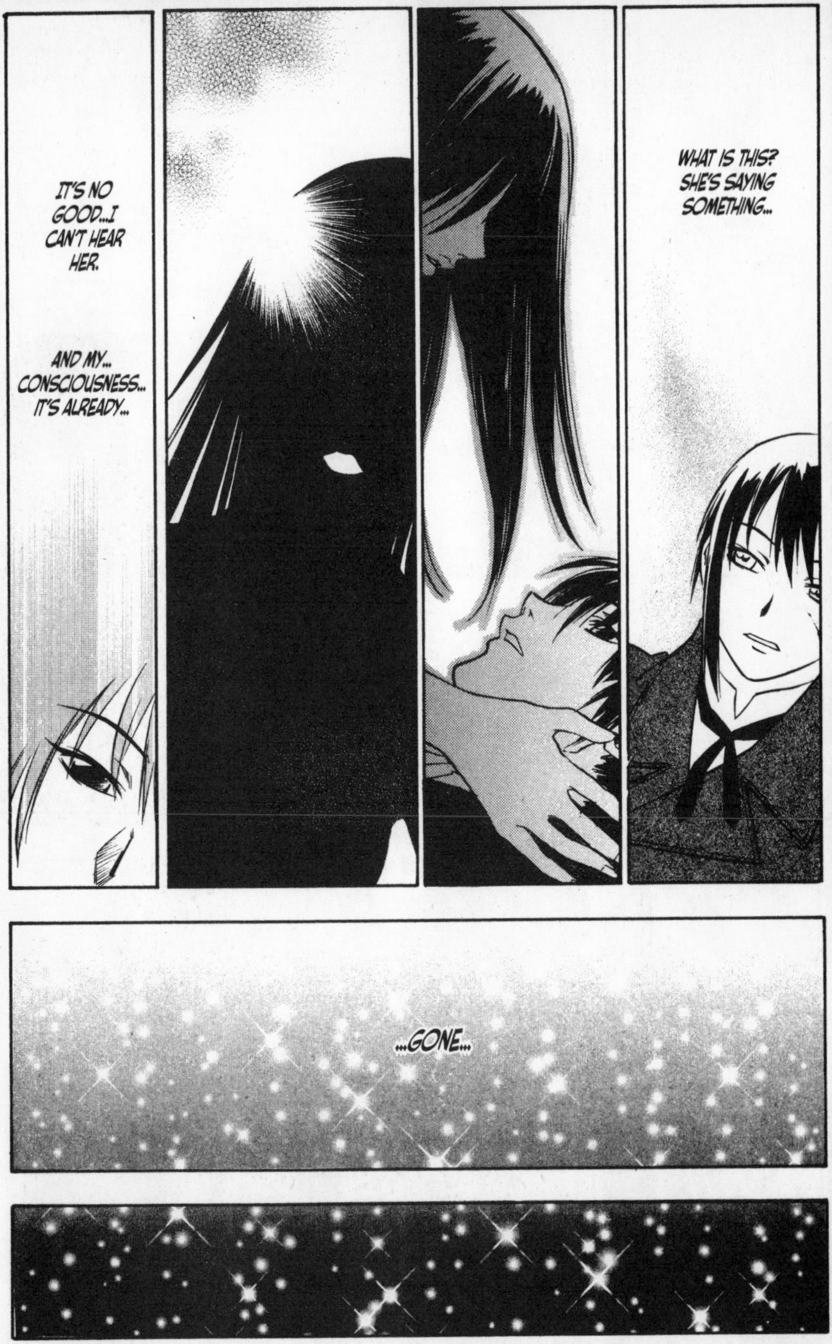
WHAT IS THIS? SHE'S SAYING SOMETHING...
IT'S NO GOOD...I CAN'T HEAR HER.
AND MY... CONSCIOUSNESS... IT'S ALREADY...
...GONE...

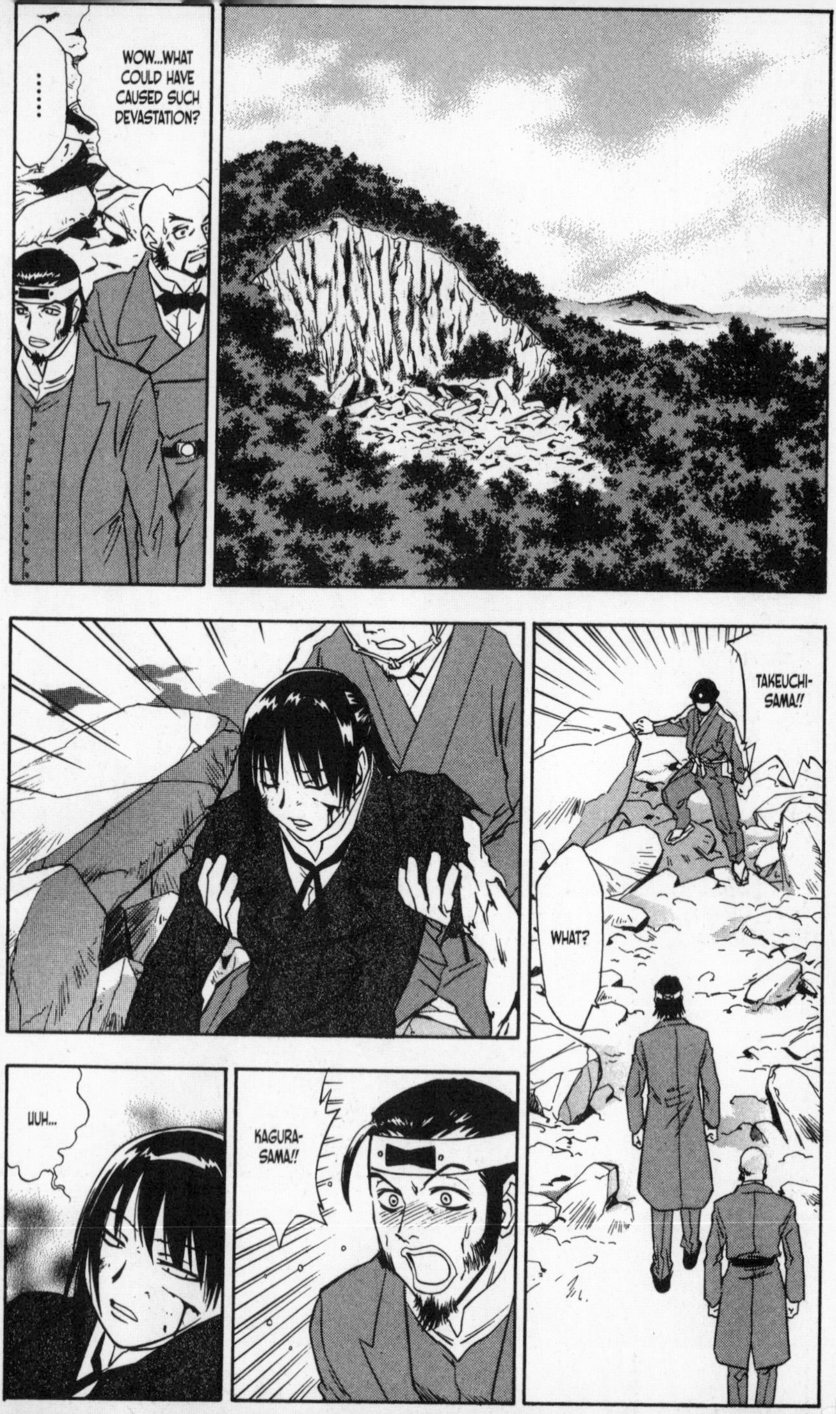
WOW...WHAT COULD HAVE CAUSED SUCH DEVASTATION?
......
TAKEUCHI-SAMA!!
WHAT?
KAGURA-SAMA!!
UUH...

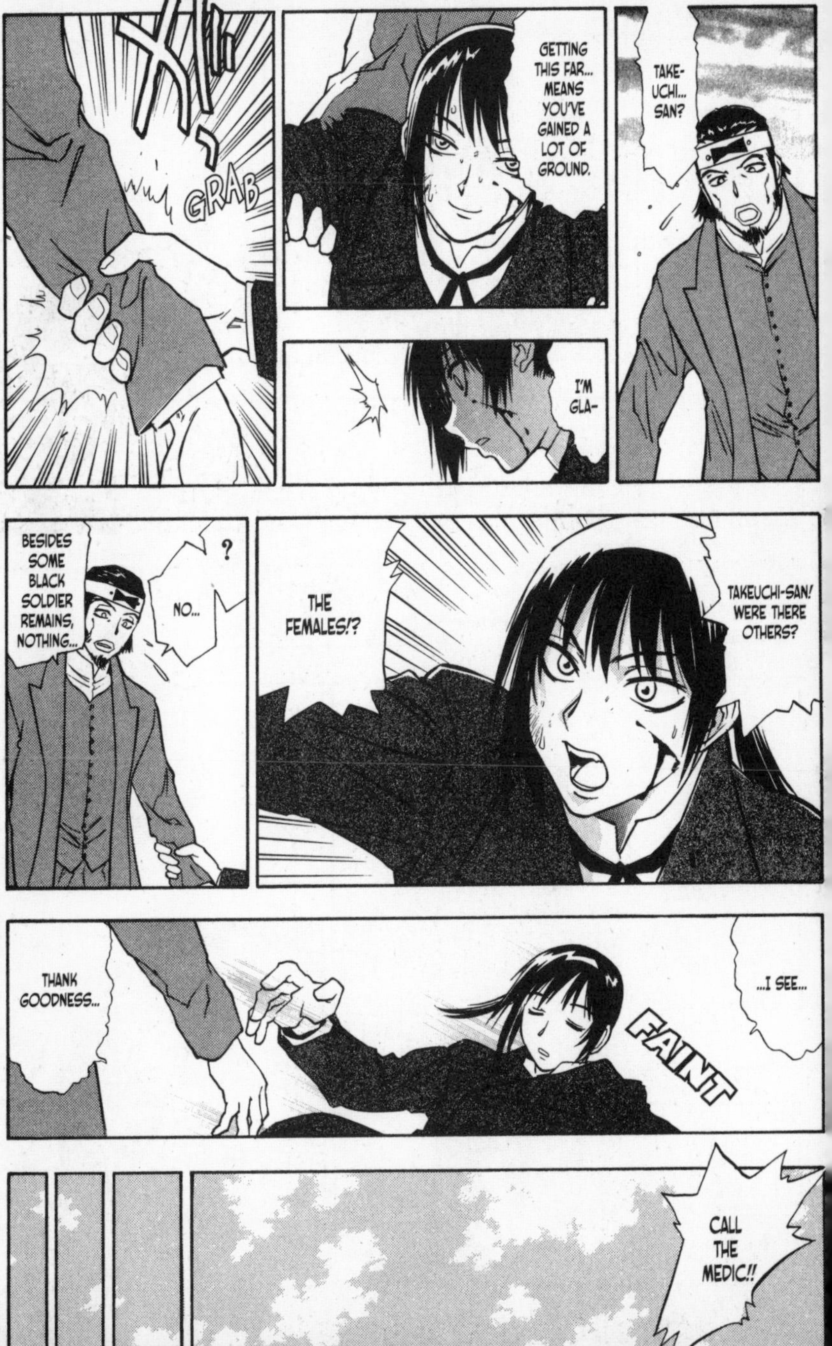
TAKE-UCHI... SAN?
GETTING THIS FAR... MEANS YOU'VE GAINED A LOT OF GROUND.
I'M GLA-
GRAB
TAKEUCHI-SAN! WERE THERE OTHERS?
THE FEMALES!?
?
NO...
BESIDES SOME BLACK SOLDIER REMAINS, NOTHING...
...I SEE...
FAINT
THANK GOODNESS...
CALL THE MEDIC!!

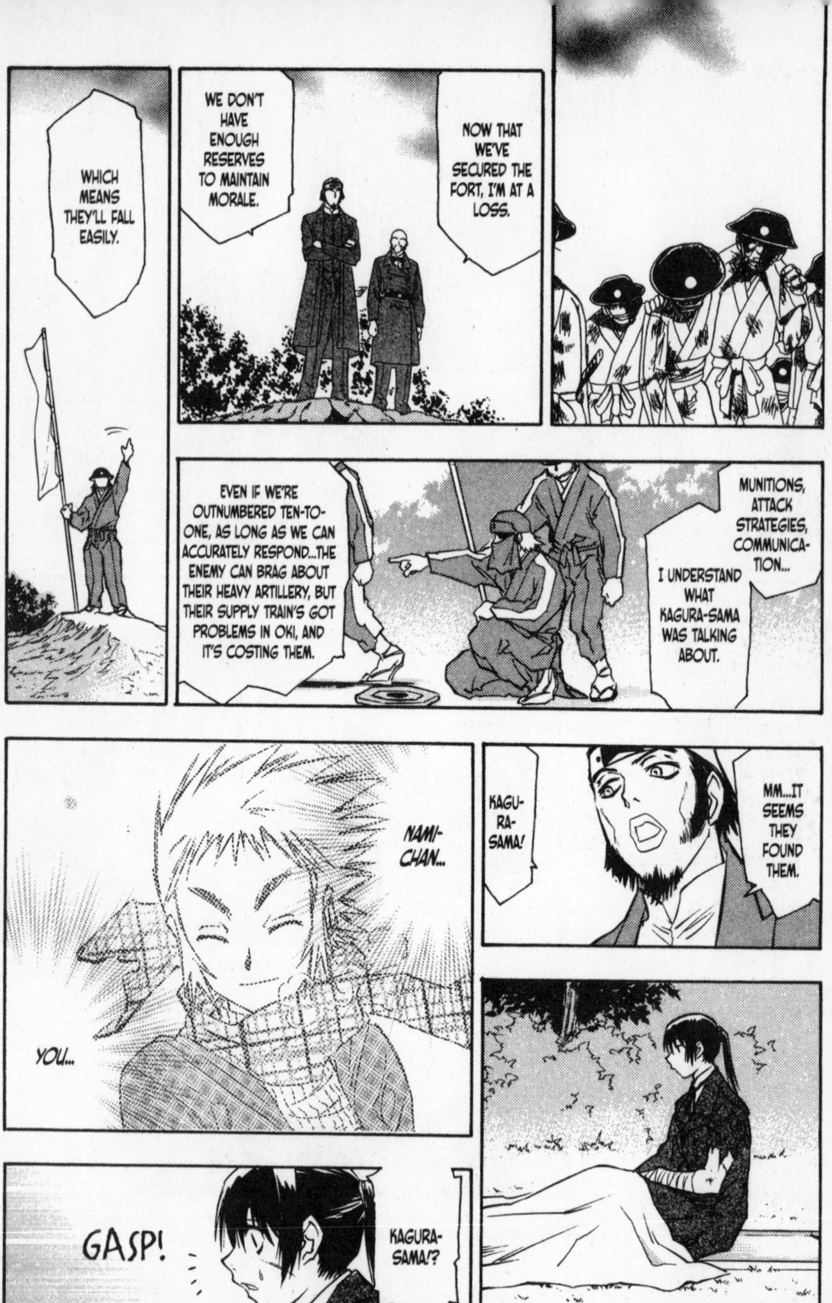
NOW THAT WE'VE SECURED THE FORT, I'M AT A LOSS.
WE DON'T HAVE ENOUGH RESERVES TO MAINTAIN MORALE.
MUNITIONS, ATTACK STRATEGIES, COMMUNICATION...
I UNDERSTAND WHAT KAGURA-SAMA WAS TALKING ABOUT.
EVEN IF WE'RE OUTNUMBERED TEN-TO-ONE, AS LONG AS WE CAN ACCURATELY RESPOND...THE ENEMY CAN BRAG ABOUT THEIR HEAVY ARTILLERY, BUT THEIR SUPPLY TRAIN'S GOT PROBLEMS IN OKI, AND IT'S COSTING THEM.
WHICH MEANS THEY'LL FALL EASILY.
MM...IT SEEMS THEY FOUND THEM.
KAGURA-SAMA!
NAMI-CHAN...
YOU...
KAGURA-SAMA!?
GASP!

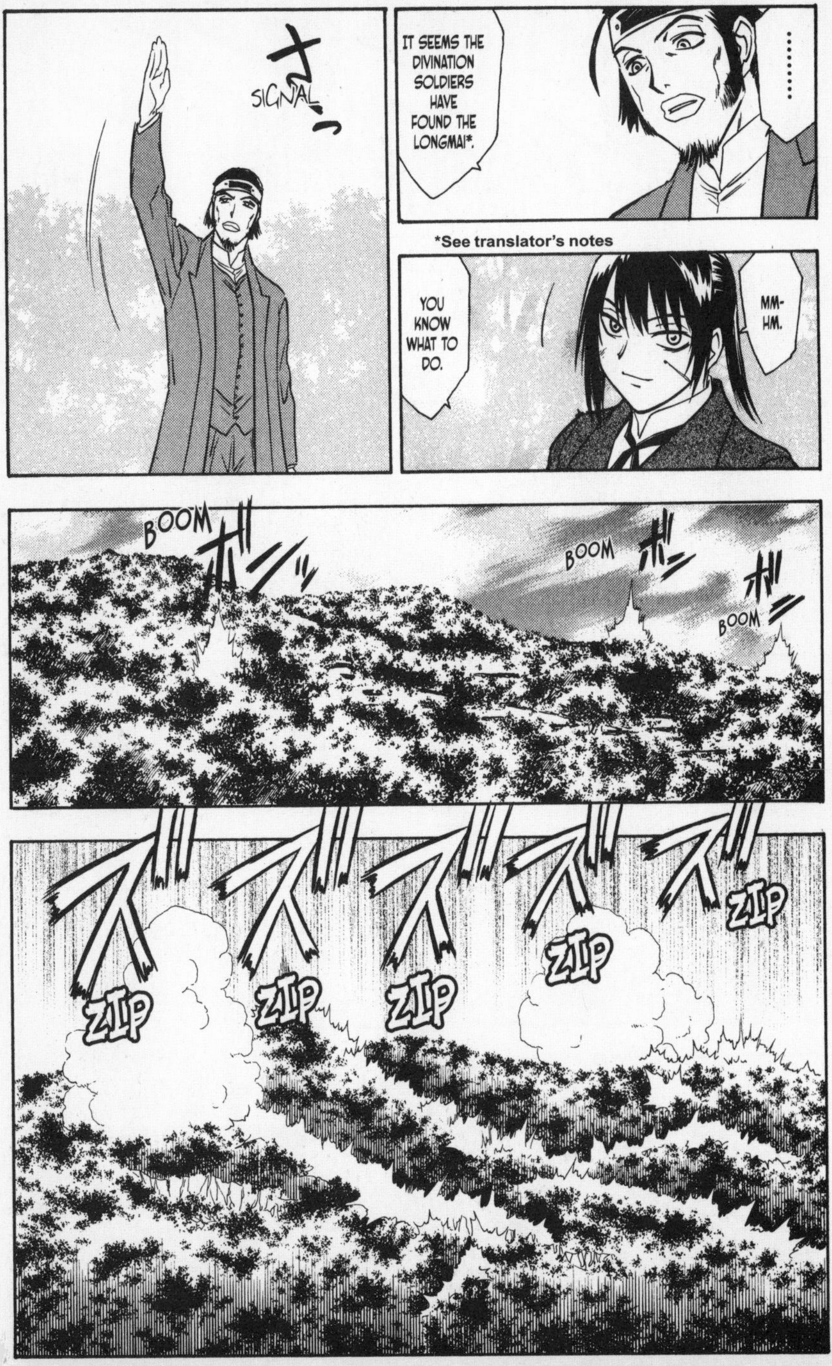
......
IT SEEMS THE DIVINATION SOLDIERS HAVE FOUND THE LONGMAI*.
*See translator's notes
MM-HM.
YOU KNOW WHAT TO DO.
さっ
SIGNAL
ボン
BOOM
ボン
BOOM
ボンッ
BOOM
ズ
ZIP
ズ
ZIP
ズ
ZIP
ズ
ZIP
ズ
ZIP

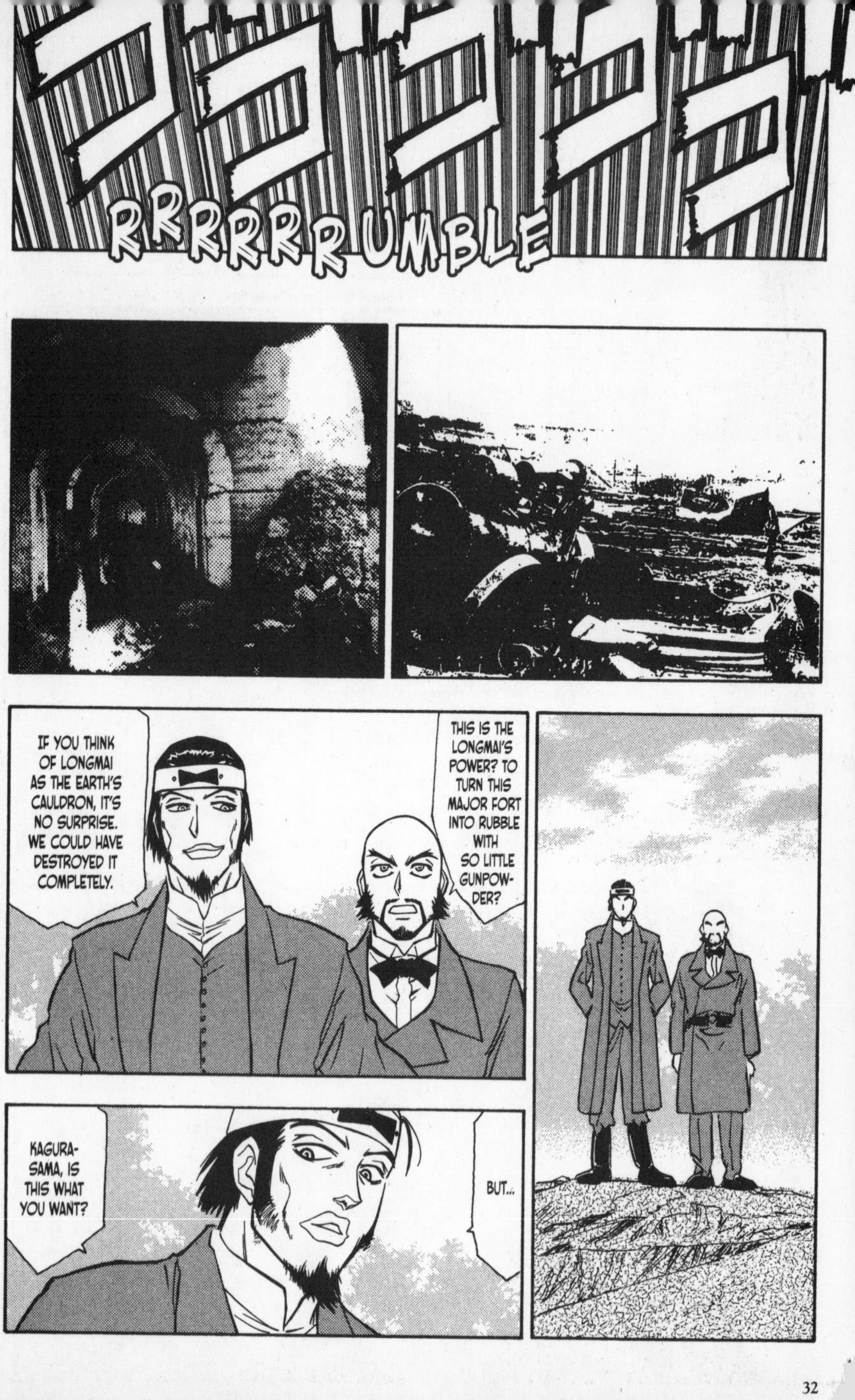
RRRRRRRUMBLE
THIS IS THE LONGMAI'S POWER? TO TURN THIS MAJOR FORT INTO RUBBLE WITH SO LITTLE GUNPOW-DER?
IF YOU THINK OF LONGMAI AS THE EARTH'S CAULDRON, IT'S NO SURPRISE. WE COULD HAVE DESTROYED IT COMPLETELY.
BUT...
KAGURA-SAMA, IS THIS WHAT YOU WANT?

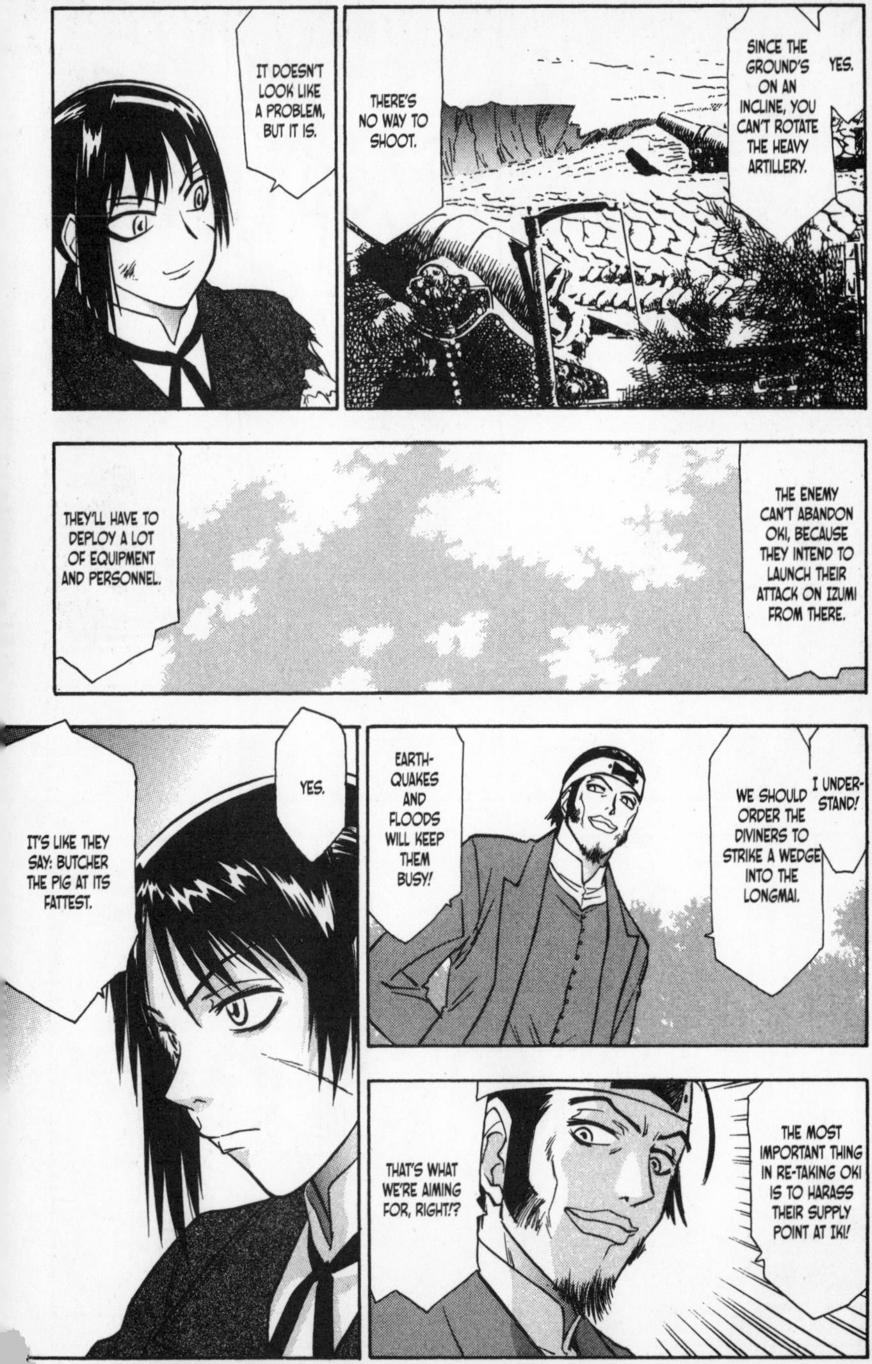
YES.
SINCE THE GROUND'S ON AN INCLINE, YOU CAN'T ROTATE THE HEAVY ARTILLERY.
THERE'S NO WAY TO SHOOT.
IT DOESN'T LOOK LIKE A PROBLEM, BUT IT IS.
THE ENEMY CAN'T ABANDON OKI, BECAUSE THEY INTEND TO LAUNCH THEIR ATTACK ON IZUMI FROM THERE.
THEY'LL HAVE TO DEPLOY A LOT OF EQUIPMENT AND PERSONNEL.
I UNDER-STAND!
WE SHOULD ORDER THE DIVINERS TO STRIKE A WEDGE INTO THE LONGMAI.
EARTH-QUAKES AND FLOODS WILL KEEP THEM BUSY!
THE MOST IMPORTANT THING IN RE-TAKING OKI IS TO HARASS THEIR SUPPLY POINT AT IKI!
THAT'S WHAT WE'RE AIMING FOR, RIGHT!?
YES.
IT'S LIKE THEY SAY: BUTCHER THE PIG AT ITS FATTEST.

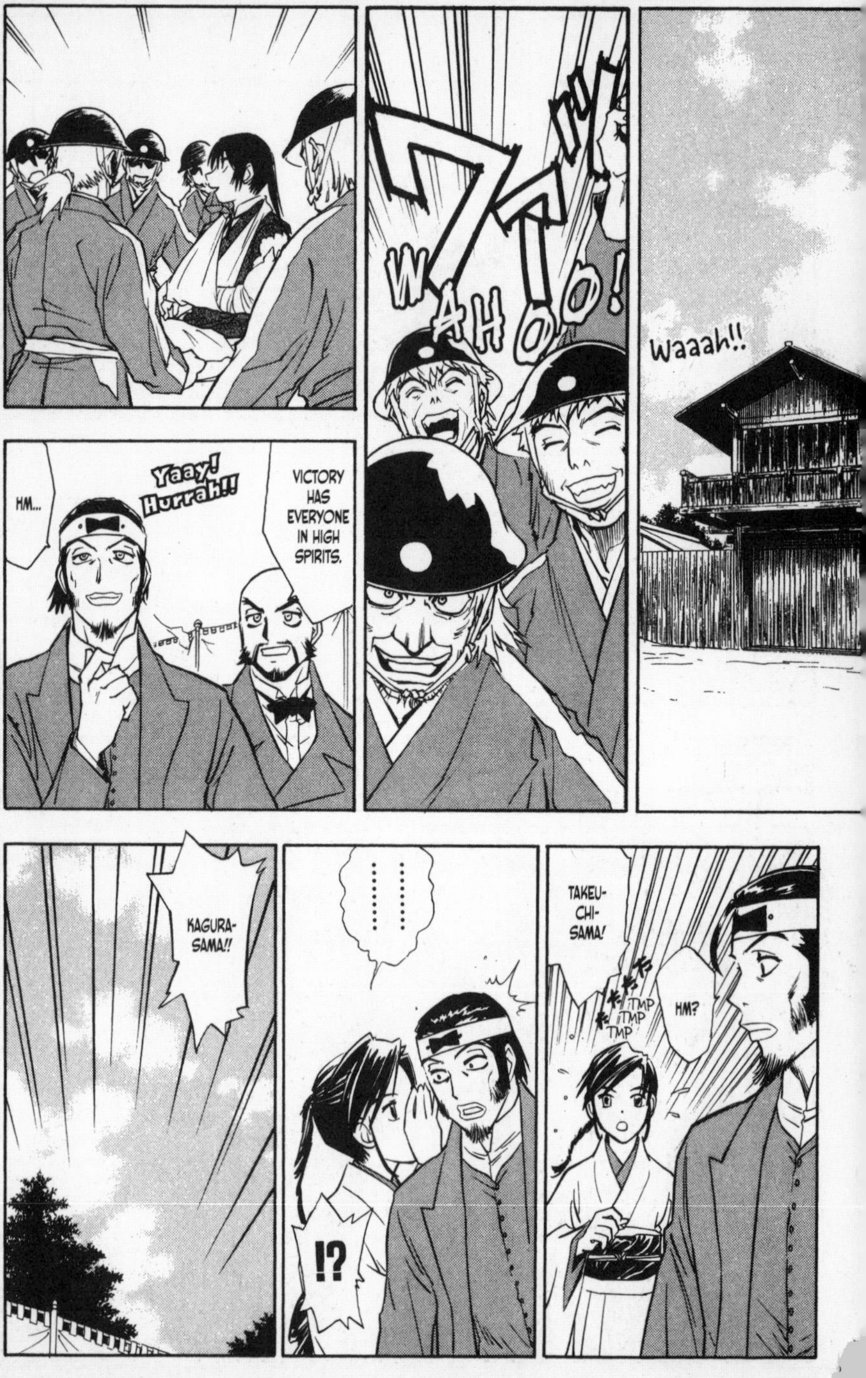
Waaah!!
WAHOO!
VICTORY HAS EVERYONE IN HIGH SPIRITS.
Yaay! Hurrah!!
HM...
TAKEU-CHI-SAMA!
TMP TMP TMP
HM?
......
!?
KAGURA-SAMA!!

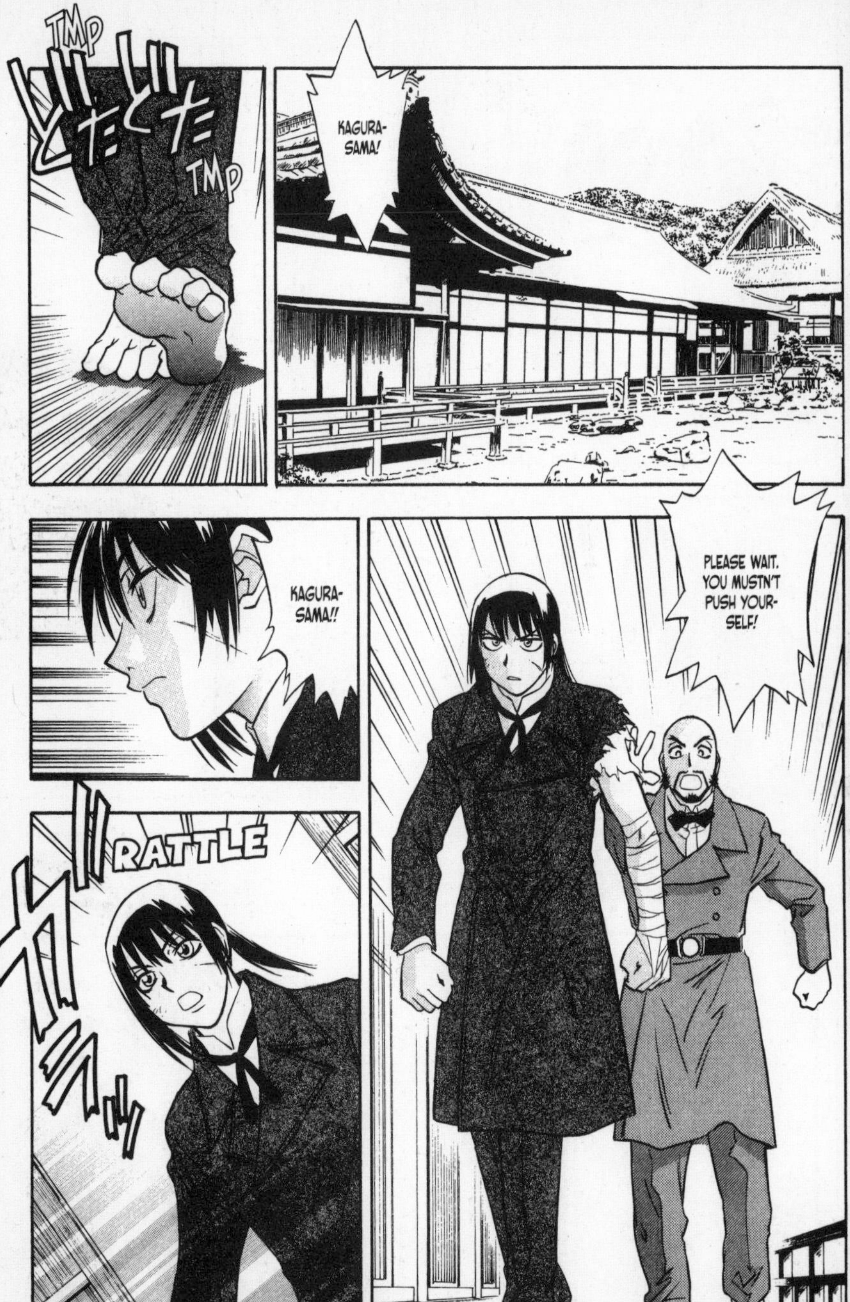
KAGURA-SAMA!
とたとた
TMP
TMP
PLEASE WAIT. YOU MUSTN'T PUSH YOUR-SELF!
KAGURA-SAMA!!
ガラッ
RATTLE

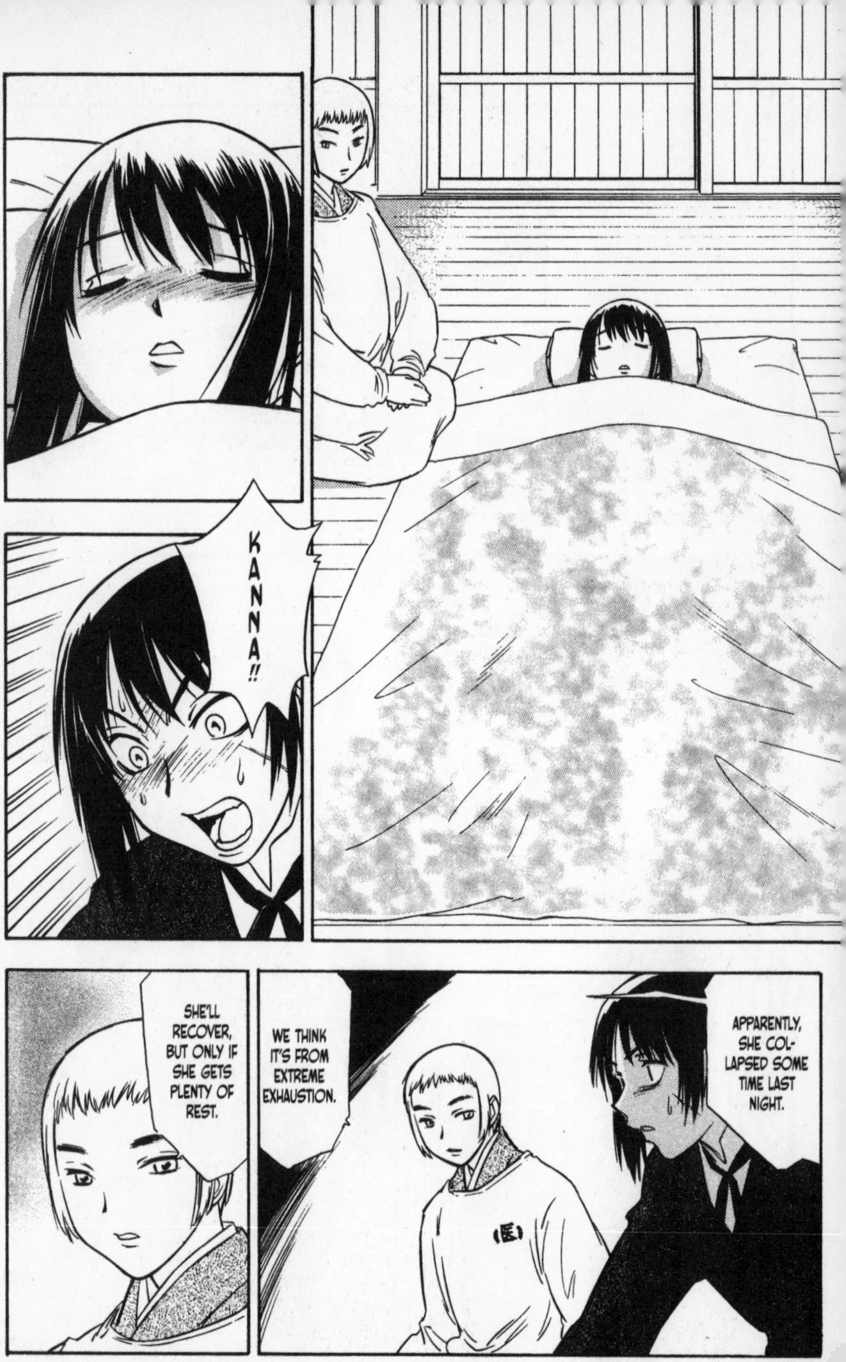
KANNA!!
APPARENTLY, SHE COL-LAPSED SOME TIME LAST NIGHT.
WE THINK IT'S FROM EXTREME EXHAUSTION.
SHE'LL RECOVER, BUT ONLY IF SHE GETS PLENTY OF REST.

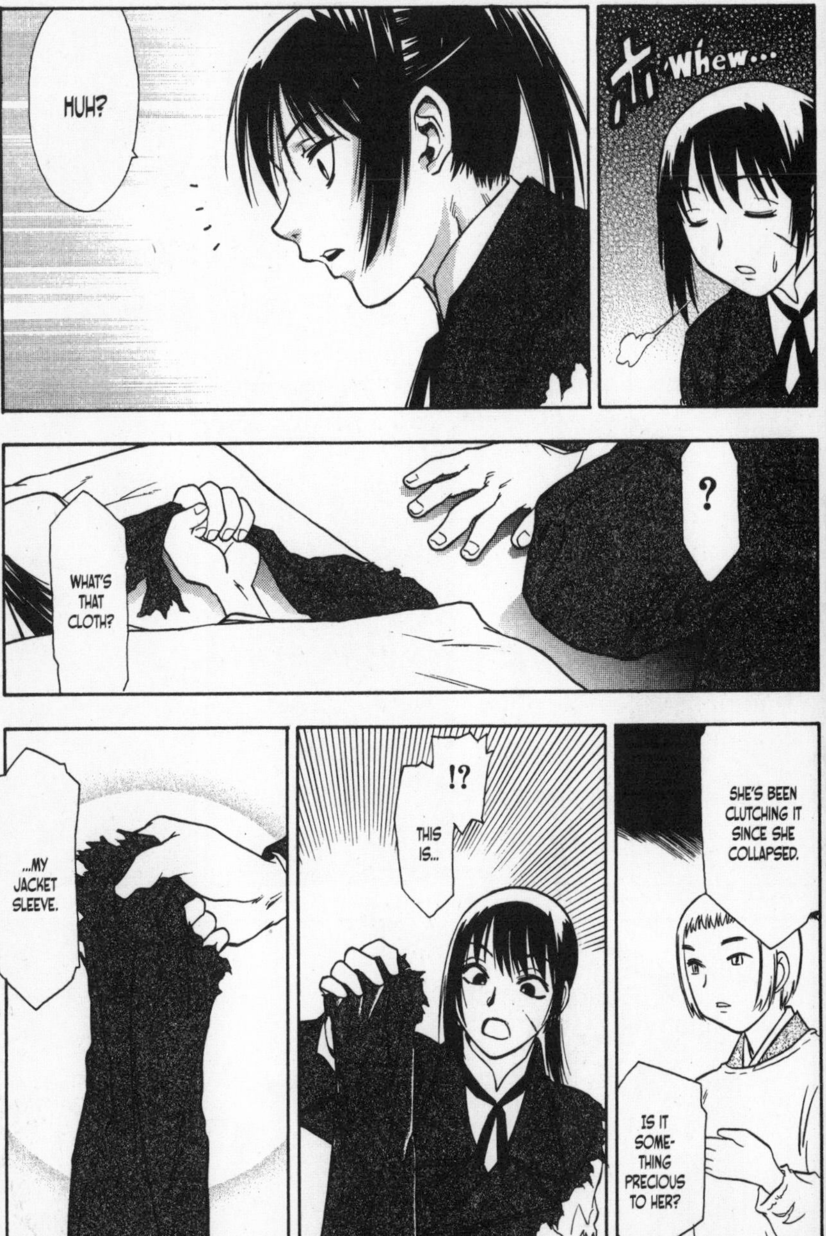
Whew...
HUH?
?
WHAT'S THAT CLOTH?
SHE'S BEEN CLUTCHING IT SINCE SHE COLLAPSED.
IS IT SOME-THING PRECIOUS TO HER?
!?
THIS IS...
...MY JACKET SLEEVE.

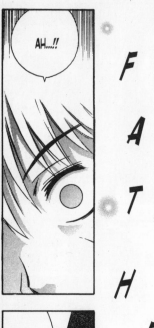

AH...!!

THEN, THAT LITTLE GIRL...

F
A
T
H
E
R

...PRO-TECTED ME.

YOU...

KANNA... THAT WAS YOU...

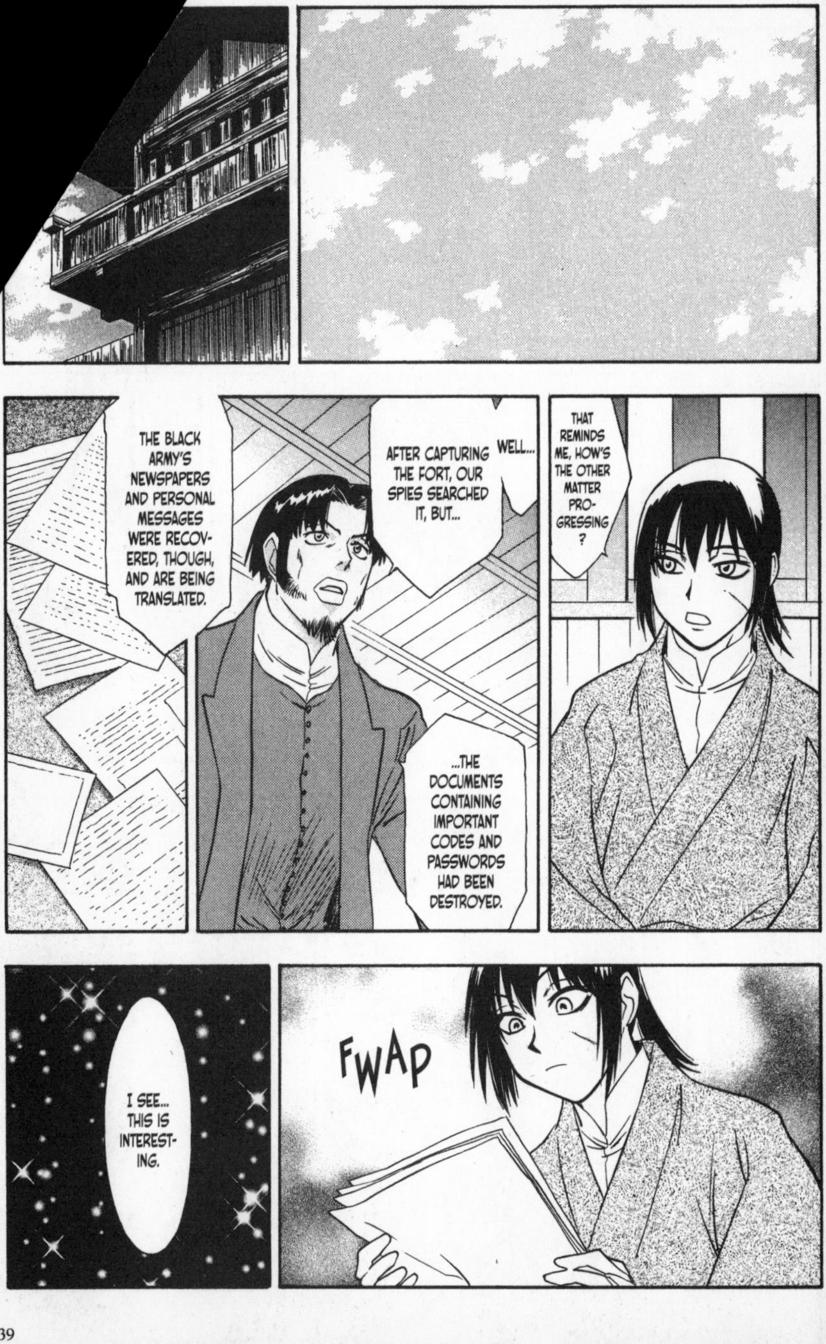
THAT REMINDS ME, HOW'S THE OTHER MATTER PROGRESSING?
WELL...
AFTER CAPTURING THE FORT, OUR SPIES SEARCHED IT, BUT...
...THE DOCUMENTS CONTAINING IMPORTANT CODES AND PASSWORDS HAD BEEN DESTROYED.
THE BLACK ARMY'S NEWSPAPERS AND PERSONAL MESSAGES WERE RECOVERED, THOUGH, AND ARE BEING TRANSLATED.
FWAP
I SEE... THIS IS INTERESTING.

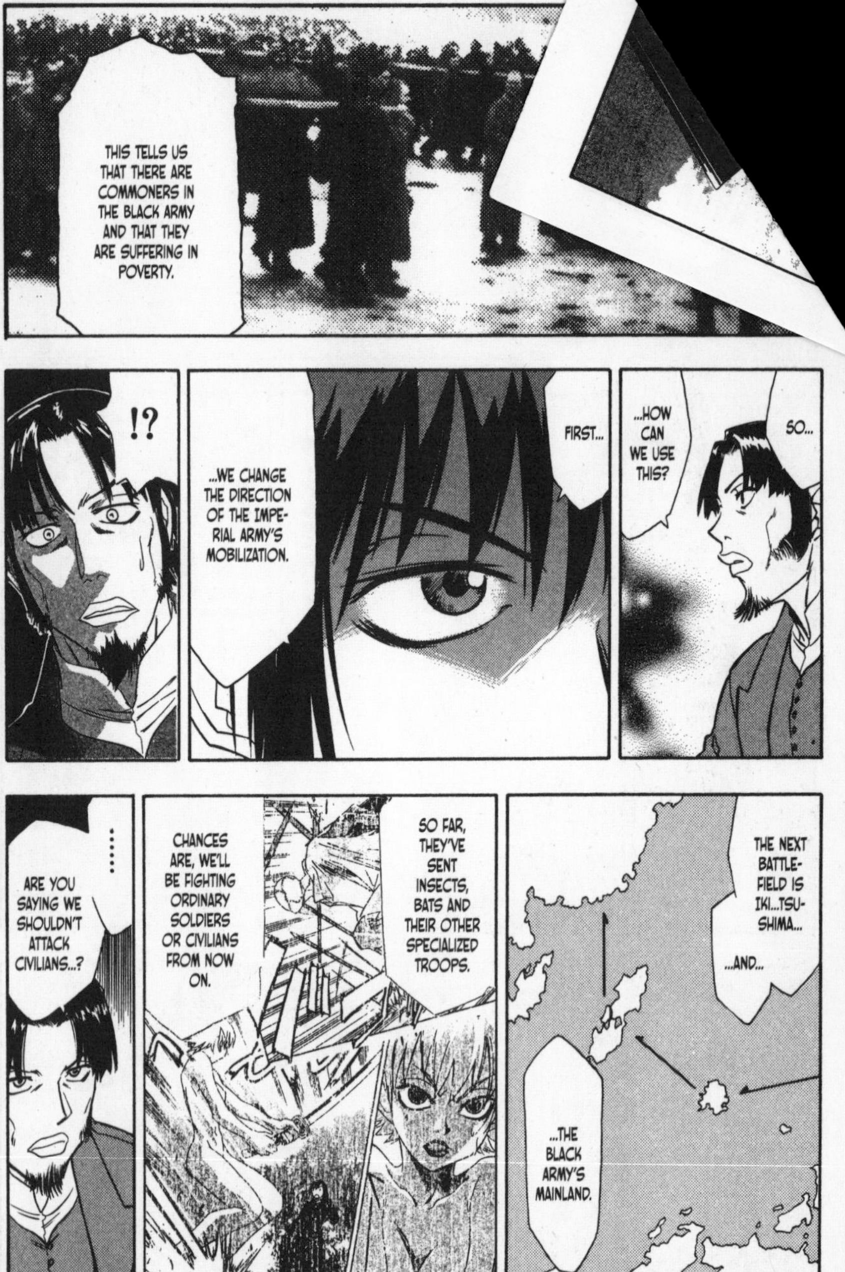
THIS TELLS US THAT THERE ARE COMMONERS IN THE BLACK ARMY AND THAT THEY ARE SUFFERING IN POVERTY.
SO...
...HOW CAN WE USE THIS?
FIRST...
...WE CHANGE THE DIRECTION OF THE IMPERIAL ARMY'S MOBILIZATION.
!?
THE NEXT BATTLEFIELD IS IKI...TSUSHIMA...
...AND...
...THE BLACK ARMY'S MAINLAND.
SO FAR, THEY'VE SENT INSECTS, BATS AND THEIR OTHER SPECIALIZED TROOPS.
CHANCES ARE, WE'LL BE FIGHTING ORDINARY SOLDIERS OR CIVILIANS FROM NOW ON.
......
ARE YOU SAYING WE SHOULDN'T ATTACK CIVILIANS...?

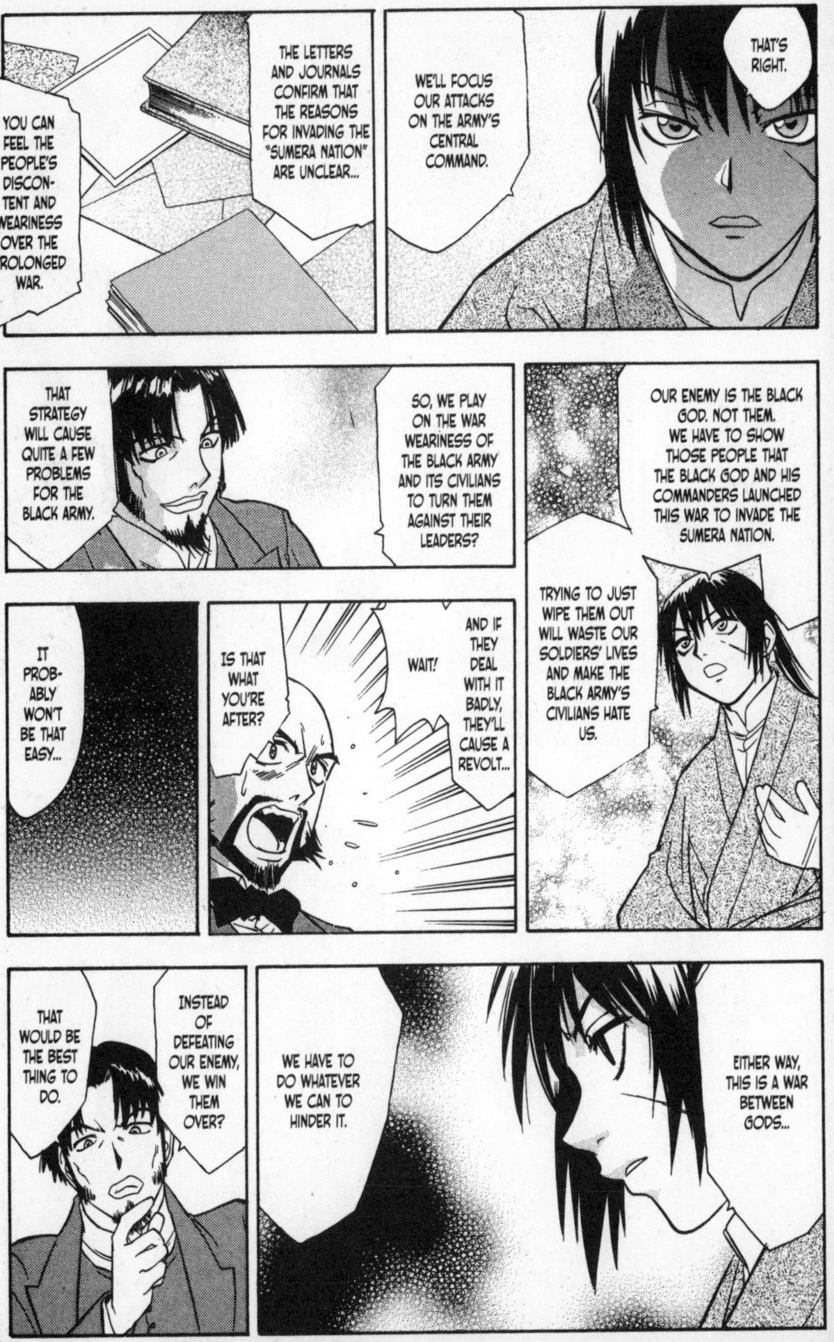
THAT'S RIGHT.
WE'LL FOCUS OUR ATTACKS ON THE ARMY'S CENTRAL COMMAND.
THE LETTERS AND JOURNALS CONFIRM THAT THE REASONS FOR INVADING THE "SUMERA NATION" ARE UNCLEAR...
YOU CAN FEEL THE PEOPLE'S DISCON-TENT AND WEARINESS OVER THE PROLONGED WAR.
OUR ENEMY IS THE BLACK GOD. NOT THEM. WE HAVE TO SHOW THOSE PEOPLE THAT THE BLACK GOD AND HIS COMMANDERS LAUNCHED THIS WAR TO INVADE THE SUMERA NATION.
TRYING TO JUST WIPE THEM OUT WILL WASTE OUR SOLDIERS' LIVES AND MAKE THE BLACK ARMY'S CIVILIANS HATE US.
SO, WE PLAY ON THE WAR WEARINESS OF THE BLACK ARMY AND ITS CIVILIANS TO TURN THEM AGAINST THEIR LEADERS?
THAT STRATEGY WILL CAUSE QUITE A FEW PROBLEMS FOR THE BLACK ARMY.
AND IF THEY DEAL WITH IT BADLY, THEY'LL CAUSE A REVOLT...
WAIT!
IS THAT WHAT YOU'RE AFTER?
IT PROB-ABLY WON'T BE THAT EASY...
EITHER WAY, THIS IS A WAR BETWEEN GODS...
WE HAVE TO DO WHATEVER WE CAN TO HINDER IT.
INSTEAD OF DEFEATING OUR ENEMY, WE WIN THEM OVER?
THAT WOULD BE THE BEST THING TO DO.

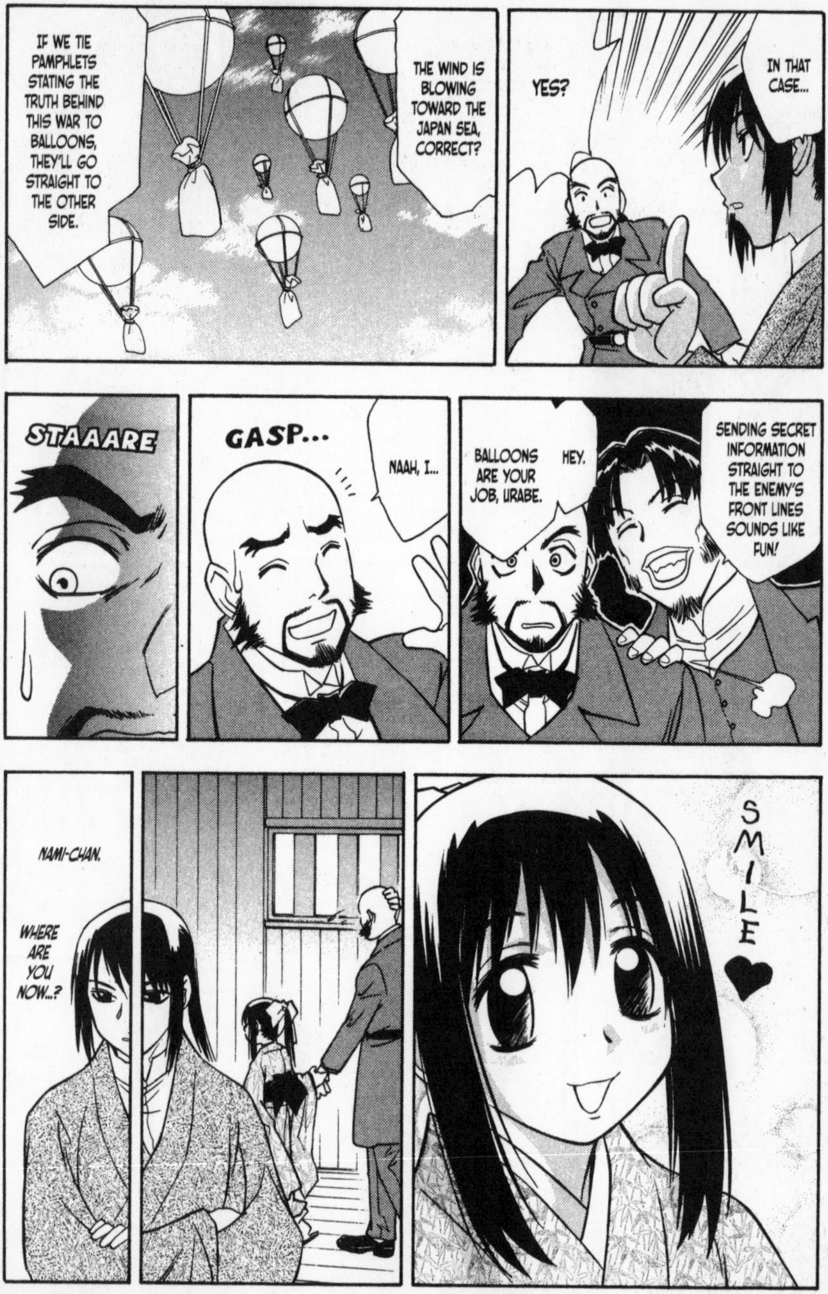
IN THAT CASE...
YES?
THE WIND IS BLOWING TOWARD THE JAPAN SEA, CORRECT?
IF WE TIE PAMPHLETS STATING THE TRUTH BEHIND THIS WAR TO BALLOONS, THEY'LL GO STRAIGHT TO THE OTHER SIDE.
SENDING SECRET INFORMATION STRAIGHT TO THE ENEMY'S FRONT LINES SOUNDS LIKE FUN!
HEY.
BALLOONS ARE YOUR JOB, URABE.
NAAH, I...
GASP...
STAAARE
SMILE
NAMI-CHAN.
WHERE ARE YOU NOW..?

Chapter 32 : OVER

神無 KANNA

Chapter 33

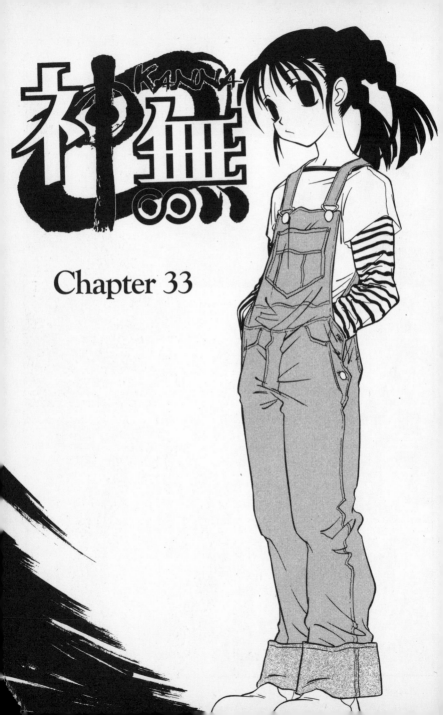

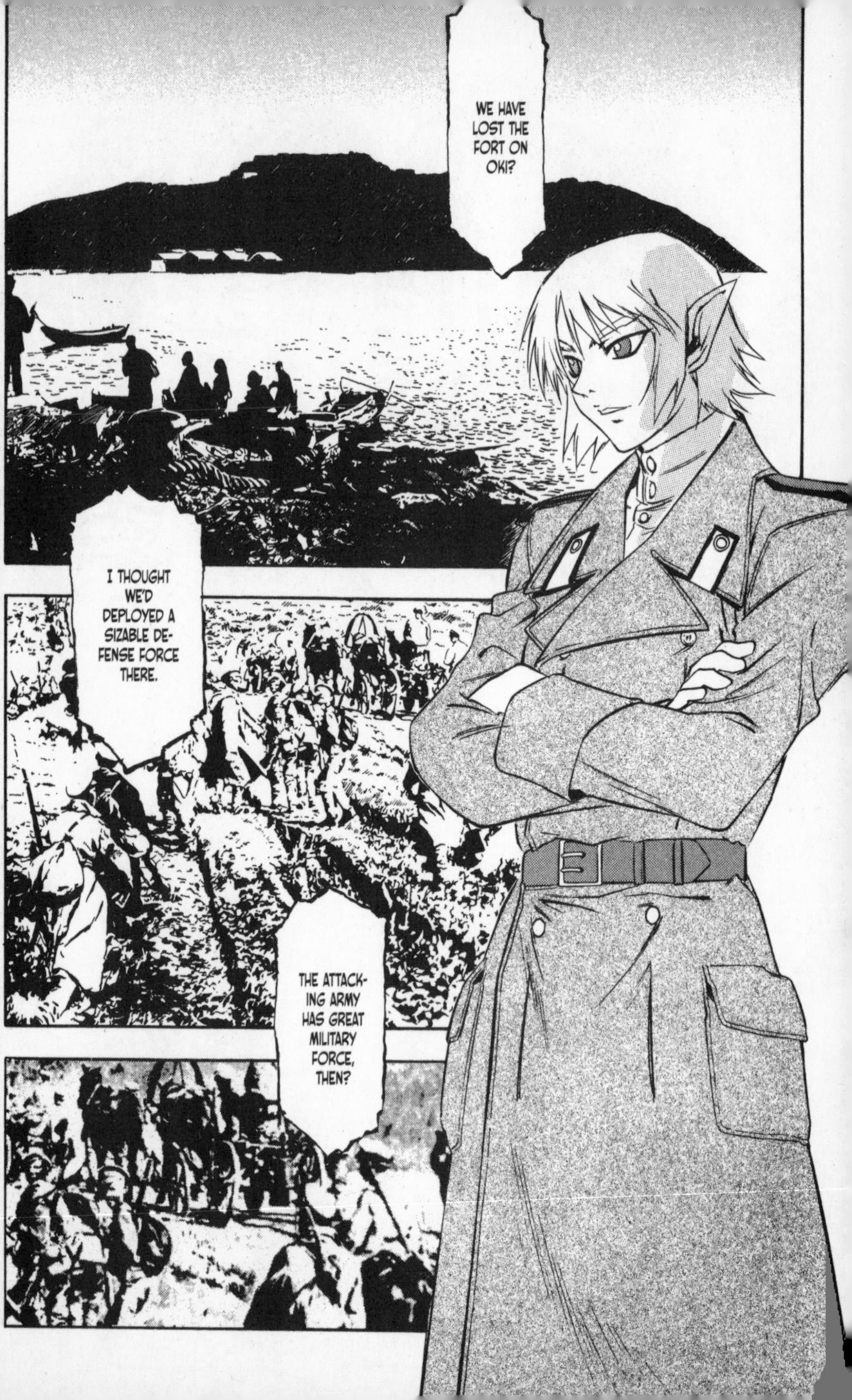
WE HAVE LOST THE FORT ON OKI?
I THOUGHT WE'D DEPLOYED A SIZABLE DE-FENSE FORCE THERE.
THE ATTACK-ING ARMY HAS GREAT MILITARY FORCE, THEN?

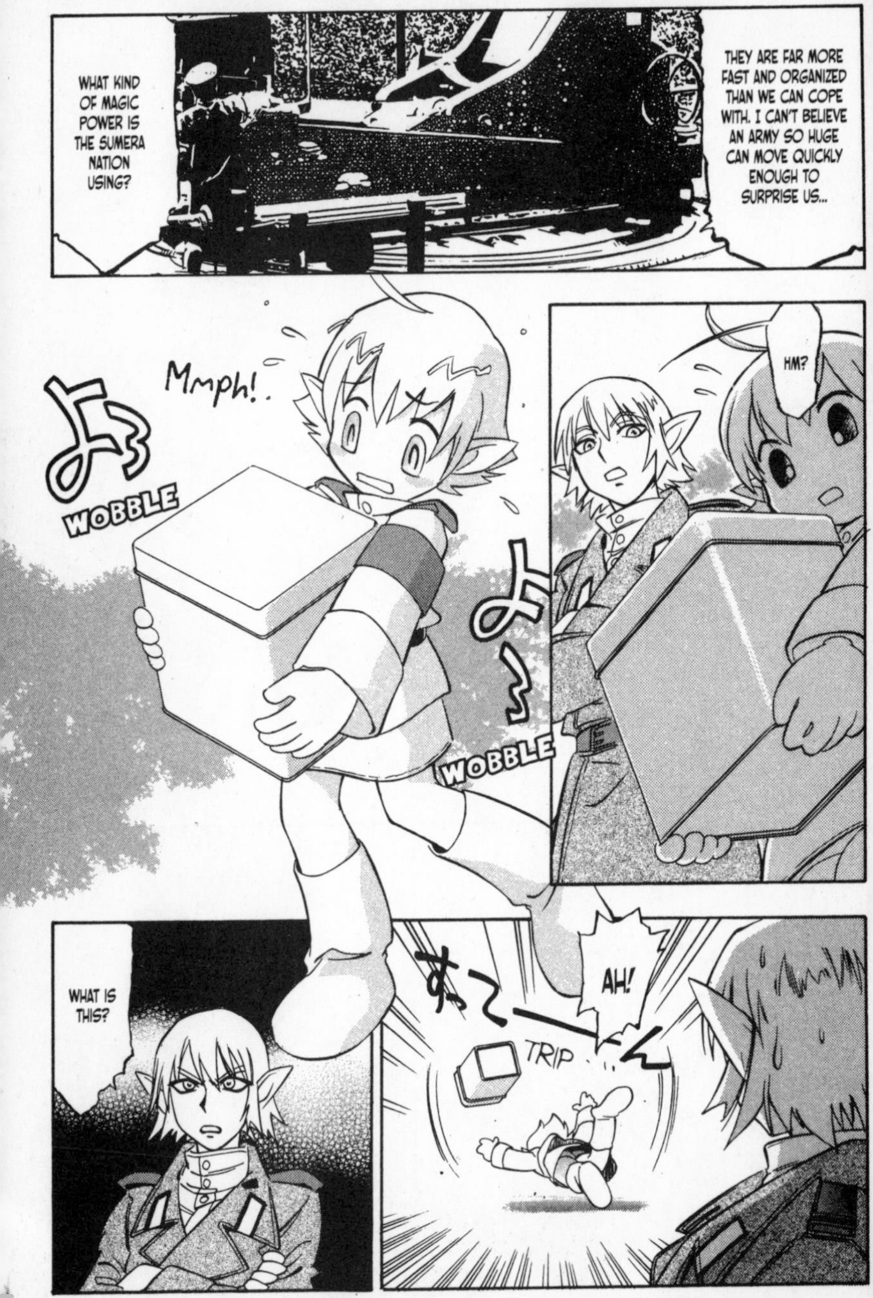
THEY ARE FAR MORE FAST AND ORGANIZED THAN WE CAN COPE WITH. I CAN'T BELIEVE AN ARMY SO HUGE CAN MOVE QUICKLY ENOUGH TO SURPRISE US...
WHAT KIND OF MAGIC POWER IS THE SUMERA NATION USING?
HM?
よろ
WOBBLE
Mmph!..
よろ
WOBBLE
AH!
すてーん
TRIP
WHAT IS THIS?

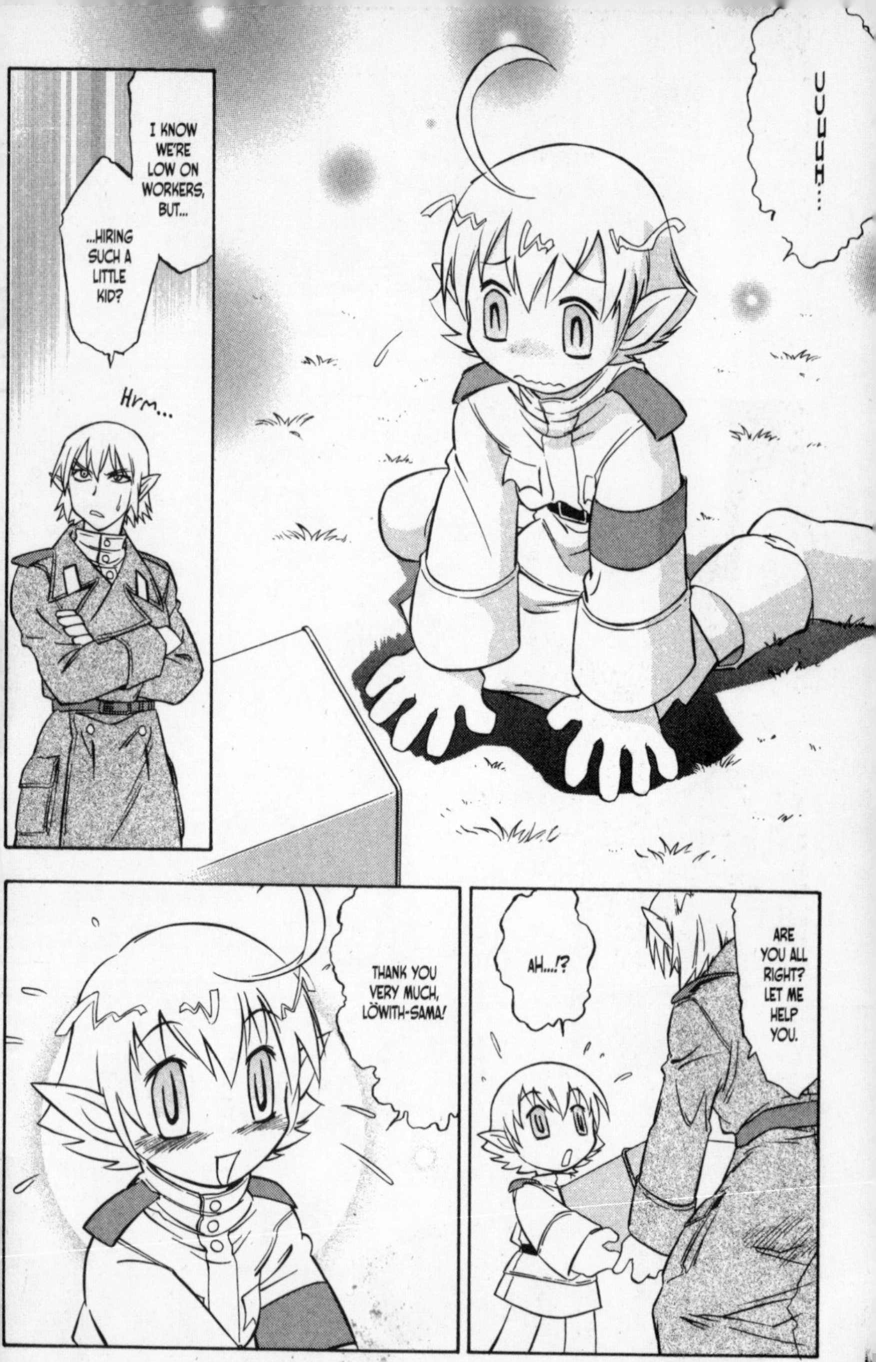
UUUUH...
I KNOW WE'RE LOW ON WORKERS, BUT...
...HIRING SUCH A LITTLE KID?
Hrm...
ARE YOU ALL RIGHT? LET ME HELP YOU.
AH...!?
THANK YOU VERY MUCH, LÖWITH-SAMA!

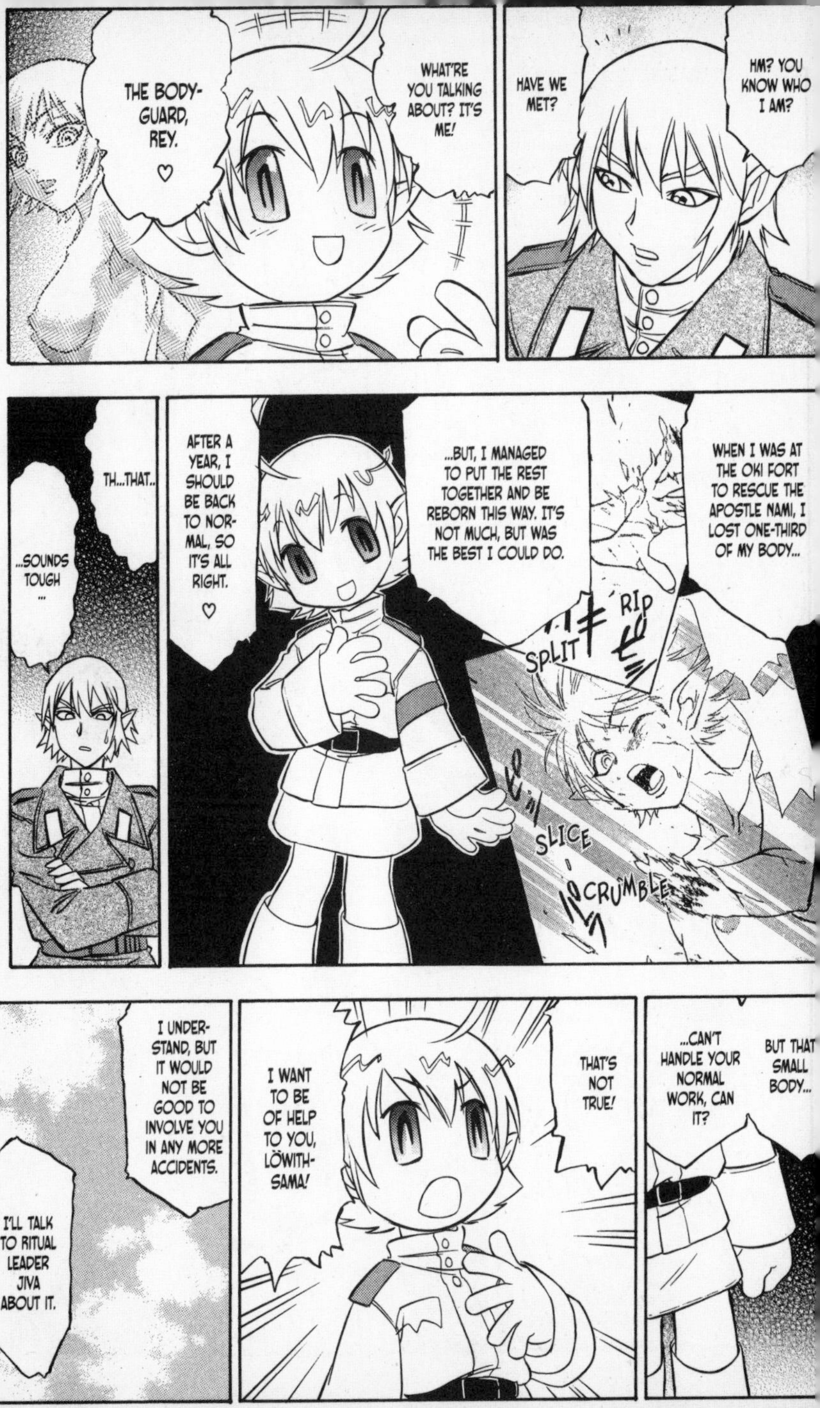
HM? YOU KNOW WHO I AM?
HAVE WE MET?
WHAT'RE YOU TALKING ABOUT? IT'S ME!
THE BODY-GUARD, REY. ♡
WHEN I WAS AT THE OKI FORT TO RESCUE THE APOSTLE NAMI, I LOST ONE-THIRD OF MY BODY...
RIP
SPLIT
SLICE
CRUMBLE
...BUT, I MANAGED TO PUT THE REST TOGETHER AND BE REBORN THIS WAY. IT'S NOT MUCH, BUT WAS THE BEST I COULD DO.
AFTER A YEAR, I SHOULD BE BACK TO NOR-MAL, SO IT'S ALL RIGHT. ♡
TH...THAT...
...SOUNDS TOUGH ...
BUT THAT SMALL BODY...
...CAN'T HANDLE YOUR NORMAL WORK, CAN IT?
THAT'S NOT TRUE!
I WANT TO BE OF HELP TO YOU, LÖWITH-SAMA!
I UNDER-STAND, BUT IT WOULD NOT BE GOOD TO INVOLVE YOU IN ANY MORE ACCIDENTS.
I'LL TALK TO RITUAL LEADER JIVA ABOUT IT.

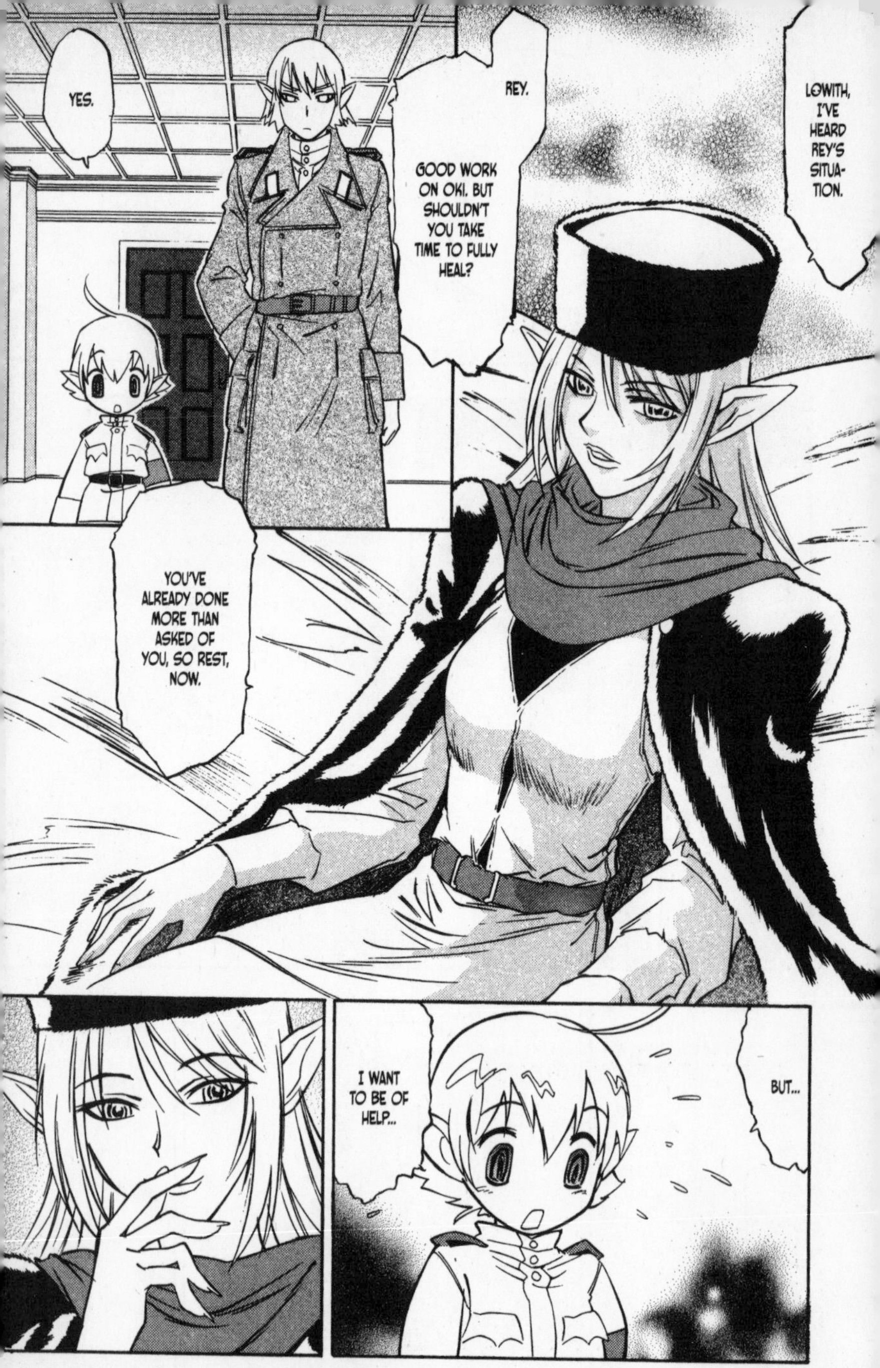
LOWITH, I'VE HEARD REY'S SITUATION.
REY.
GOOD WORK ON OKI. BUT SHOULDN'T YOU TAKE TIME TO FULLY HEAL?
YES.
YOU'VE ALREADY DONE MORE THAN ASKED OF YOU, SO REST, NOW.
BUT...
I WANT TO BE OF HELP...

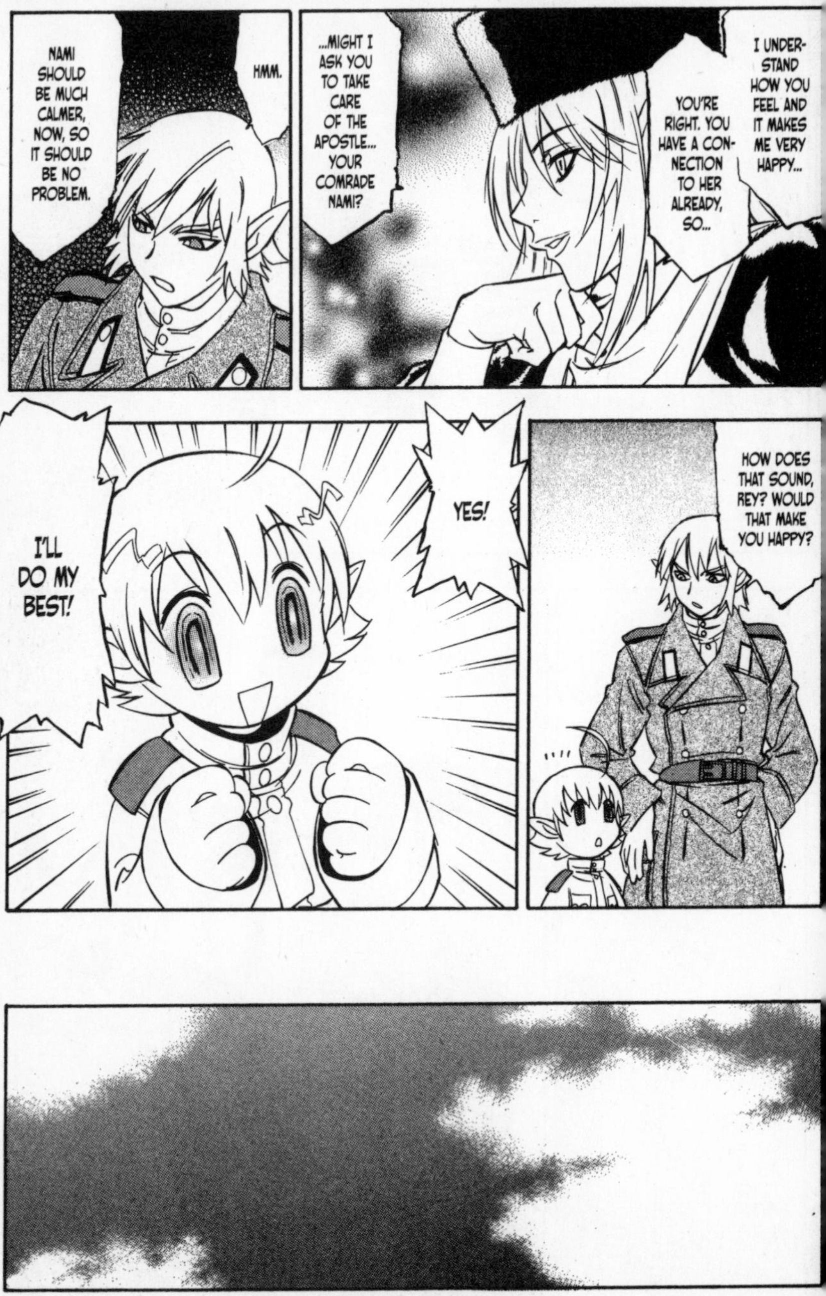
I UNDER-STAND HOW YOU FEEL AND IT MAKES ME VERY HAPPY...
YOU'RE RIGHT. YOU HAVE A CON-NECTION TO HER ALREADY, SO...
...MIGHT I ASK YOU TO TAKE CARE OF THE APOSTLE... YOUR COMRADE NAMI?
HMM.
NAMI SHOULD BE MUCH CALMER, NOW, SO IT SHOULD BE NO PROBLEM.
HOW DOES THAT SOUND, REY? WOULD THAT MAKE YOU HAPPY?
YES!
I'LL DO MY BEST!

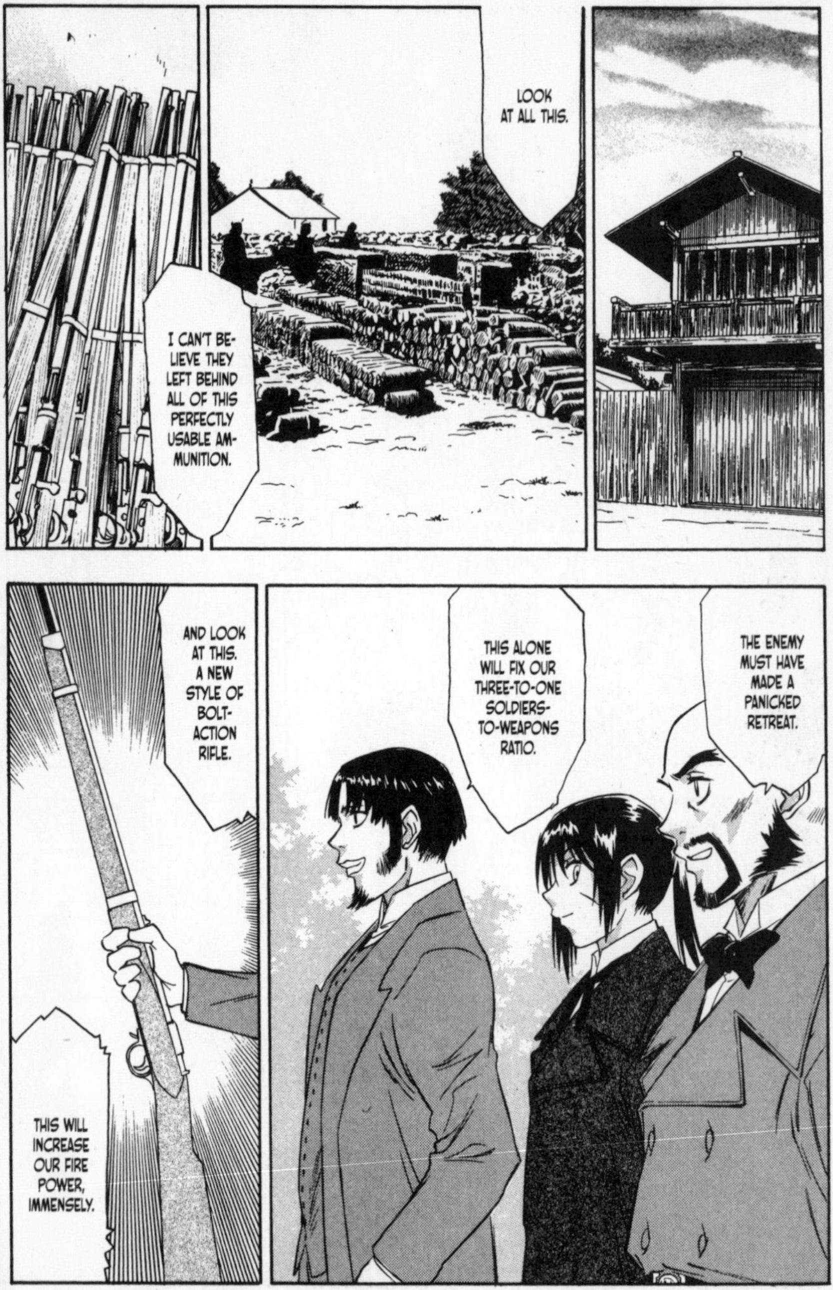
LOOK AT ALL THIS.
I CAN'T BE-LIEVE THEY LEFT BEHIND ALL OF THIS PERFECTLY USABLE AM-MUNITION.
THE ENEMY MUST HAVE MADE A PANICKED RETREAT.
THIS ALONE WILL FIX OUR THREE-TO-ONE SOLDIERS-TO-WEAPONS RATIO.
AND LOOK AT THIS. A NEW STYLE OF BOLT-ACTION RIFLE.
THIS WILL INCREASE OUR FIRE POWER, IMMENSELY.

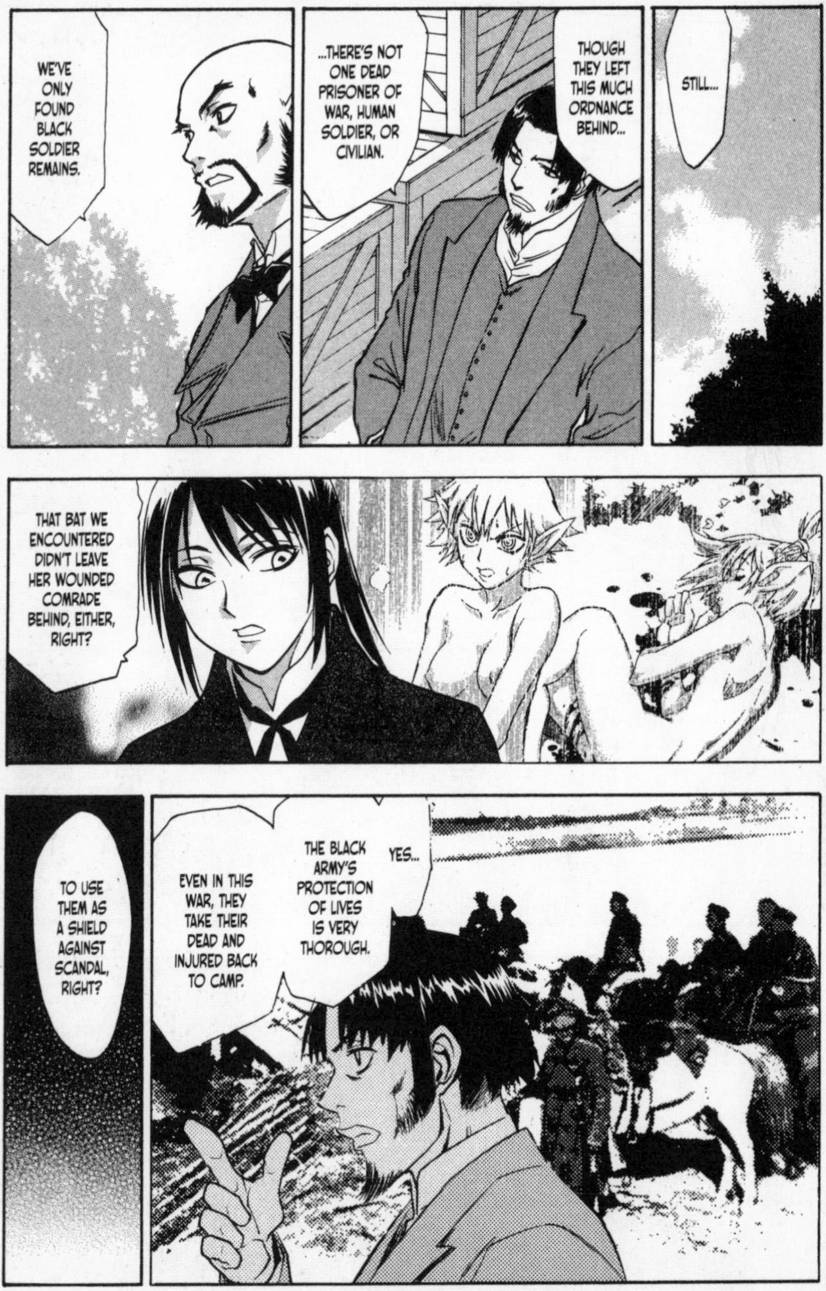
STILL...
THOUGH THEY LEFT THIS MUCH ORDNANCE BEHIND...
...THERE'S NOT ONE DEAD PRISONER OF WAR, HUMAN SOLDIER, OR CIVILIAN.
WE'VE ONLY FOUND BLACK SOLDIER REMAINS.
THAT BAT WE ENCOUNTERED DIDN'T LEAVE HER WOUNDED COMRADE BEHIND, EITHER, RIGHT?
YES...
THE BLACK ARMY'S PROTECTION OF LIVES IS VERY THOROUGH.
EVEN IN THIS WAR, THEY TAKE THEIR DEAD AND INJURED BACK TO CAMP.
TO USE THEM AS A SHIELD AGAINST SCANDAL, RIGHT?

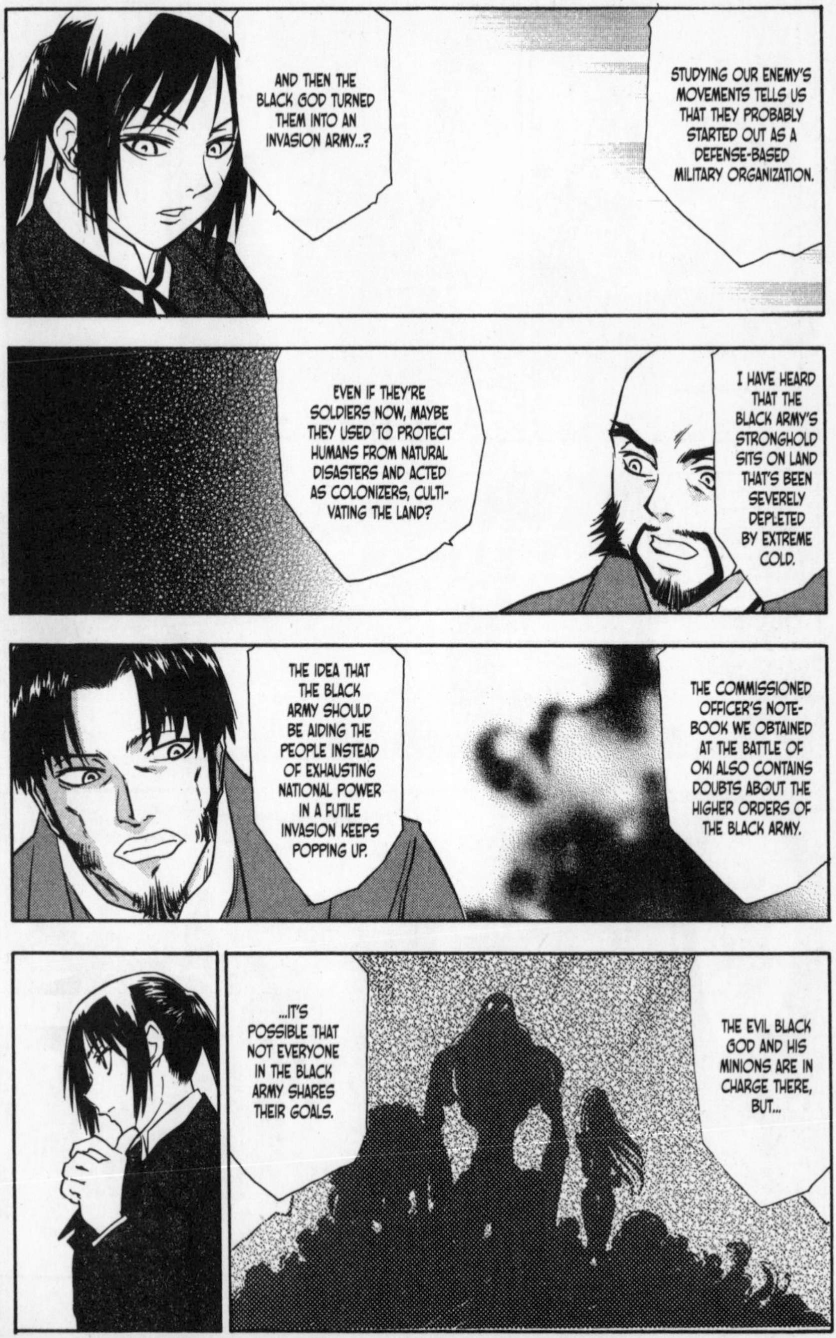
STUDYING OUR ENEMY'S MOVEMENTS TELLS US THAT THEY PROBABLY STARTED OUT AS A DEFENSE-BASED MILITARY ORGANIZATION.
AND THEN THE BLACK GOD TURNED THEM INTO AN INVASION ARMY...?
I HAVE HEARD THAT THE BLACK ARMY'S STRONGHOLD SITS ON LAND THAT'S BEEN SEVERELY DEPLETED BY EXTREME COLD.
EVEN IF THEY'RE SOLDIERS NOW, MAYBE THEY USED TO PROTECT HUMANS FROM NATURAL DISASTERS AND ACTED AS COLONIZERS, CULTI-VATING THE LAND?
THE COMMISSIONED OFFICER'S NOTE-BOOK WE OBTAINED AT THE BATTLE OF OKI ALSO CONTAINS DOUBTS ABOUT THE HIGHER ORDERS OF THE BLACK ARMY.
THE IDEA THAT THE BLACK ARMY SHOULD BE AIDING THE PEOPLE INSTEAD OF EXHAUSTING NATIONAL POWER IN A FUTILE INVASION KEEPS POPPING UP.
THE EVIL BLACK GOD AND HIS MINIONS ARE IN CHARGE THERE, BUT...
...IT'S POSSIBLE THAT NOT EVERYONE IN THE BLACK ARMY SHARES THEIR GOALS.

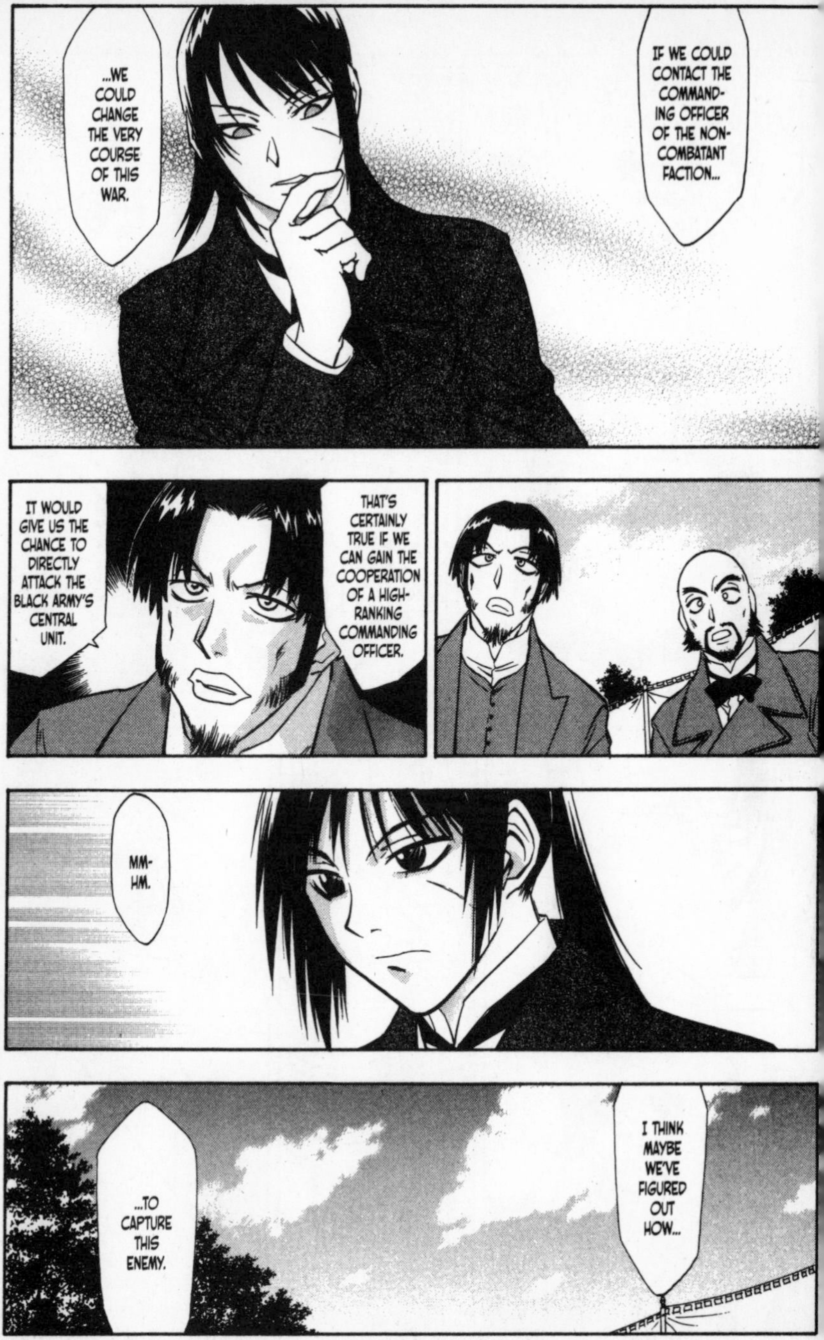
IF WE COULD CONTACT THE COMMAND-ING OFFICER OF THE NON-COMBATANT FACTION...
...WE COULD CHANGE THE VERY COURSE OF THIS WAR.
THAT'S CERTAINLY TRUE IF WE CAN GAIN THE COOPERATION OF A HIGH-RANKING COMMANDING OFFICER.
IT WOULD GIVE US THE CHANCE TO DIRECTLY ATTACK THE BLACK ARMY'S CENTRAL UNIT.
MM-HM.
I THINK MAYBE WE'VE FIGURED OUT HOW...
...TO CAPTURE THIS ENEMY.

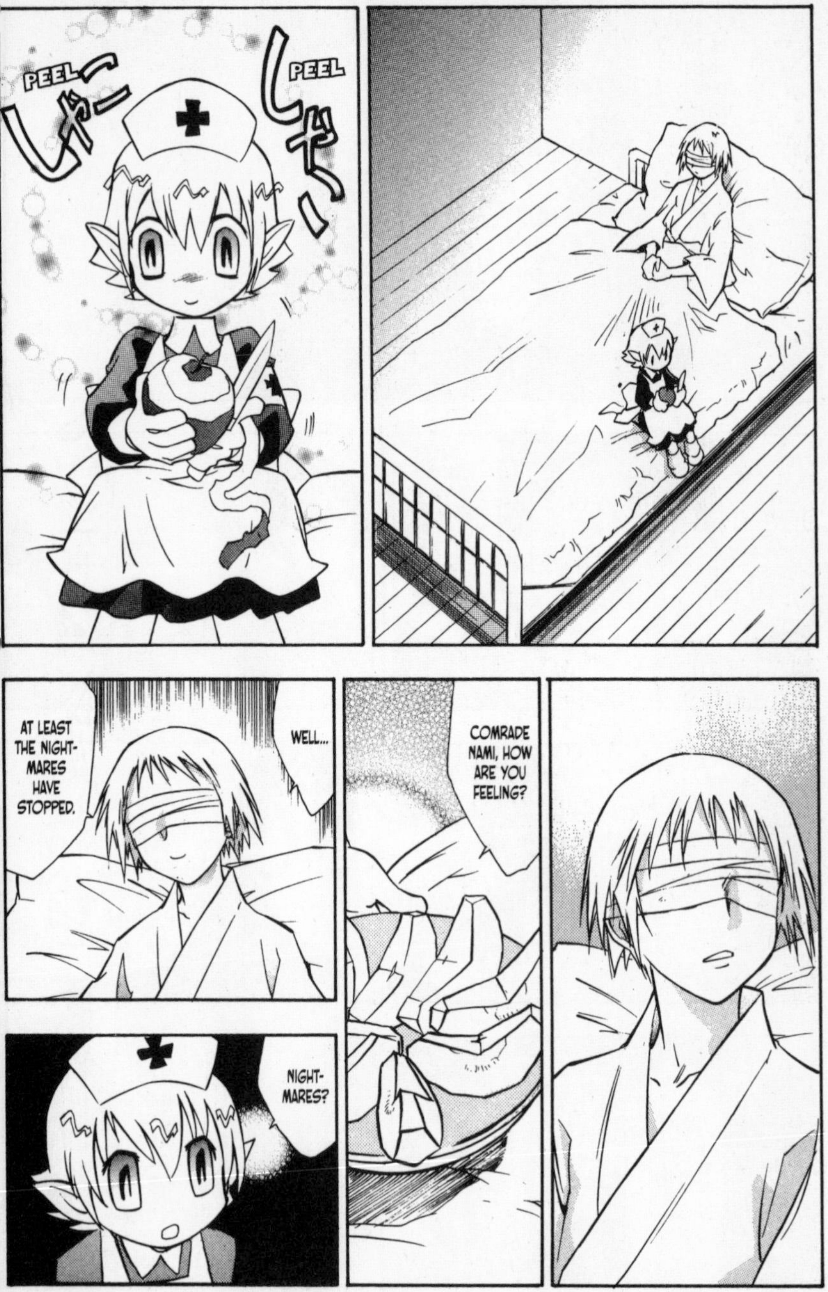
PEEL
PEEL
COMRADE NAMI, HOW ARE YOU FEELING?
WELL...
AT LEAST THE NIGHT-MARES HAVE STOPPED.
NIGHT-MARES?

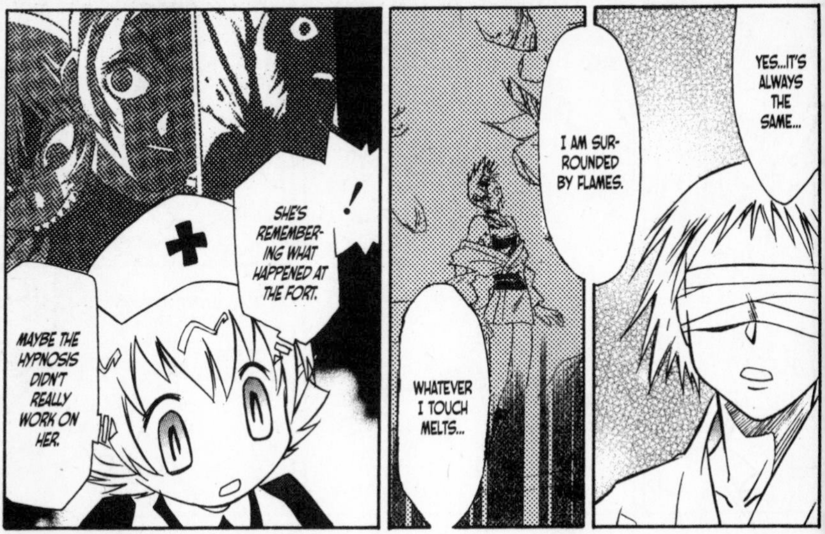
YES...IT'S ALWAYS THE SAME...
I AM SURROUNDED BY FLAMES.
WHATEVER I TOUCH MELTS...
!
SHE'S REMEMBERING WHAT HAPPENED AT THE FORT.
MAYBE THE HYPNOSIS DIDN'T REALLY WORK ON HER.

*Hypnosis: Controlling another's mind.

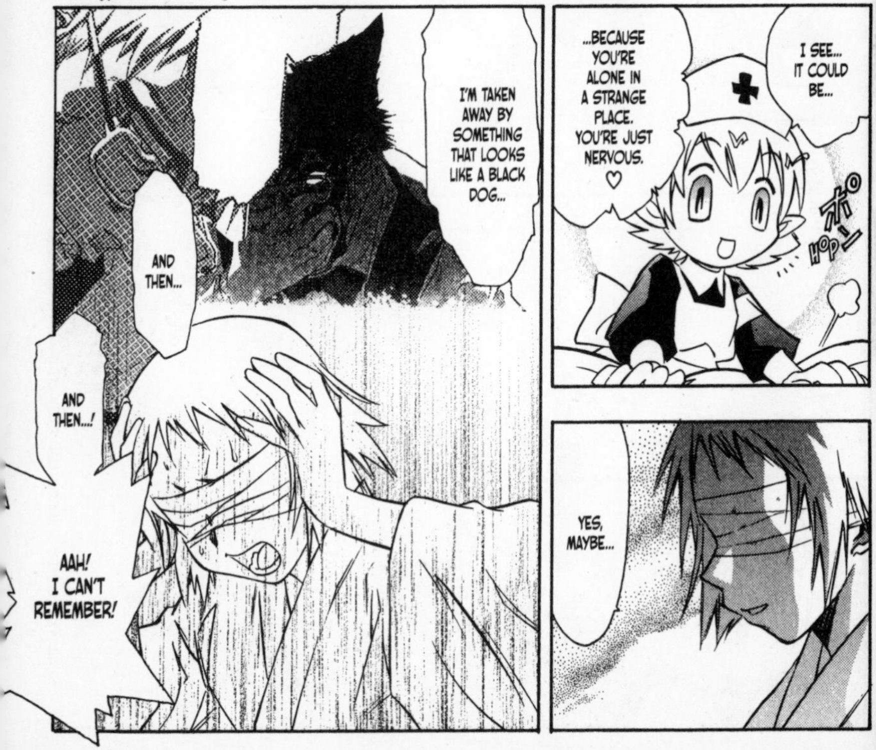
I SEE... IT COULD BE...
...BECAUSE YOU'RE ALONE IN A STRANGE PLACE. YOU'RE JUST NERVOUS. ♡
HOP
YES, MAYBE...
I'M TAKEN AWAY BY SOMETHING THAT LOOKS LIKE A BLACK DOG...
AND THEN...
AND THEN...!
AAH! I CAN'T REMEMBER!

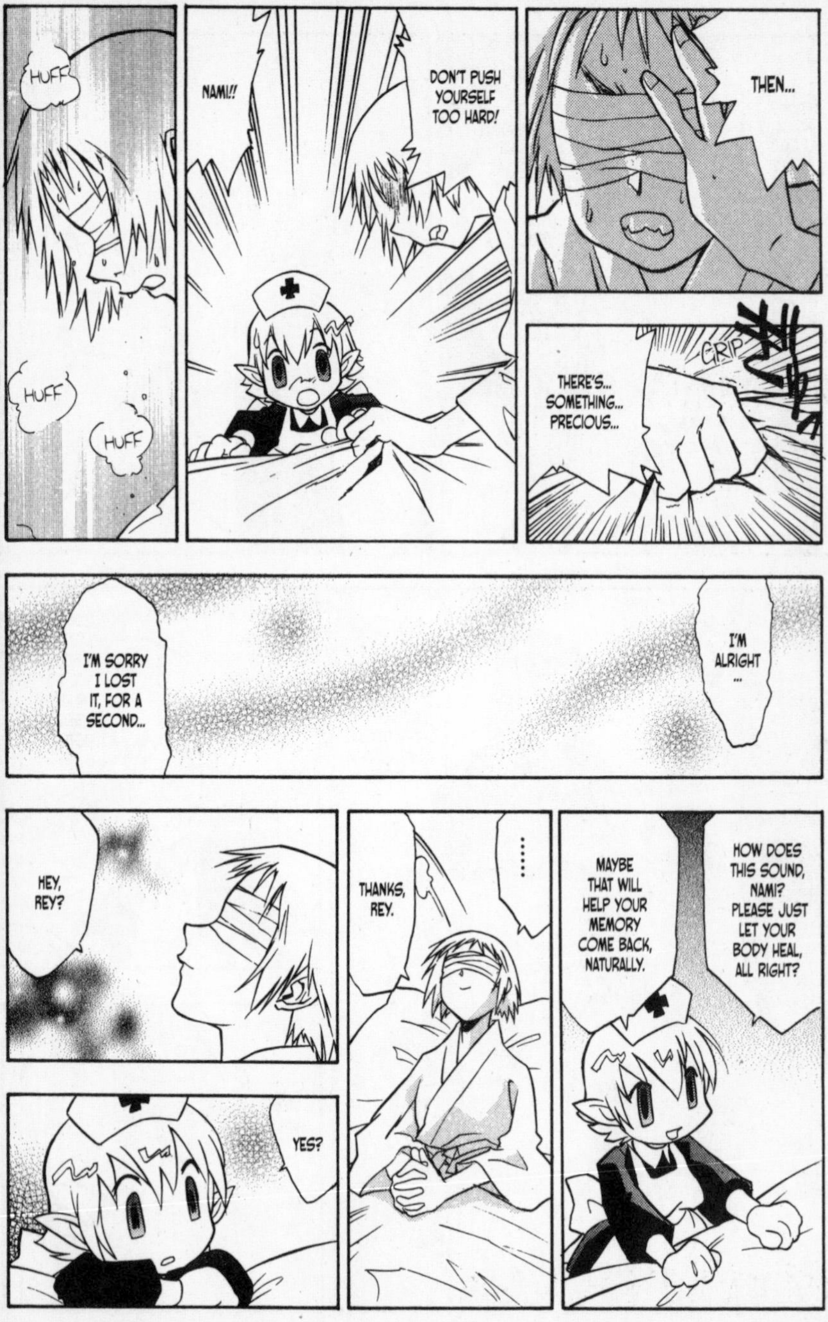
THEN...
THERE'S... SOMETHING... PRECIOUS...
GRIP
DON'T PUSH YOURSELF TOO HARD!
NAMI!!
HUFF
HUFF
HUFF
I'M ALRIGHT ...
I'M SORRY I LOST IT, FOR A SECOND...
HOW DOES THIS SOUND, NAMI? PLEASE JUST LET YOUR BODY HEAL, ALL RIGHT?
MAYBE THAT WILL HELP YOUR MEMORY COME BACK, NATURALLY.
......
THANKS, REY.
HEY, REY?
YES?

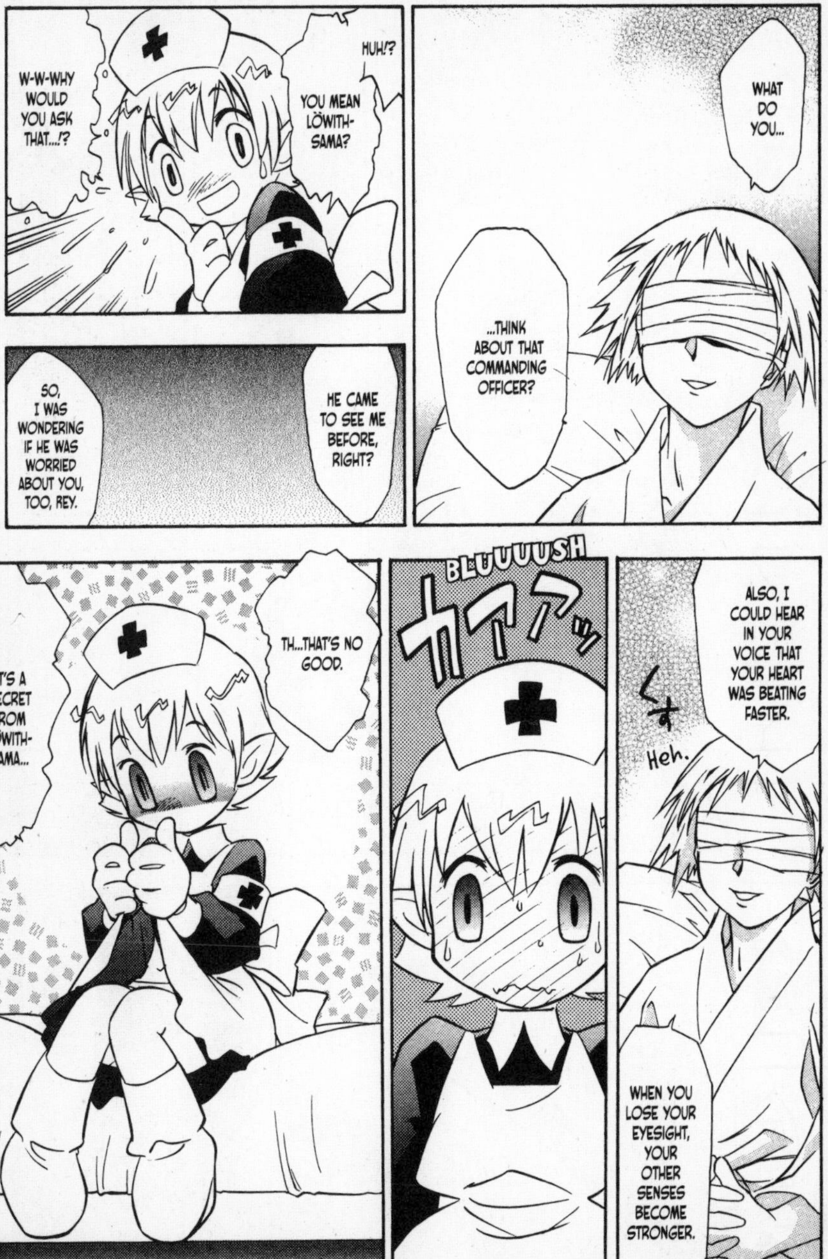
WHAT DO YOU...
...THINK ABOUT THAT COMMANDING OFFICER?
HUH!?
YOU MEAN LÖWITH-SAMA?
W-W-WHY WOULD YOU ASK THAT...!?
HE CAME TO SEE ME BEFORE, RIGHT?
SO, I WAS WONDERING IF HE WAS WORRIED ABOUT YOU, TOO, REY.
ALSO, I COULD HEAR IN YOUR VOICE THAT YOUR HEART WAS BEATING FASTER.
くす
Heh.
WHEN YOU LOSE YOUR EYESIGHT, YOUR OTHER SENSES BECOME STRONGER.
BLUUUUSH
カアアッ
TH...THAT'S NO GOOD.
IT'S A SECRET FROM LÖWITH-SAMA...

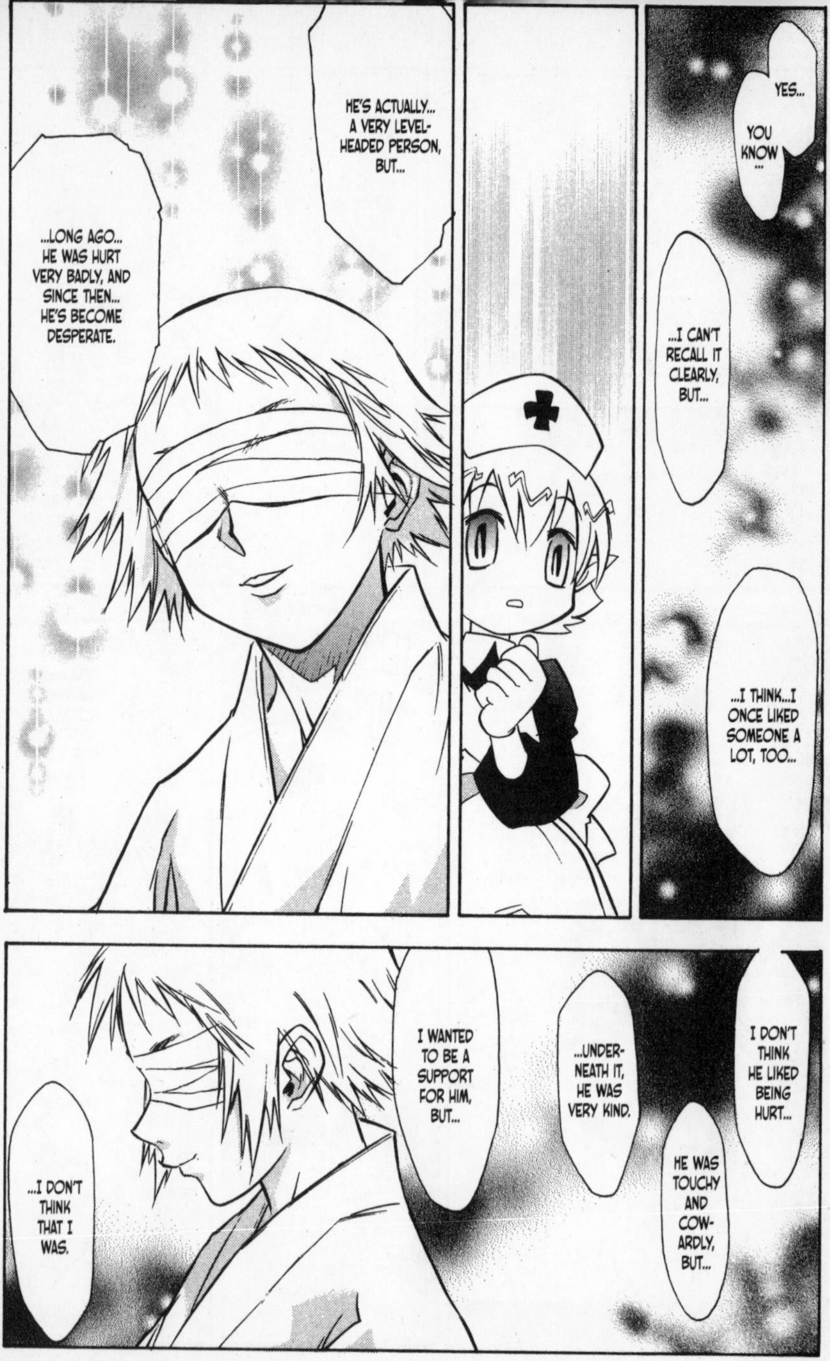
YES...
YOU KNOW...
...I CAN'T RECALL IT CLEARLY, BUT...
...I THINK...I ONCE LIKED SOMEONE A LOT, TOO...
HE'S ACTUALLY... A VERY LEVEL-HEADED PERSON, BUT...
...LONG AGO... HE WAS HURT VERY BADLY, AND SINCE THEN... HE'S BECOME DESPERATE.
I DON'T THINK HE LIKED BEING HURT...
HE WAS TOUCHY AND COW-ARDLY, BUT...
...UNDER-NEATH IT, HE WAS VERY KIND.
I WANTED TO BE A SUPPORT FOR HIM, BUT...
...I DON'T THINK THAT I WAS.

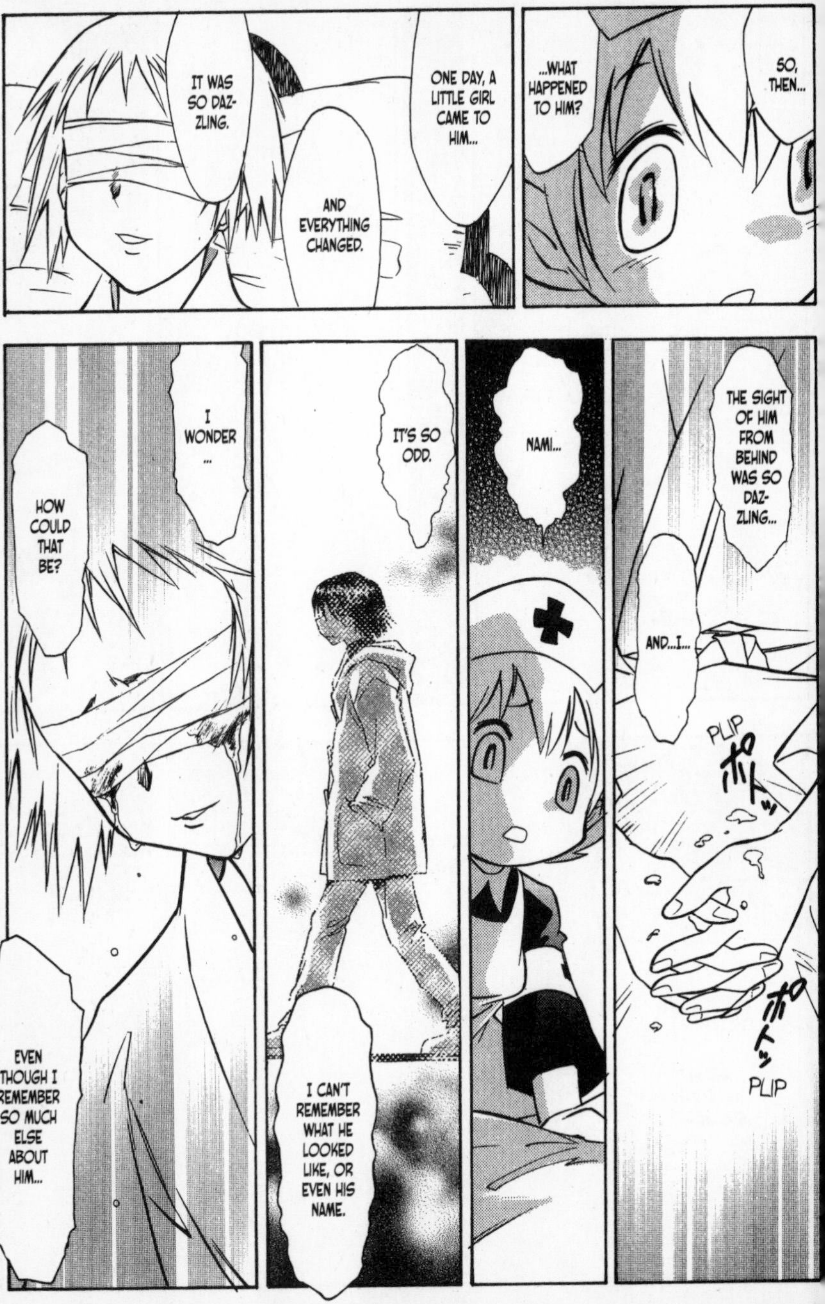
SO, THEN...
...WHAT HAPPENED TO HIM?
ONE DAY, A LITTLE GIRL CAME TO HIM...
AND EVERYTHING CHANGED.
IT WAS SO DAZ-ZLING.
THE SIGHT OF HIM FROM BEHIND WAS SO DAZ-ZLING...
AND...I...
PLIP
PLIP
NAMI...
IT'S SO ODD.
I CAN'T REMEMBER WHAT HE LOOKED LIKE, OR EVEN HIS NAME.
I WONDER ...
HOW COULD THAT BE?
EVEN THOUGH I REMEMBER SO MUCH ELSE ABOUT HIM...

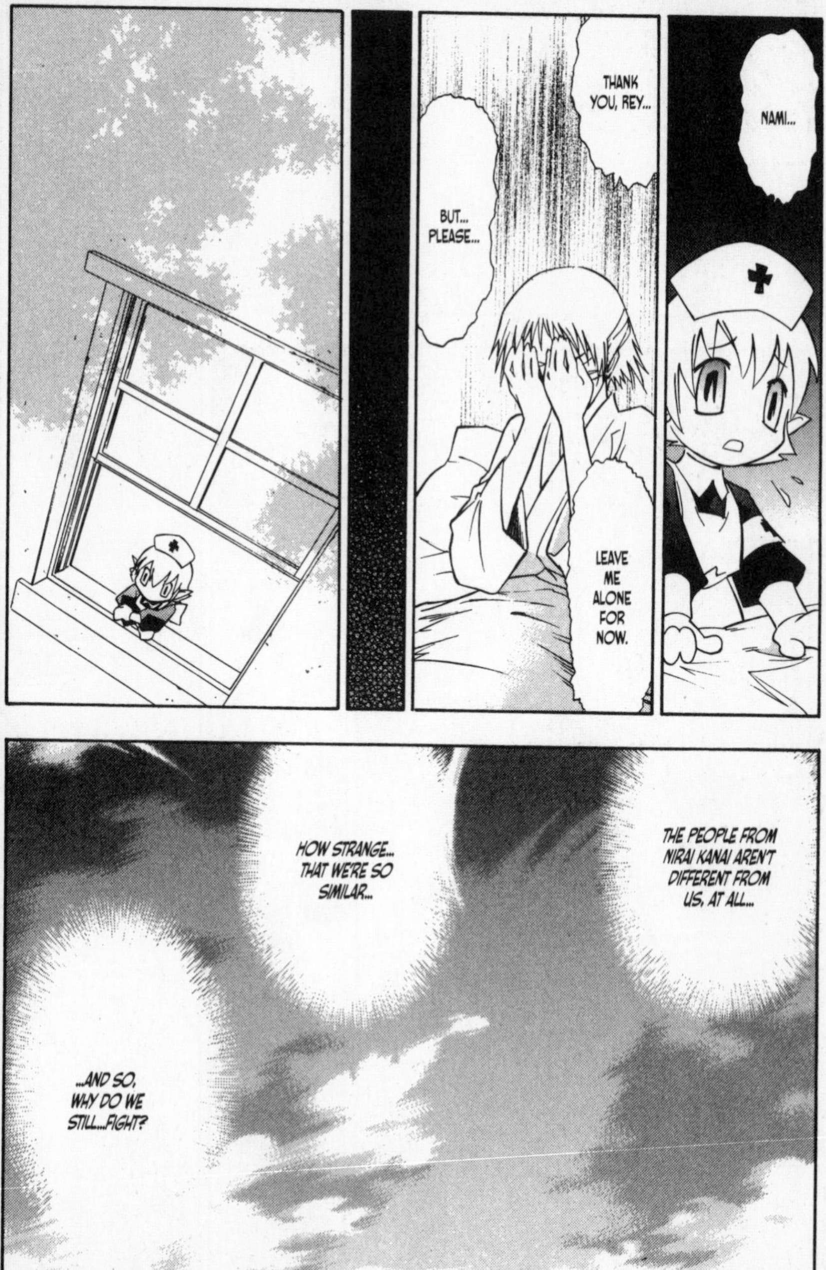
NAMI...
THANK YOU, REY...
BUT... PLEASE...
LEAVE ME ALONE FOR NOW.
THE PEOPLE FROM NIRAI KANAI AREN'T DIFFERENT FROM US, AT ALL...
HOW STRANGE... THAT WE'RE SO SIMILAR...
...AND SO, WHY DO WE STILL...FIGHT?

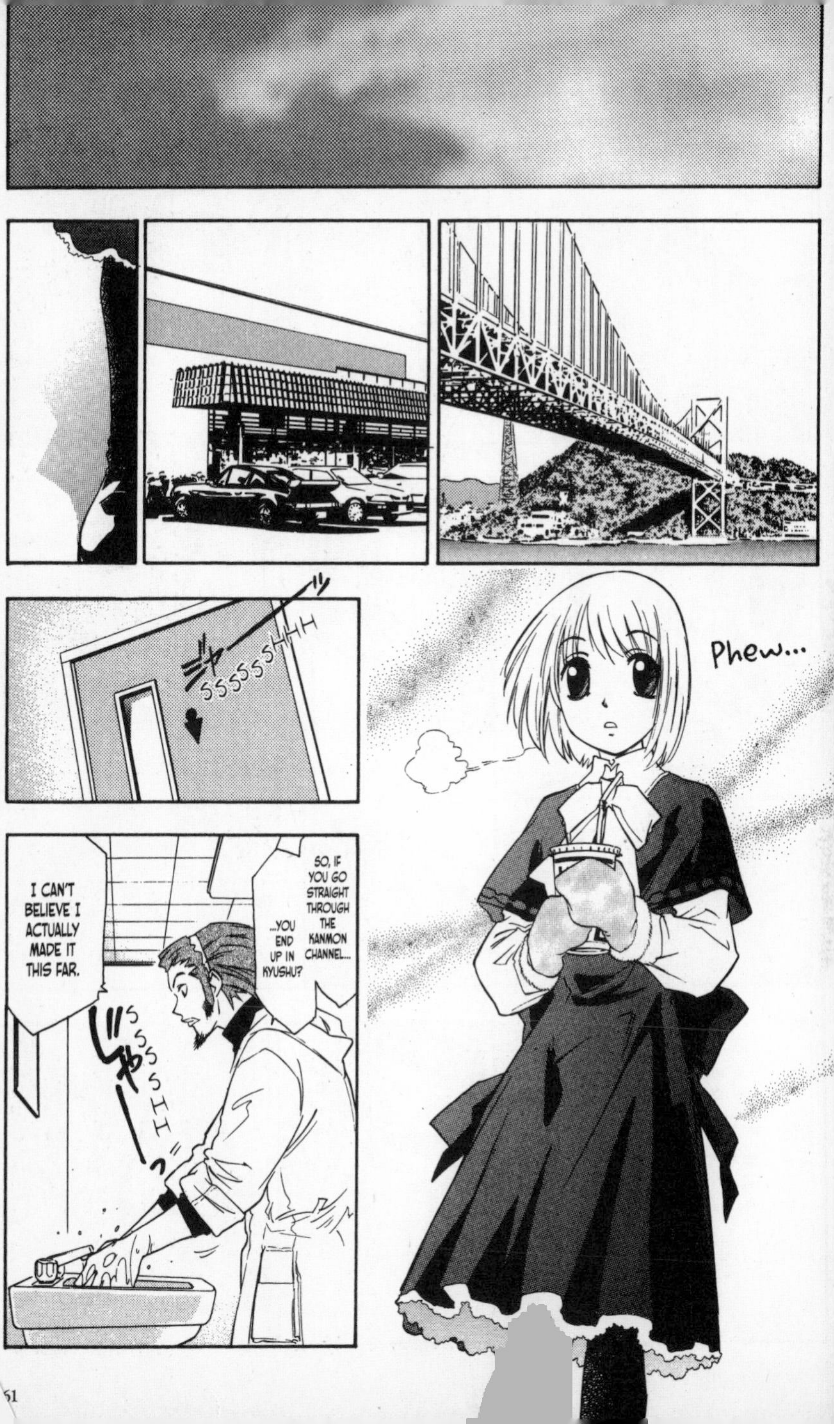
Phew...
SSSSSSHHH
SO, IF YOU GO STRAIGHT THROUGH THE KANMON CHANNEL...
...YOU END UP IN KYUSHU?
I CAN'T BELIEVE I ACTUALLY MADE IT THIS FAR.
SSSSHHH

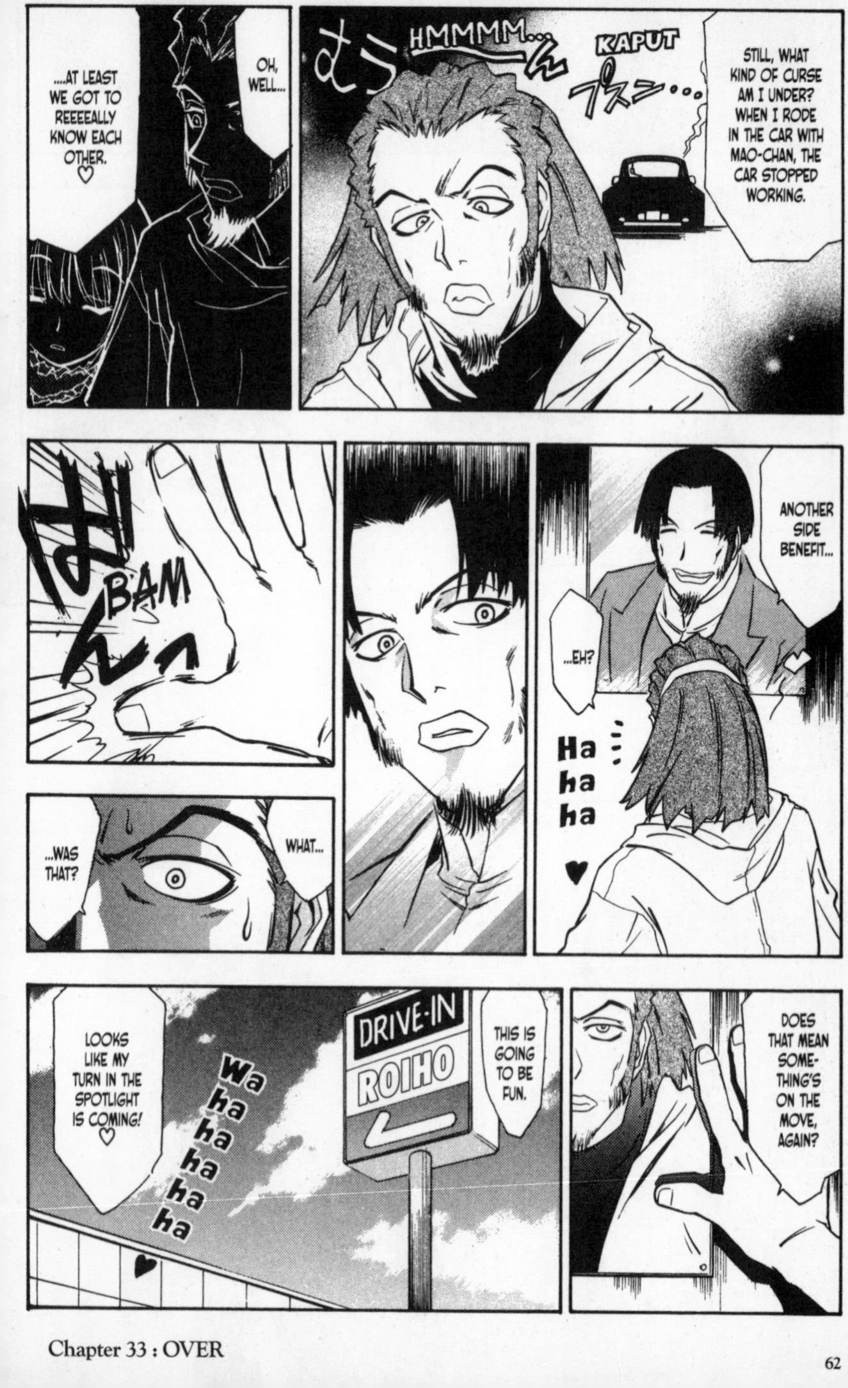
HMMMM...
KAPUT
STILL, WHAT KIND OF CURSE AM I UNDER? WHEN I RODE IN THE CAR WITH MAO-CHAN, THE CAR STOPPED WORKING.
OH, WELL...
....AT LEAST WE GOT TO REEEEALLY KNOW EACH OTHER. ♡
ANOTHER SIDE BENEFIT...
...EH?
Ha ha ha ♥
BAM
WHAT...
...WAS THAT?
DOES THAT MEAN SOME-THING'S ON THE MOVE, AGAIN?
THIS IS GOING TO BE FUN.
DRIVE-IN
ROIHO
LOOKS LIKE MY TURN IN THE SPOTLIGHT IS COMING! ♡
Wa ha ha ha ha ha ha ♥

Chapter 34

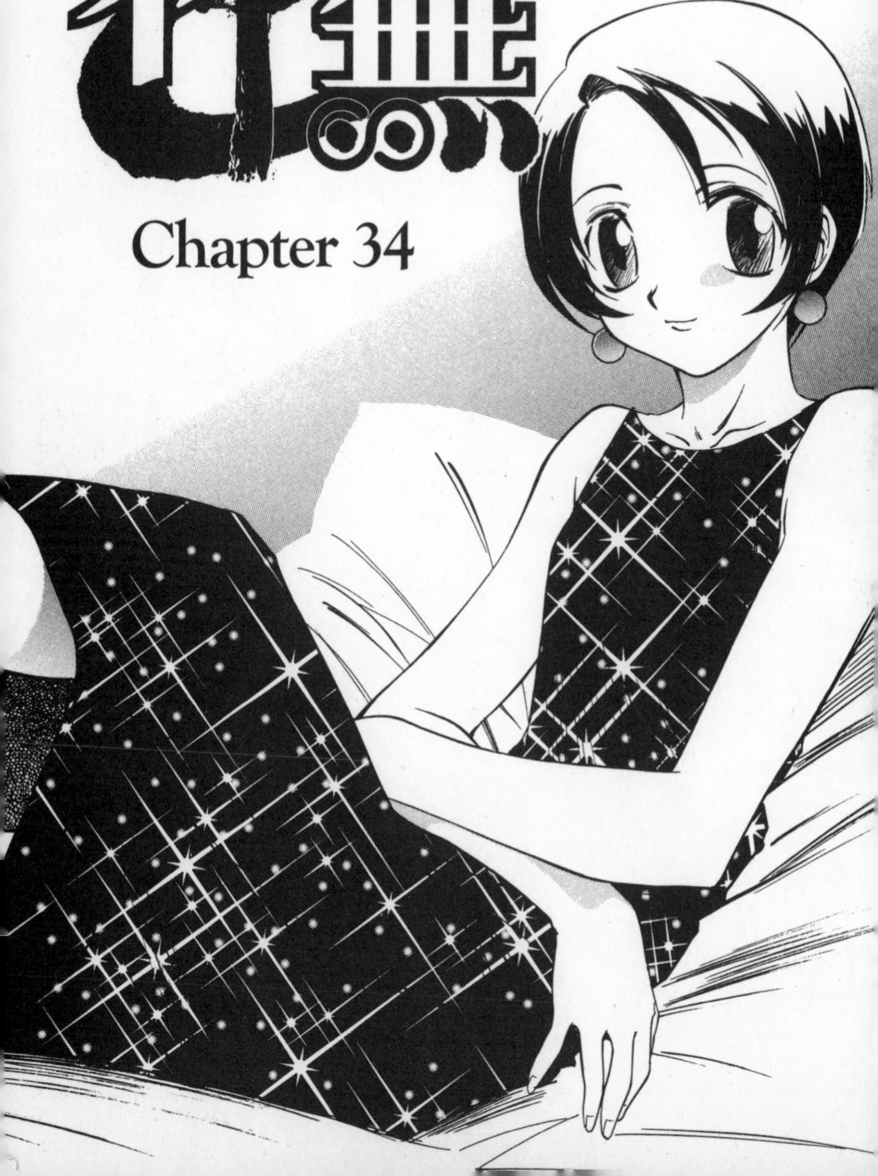

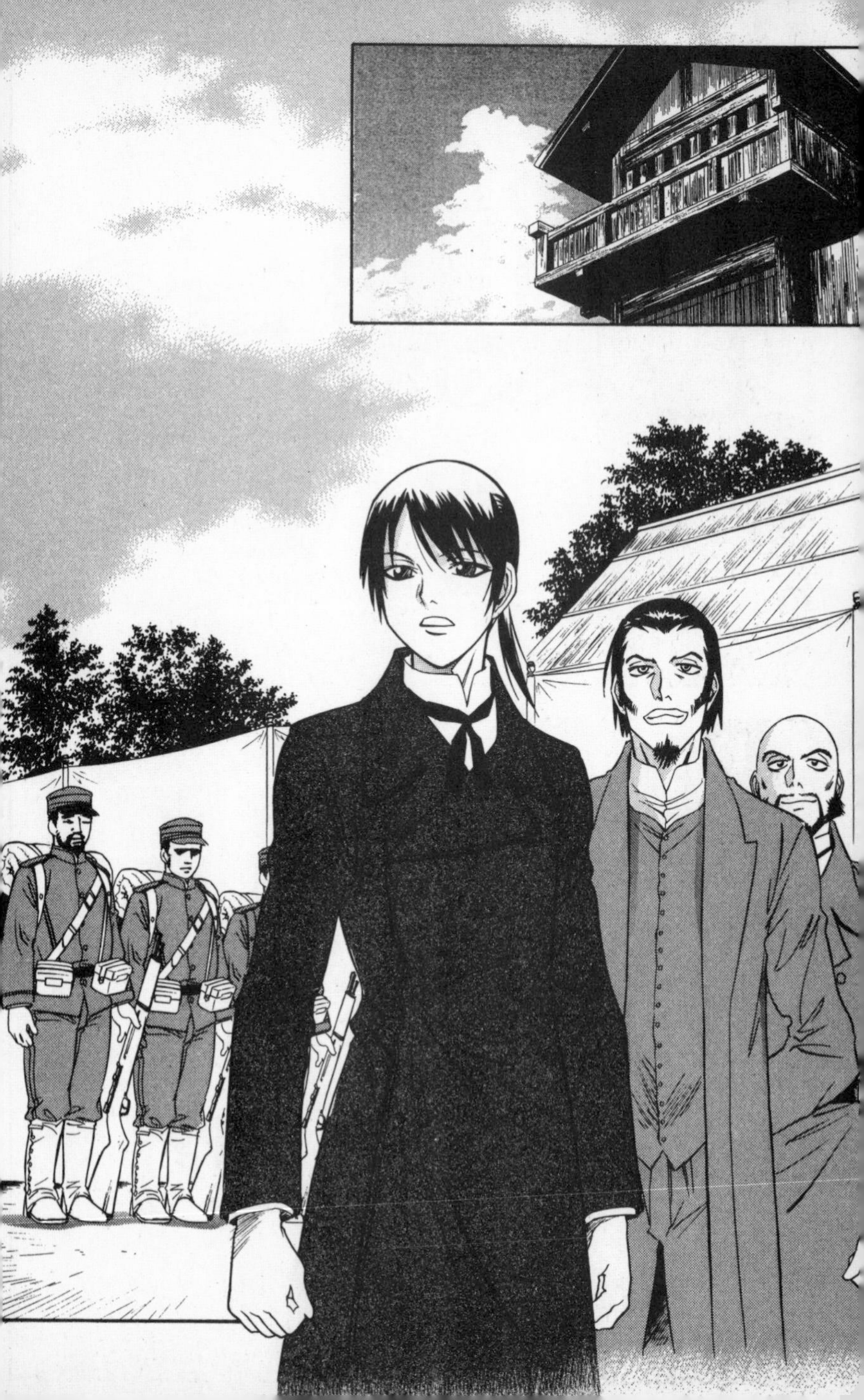

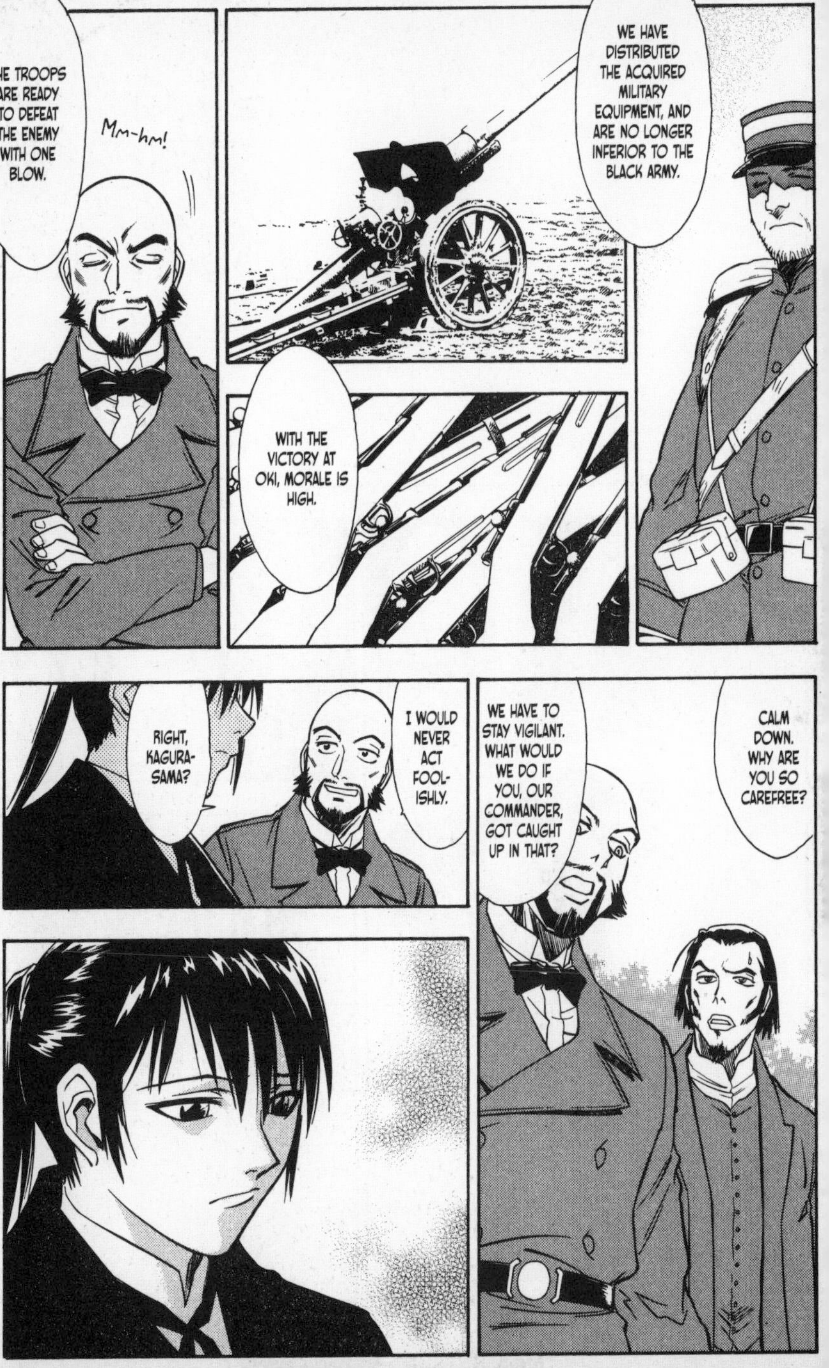
WE HAVE DISTRIBUTED THE ACQUIRED MILITARY EQUIPMENT, AND ARE NO LONGER INFERIOR TO THE BLACK ARMY.
WITH THE VICTORY AT OKI, MORALE IS HIGH.
THE TROOPS ARE READY TO DEFEAT THE ENEMY WITH ONE BLOW.
Mm-hm!
CALM DOWN. WHY ARE YOU SO CAREFREE?
WE HAVE TO STAY VIGILANT. WHAT WOULD WE DO IF YOU, OUR COMMANDER, GOT CAUGHT UP IN THAT?
I WOULD NEVER ACT FOOL-ISHLY.
RIGHT, KAGURA-SAMA?

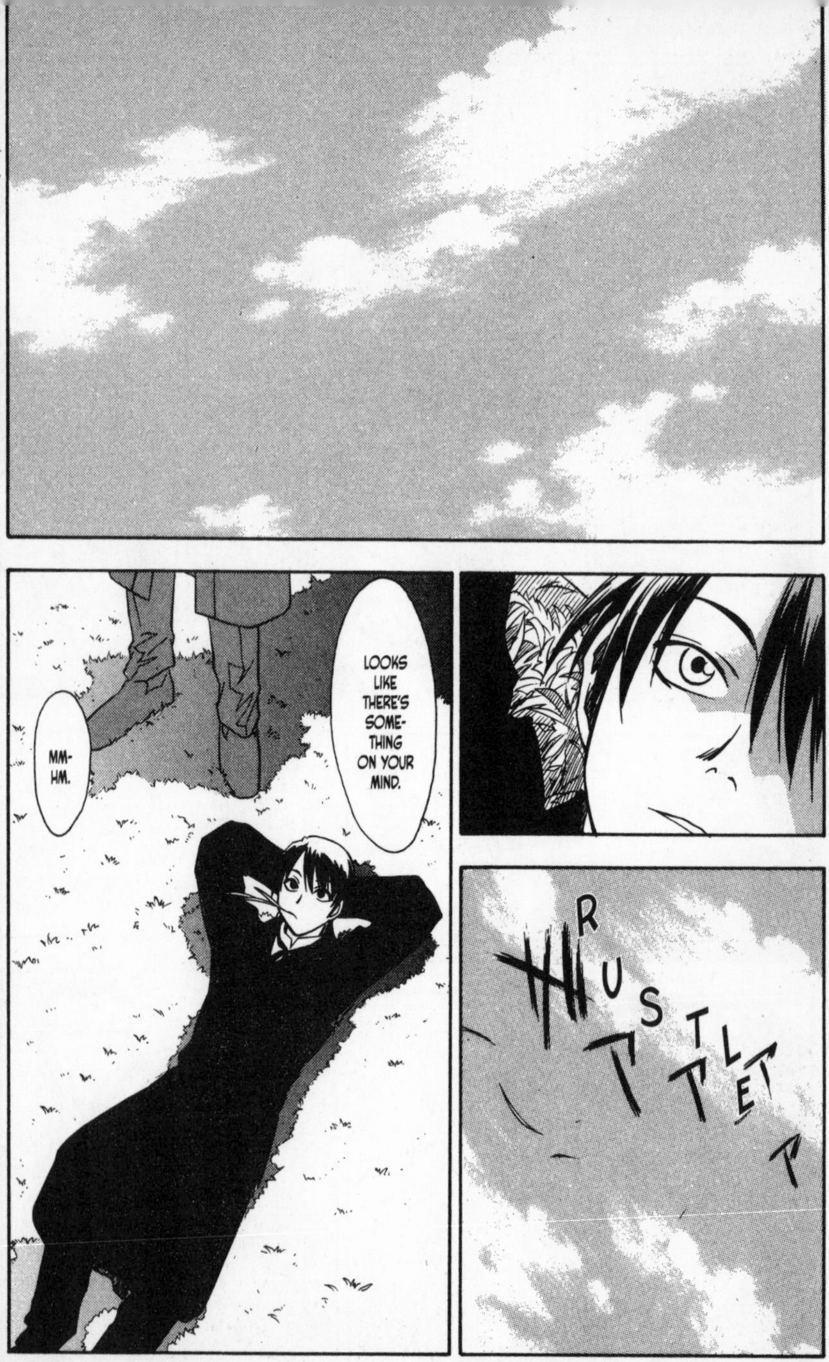
RUSTLE
LOOKS LIKE THERE'S SOME-THING ON YOUR MIND.
MM-HM.

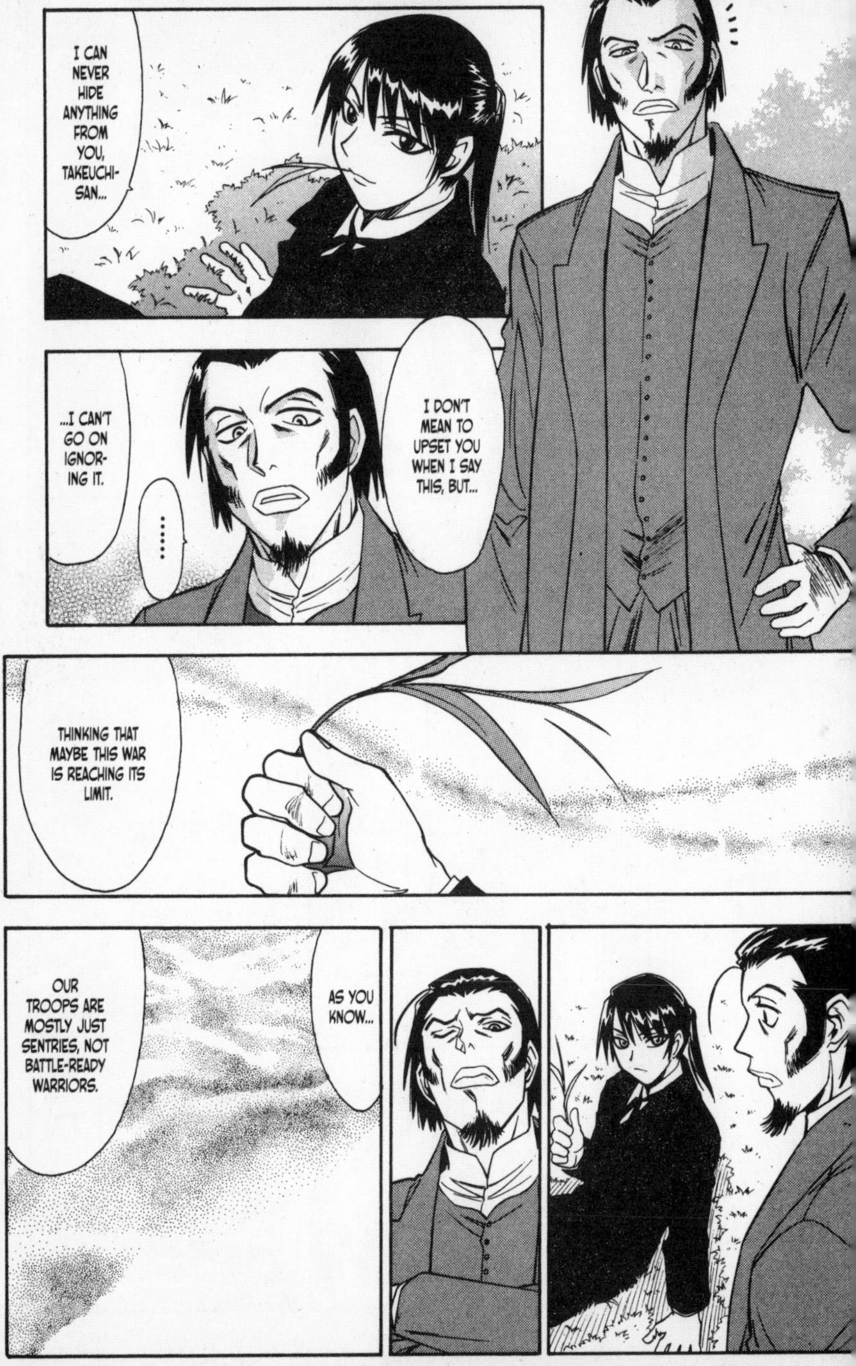
I CAN NEVER HIDE ANYTHING FROM YOU, TAKEUCHI-SAN...
I DON'T MEAN TO UPSET YOU WHEN I SAY THIS, BUT...
......
...I CAN'T GO ON IGNORING IT.
THINKING THAT MAYBE THIS WAR IS REACHING ITS LIMIT.
AS YOU KNOW...
OUR TROOPS ARE MOSTLY JUST SENTRIES, NOT BATTLE-READY WARRIORS.

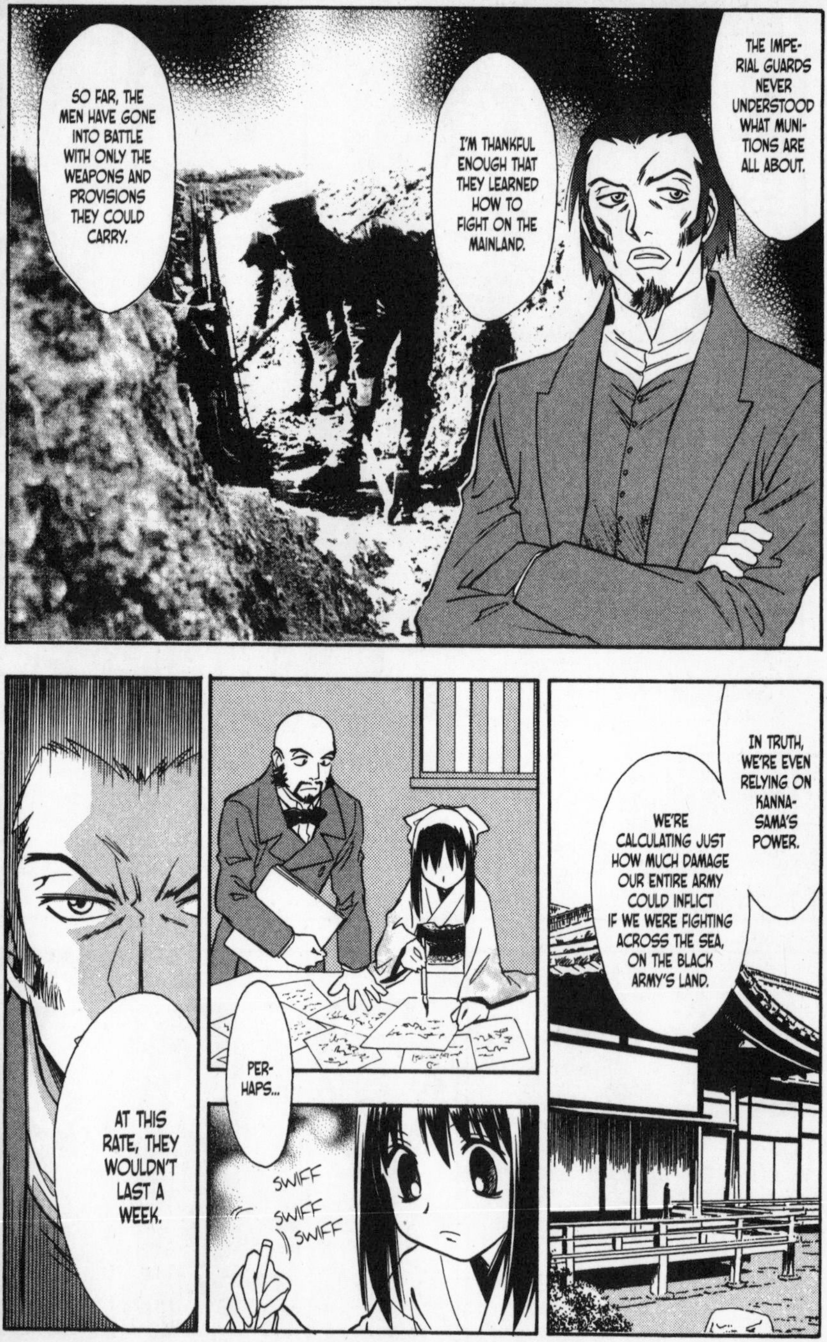
THE IMPERIAL GUARDS NEVER UNDERSTOOD WHAT MUNITIONS ARE ALL ABOUT.
I'M THANKFUL ENOUGH THAT THEY LEARNED HOW TO FIGHT ON THE MAINLAND.
SO FAR, THE MEN HAVE GONE INTO BATTLE WITH ONLY THE WEAPONS AND PROVISIONS THEY COULD CARRY.
IN TRUTH, WE'RE EVEN RELYING ON KANNA-SAMA'S POWER.
WE'RE CALCULATING JUST HOW MUCH DAMAGE OUR ENTIRE ARMY COULD INFLICT IF WE WERE FIGHTING ACROSS THE SEA, ON THE BLACK ARMY'S LAND.
PER-HAPS...
SWIFF
SWIFF
SWIFF
AT THIS RATE, THEY WOULDN'T LAST A WEEK.

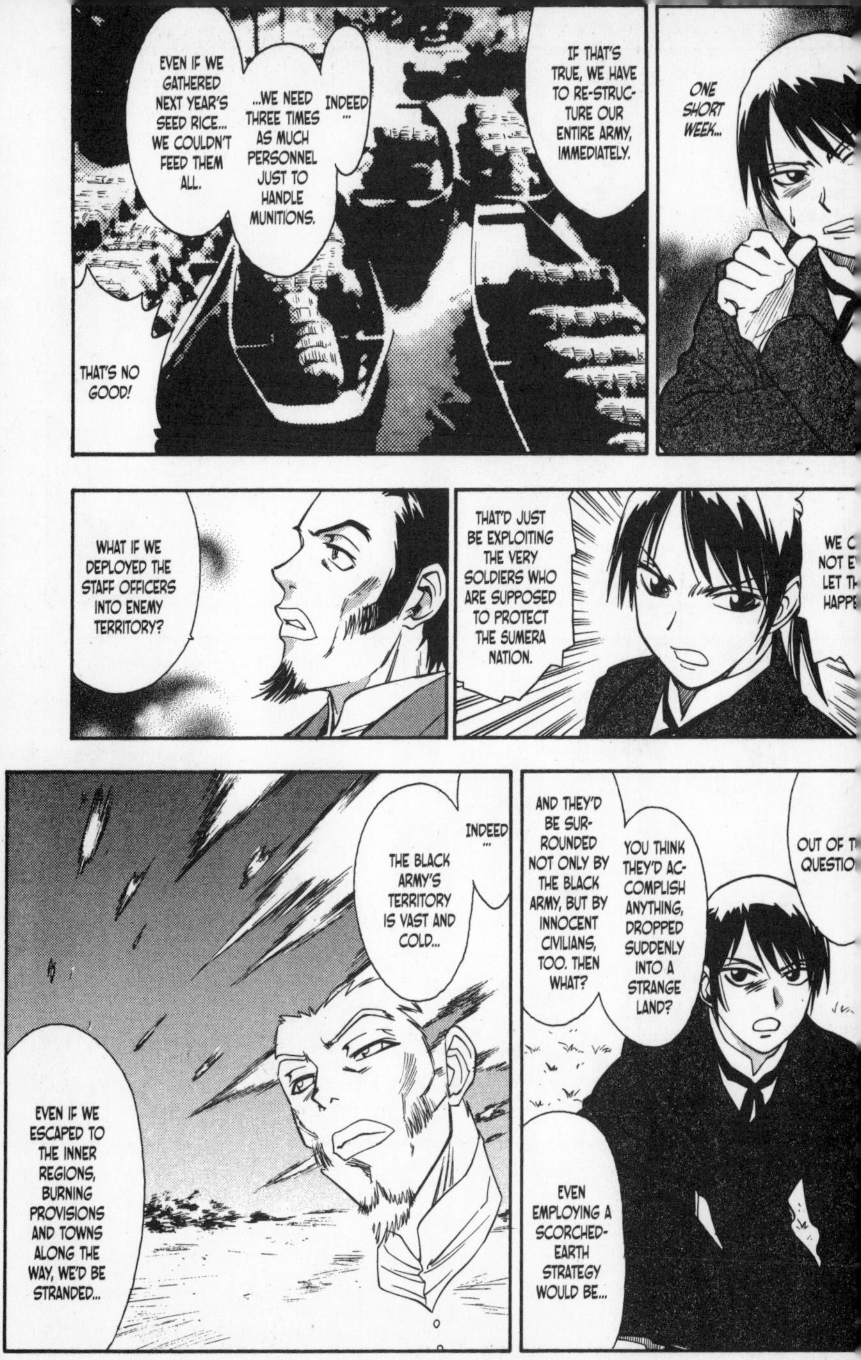
ONE SHORT WEEK...
IF THAT'S TRUE, WE HAVE TO RE-STRUCTURE OUR ENTIRE ARMY, IMMEDIATELY.
INDEED...
...WE NEED THREE TIMES AS MUCH PERSONNEL JUST TO HANDLE MUNITIONS.
EVEN IF WE GATHERED NEXT YEAR'S SEED RICE... WE COULDN'T FEED THEM ALL.
THAT'S NO GOOD!
WE C NOT E LET TH HAPPE
THAT'D JUST BE EXPLOITING THE VERY SOLDIERS WHO ARE SUPPOSED TO PROTECT THE SUMERA NATION.
WHAT IF WE DEPLOYED THE STAFF OFFICERS INTO ENEMY TERRITORY?
OUT OF T QUESTIO
YOU THINK THEY'D ACCOMPLISH ANYTHING, DROPPED SUDDENLY INTO A STRANGE LAND?
AND THEY'D BE SURROUNDED NOT ONLY BY THE BLACK ARMY, BUT BY INNOCENT CIVILIANS, TOO. THEN WHAT?
EVEN EMPLOYING A SCORCHED-EARTH STRATEGY WOULD BE...
INDEED...
THE BLACK ARMY'S TERRITORY IS VAST AND COLD...
EVEN IF WE ESCAPED TO THE INNER REGIONS, BURNING PROVISIONS AND TOWNS ALONG THE WAY, WE'D BE STRANDED...

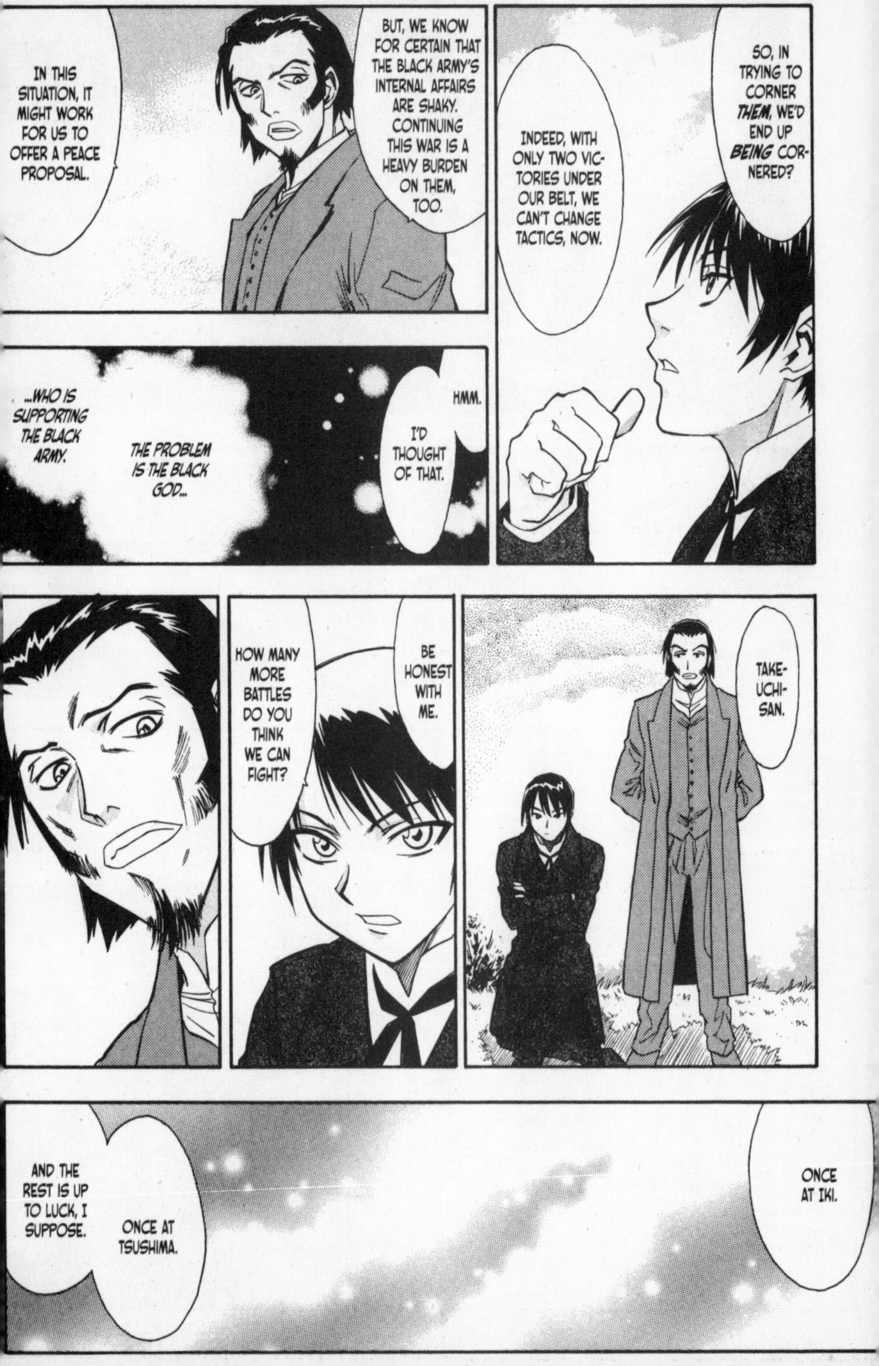
SO, IN TRYING TO CORNER *THEM*, WE'D END UP *BEING* CORNERED?
INDEED, WITH ONLY TWO VICTORIES UNDER OUR BELT, WE CAN'T CHANGE TACTICS, NOW.
BUT, WE KNOW FOR CERTAIN THAT THE BLACK ARMY'S INTERNAL AFFAIRS ARE SHAKY. CONTINUING THIS WAR IS A HEAVY BURDEN ON THEM, TOO.
IN THIS SITUATION, IT MIGHT WORK FOR US TO OFFER A PEACE PROPOSAL.
HMM.
I'D THOUGHT OF THAT.
THE PROBLEM IS THE BLACK GOD...
...WHO IS SUPPORTING THE BLACK ARMY.
TAKE-UCHI-SAN.
BE HONEST WITH ME.
HOW MANY MORE BATTLES DO YOU THINK WE CAN FIGHT?
ONCE AT IKI.
ONCE AT TSUSHIMA.
AND THE REST IS UP TO LUCK, I SUPPOSE.

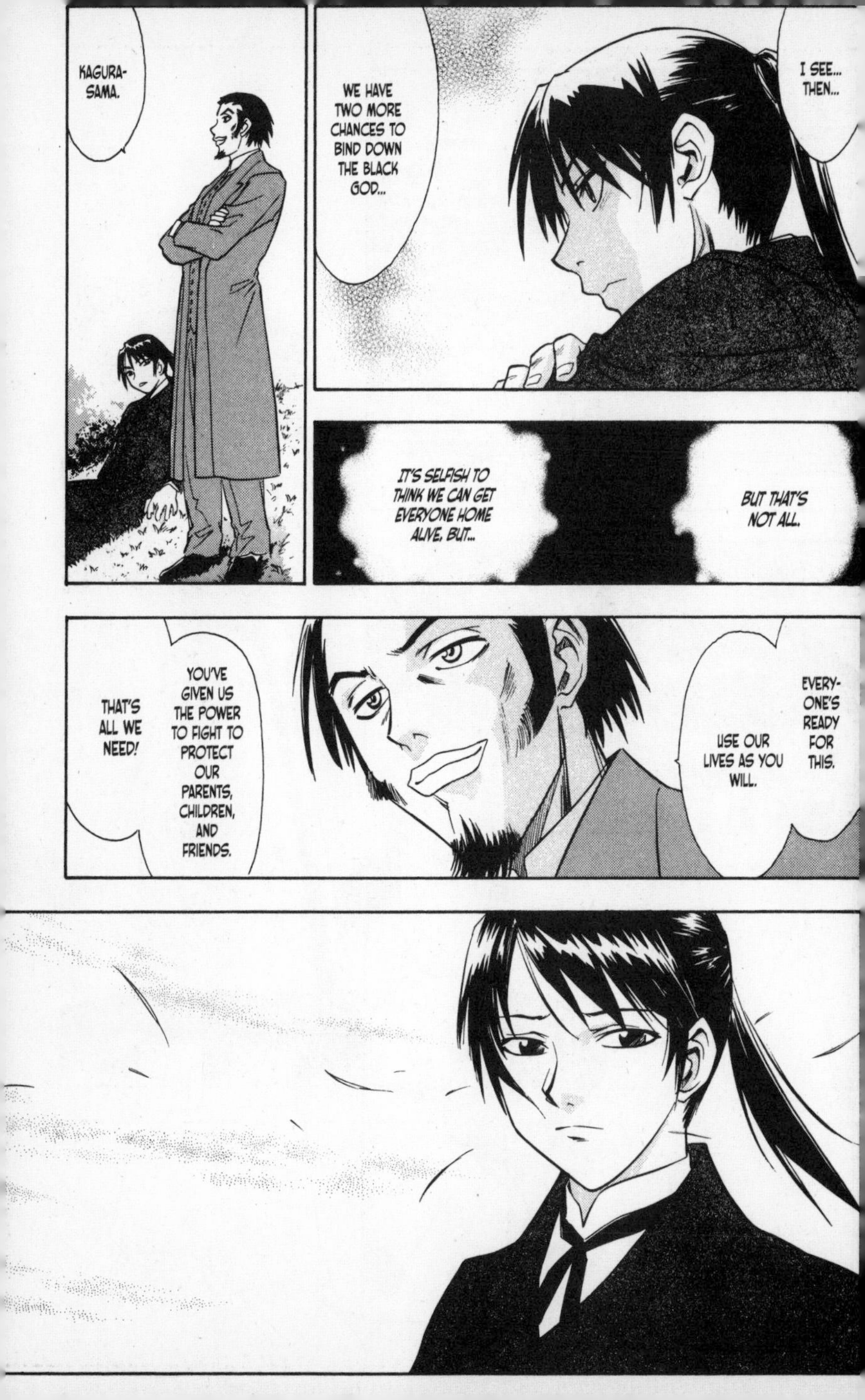
I SEE... THEN...
WE HAVE TWO MORE CHANCES TO BIND DOWN THE BLACK GOD...
BUT THAT'S NOT ALL.
IT'S SELFISH TO THINK WE CAN GET EVERYONE HOME ALIVE, BUT...
KAGURA-SAMA.
EVERYONE'S READY FOR THIS.
USE OUR LIVES AS YOU WILL.
YOU'VE GIVEN US THE POWER TO FIGHT TO PROTECT OUR PARENTS, CHILDREN, AND FRIENDS.
THAT'S ALL WE NEED!

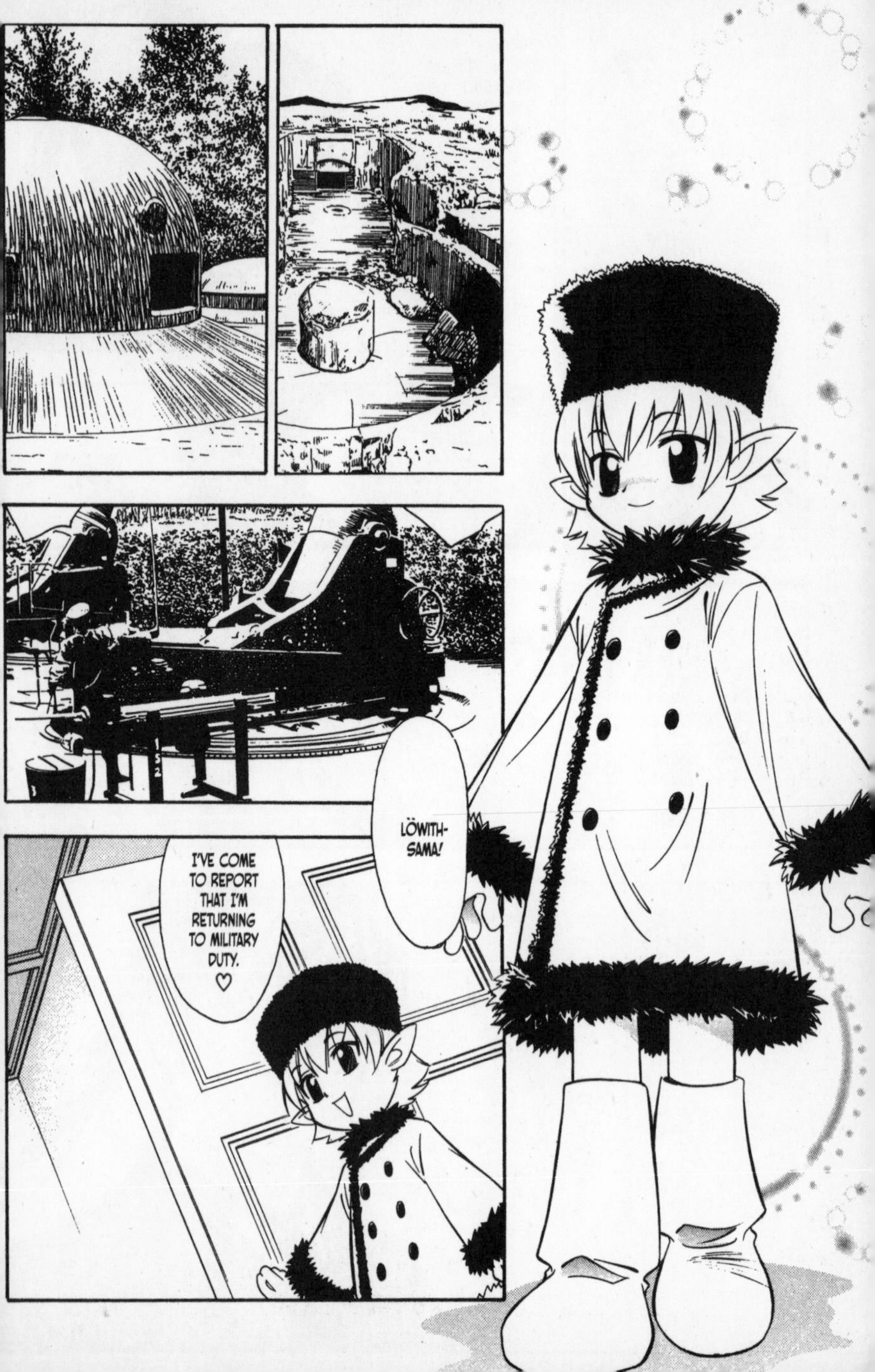
LÖWITH-SAMA!
I'VE COME TO REPORT THAT I'M RETURNING TO MILITARY DUTY. ♡

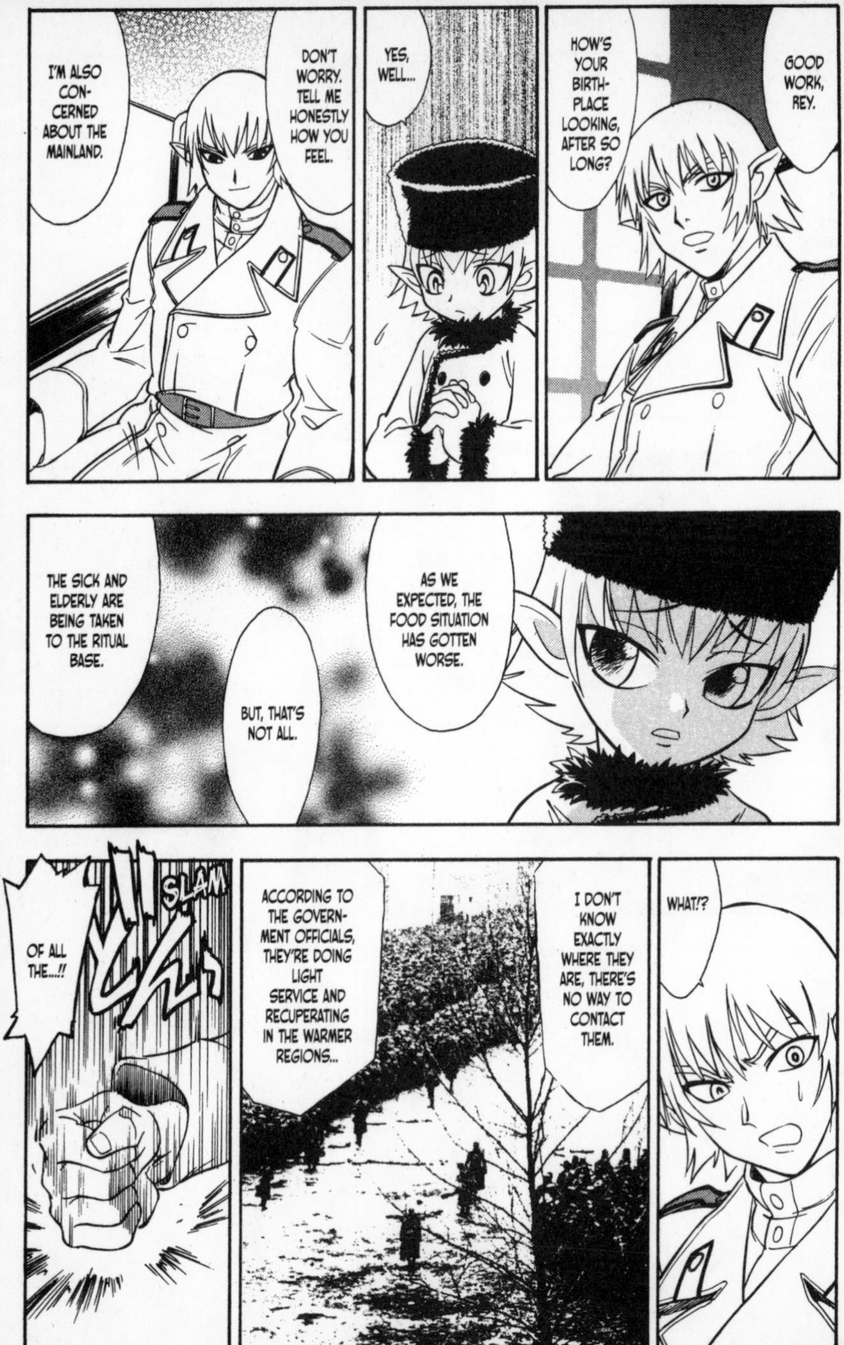
GOOD WORK, REY.
HOW'S YOUR BIRTH-PLACE LOOKING, AFTER SO LONG?
YES, WELL...
DON'T WORRY. TELL ME HONESTLY HOW YOU FEEL.
I'M ALSO CON-CERNED ABOUT THE MAINLAND.
AS WE EXPECTED, THE FOOD SITUATION HAS GOTTEN WORSE.
BUT, THAT'S NOT ALL.
THE SICK AND ELDERLY ARE BEING TAKEN TO THE RITUAL BASE.
WHAT!?
I DON'T KNOW EXACTLY WHERE THEY ARE, THERE'S NO WAY TO CONTACT THEM.
ACCORDING TO THE GOVERN-MENT OFFICIALS, THEY'RE DOING LIGHT SERVICE AND RECUPERATING IN THE WARMER REGIONS...
SLAM
OF ALL THE...!!

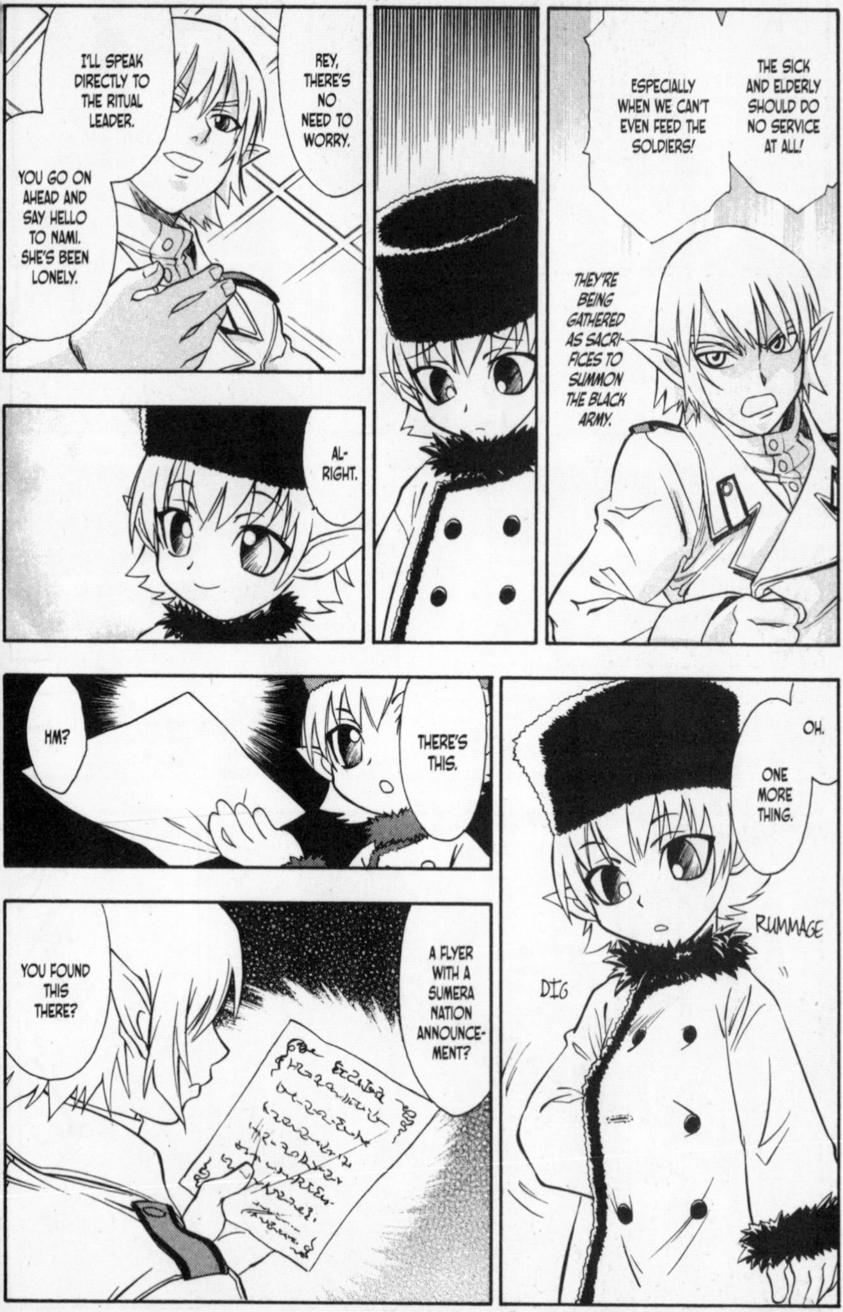

THE SICK AND ELDERLY SHOULD DO NO SERVICE AT ALL!
ESPECIALLY WHEN WE CAN'T EVEN FEED THE SOLDIERS!
THEY'RE BEING GATHERED AS SACRI-FICES TO SUMMON THE BLACK ARMY.
REY, THERE'S NO NEED TO WORRY.
I'LL SPEAK DIRECTLY TO THE RITUAL LEADER.
YOU GO ON AHEAD AND SAY HELLO TO NAMI. SHE'S BEEN LONELY.
AL-RIGHT.
OH.
ONE MORE THING.
RUMMAGE
DIG
THERE'S THIS.
HM?
A FLYER WITH A SUMERA NATION ANNOUNCE-MENT?
YOU FOUND THIS THERE?

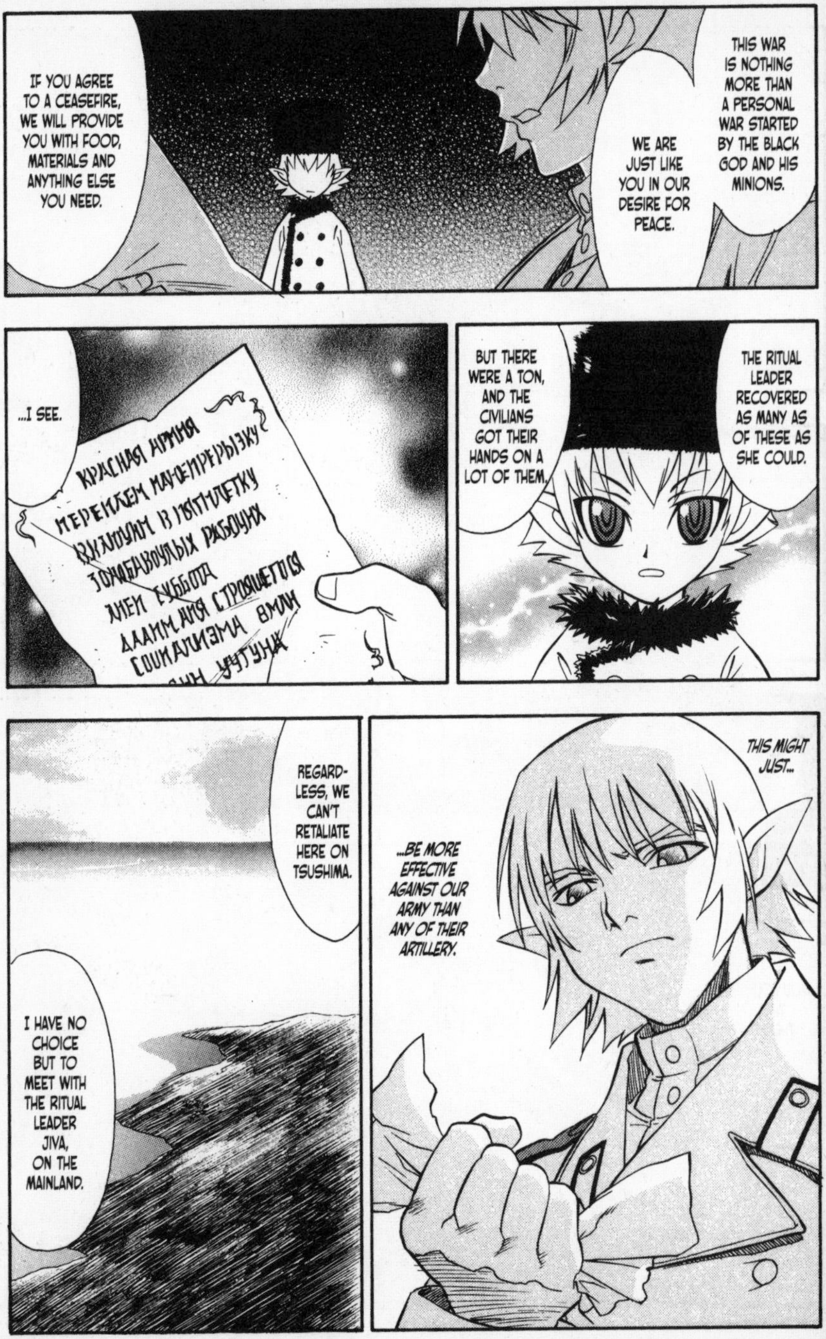
THIS WAR IS NOTHING MORE THAN A PERSONAL WAR STARTED BY THE BLACK GOD AND HIS MINIONS.
WE ARE JUST LIKE YOU IN OUR DESIRE FOR PEACE.
IF YOU AGREE TO A CEASEFIRE, WE WILL PROVIDE YOU WITH FOOD, MATERIALS AND ANYTHING ELSE YOU NEED.
THE RITUAL LEADER RECOVERED AS MANY AS OF THESE AS SHE COULD.
BUT THERE WERE A TON, AND THE CIVILIANS GOT THEIR HANDS ON A LOT OF THEM.
...I SEE.
КРАСНАЯ АРМИЯ
THIS MIGHT JUST...
...BE MORE EFFECTIVE AGAINST OUR ARMY THAN ANY OF THEIR ARTILLERY.
REGARD-LESS, WE CAN'T RETALIATE HERE ON TSUSHIMA.
I HAVE NO CHOICE BUT TO MEET WITH THE RITUAL LEADER JIVA, ON THE MAINLAND.

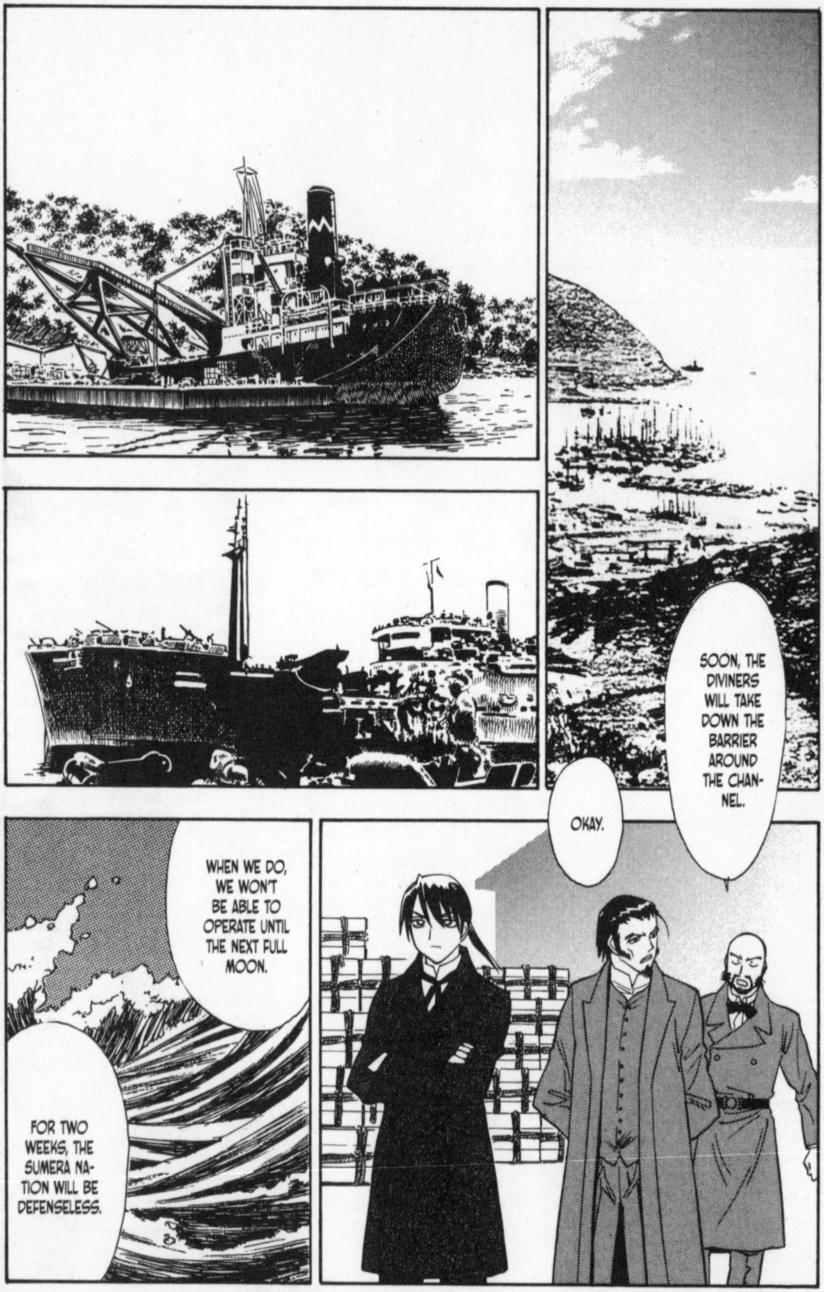
SOON, THE DIVINERS WILL TAKE DOWN THE BARRIER AROUND THE CHAN-NEL.
OKAY.
WHEN WE DO, WE WON'T BE ABLE TO OPERATE UNTIL THE NEXT FULL MOON.
FOR TWO WEEKS, THE SUMERA NA-TION WILL BE DEFENSELESS.

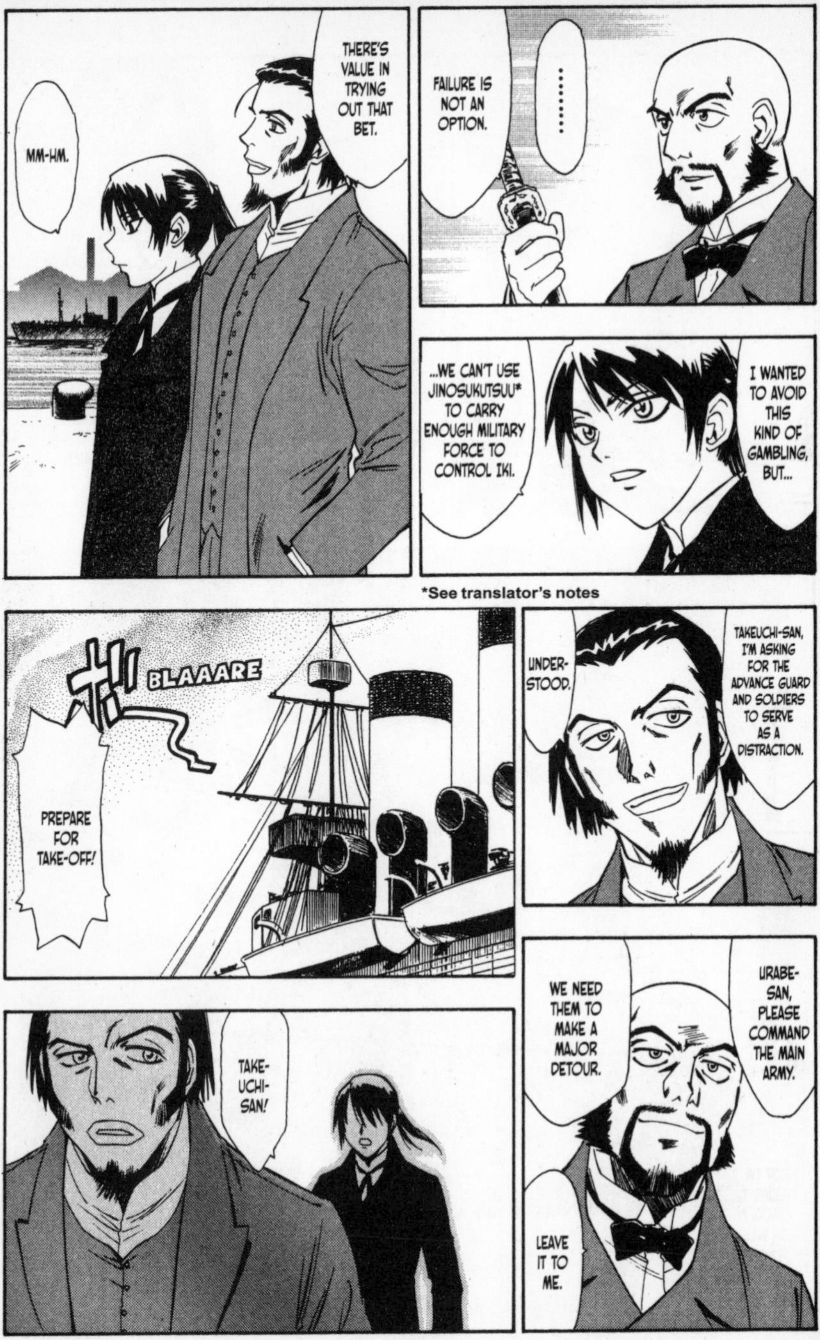
……
FAILURE IS NOT AN OPTION.
I WANTED TO AVOID THIS KIND OF GAMBLING, BUT...
...WE CAN'T USE JINOSUKUTSUU* TO CARRY ENOUGH MILITARY FORCE TO CONTROL IKI.
THERE'S VALUE IN TRYING OUT THAT BET.
MM-HM.
*See translator's notes
TAKEUCHI-SAN, I'M ASKING FOR THE ADVANCE GUARD AND SOLDIERS TO SERVE AS A DISTRACTION.
UNDER-STOOD.
URABE-SAN, PLEASE COMMAND THE MAIN ARMY.
WE NEED THEM TO MAKE A MAJOR DETOUR.
LEAVE IT TO ME.
BLAAARE
PREPARE FOR TAKE-OFF!
TAKE-UCHI-SAN!

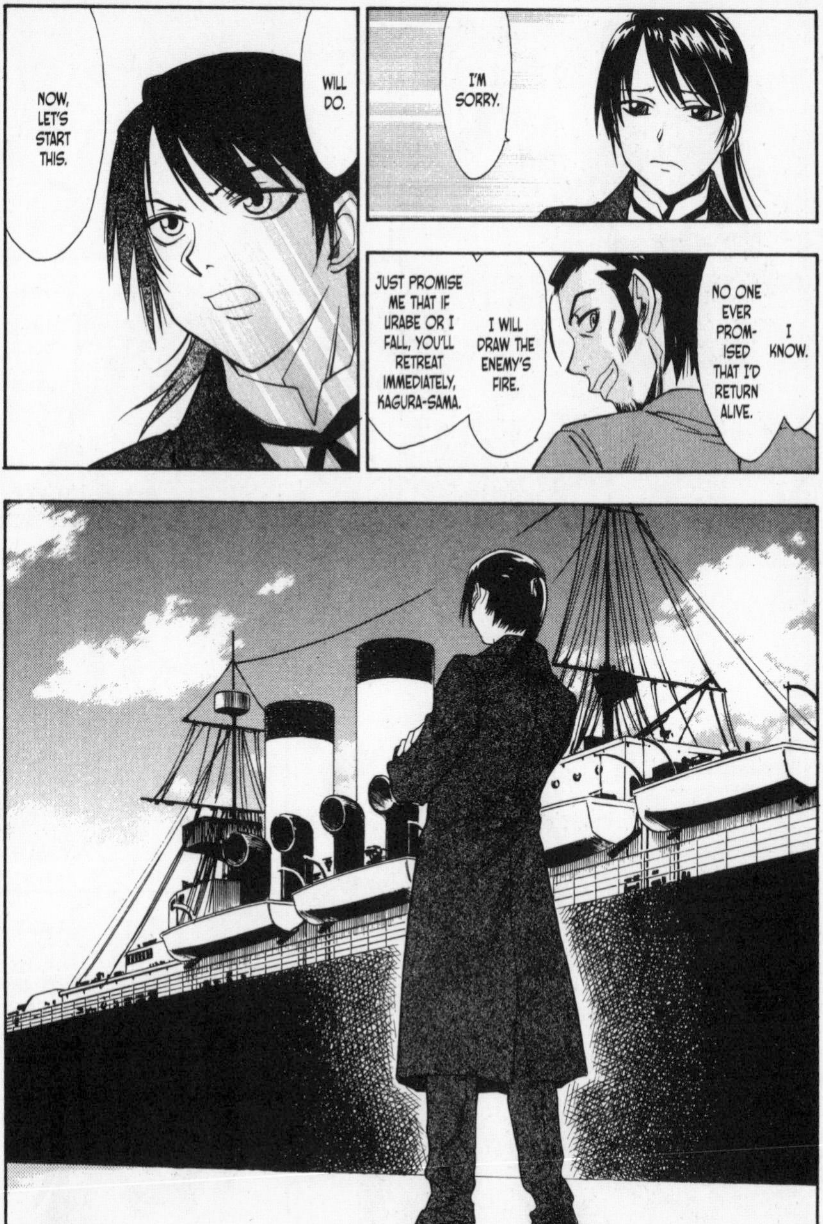
I'M SORRY.
I KNOW.
NO ONE EVER PROMISED THAT I'D RETURN ALIVE.
I WILL DRAW THE ENEMY'S FIRE.
JUST PROMISE ME THAT IF URABE OR I FALL, YOU'LL RETREAT IMMEDIATELY, KAGURA-SAMA.
WILL DO.
NOW, LET'S START THIS.

Chapter 34 : OVER

神無 KANNA

Chapter 35

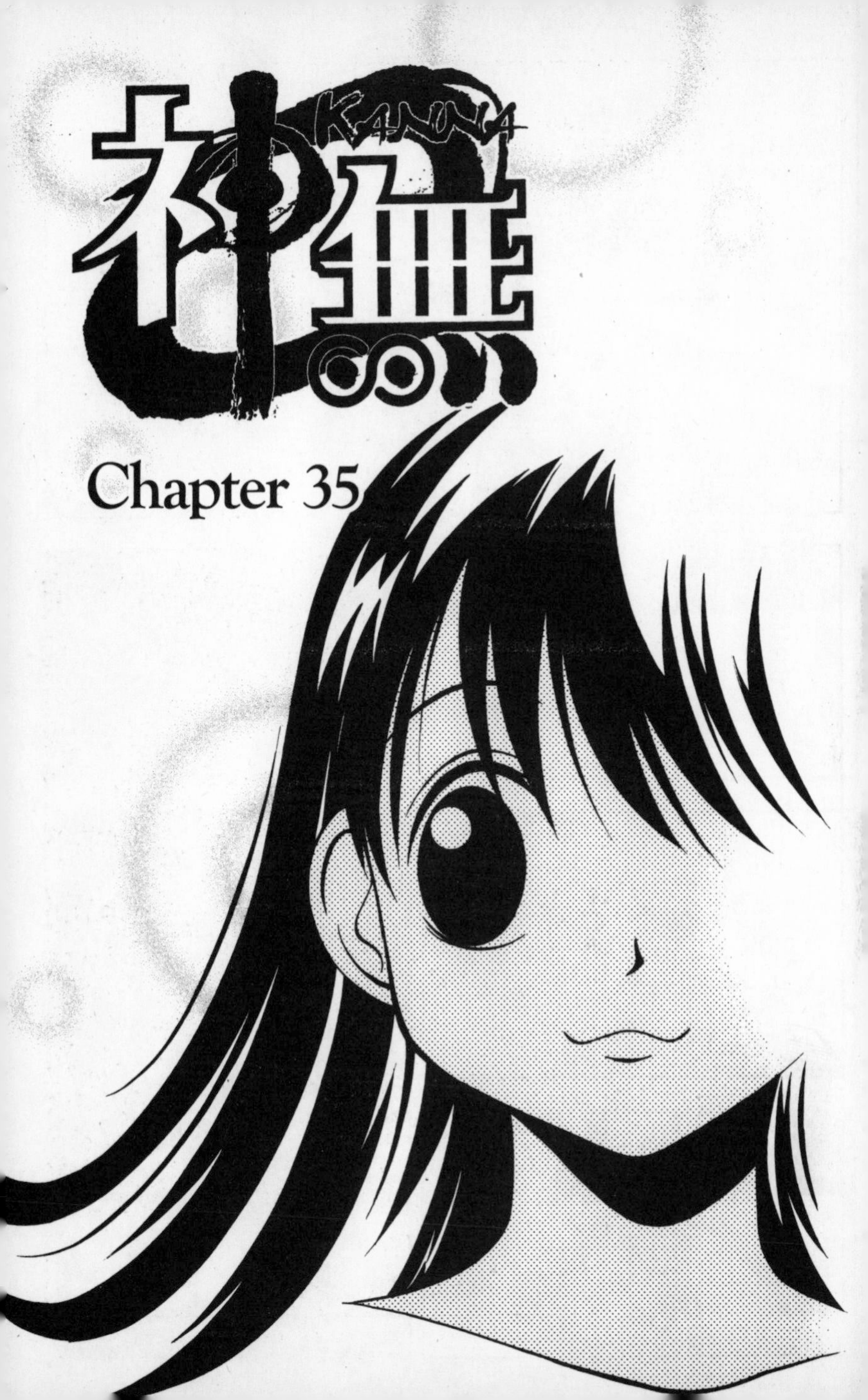

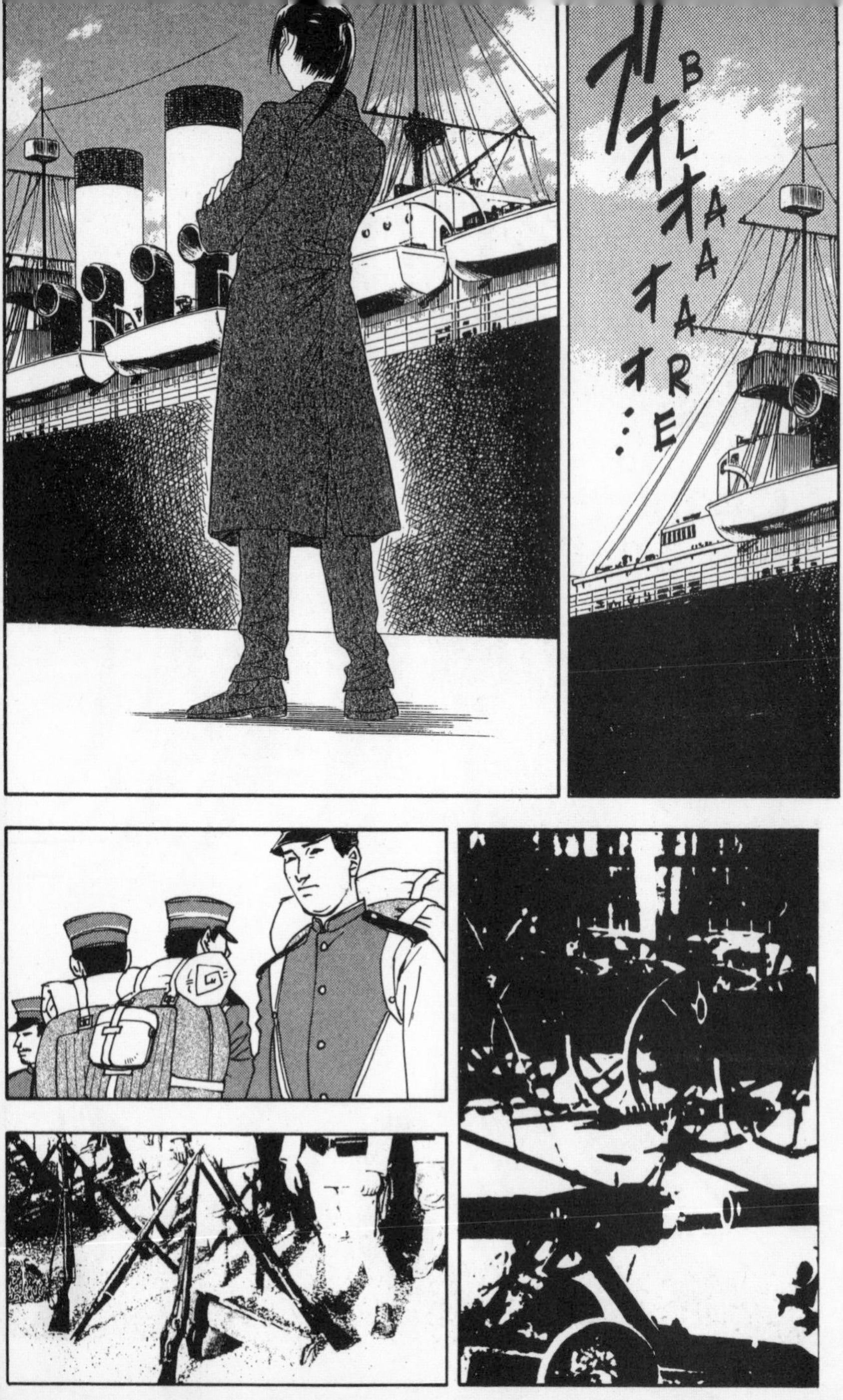
BLAAARE...

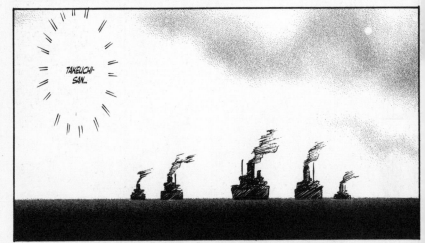

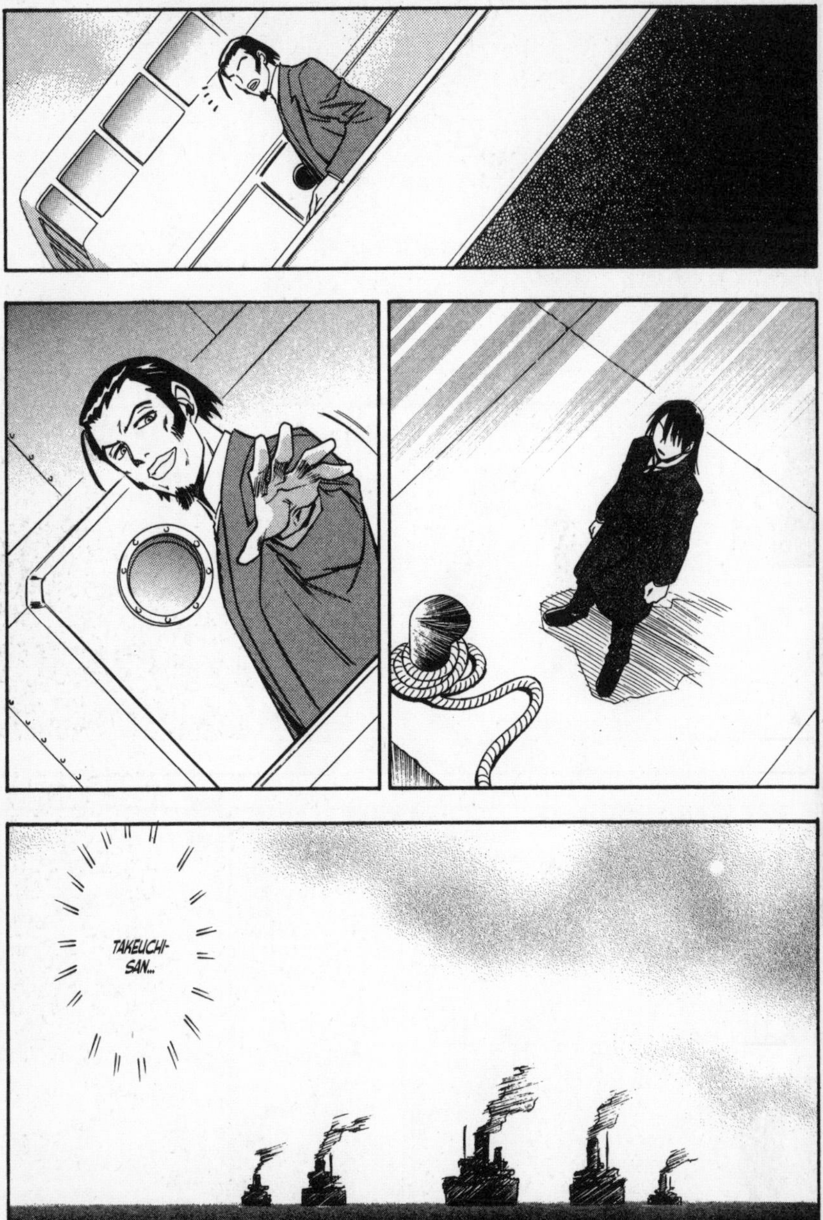
TAKEUCHI-SAN...

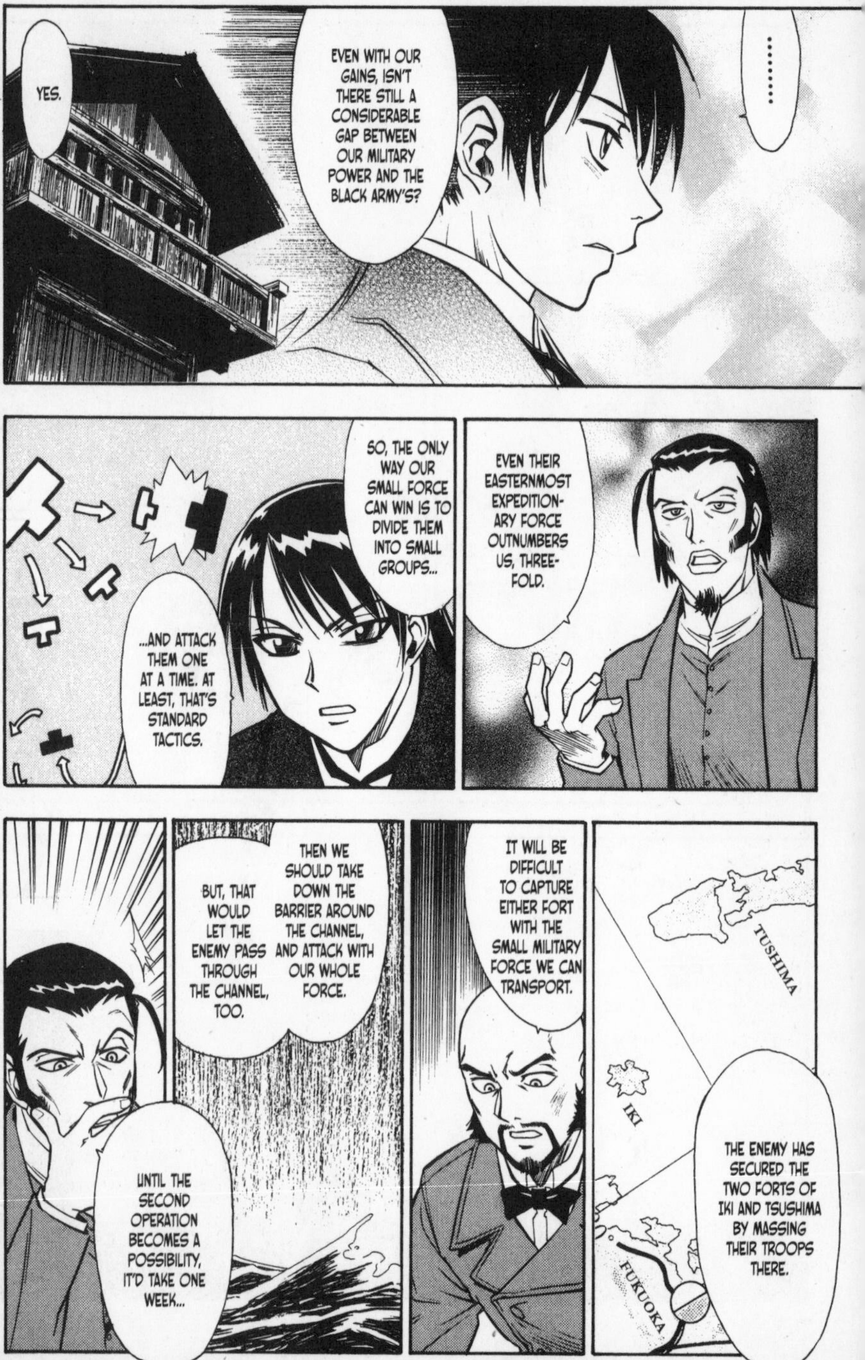

......
EVEN WITH OUR GAINS, ISN'T THERE STILL A CONSIDERABLE GAP BETWEEN OUR MILITARY POWER AND THE BLACK ARMY'S?
YES.
EVEN THEIR EASTERNMOST EXPEDITION-ARY FORCE OUTNUMBERS US, THREE-FOLD.
SO, THE ONLY WAY OUR SMALL FORCE CAN WIN IS TO DIVIDE THEM INTO SMALL GROUPS...
...AND ATTACK THEM ONE AT A TIME. AT LEAST, THAT'S STANDARD TACTICS.
TUSHIMA
IKI
FUKUOKA
THE ENEMY HAS SECURED THE TWO FORTS OF IKI AND TSUSHIMA BY MASSING THEIR TROOPS THERE.
IT WILL BE DIFFICULT TO CAPTURE EITHER FORT WITH THE SMALL MILITARY FORCE WE CAN TRANSPORT.
THEN WE SHOULD TAKE DOWN THE BARRIER AROUND THE CHANNEL, AND ATTACK WITH OUR WHOLE FORCE.
BUT, THAT WOULD LET THE ENEMY PASS THROUGH THE CHANNEL, TOO.
UNTIL THE SECOND OPERATION BECOMES A POSSIBILITY, IT'D TAKE ONE WEEK...

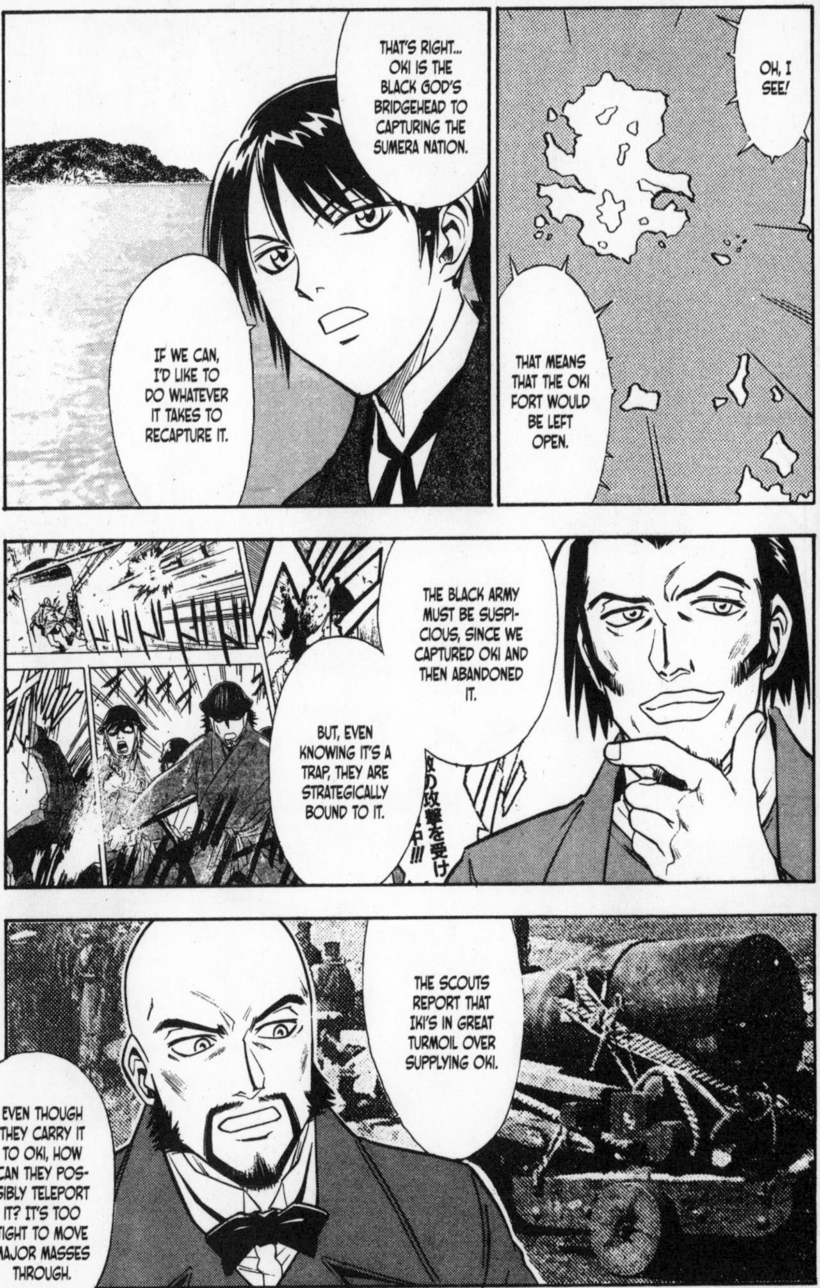
OH, I SEE!
THAT MEANS THAT THE OKI FORT WOULD BE LEFT OPEN.
THAT'S RIGHT... OKI IS THE BLACK GOD'S BRIDGEHEAD TO CAPTURING THE SUMERA NATION.
IF WE CAN, I'D LIKE TO DO WHATEVER IT TAKES TO RECAPTURE IT.
THE BLACK ARMY MUST BE SUSPI- CIOUS, SINCE WE CAPTURED OKI AND THEN ABANDONED IT.
BUT, EVEN KNOWING IT'S A TRAP, THEY ARE STRATEGICALLY BOUND TO IT.
THE SCOUTS REPORT THAT IKI'S IN GREAT TURMOIL OVER SUPPLYING OKI.
EVEN THOUGH THEY CARRY IT TO OKI, HOW CAN THEY POS- SIBLY TELEPORT IT? IT'S TOO TIGHT TO MOVE MAJOR MASSES THROUGH.

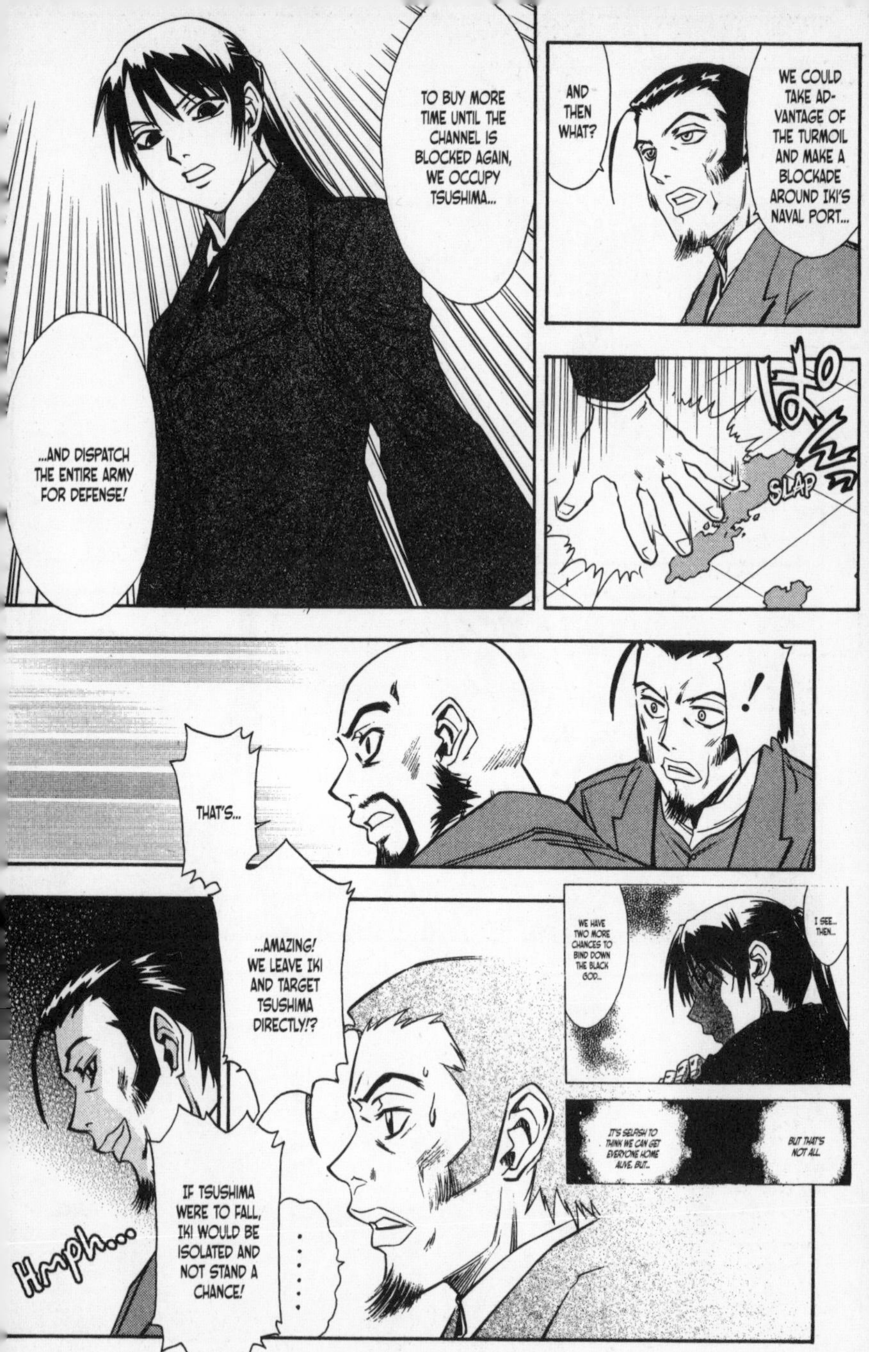
WE COULD TAKE AD-VANTAGE OF THE TURMOIL AND MAKE A BLOCKADE AROUND IKI'S NAVAL PORT...
AND THEN WHAT?
SLAP
TO BUY MORE TIME UNTIL THE CHANNEL IS BLOCKED AGAIN, WE OCCUPY TSUSHIMA...
...AND DISPATCH THE ENTIRE ARMY FOR DEFENSE!
!
THAT'S...
I SEE... THEN...
WE HAVE TWO MORE CHANCES TO BIND DOWN THE BLACK GOD...
BUT THAT'S NOT ALL.
IT'S SELFISH TO THINK WE CAN GET EVERYONE HOME ALIVE, BUT...
...AMAZING! WE LEAVE IKI AND TARGET TSUSHIMA DIRECTLY!?
IF TSUSHIMA WERE TO FALL, IKI WOULD BE ISOLATED AND NOT STAND A CHANCE!
......
Hmph...

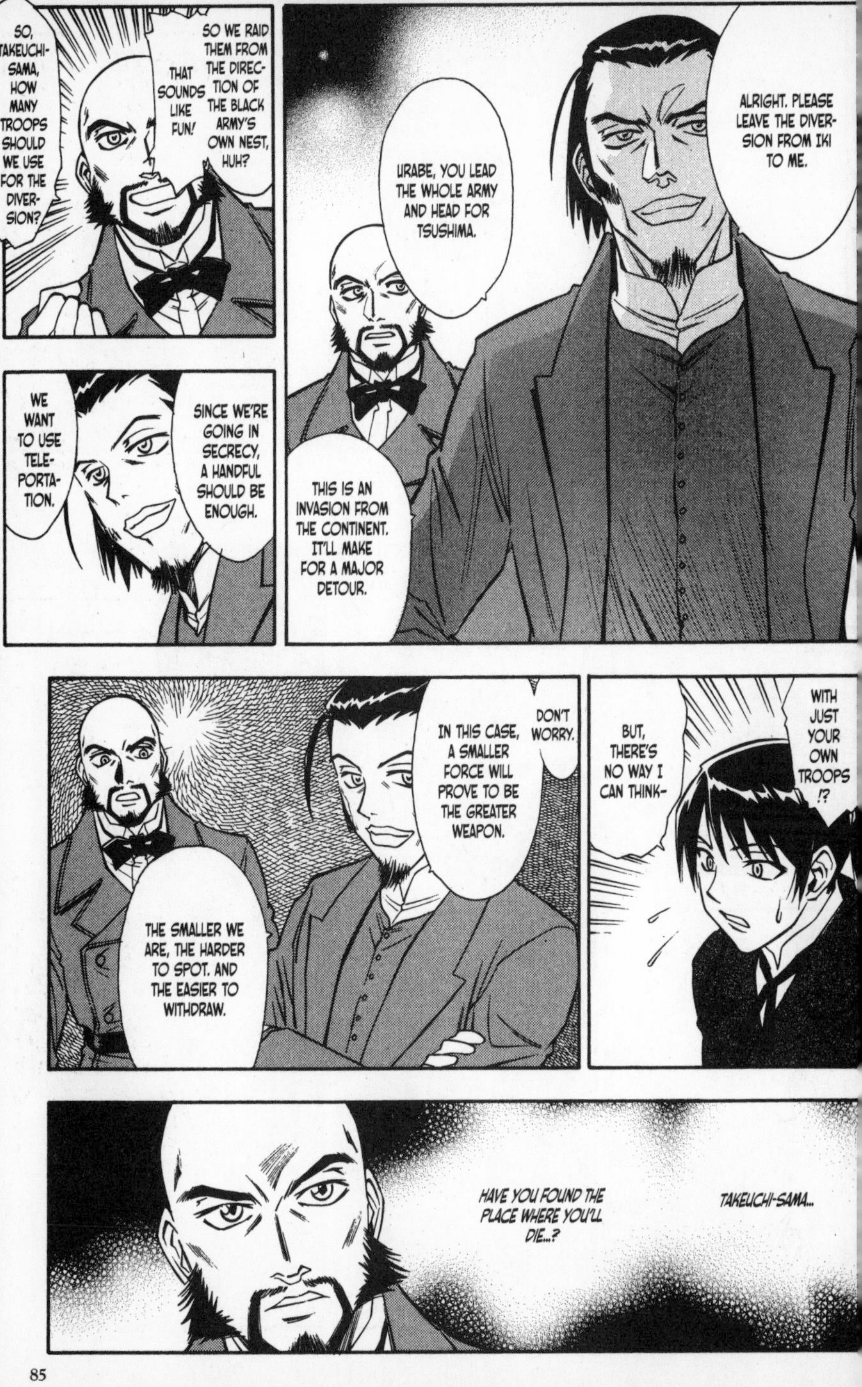
ALRIGHT. PLEASE LEAVE THE DIVERSION FROM IKI TO ME.
URABE, YOU LEAD THE WHOLE ARMY AND HEAD FOR TSUSHIMA.
THIS IS AN INVASION FROM THE CONTINENT. IT'LL MAKE FOR A MAJOR DETOUR.
SO WE RAID THEM FROM THE DIRECTION OF THE BLACK ARMY'S OWN NEST, HUH?
THAT SOUNDS LIKE FUN!
SO, TAKEUCHI-SAMA, HOW MANY TROOPS SHOULD WE USE FOR THE DIVERSION?
SINCE WE'RE GOING IN SECRECY, A HANDFUL SHOULD BE ENOUGH.
WE WANT TO USE TELEPORTATION.
WITH JUST YOUR OWN TROOPS!?
BUT, THERE'S NO WAY I CAN THINK-
DON'T WORRY.
IN THIS CASE, A SMALLER FORCE WILL PROVE TO BE THE GREATER WEAPON.
THE SMALLER WE ARE, THE HARDER TO SPOT. AND THE EASIER TO WITHDRAW.
TAKEUCHI-SAMA...
HAVE YOU FOUND THE PLACE WHERE YOU'LL DIE...?

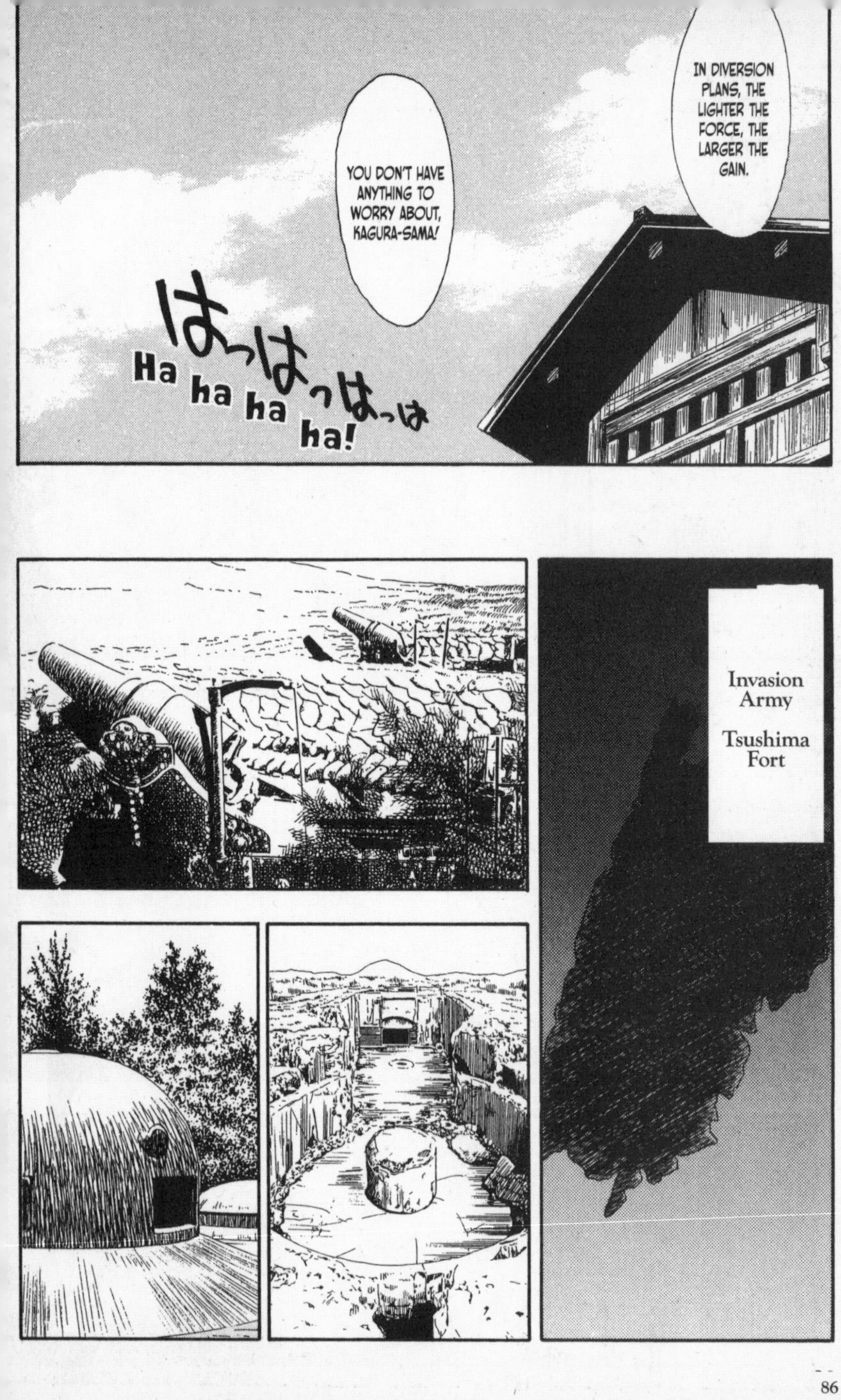
IN DIVERSION PLANS, THE LIGHTER THE FORCE, THE LARGER THE GAIN.
YOU DON'T HAVE ANYTHING TO WORRY ABOUT, KAGURA-SAMA!
はっはっはっは
Ha ha ha ha!
Invasion Army
Tsushima Fort

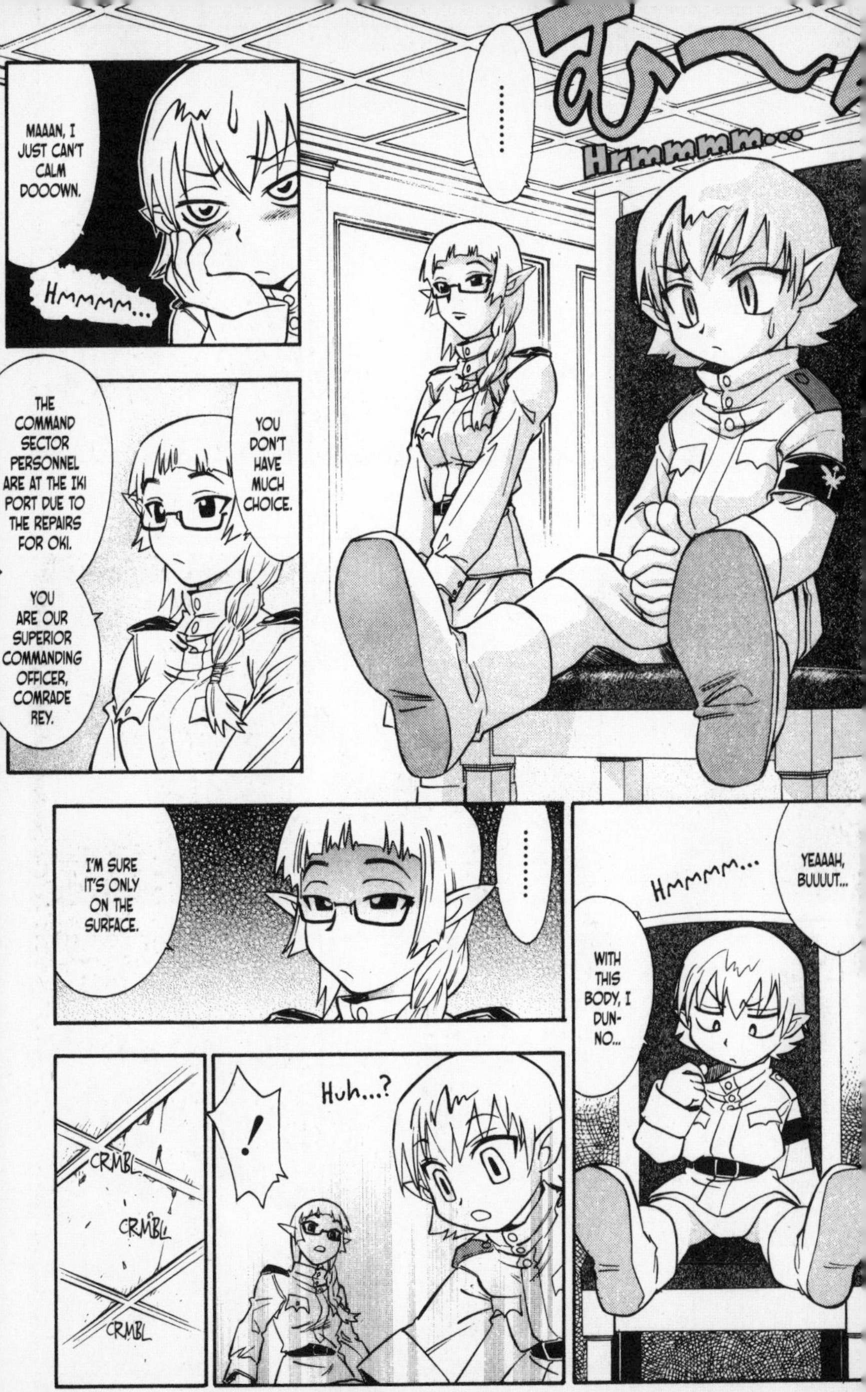
......
Hrmmmmm...
MAAAN, I JUST CAN'T CALM DOOOWN.
Hmmmm...
YOU DON'T HAVE MUCH CHOICE.
THE COMMAND SECTOR PERSONNEL ARE AT THE IKI PORT DUE TO THE REPAIRS FOR OKI.
YOU ARE OUR SUPERIOR COMMANDING OFFICER, COMRADE REY.
YEAAAH, BUUUT...
Hmmmm...
WITH THIS BODY, I DUN-NO...
......
I'M SURE IT'S ONLY ON THE SURFACE.
!
Huh...?
CRMBL
CRMBL
CRMBL

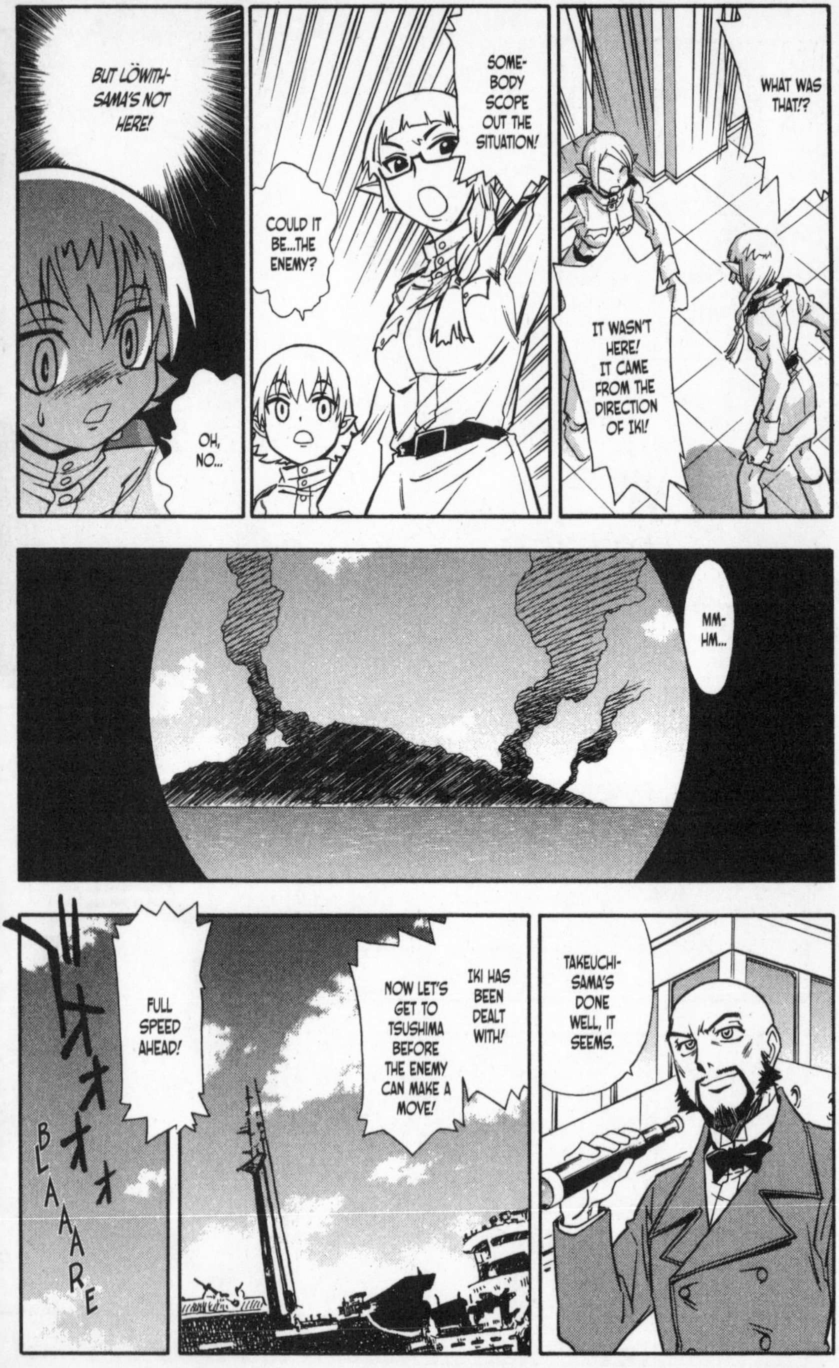
WHAT WAS THAT!?
IT WASN'T HERE! IT CAME FROM THE DIRECTION OF IKI!
SOME-BODY SCOPE OUT THE SITUATION!
COULD IT BE...THE ENEMY?
BUT LÖWITH-SAMA'S NOT HERE!
OH, NO...
MM-HM...
TAKEUCHI-SAMA'S DONE WELL, IT SEEMS.
IKI HAS BEEN DEALT WITH!
NOW LET'S GET TO TSUSHIMA BEFORE THE ENEMY CAN MAKE A MOVE!
FULL SPEED AHEAD!
BLAAARE

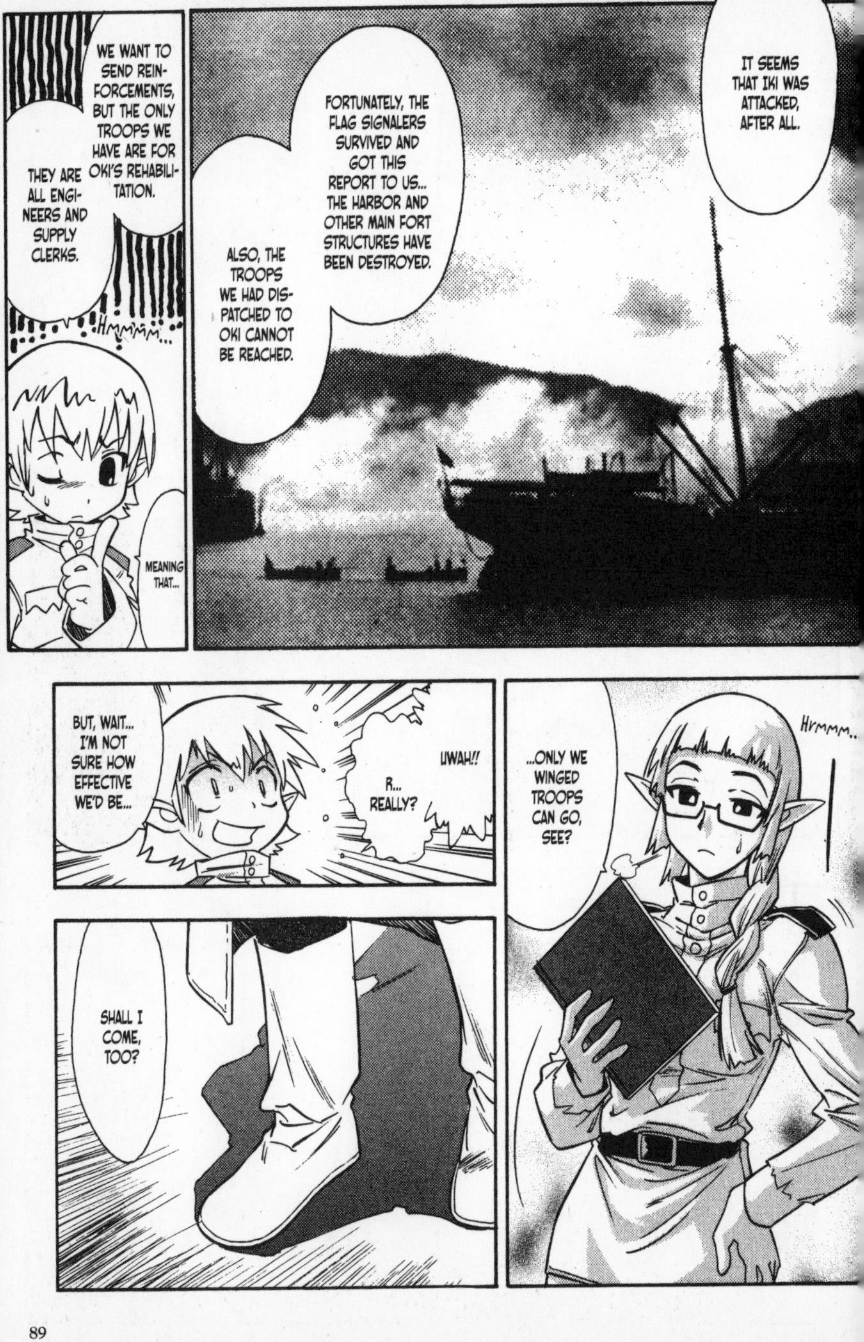
IT SEEMS THAT IKI WAS ATTACKED, AFTER ALL.
FORTUNATELY, THE FLAG SIGNALERS SURVIVED AND GOT THIS REPORT TO US... THE HARBOR AND OTHER MAIN FORT STRUCTURES HAVE BEEN DESTROYED.
ALSO, THE TROOPS WE HAD DIS-PATCHED TO OKI CANNOT BE REACHED.
WE WANT TO SEND REIN-FORCEMENTS, BUT THE ONLY TROOPS WE HAVE ARE FOR OKI'S REHABILI-TATION.
THEY ARE ALL ENGI-NEERS AND SUPPLY CLERKS.
HMMMM...
MEANING THAT...
HRMMM...
...ONLY WE WINGED TROOPS CAN GO, SEE?
UWAH!!
R... REALLY?
BUT, WAIT... I'M NOT SURE HOW EFFECTIVE WE'D BE...
SHALL I COME, TOO?

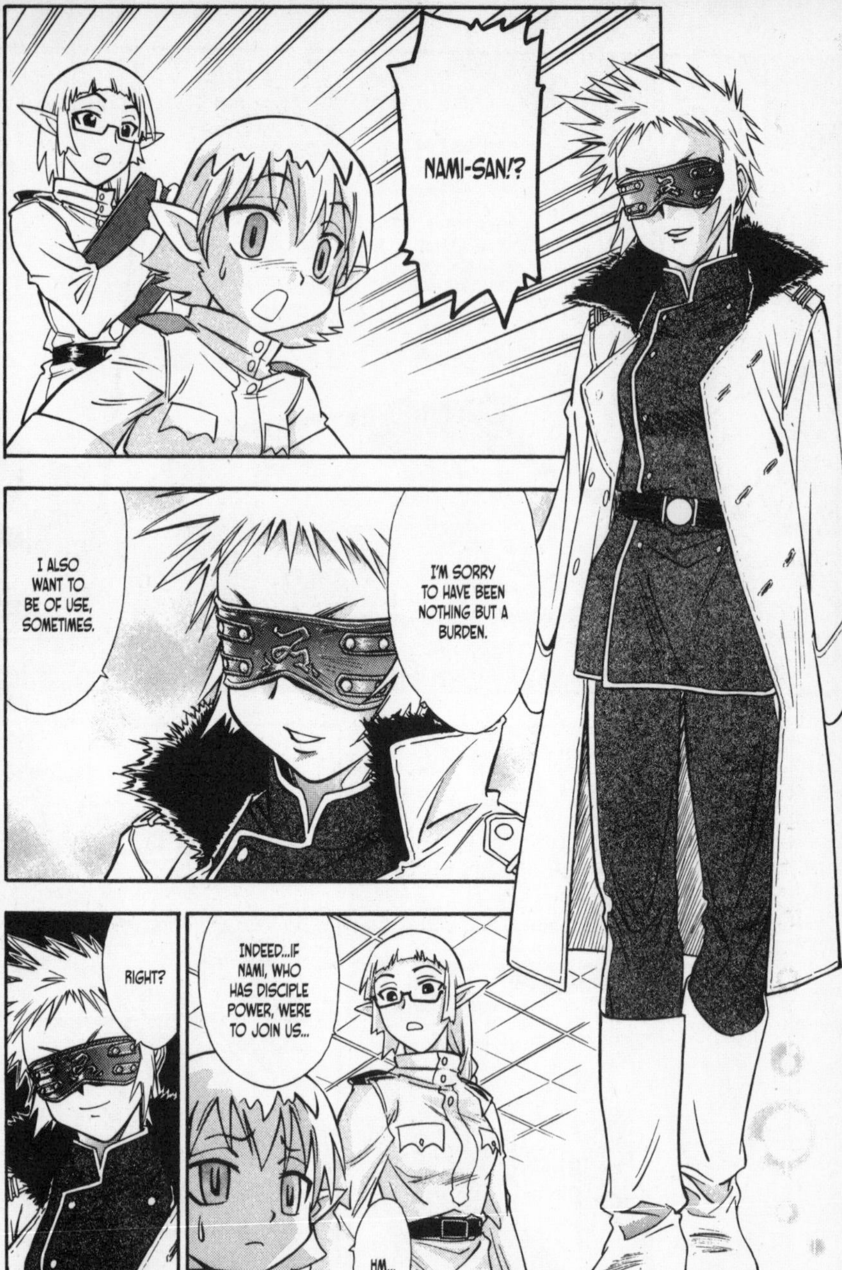
NAMI-SAN!?
I'M SORRY TO HAVE BEEN NOTHING BUT A BURDEN.
I ALSO WANT TO BE OF USE, SOMETIMES.
INDEED...IF NAMI, WHO HAS DISCIPLE POWER, WERE TO JOIN US...
HM...
RIGHT?

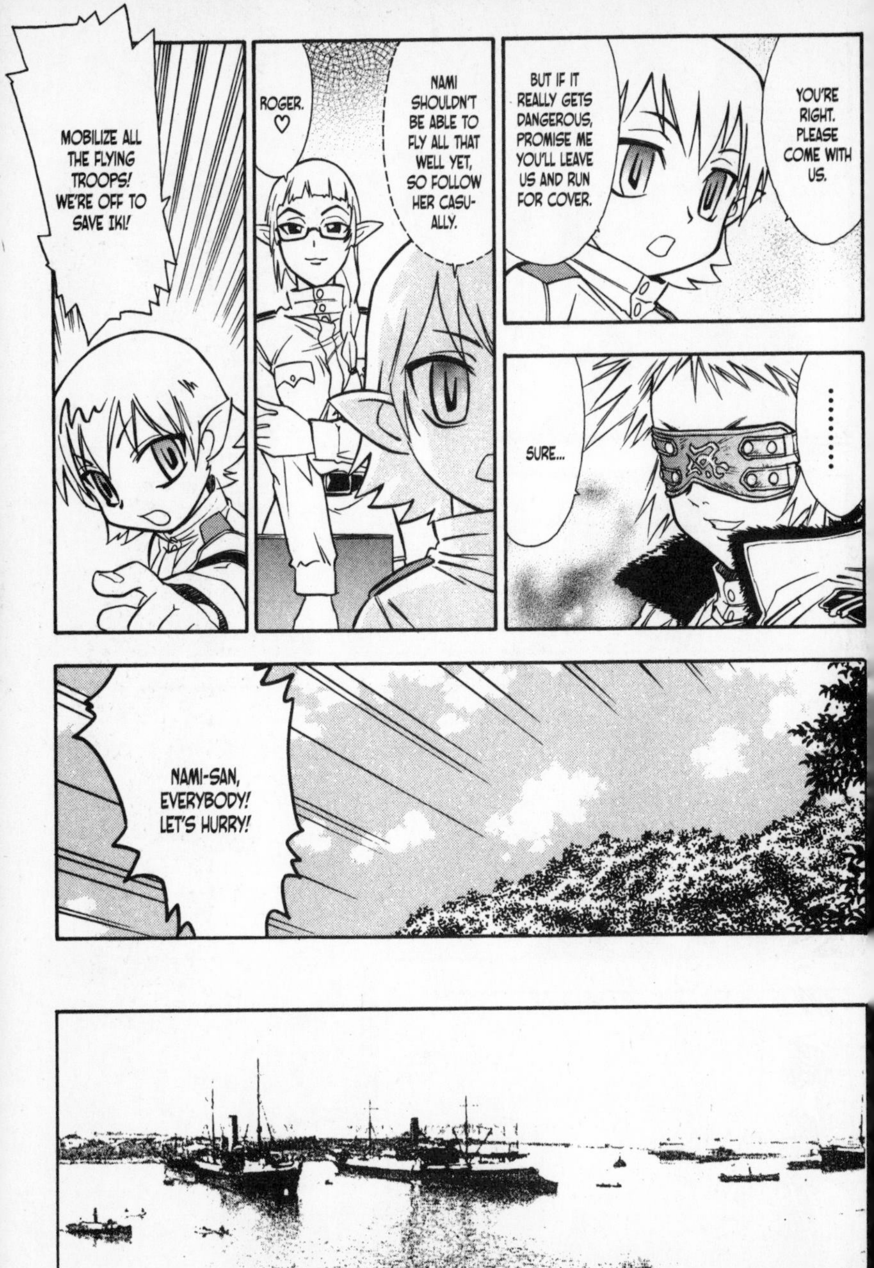
YOU'RE RIGHT. PLEASE COME WITH US.
BUT IF IT REALLY GETS DANGEROUS, PROMISE ME YOU'LL LEAVE US AND RUN FOR COVER.
......
SURE...
NAMI SHOULDN'T BE ABLE TO FLY ALL THAT WELL YET, SO FOLLOW HER CASU-ALLY.
ROGER. ♡
MOBILIZE ALL THE FLYING TROOPS! WE'RE OFF TO SAVE IKI!
NAMI-SAN, EVERYBODY! LET'S HURRY!

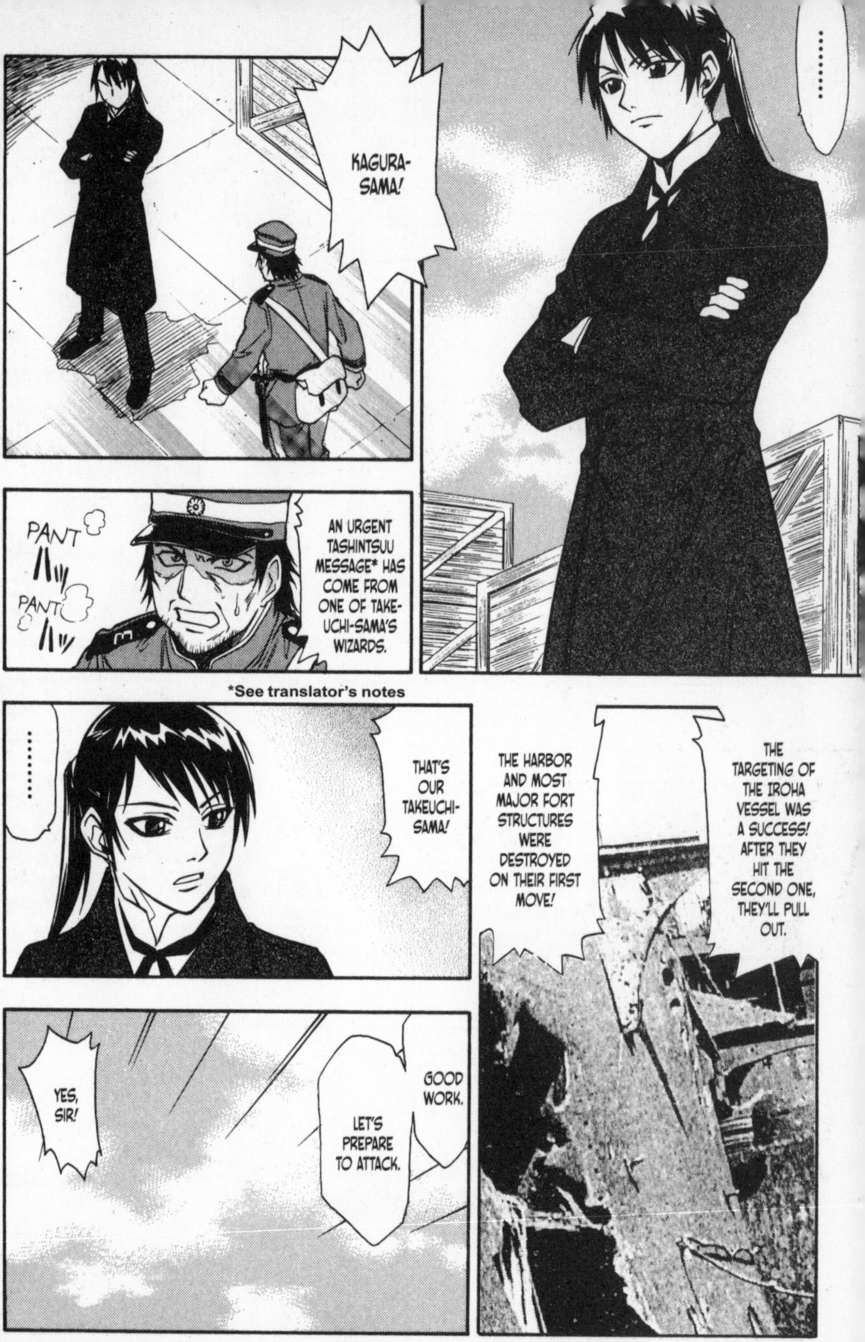
......
KAGURA-SAMA!
AN URGENT TASHINTSUU MESSAGE* HAS COME FROM ONE OF TAKE-UCHI-SAMA'S WIZARDS.
PANT ハッ
PANT ハッ
THE TARGETING OF THE IROHA VESSEL WAS A SUCCESS! AFTER THEY HIT THE SECOND ONE, THEY'LL PULL OUT.
THE HARBOR AND MOST MAJOR FORT STRUCTURES WERE DESTROYED ON THEIR FIRST MOVE!
......
THAT'S OUR TAKEUCHI-SAMA!
GOOD WORK.
LET'S PREPARE TO ATTACK.
YES, SIR!

*See translator's notes

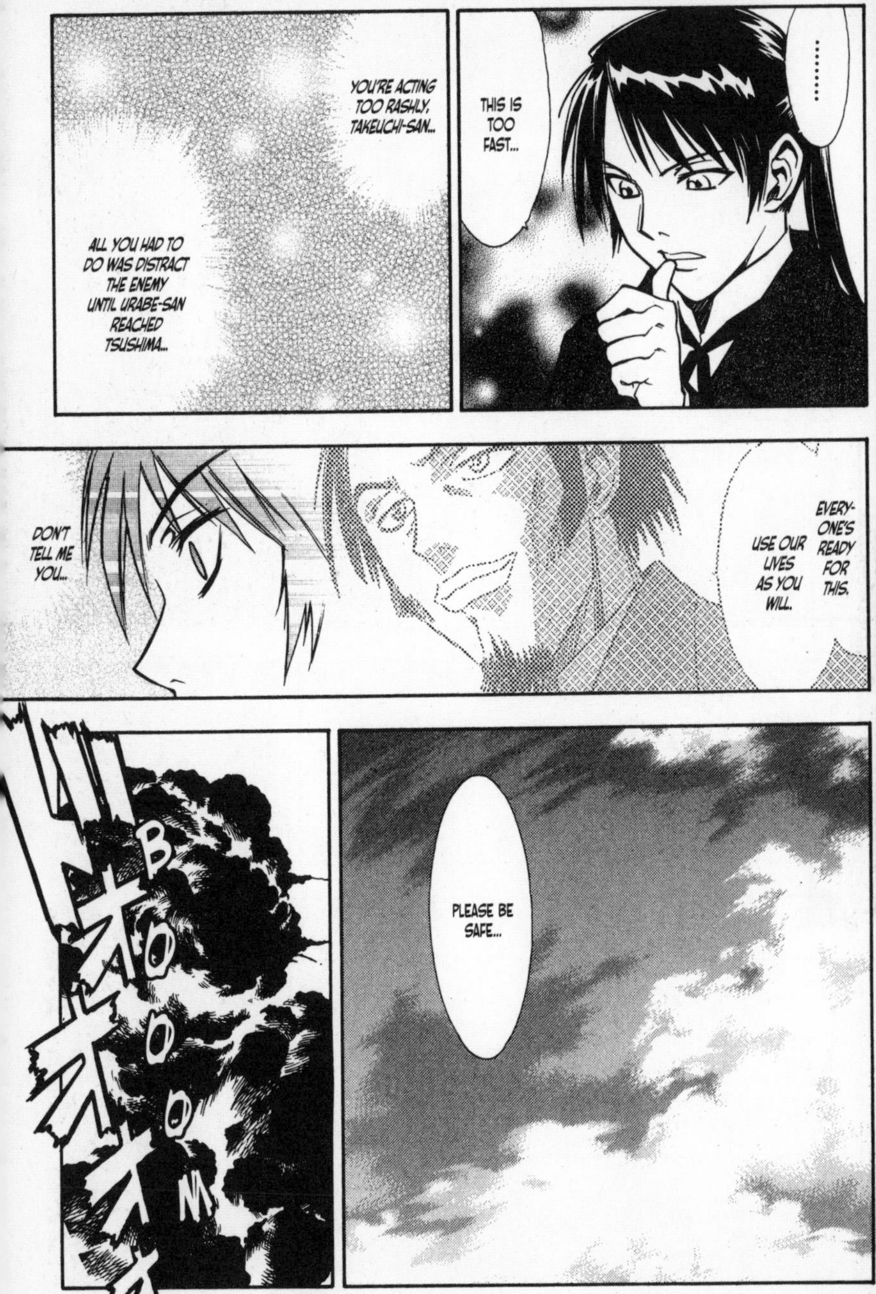

......
THIS IS TOO FAST...
YOU'RE ACTING TOO RASHLY, TAKEUCHI-SAN...
ALL YOU HAD TO DO WAS DISTRACT THE ENEMY UNTIL URABE-SAN REACHED TSUSHIMA...
EVERYONE'S READY FOR THIS.
USE OUR LIVES AS YOU WILL.
DON'T TELL ME YOU...
PLEASE BE SAFE...
BOOOOM

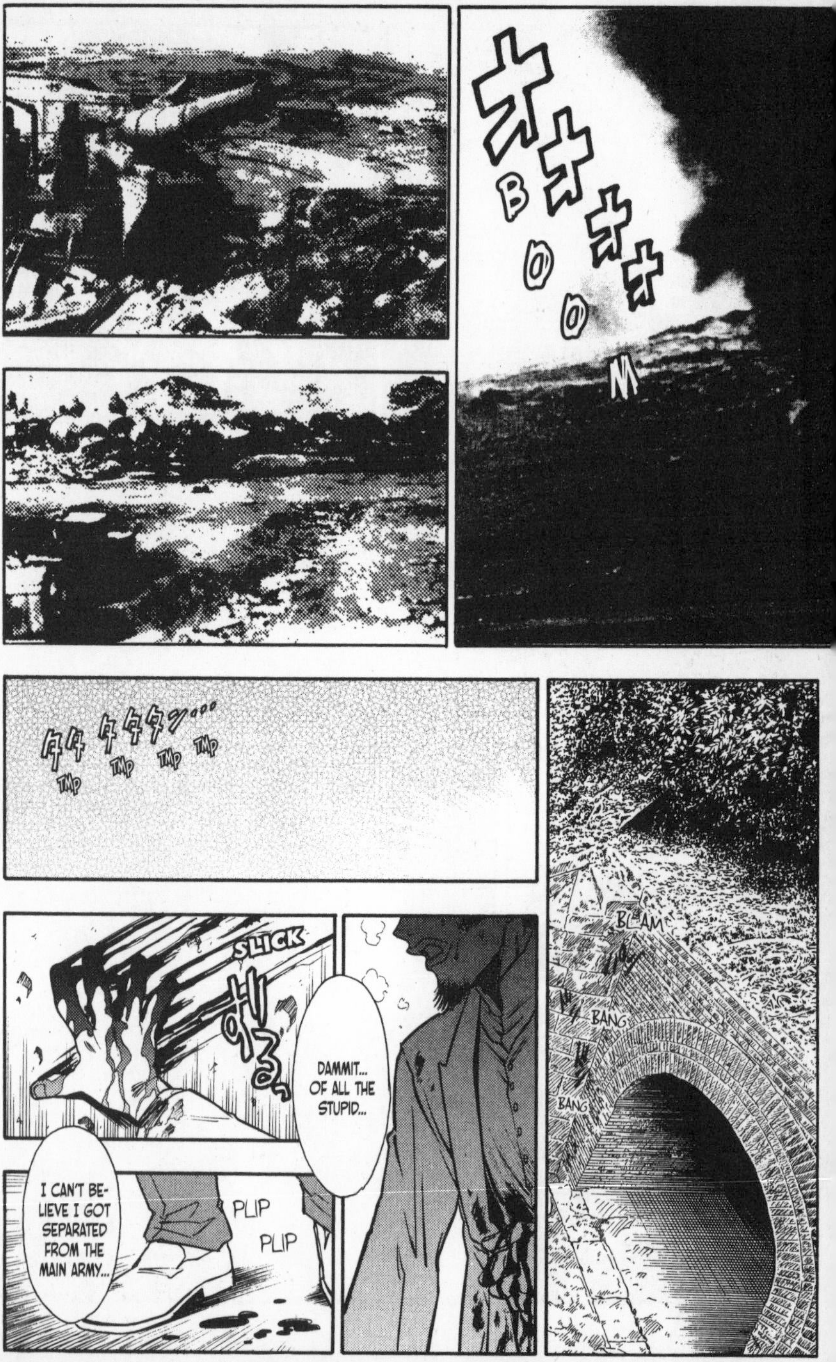
BOOOM
BLAM
BANG
BANG
TMP TMP TMP TMP
DAMMIT... OF ALL THE STUPID...
SLICK
I CAN'T BE-LIEVE I GOT SEPARATED FROM THE MAIN ARMY...
PLIP
PLIP

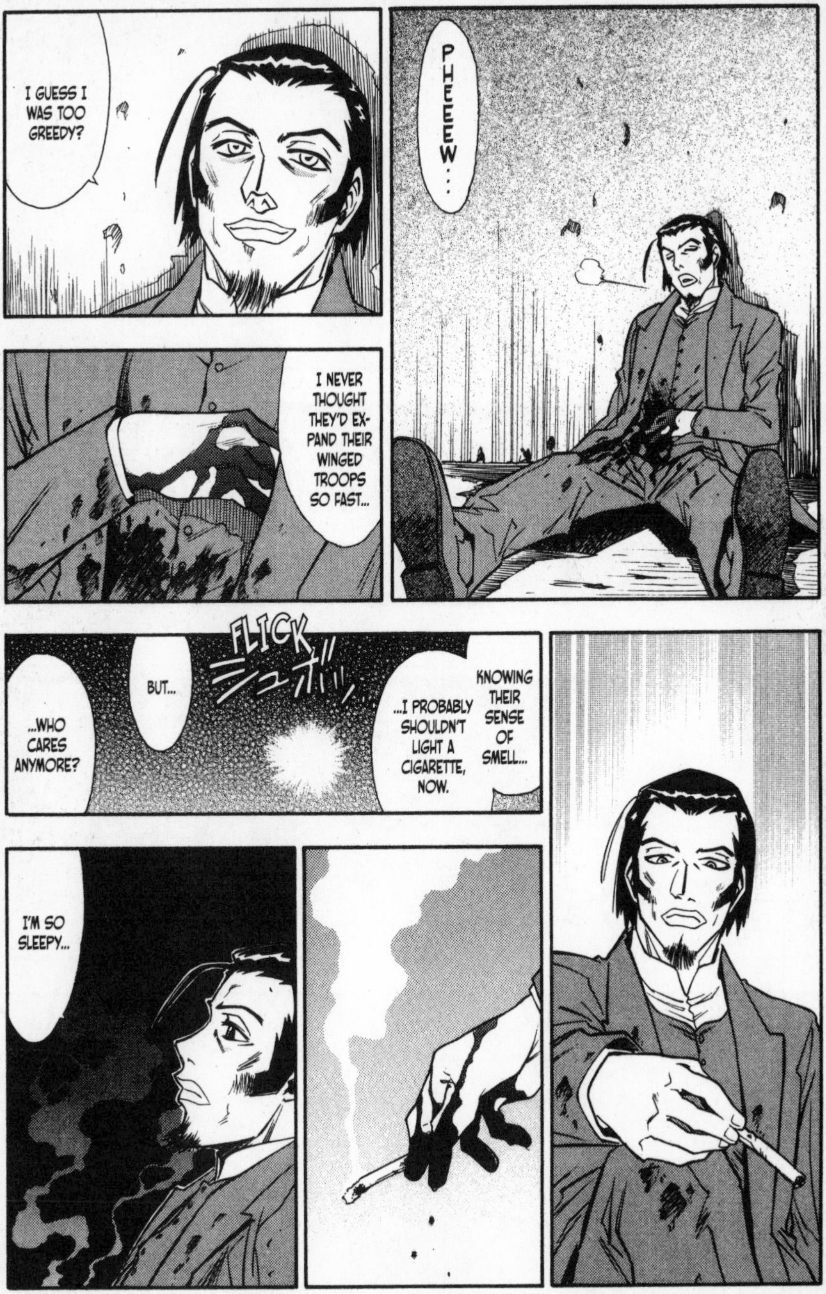
PHEEEW...
I GUESS I WAS TOO GREEDY?
I NEVER THOUGHT THEY'D EXPAND THEIR WINGED TROOPS SO FAST...
KNOWING THEIR SENSE OF SMELL...
...I PROBABLY SHOULDN'T LIGHT A CIGARETTE, NOW.
FLICK
シュボッ
BUT...
...WHO CARES ANYMORE?
I'M SO SLEEPY...

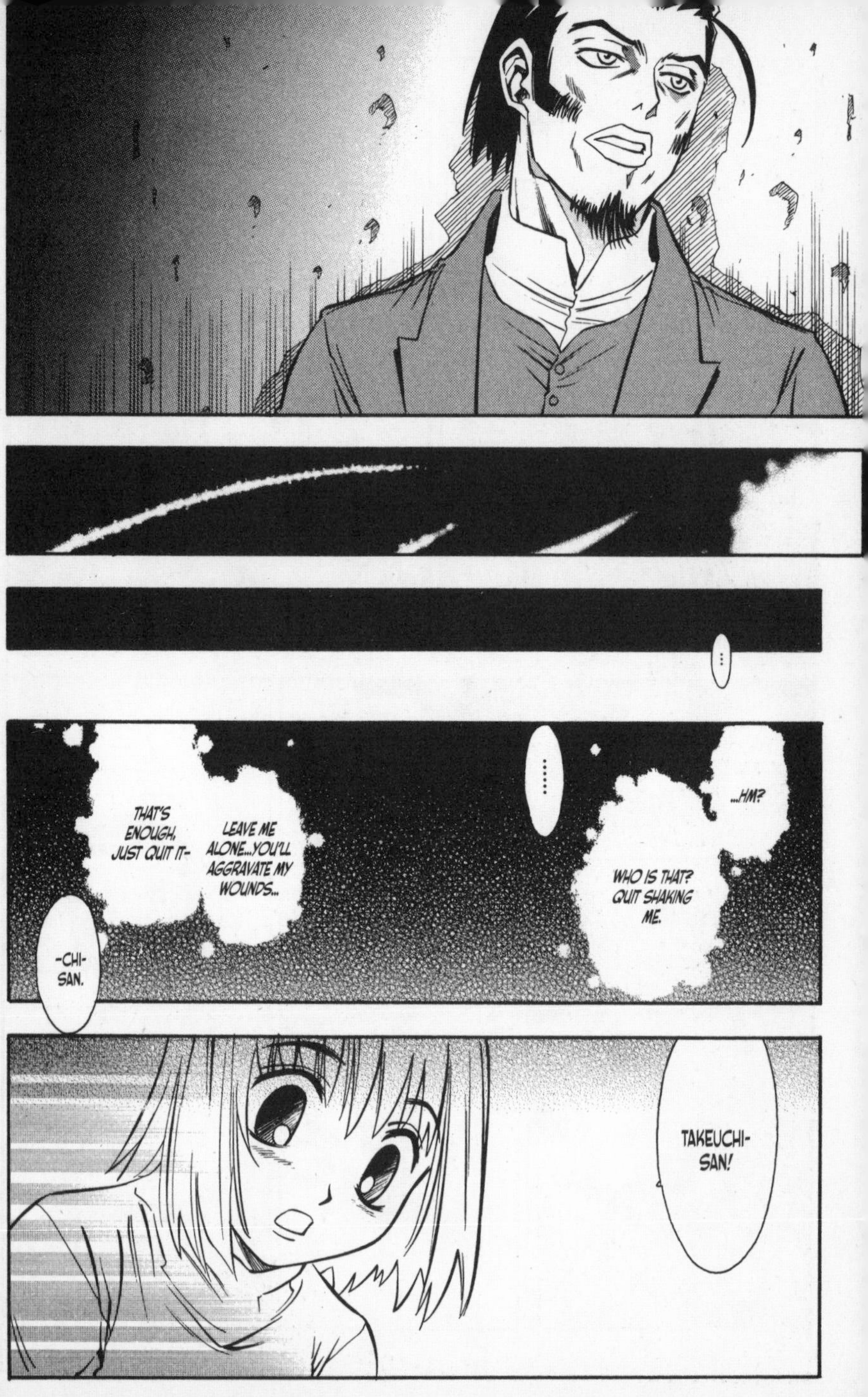
…
...HM?
WHO IS THAT? QUIT SHAKING ME.
......
LEAVE ME ALONE...YOU'LL AGGRAVATE MY WOUNDS...
THAT'S ENOUGH. JUST QUIT IT-
-CHI-SAN.
TAKEUCHI-SAN!

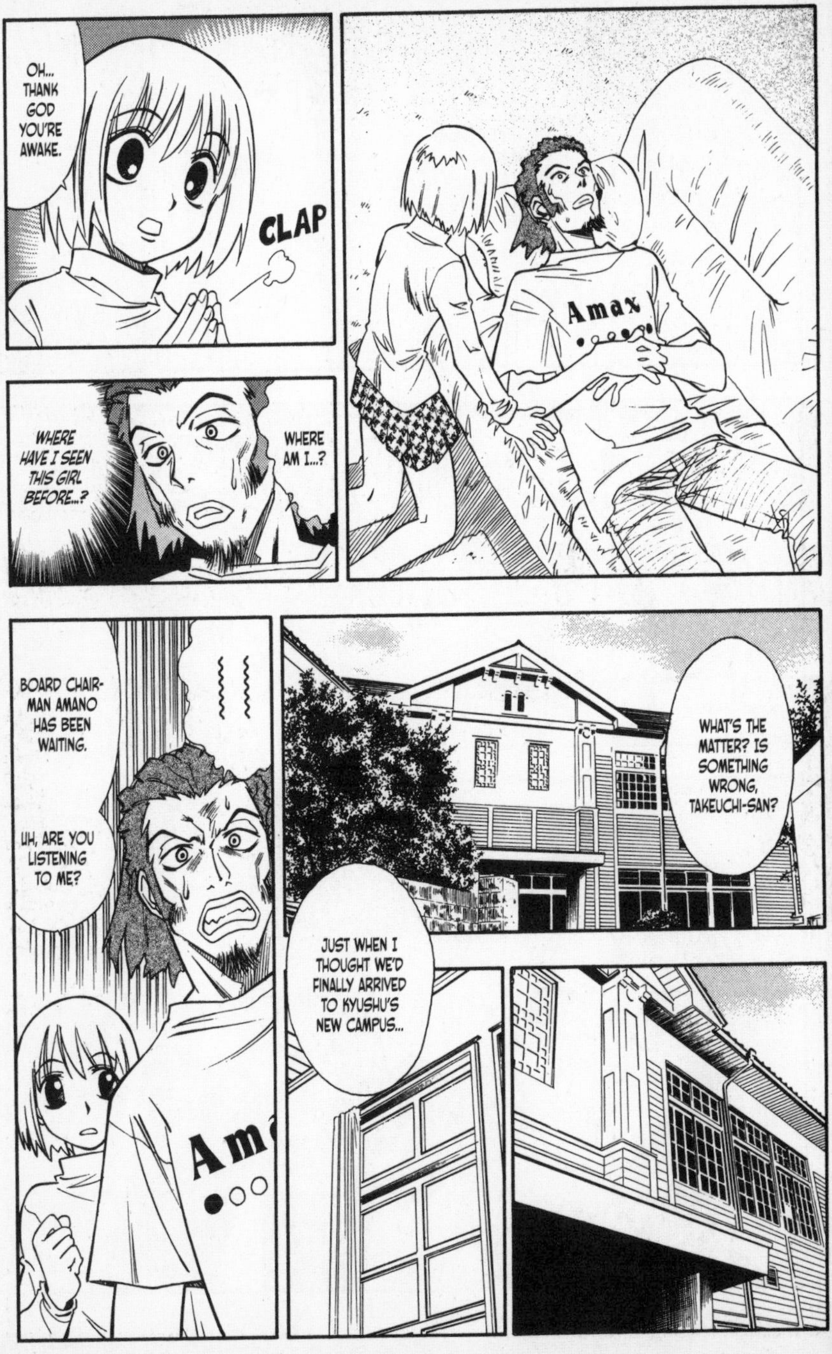
OH... THANK GOD YOU'RE AWAKE.
CLAP
WHERE AM I...?
WHERE HAVE I SEEN THIS GIRL BEFORE...?
WHAT'S THE MATTER? IS SOMETHING WRONG, TAKEUCHI-SAN?
JUST WHEN I THOUGHT WE'D FINALLY ARRIVED TO KYUSHU'S NEW CAMPUS...
BOARD CHAIR-MAN AMANO HAS BEEN WAITING.
UH, ARE YOU LISTENING TO ME?

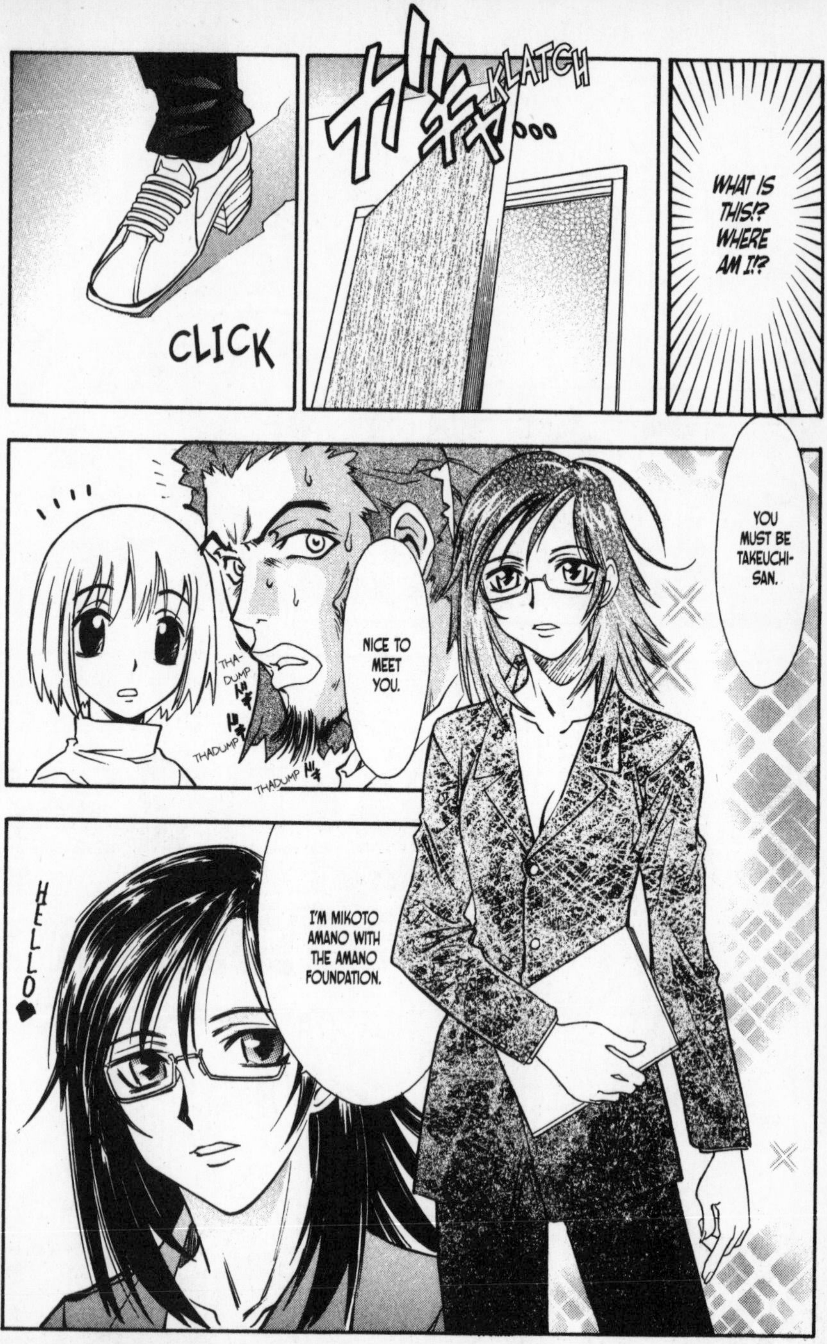
WHAT IS THIS!? WHERE AM I!?
KLATCH...
CLICK
YOU MUST BE TAKEUCHI-SAN.
NICE TO MEET YOU.
THA-DUMP
THADUMP
THADUMP
I'M MIKOTO AMANO WITH THE AMANO FOUNDATION.
HELLO

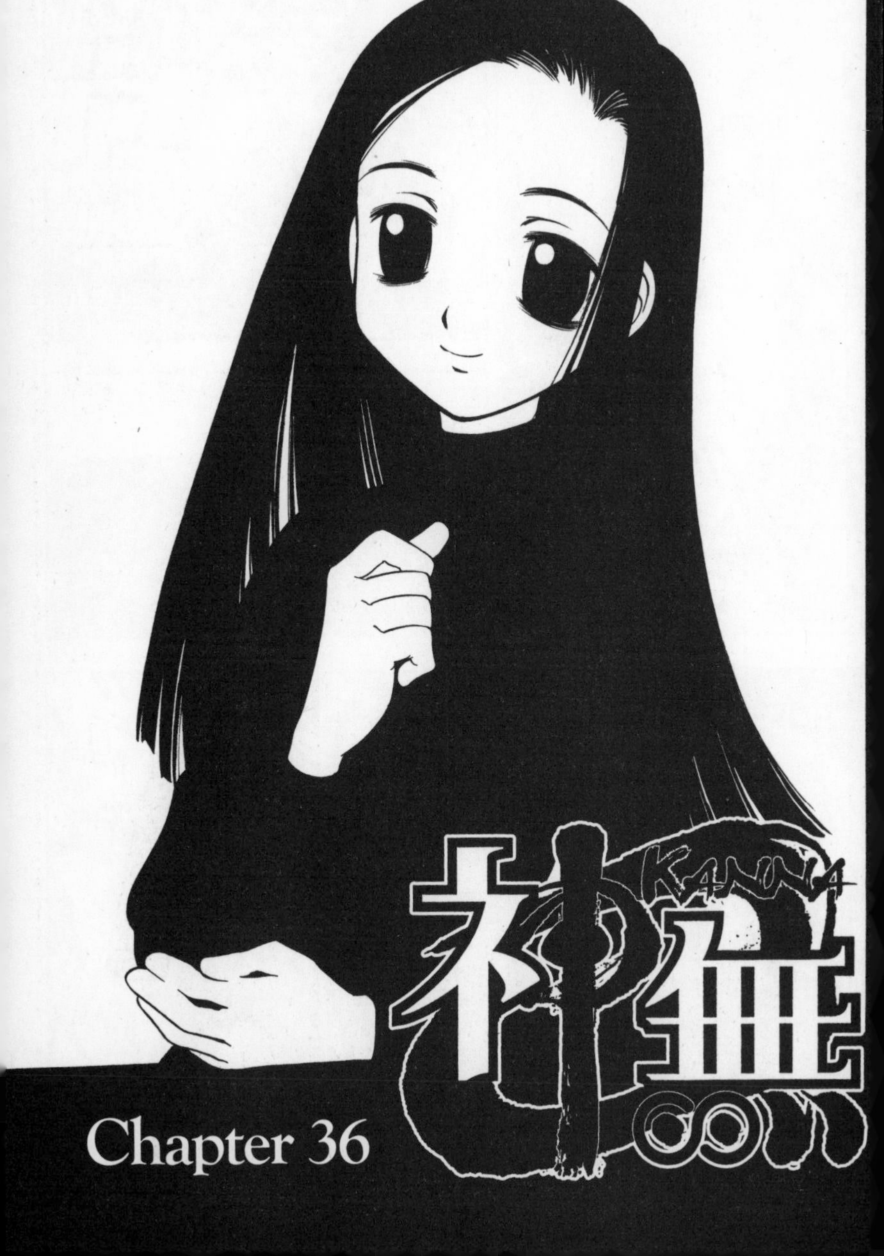
KANNA
神無
Chapter 36

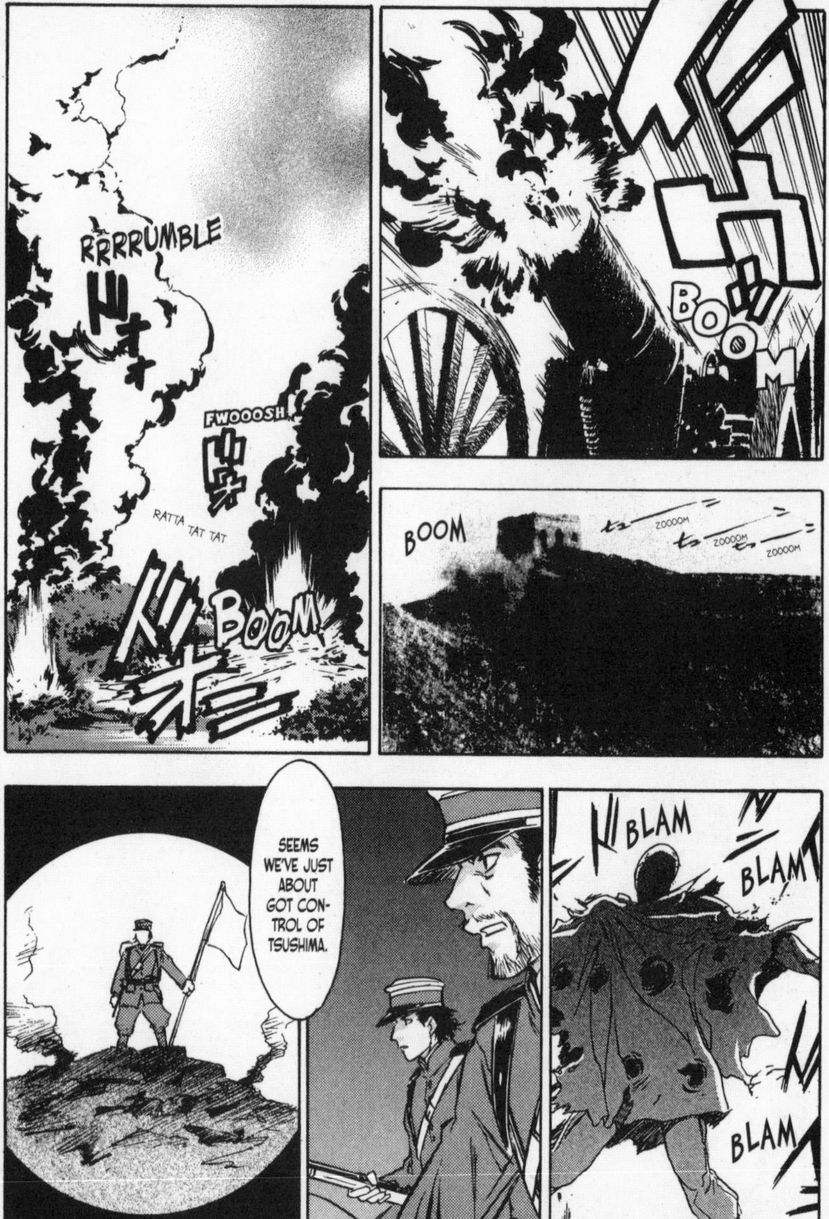
BOOM
BOOM
ZOOOOM
ZOOOOM
ZOOOOM
RRRRUMBLE
FWOOOSH
RATTA TAT TAT
BOOM
BLAM
BLAM
BLAM
SEEMS WE'VE JUST ABOUT GOT CON-TROL OF TSUSHIMA.

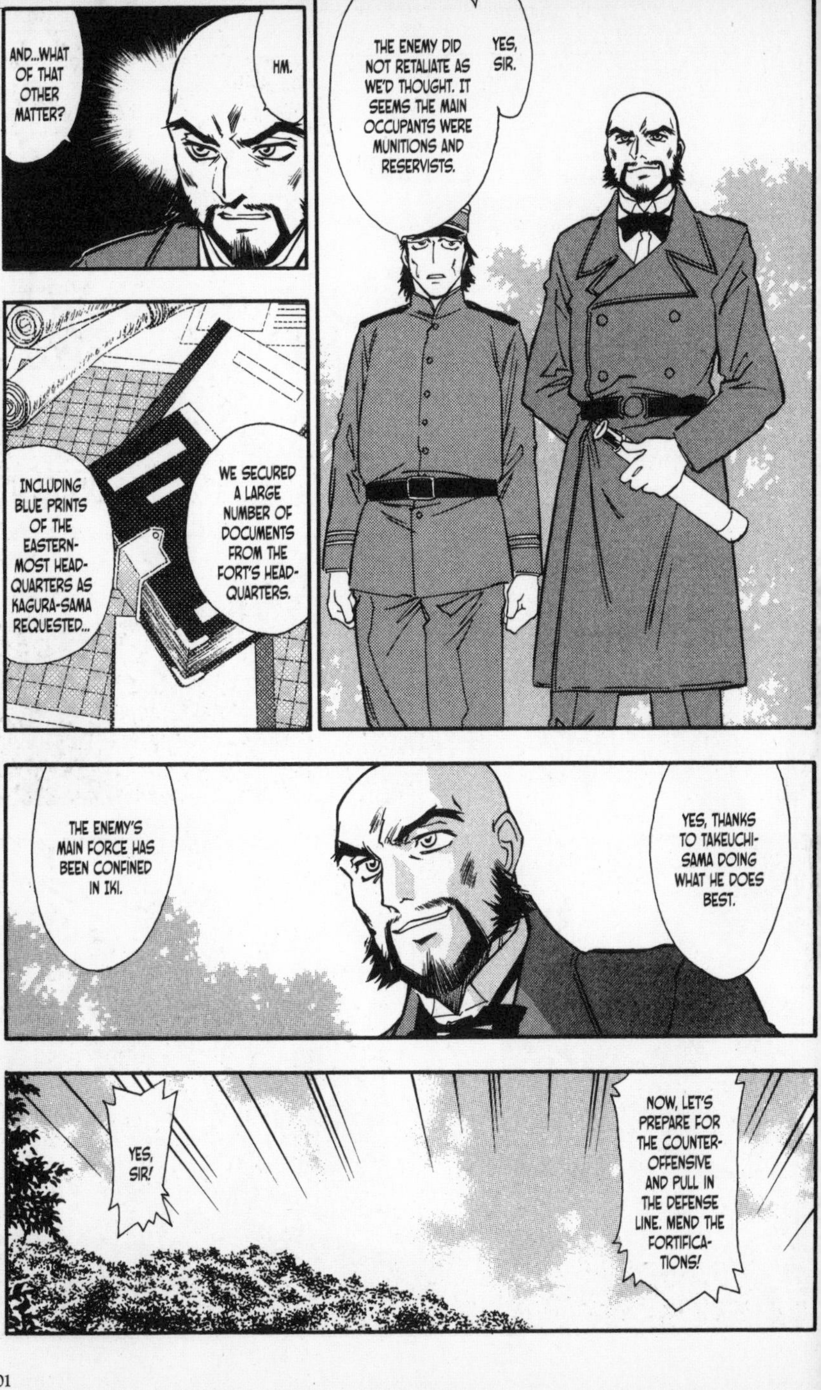
YES, SIR.
THE ENEMY DID NOT RETALIATE AS WE'D THOUGHT. IT SEEMS THE MAIN OCCUPANTS WERE MUNITIONS AND RESERVISTS.
HM.
AND...WHAT OF THAT OTHER MATTER?
WE SECURED A LARGE NUMBER OF DOCUMENTS FROM THE FORT'S HEAD-QUARTERS.
INCLUDING BLUE PRINTS OF THE EASTERN-MOST HEAD-QUARTERS AS KAGURA-SAMA REQUESTED...
YES, THANKS TO TAKEUCHI-SAMA DOING WHAT HE DOES BEST.
THE ENEMY'S MAIN FORCE HAS BEEN CONFINED IN IKI.
NOW, LET'S PREPARE FOR THE COUNTER-OFFENSIVE AND PULL IN THE DEFENSE LINE. MEND THE FORTIFICA-TIONS!
YES, SIR!

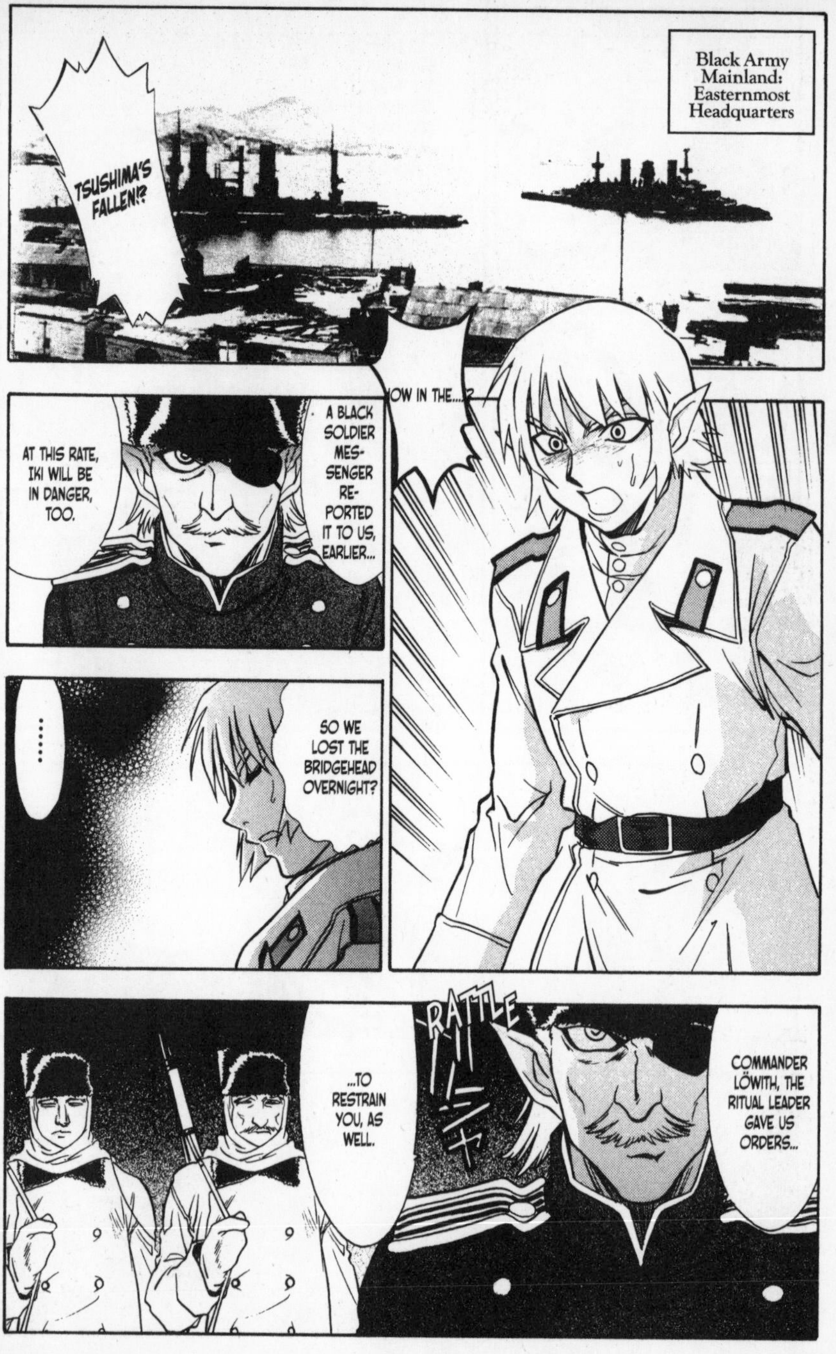
Black Army Mainland: Easternmost Headquarters
TSUSHIMA'S FALLEN!?
HOW IN THE...!?
A BLACK SOLDIER MES-SENGER RE-PORTED IT TO US, EARLIER...
AT THIS RATE, IKI WILL BE IN DANGER, TOO.
SO WE LOST THE BRIDGEHEAD OVERNIGHT?
......
COMMANDER LÖWITH, THE RITUAL LEADER GAVE US ORDERS...
RATTLE
...TO RESTRAIN YOU, AS WELL.

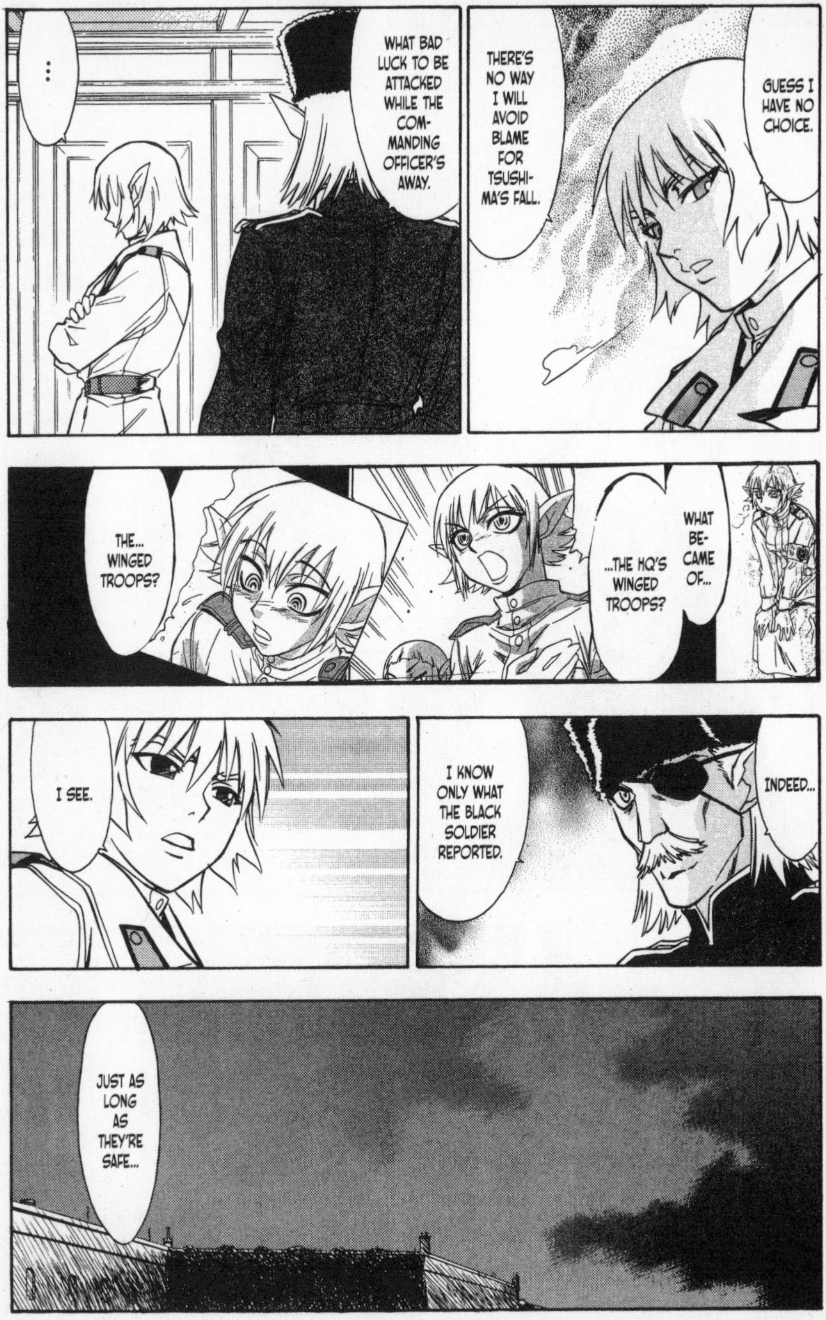
GUESS I HAVE NO CHOICE.
THERE'S NO WAY I WILL AVOID BLAME FOR TSUSHIMA'S FALL.
WHAT BAD LUCK TO BE ATTACKED WHILE THE COMMANDING OFFICER'S AWAY.
...
WHAT BECAME OF...
...THE HQ'S WINGED TROOPS?
THE... WINGED TROOPS?
INDEED...
I KNOW ONLY WHAT THE BLACK SOLDIER REPORTED.
I SEE.
JUST AS LONG AS THEY'RE SAFE...

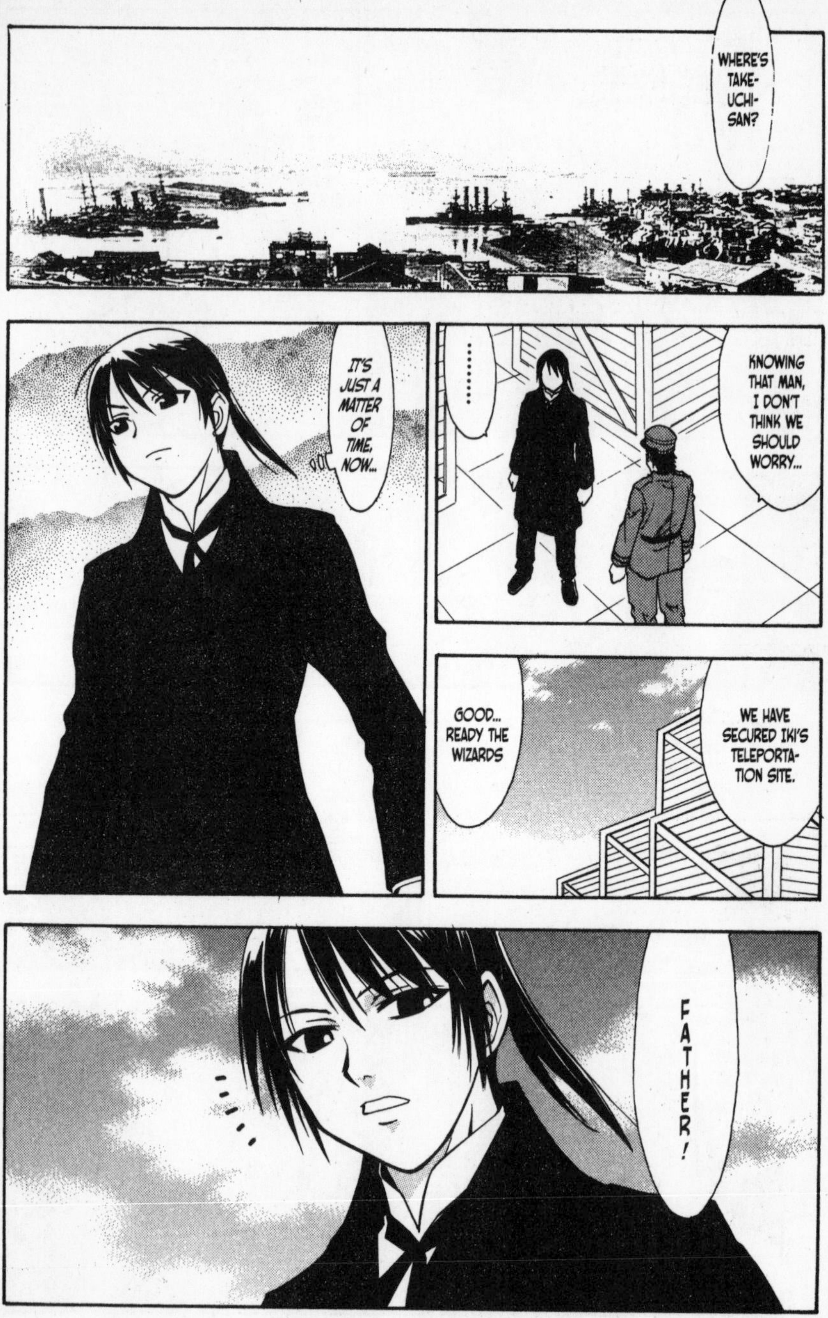
WHERE'S TAKE-UCHI-SAN?
KNOWING THAT MAN, I DON'T THINK WE SHOULD WORRY...
......
WE HAVE SECURED IKI'S TELEPORTA-TION SITE.
GOOD... READY THE WIZARDS
IT'S JUST A MATTER OF TIME, NOW...
FATHER!
...

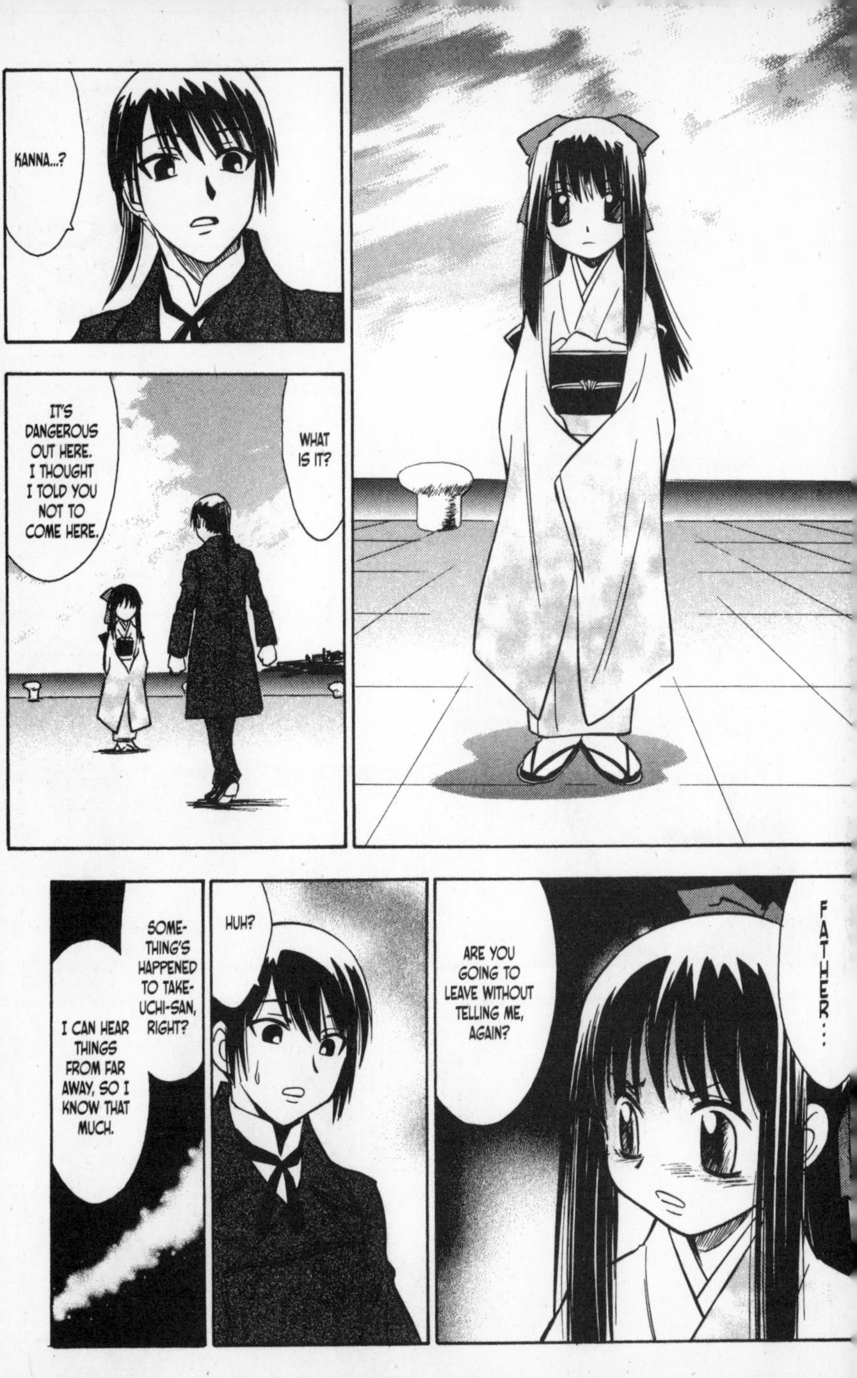
KANNA...?
WHAT IS IT?
IT'S DANGEROUS OUT HERE. I THOUGHT I TOLD YOU NOT TO COME HERE.
FATHER...
ARE YOU GOING TO LEAVE WITHOUT TELLING ME, AGAIN?
HUH?
SOME-THING'S HAPPENED TO TAKE-UCHI-SAN, RIGHT?
I CAN HEAR THINGS FROM FAR AWAY, SO I KNOW THAT MUCH.

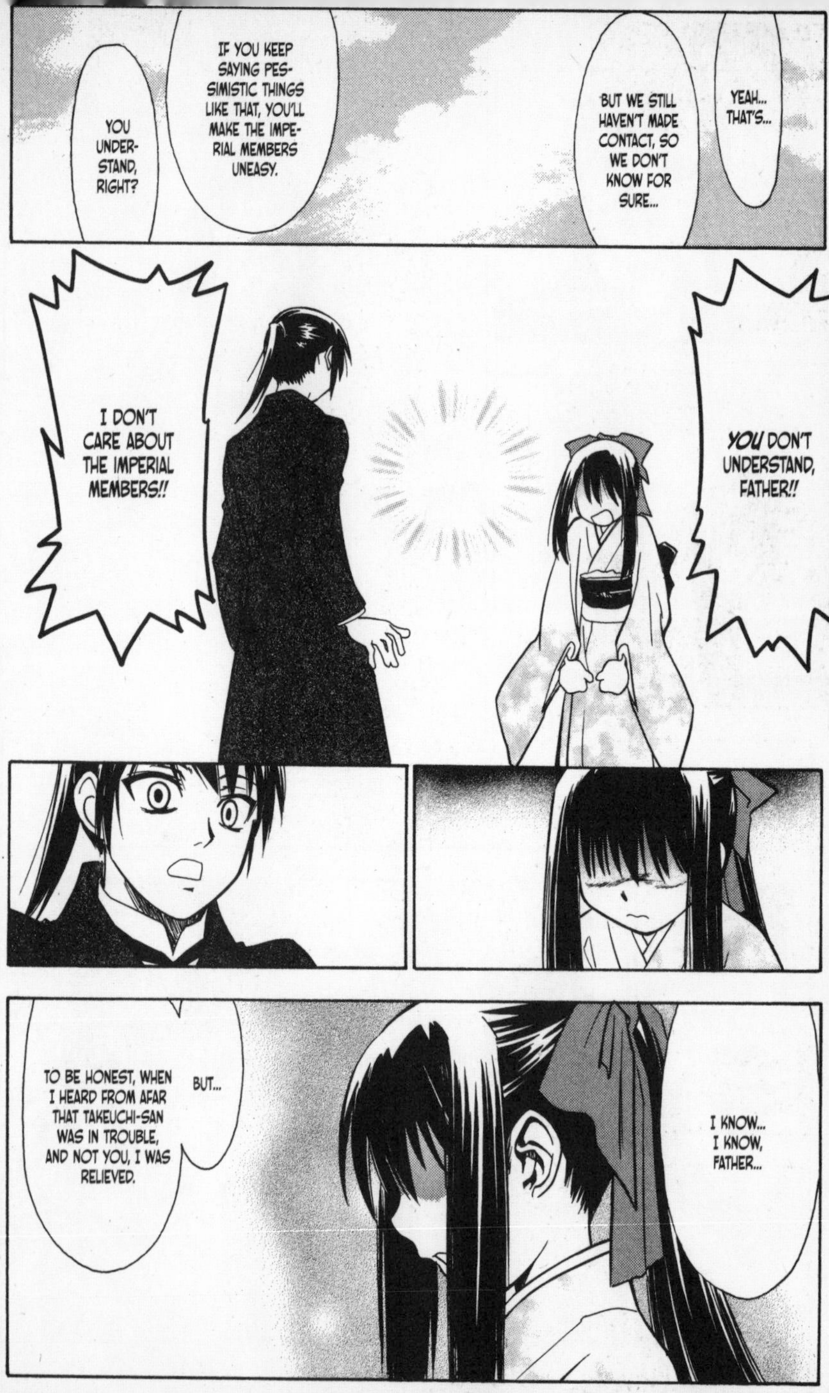
YEAH... THAT'S...
BUT WE STILL HAVEN'T MADE CONTACT, SO WE DON'T KNOW FOR SURE...
IF YOU KEEP SAYING PES-SIMISTIC THINGS LIKE THAT, YOU'LL MAKE THE IMPE-RIAL MEMBERS UNEASY.
YOU UNDER-STAND, RIGHT?
YOU DON'T UNDERSTAND, FATHER!!
I DON'T CARE ABOUT THE IMPERIAL MEMBERS!!
I KNOW... I KNOW, FATHER...
BUT...
TO BE HONEST, WHEN I HEARD FROM AFAR THAT TAKEUCHI-SAN WAS IN TROUBLE, AND NOT YOU, I WAS RELIEVED.

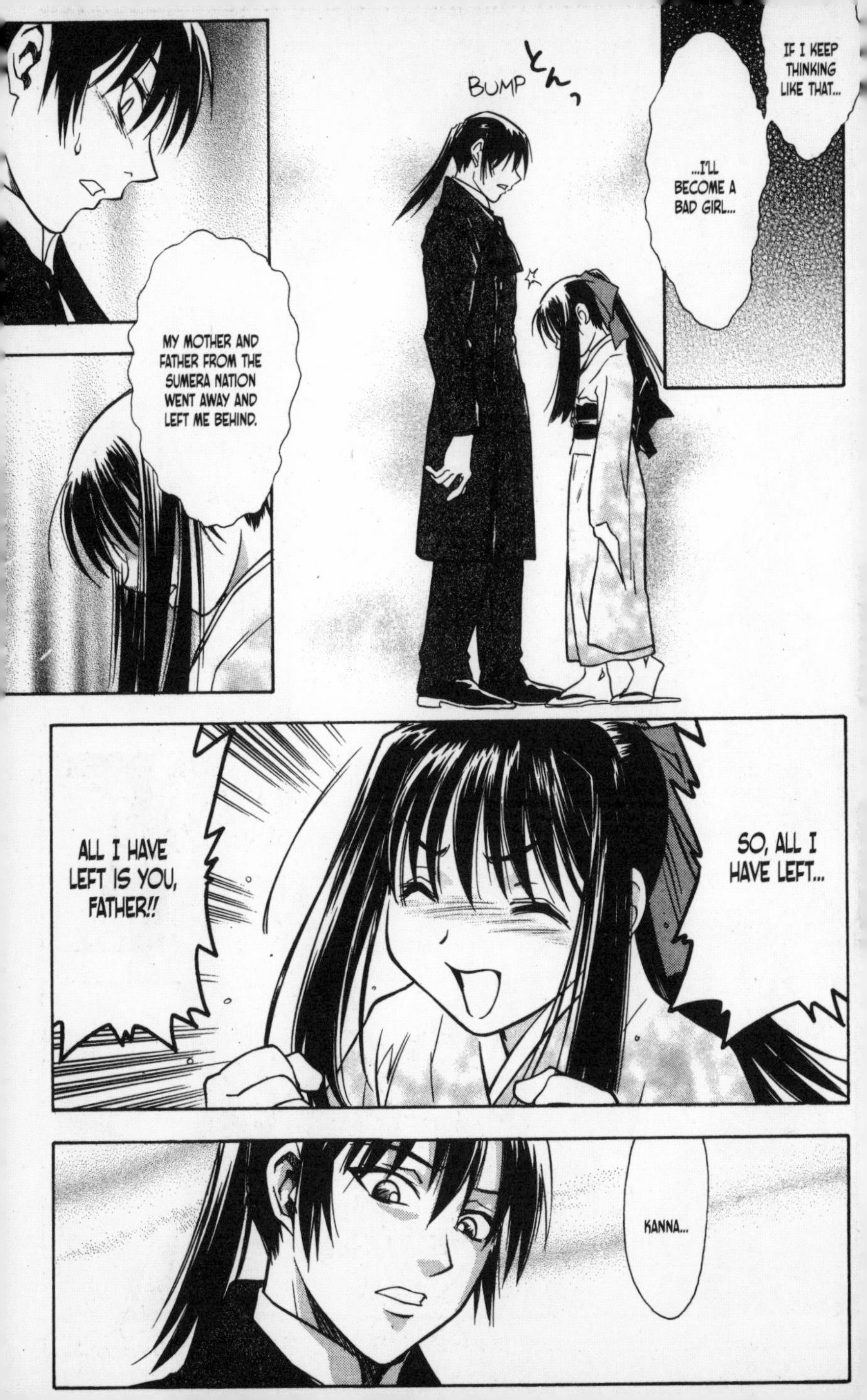
IF I KEEP THINKING LIKE THAT...
...I'LL BECOME A BAD GIRL...
BUMP
とんっ
MY MOTHER AND FATHER FROM THE SUMERA NATION WENT AWAY AND LEFT ME BEHIND.
SO, ALL I HAVE LEFT...
ALL I HAVE LEFT IS YOU, FATHER!!
KANNA...

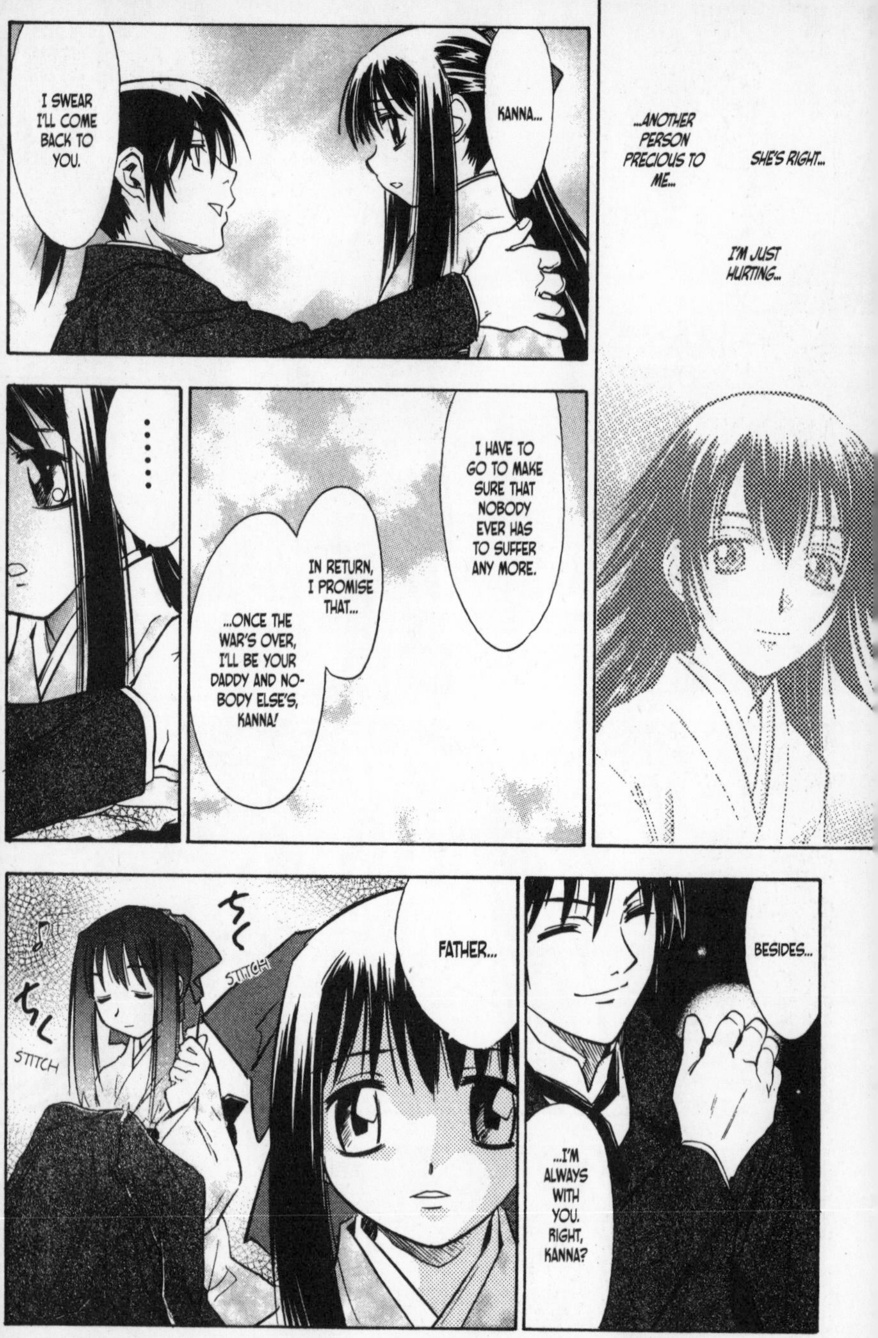
SHE'S RIGHT...
I'M JUST HURTING...
...ANOTHER PERSON PRECIOUS TO ME...
KANNA...
I SWEAR I'LL COME BACK TO YOU.
I HAVE TO GO TO MAKE SURE THAT NOBODY EVER HAS TO SUFFER ANY MORE.
IN RETURN, I PROMISE THAT...
...ONCE THE WAR'S OVER, I'LL BE YOUR DADDY AND NO-BODY ELSE'S, KANNA!
......
BESIDES...
...I'M ALWAYS WITH YOU. RIGHT, KANNA?
FATHER...
ちく
STITCH
ちく
STITCH

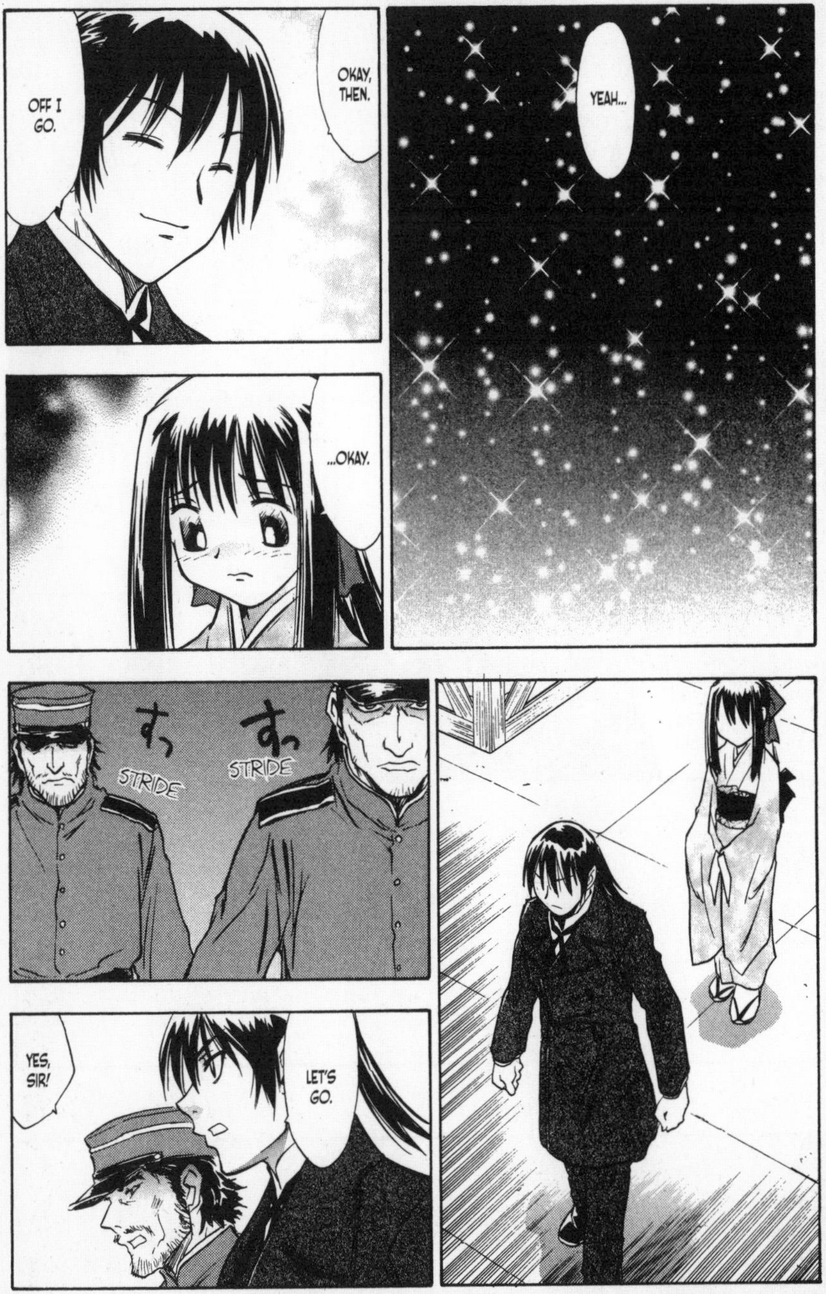
YEAH...
OKAY, THEN.
OFF I GO.
...OKAY.
すっ
STRIDE
すっ
STRIDE
LET'S GO.
YES, SIR!

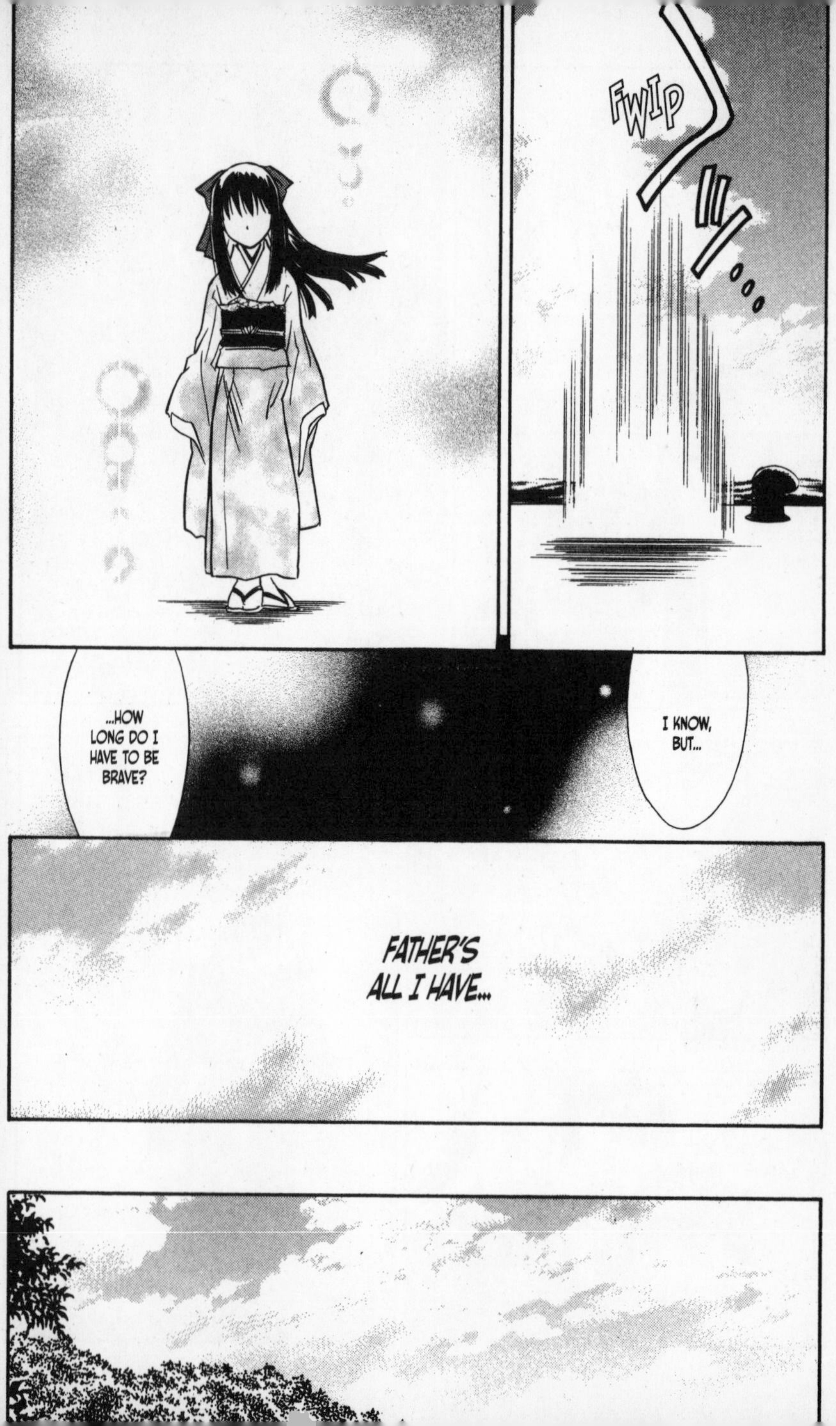
FWIP
I KNOW, BUT...
...HOW LONG DO I HAVE TO BE BRAVE?
FATHER'S ALL I HAVE...

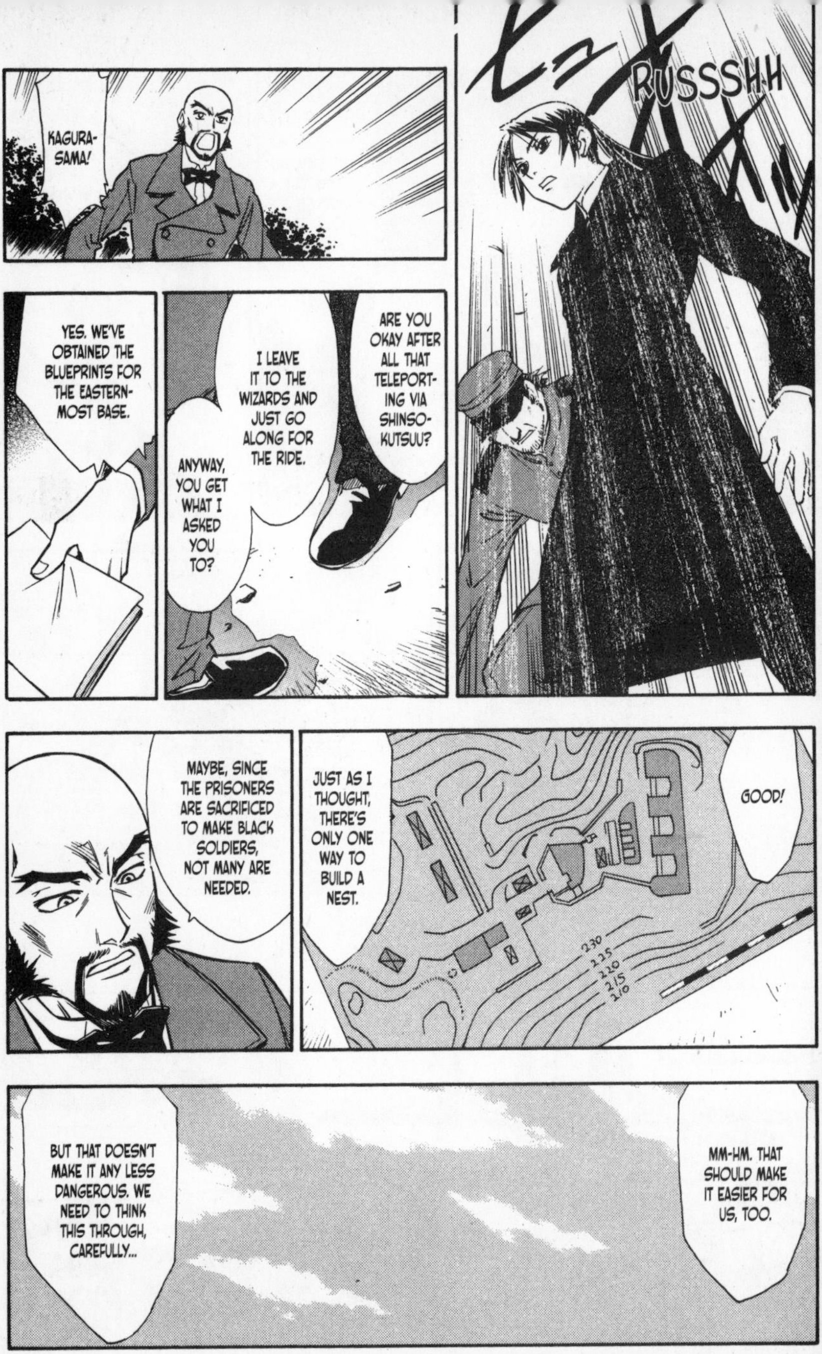
RUSSSHH
KAGURA-SAMA!
ARE YOU OKAY AFTER ALL THAT TELEPORTING VIA SHINSO-KUTSUU?
I LEAVE IT TO THE WIZARDS AND JUST GO ALONG FOR THE RIDE.
ANYWAY, YOU GET WHAT I ASKED YOU TO?
YES. WE'VE OBTAINED THE BLUEPRINTS FOR THE EASTERN-MOST BASE.
GOOD!
JUST AS I THOUGHT, THERE'S ONLY ONE WAY TO BUILD A NEST.
230
225
220
215
210
MAYBE, SINCE THE PRISONERS ARE SACRIFICED TO MAKE BLACK SOLDIERS, NOT MANY ARE NEEDED.
MM-HM. THAT SHOULD MAKE IT EASIER FOR US, TOO.
BUT THAT DOESN'T MAKE IT ANY LESS DANGEROUS. WE NEED TO THINK THIS THROUGH, CAREFULLY...

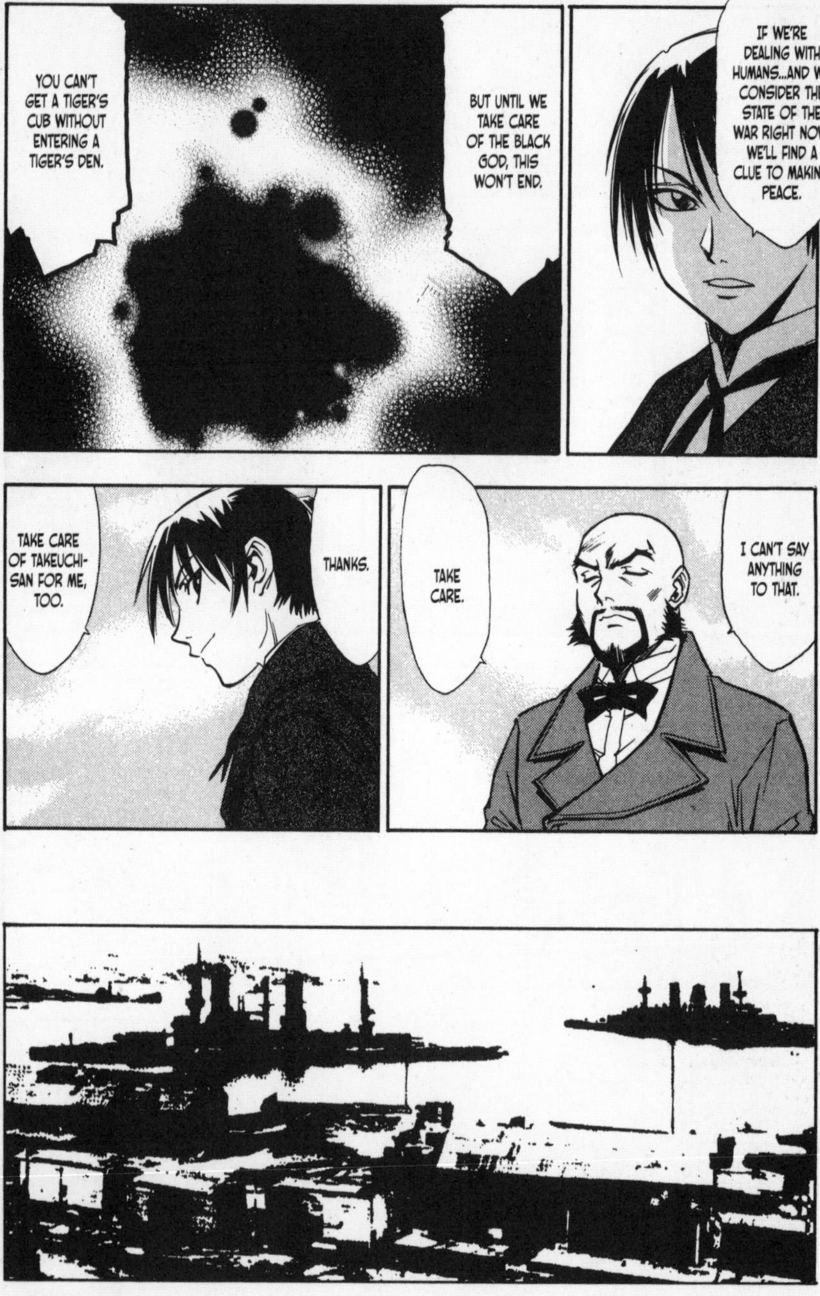
IF WE'RE DEALING WITH HUMANS...AND WE CONSIDER THE STATE OF THE WAR RIGHT NOW, WE'LL FIND A CLUE TO MAKING PEACE.
BUT UNTIL WE TAKE CARE OF THE BLACK GOD, THIS WON'T END.
YOU CAN'T GET A TIGER'S CUB WITHOUT ENTERING A TIGER'S DEN.
I CAN'T SAY ANYTHING TO THAT.
TAKE CARE.
THANKS.
TAKE CARE OF TAKEUCHI-SAN FOR ME, TOO.

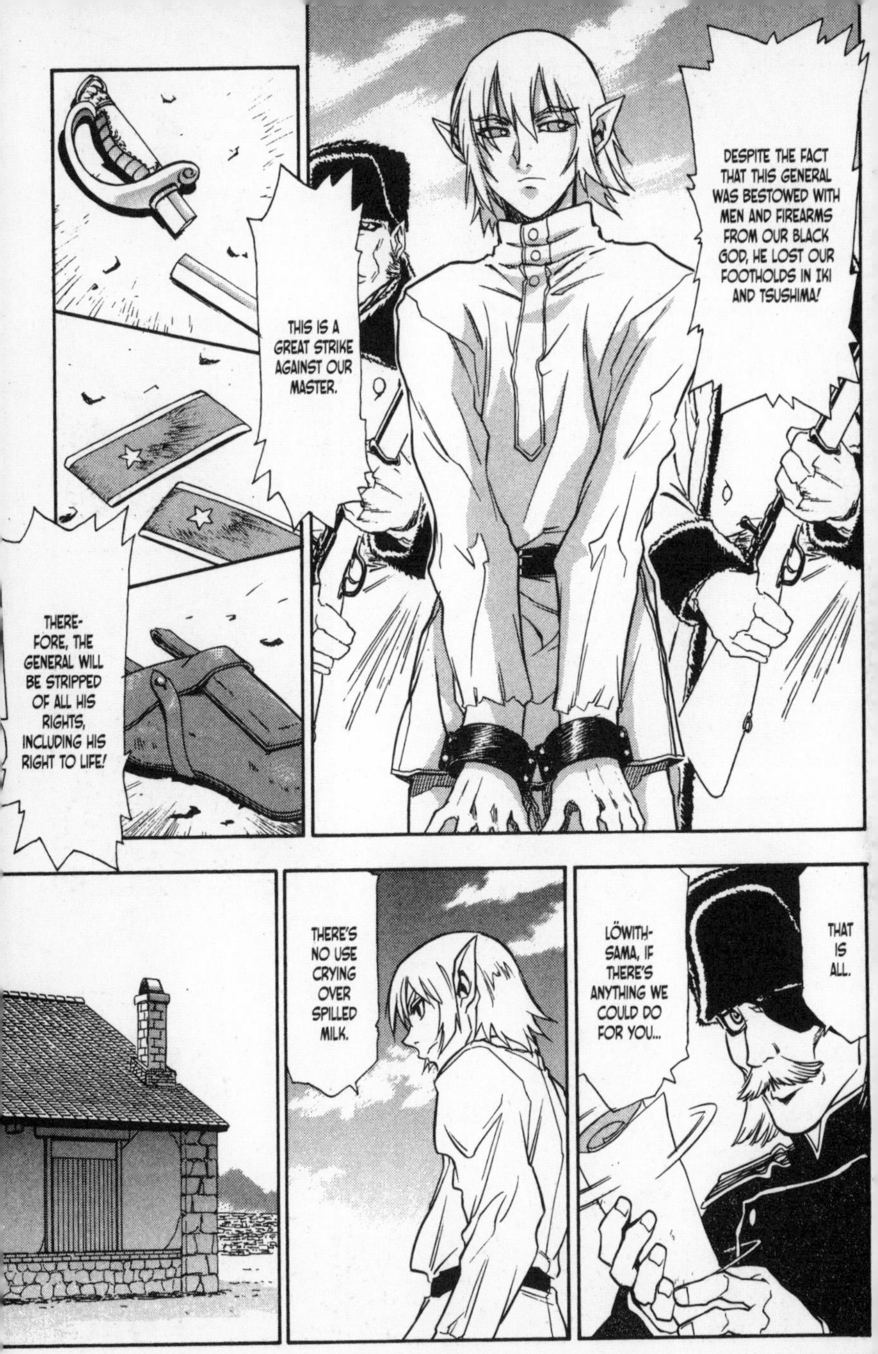
DESPITE THE FACT THAT THIS GENERAL WAS BESTOWED WITH MEN AND FIREARMS FROM OUR BLACK GOD, HE LOST OUR FOOTHOLDS IN IKI AND TSUSHIMA!
THIS IS A GREAT STRIKE AGAINST OUR MASTER.
THERE-FORE, THE GENERAL WILL BE STRIPPED OF ALL HIS RIGHTS, INCLUDING HIS RIGHT TO LIFE!
THAT IS ALL.
LÖWITH-SAMA, IF THERE'S ANYTHING WE COULD DO FOR YOU...
THERE'S NO USE CRYING OVER SPILLED MILK.

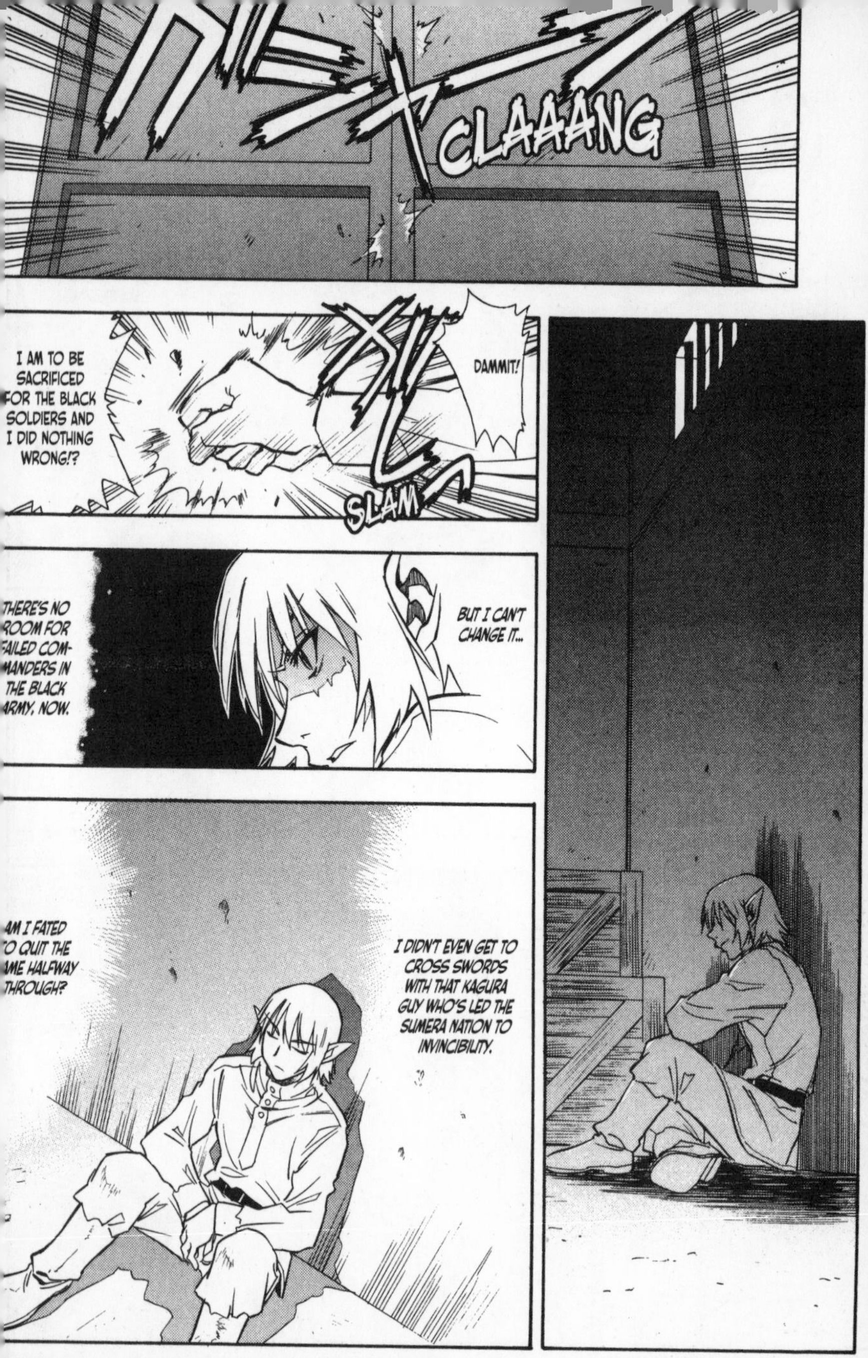
CLAAANG
DAMMIT!
SLAM
I AM TO BE SACRIFICED FOR THE BLACK SOLDIERS AND I DID NOTHING WRONG!?
BUT I CAN'T CHANGE IT...
THERE'S NO ROOM FOR AILED COM-MANDERS IN THE BLACK ARMY, NOW.
I DIDN'T EVEN GET TO CROSS SWORDS WITH THAT KAGURA GUY WHO'S LED THE SUMERA NATION TO INVINCIBILITY.
AM I FATED O QUIT THE AME HALFWAY THROUGH?

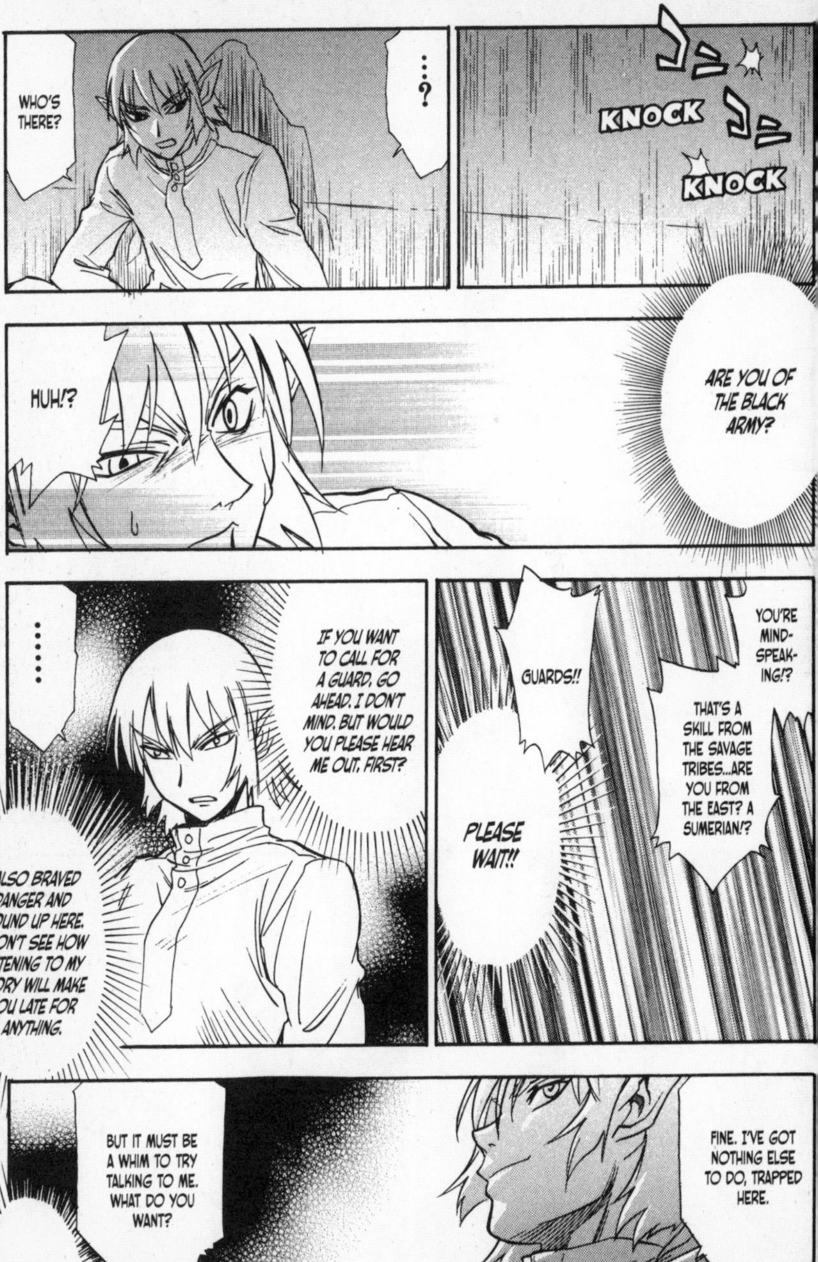
KNOCK
KNOCK
...?
WHO'S THERE?
ARE YOU OF THE BLACK ARMY?
HUH!?
YOU'RE MIND-SPEAKING!?
THAT'S A SKILL FROM THE SAVAGE TRIBES...ARE YOU FROM THE EAST? A SUMERIAN!?
GUARDS!!
PLEASE WAIT!!
IF YOU WANT TO CALL FOR A GUARD, GO AHEAD. I DON'T MIND. BUT WOULD YOU PLEASE HEAR ME OUT, FIRST?
......
I ALSO BRAVED DANGER AND WOUND UP HERE. I DON'T SEE HOW LISTENING TO MY STORY WILL MAKE YOU LATE FOR ANYTHING.
FINE. I'VE GOT NOTHING ELSE TO DO, TRAPPED HERE.
BUT IT MUST BE A WHIM TO TRY TALKING TO ME. WHAT DO YOU WANT?
THE TRUTH IS...

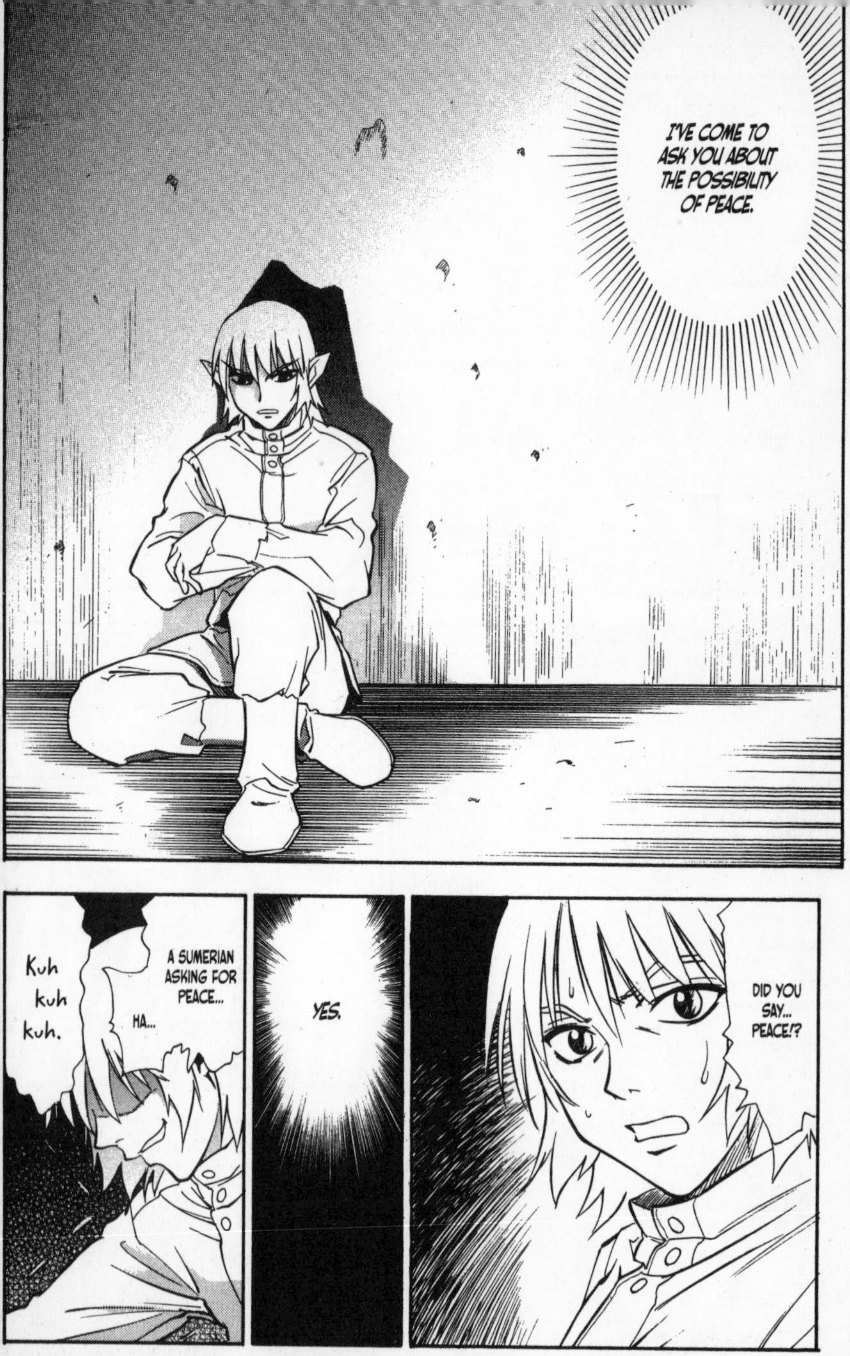
I'VE COME TO ASK YOU ABOUT THE POSSIBILITY OF PEACE.
DID YOU SAY... PEACE!?
YES.
A SUMERIAN ASKING FOR PEACE...
HA...
Kuh kuh kuh.

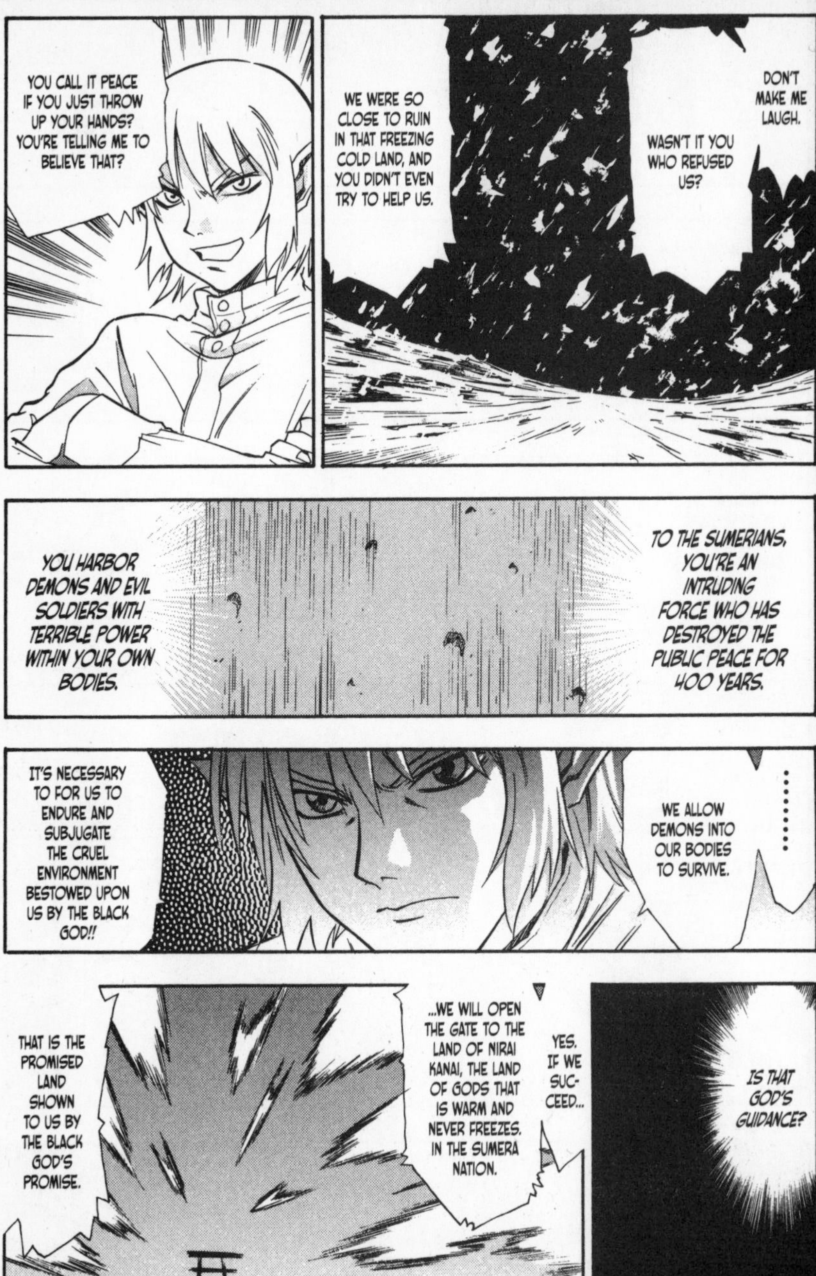
DON'T MAKE ME LAUGH.
WASN'T IT YOU WHO REFUSED US?
WE WERE SO CLOSE TO RUIN IN THAT FREEZING COLD LAND, AND YOU DIDN'T EVEN TRY TO HELP US.
YOU CALL IT PEACE IF YOU JUST THROW UP YOUR HANDS? YOU'RE TELLING ME TO BELIEVE THAT?
TO THE SUMERIANS, YOU'RE AN INTRUDING FORCE WHO HAS DESTROYED THE PUBLIC PEACE FOR 400 YEARS.
YOU HARBOR DEMONS AND EVIL SOLDIERS WITH TERRIBLE POWER WITHIN YOUR OWN BODIES.
....
WE ALLOW DEMONS INTO OUR BODIES TO SURVIVE.
IT'S NECESSARY TO FOR US TO ENDURE AND SUBJUGATE THE CRUEL ENVIRONMENT BESTOWED UPON US BY THE BLACK GOD!!
IS THAT GOD'S GUIDANCE?
YES. IF WE SUC-CEED...
...WE WILL OPEN THE GATE TO THE LAND OF NIRAI KANAI, THE LAND OF GODS THAT IS WARM AND NEVER FREEZES. IN THE SUMERA NATION.
THAT IS THE PROMISED LAND SHOWN TO US BY THE BLACK GOD'S PROMISE.

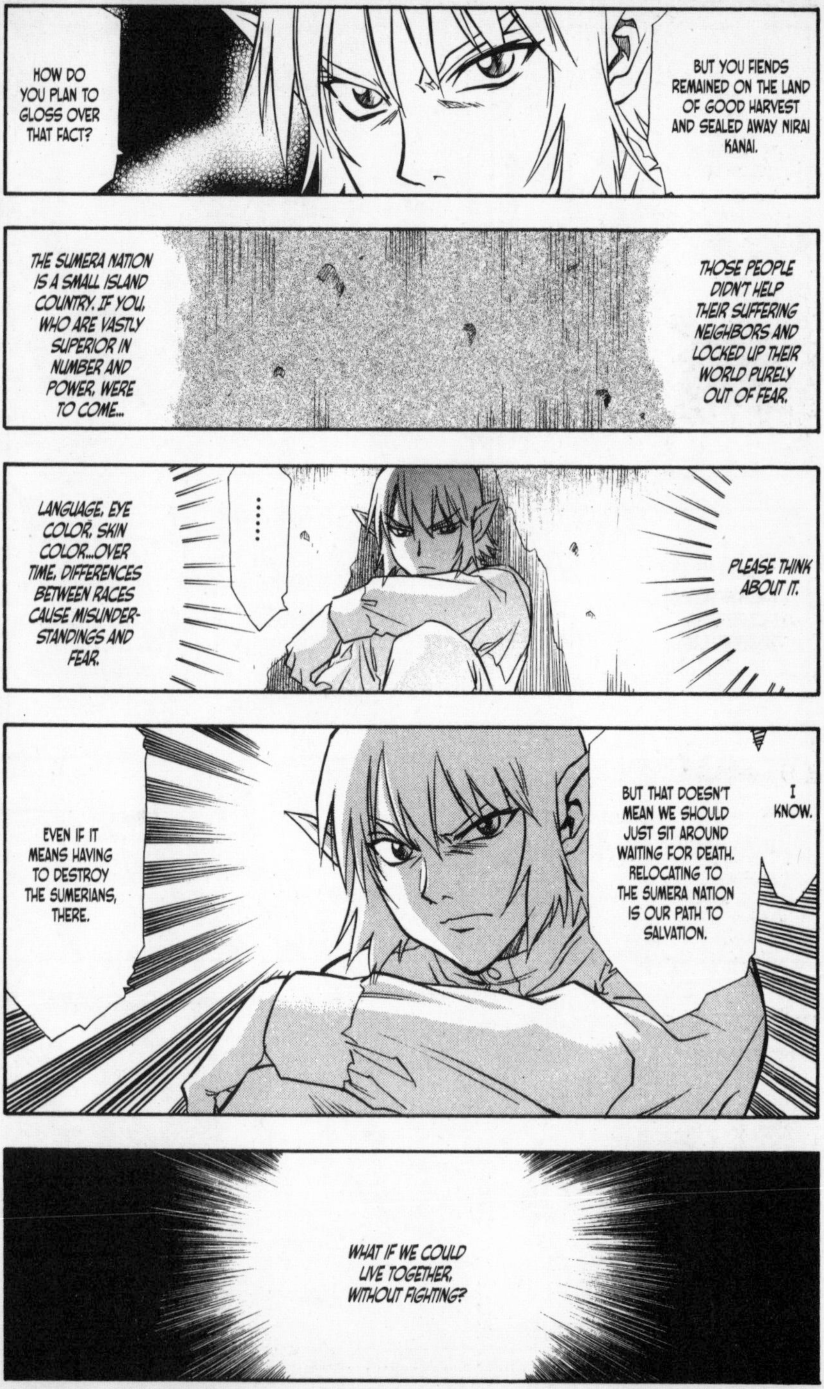

BUT YOU FIENDS REMAINED ON THE LAND OF GOOD HARVEST AND SEALED AWAY NIRAI KANAI.
HOW DO YOU PLAN TO GLOSS OVER THAT FACT?
THOSE PEOPLE DIDN'T HELP THEIR SUFFERING NEIGHBORS AND LOCKED UP THEIR WORLD PURELY OUT OF FEAR.
THE SUMERA NATION IS A SMALL ISLAND COUNTRY. IF YOU, WHO ARE VASTLY SUPERIOR IN NUMBER AND POWER, WERE TO COME...
PLEASE THINK ABOUT IT.
......
LANGUAGE, EYE COLOR, SKIN COLOR...OVER TIME, DIFFERENCES BETWEEN RACES CAUSE MISUNDER-STANDINGS AND FEAR.
I KNOW.
BUT THAT DOESN'T MEAN WE SHOULD JUST SIT AROUND WAITING FOR DEATH. RELOCATING TO THE SUMERA NATION IS OUR PATH TO SALVATION.
EVEN IF IT MEANS HAVING TO DESTROY THE SUMERIANS, THERE.
WHAT IF WE COULD LIVE TOGETHER, WITHOUT FIGHTING?

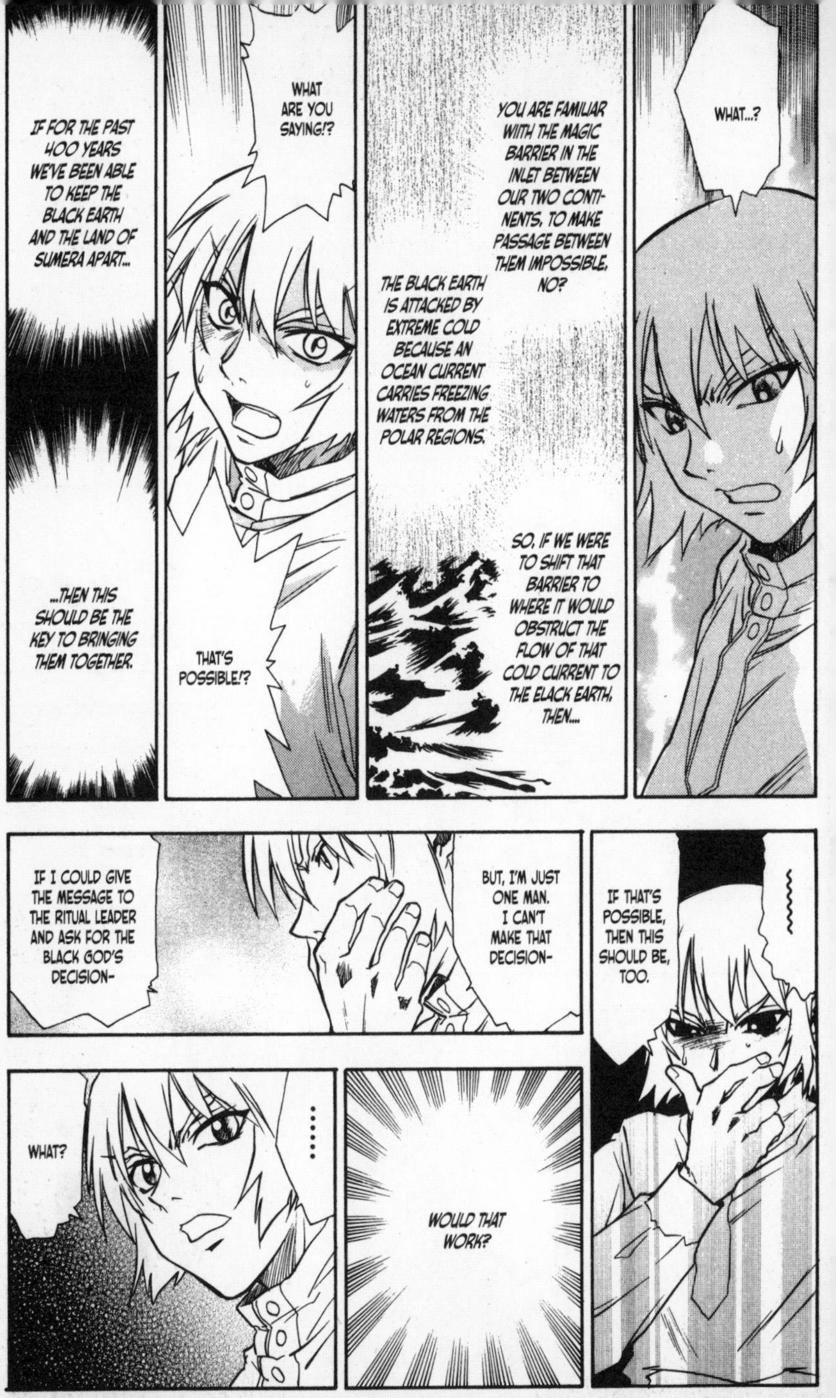
WHAT...?
YOU ARE FAMILIAR WITH THE MAGIC BARRIER IN THE INLET BETWEEN OUR TWO CONTINENTS, TO MAKE PASSAGE BETWEEN THEM IMPOSSIBLE, NO?
THE BLACK EARTH IS ATTACKED BY EXTREME COLD BECAUSE AN OCEAN CURRENT CARRIES FREEZING WATERS FROM THE POLAR REGIONS.
SO, IF WE WERE TO SHIFT THAT BARRIER TO WHERE IT WOULD OBSTRUCT THE FLOW OF THAT COLD CURRENT TO THE ELACK EARTH, THEN....
WHAT ARE YOU SAYING!?
THAT'S POSSIBLE!?
IF FOR THE PAST 400 YEARS WE'VE BEEN ABLE TO KEEP THE BLACK EARTH AND THE LAND OF SUMERA APART...
...THEN THIS SHOULD BE THE KEY TO BRINGING THEM TOGETHER.
IF THAT'S POSSIBLE, THEN THIS SHOULD BE, TOO.
BUT, I'M JUST ONE MAN. I CAN'T MAKE THAT DECISION-
IF I COULD GIVE THE MESSAGE TO THE RITUAL LEADER AND ASK FOR THE BLACK GOD'S DECISION-
WOULD THAT WORK?
......
WHAT?

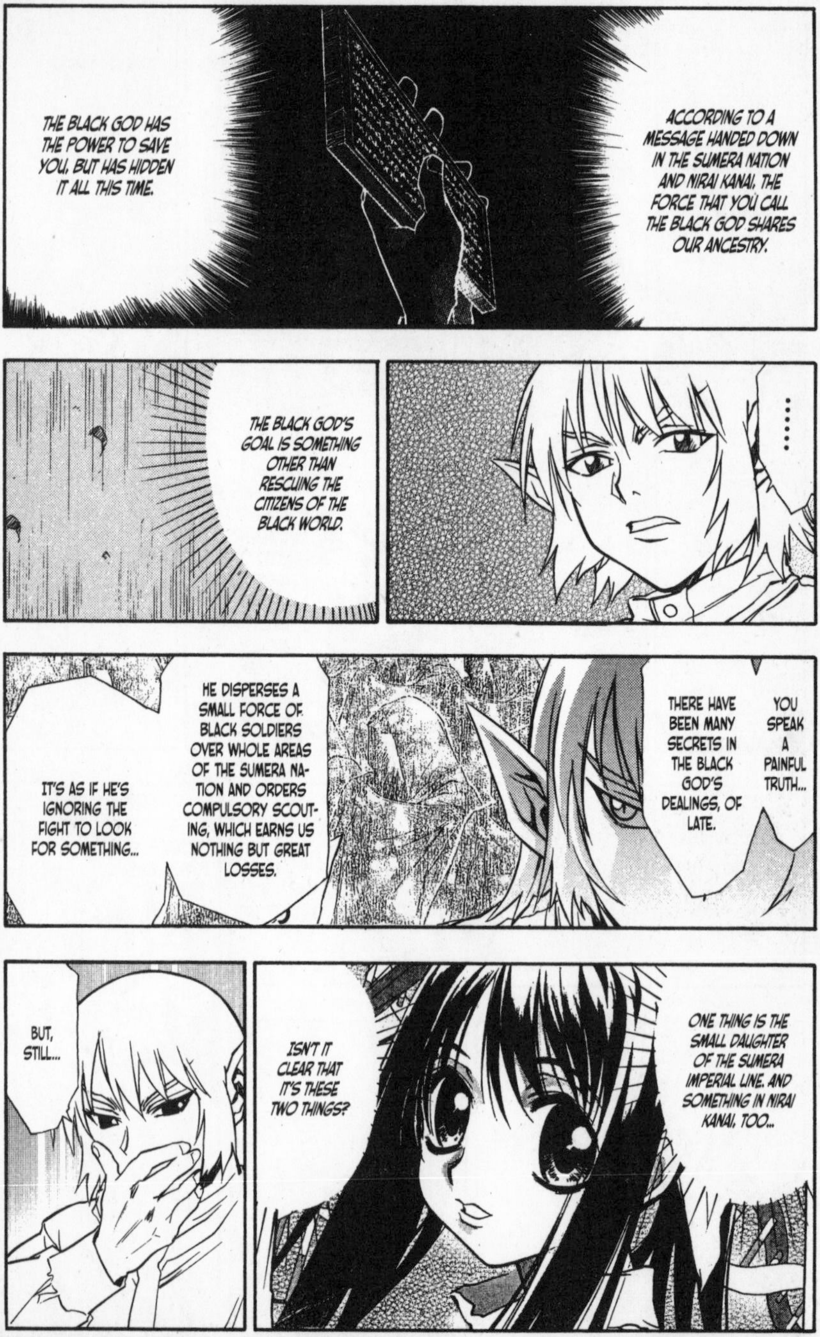
ACCORDING TO A MESSAGE HANDED DOWN IN THE SUMERA NATION AND NIRAI KANAI, THE FORCE THAT YOU CALL THE BLACK GOD SHARES OUR ANCESTRY.
THE BLACK GOD HAS THE POWER TO SAVE YOU, BUT HAS HIDDEN IT ALL THIS TIME.
......
THE BLACK GOD'S GOAL IS SOMETHING OTHER THAN RESCUING THE CITIZENS OF THE BLACK WORLD.
YOU SPEAK A PAINFUL TRUTH...
THERE HAVE BEEN MANY SECRETS IN THE BLACK GOD'S DEALINGS, OF LATE.
HE DISPERSES A SMALL FORCE OF BLACK SOLDIERS OVER WHOLE AREAS OF THE SUMERA NATION AND ORDERS COMPULSORY SCOUTING, WHICH EARNS US NOTHING BUT GREAT LOSSES.
IT'S AS IF HE'S IGNORING THE FIGHT TO LOOK FOR SOMETHING...
ONE THING IS THE SMALL DAUGHTER OF THE SUMERA IMPERIAL LINE, AND SOMETHING IN NIRAI KANAI, TOO...
ISN'T IT CLEAR THAT IT'S THESE TWO THINGS?
BUT, STILL...

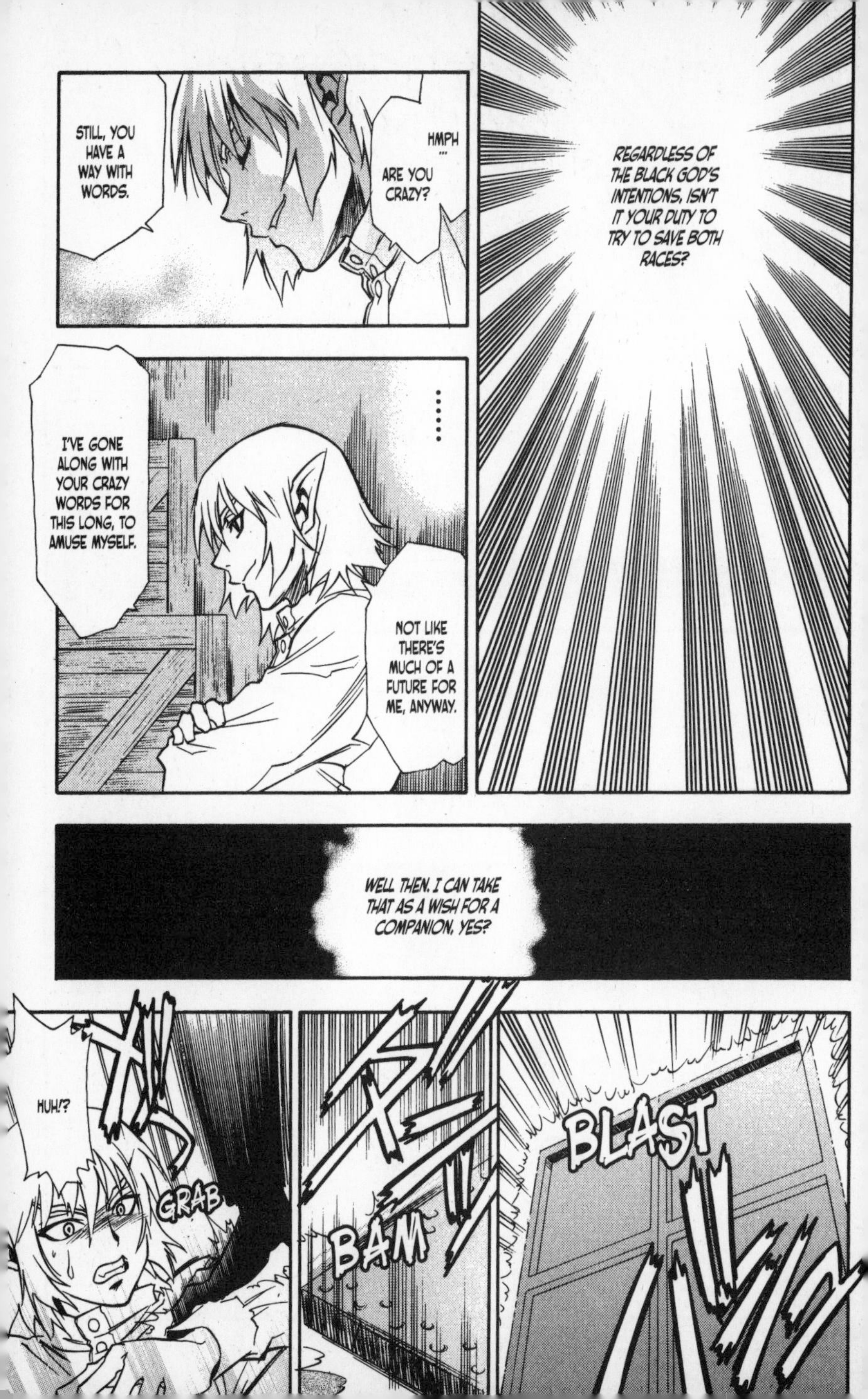
REGARDLESS OF THE BLACK GOD'S INTENTIONS, ISN'T IT YOUR DUTY TO TRY TO SAVE BOTH RACES?
HMPH...
ARE YOU CRAZY?
STILL, YOU HAVE A WAY WITH WORDS.
......
I'VE GONE ALONG WITH YOUR CRAZY WORDS FOR THIS LONG, TO AMUSE MYSELF.
NOT LIKE THERE'S MUCH OF A FUTURE FOR ME, ANYWAY.
WELL THEN. I CAN TAKE THAT AS A WISH FOR A COMPANION, YES?
BLAST
BAM
HUH!?
GRAB

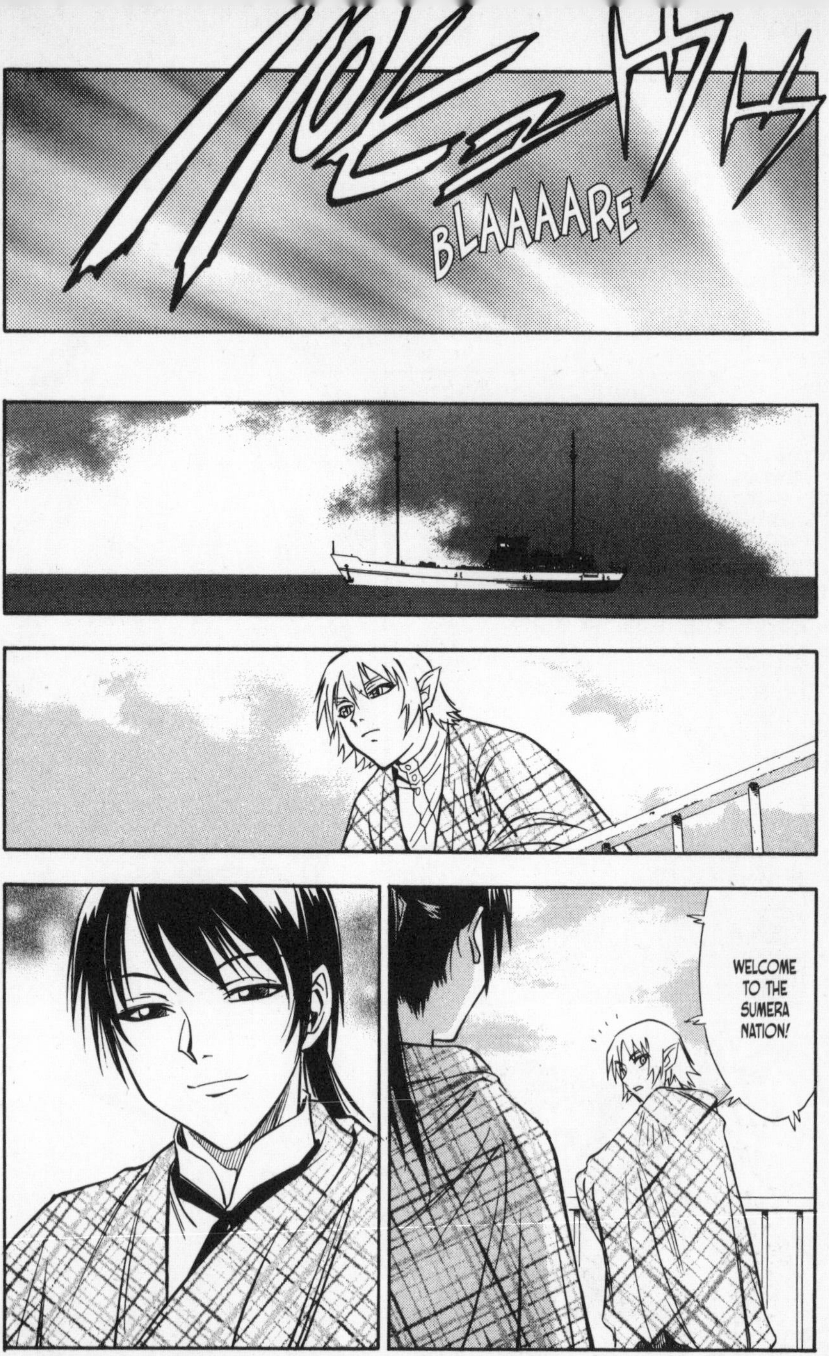
BLAAAARE
WELCOME TO THE SUMERA NATION!

Chapter 36 : OVER

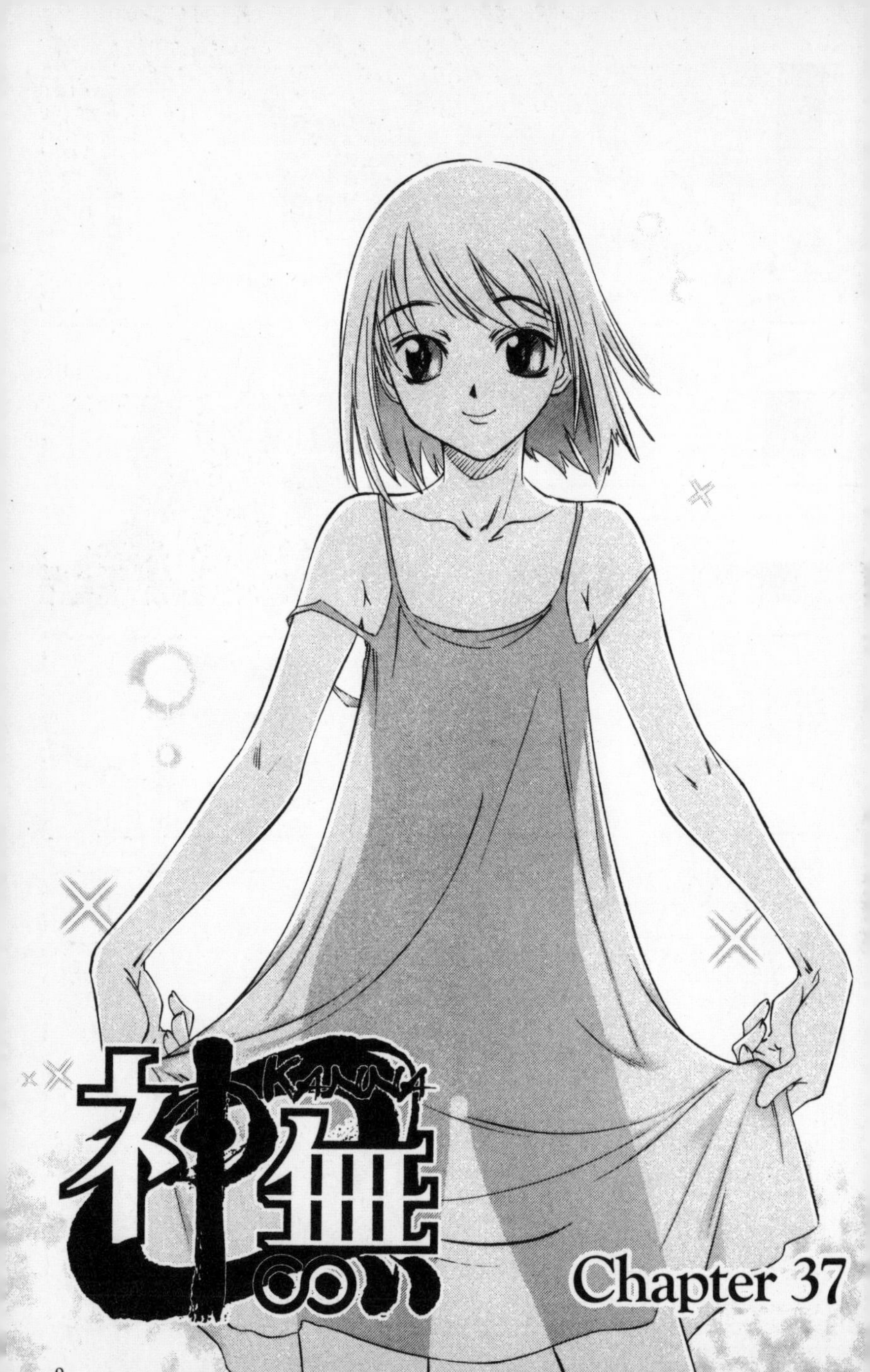
神無
KANNA

Chapter 37

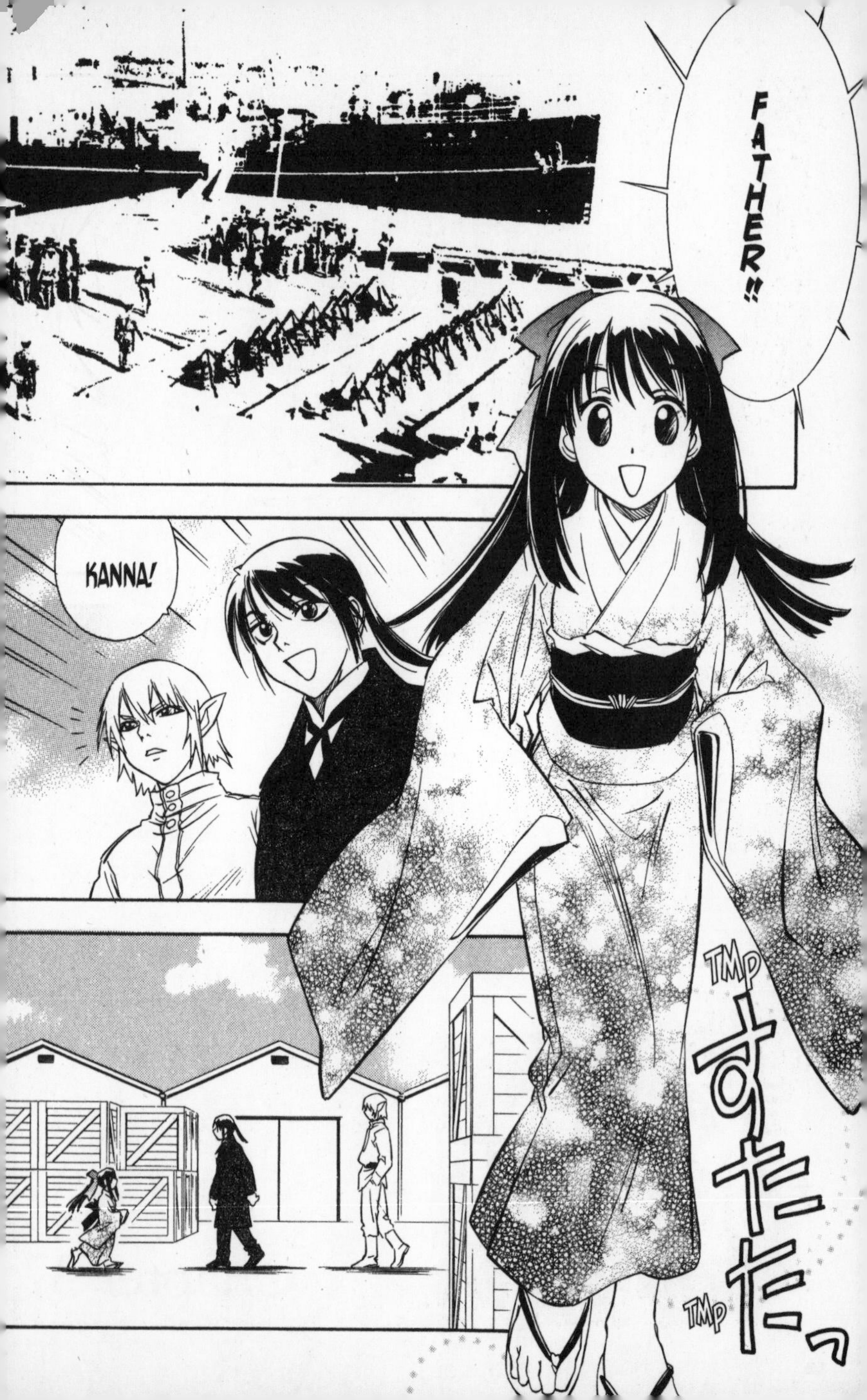
FATHER!!
KANNA!
TMP
すたたっ
TMP

FATHER?..

KANNA?

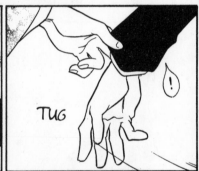

TUG

!

AH...

SURE...

...LEAVE ME AGAIN.

DON'T...

THIS LITTLE GIRL?

KAGURA SAID THE BLACK GOD IS AFTER HER, BUT...?

STEP

WHO IS THIS MAN?

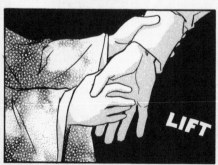

LIFT

THIS IS MY VERY SPECIAL GUEST.

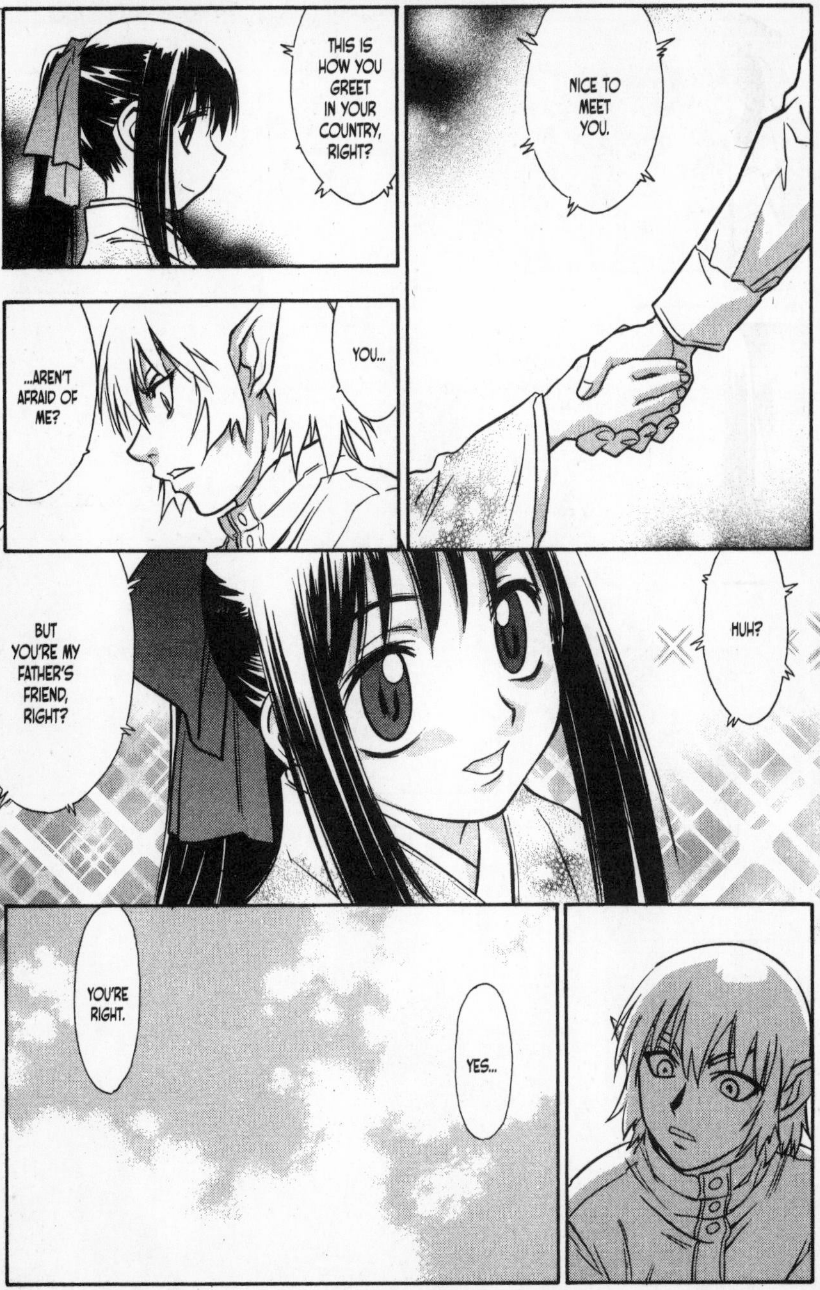
NICE TO MEET YOU.
THIS IS HOW YOU GREET IN YOUR COUNTRY, RIGHT?
YOU...
...AREN'T AFRAID OF ME?
HUH?
BUT YOU'RE MY FATHER'S FRIEND, RIGHT?
YES...
YOU'RE RIGHT.

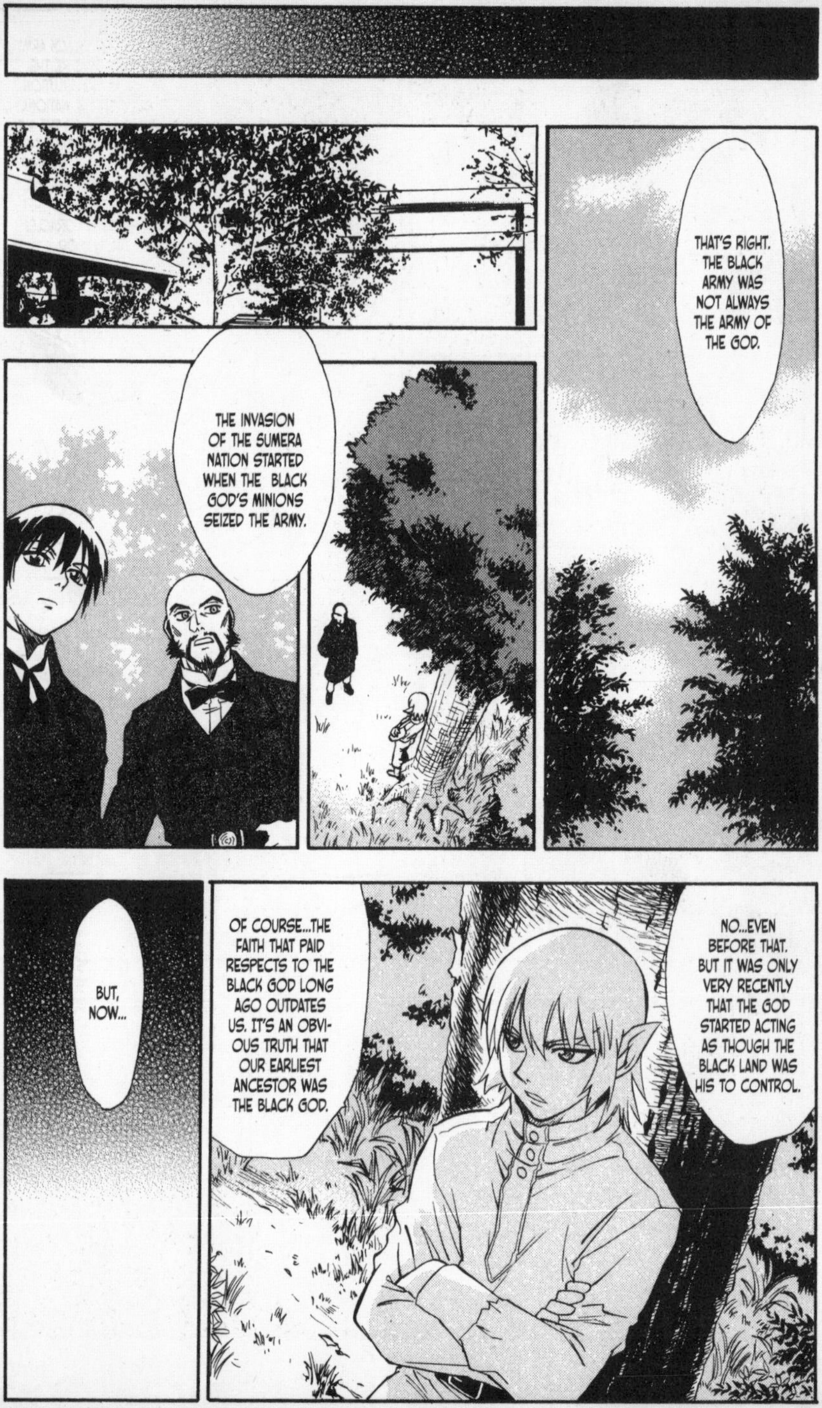
THAT'S RIGHT. THE BLACK ARMY WAS NOT ALWAYS THE ARMY OF THE GOD.
THE INVASION OF THE SUMERA NATION STARTED WHEN THE BLACK GOD'S MINIONS SEIZED THE ARMY.
NO...EVEN BEFORE THAT. BUT IT WAS ONLY VERY RECENTLY THAT THE GOD STARTED ACTING AS THOUGH THE BLACK LAND WAS HIS TO CONTROL.
OF COURSE...THE FAITH THAT PAID RESPECTS TO THE BLACK GOD LONG AGO OUTDATES US. IT'S AN OBVIOUS TRUTH THAT OUR EARLIEST ANCESTOR WAS THE BLACK GOD.
BUT, NOW...

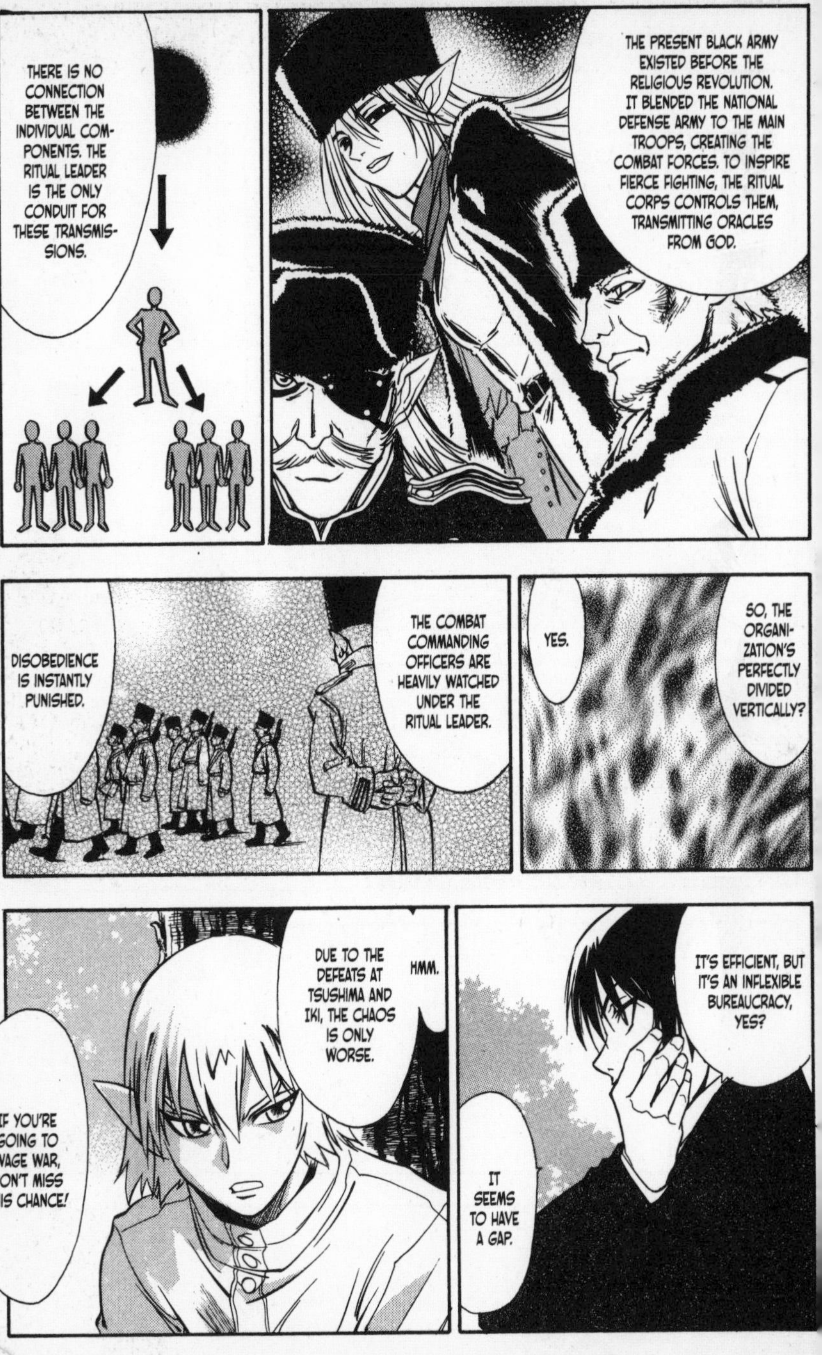
THE PRESENT BLACK ARMY EXISTED BEFORE THE RELIGIOUS REVOLUTION. IT BLENDED THE NATIONAL DEFENSE ARMY TO THE MAIN TROOPS, CREATING THE COMBAT FORCES. TO INSPIRE FIERCE FIGHTING, THE RITUAL CORPS CONTROLS THEM, TRANSMITTING ORACLES FROM GOD.
THERE IS NO CONNECTION BETWEEN THE INDIVIDUAL COMPONENTS. THE RITUAL LEADER IS THE ONLY CONDUIT FOR THESE TRANSMISSIONS.
SO, THE ORGANIZATION'S PERFECTLY DIVIDED VERTICALLY?
YES.
THE COMBAT COMMANDING OFFICERS ARE HEAVILY WATCHED UNDER THE RITUAL LEADER.
DISOBEDIENCE IS INSTANTLY PUNISHED.
IT'S EFFICIENT, BUT IT'S AN INFLEXIBLE BUREAUCRACY, YES?
IT SEEMS TO HAVE A GAP.
HMM.
DUE TO THE DEFEATS AT TSUSHIMA AND IKI, THE CHAOS IS ONLY WORSE.
IF YOU'RE GOING TO WAGE WAR, DON'T MISS THIS CHANCE!

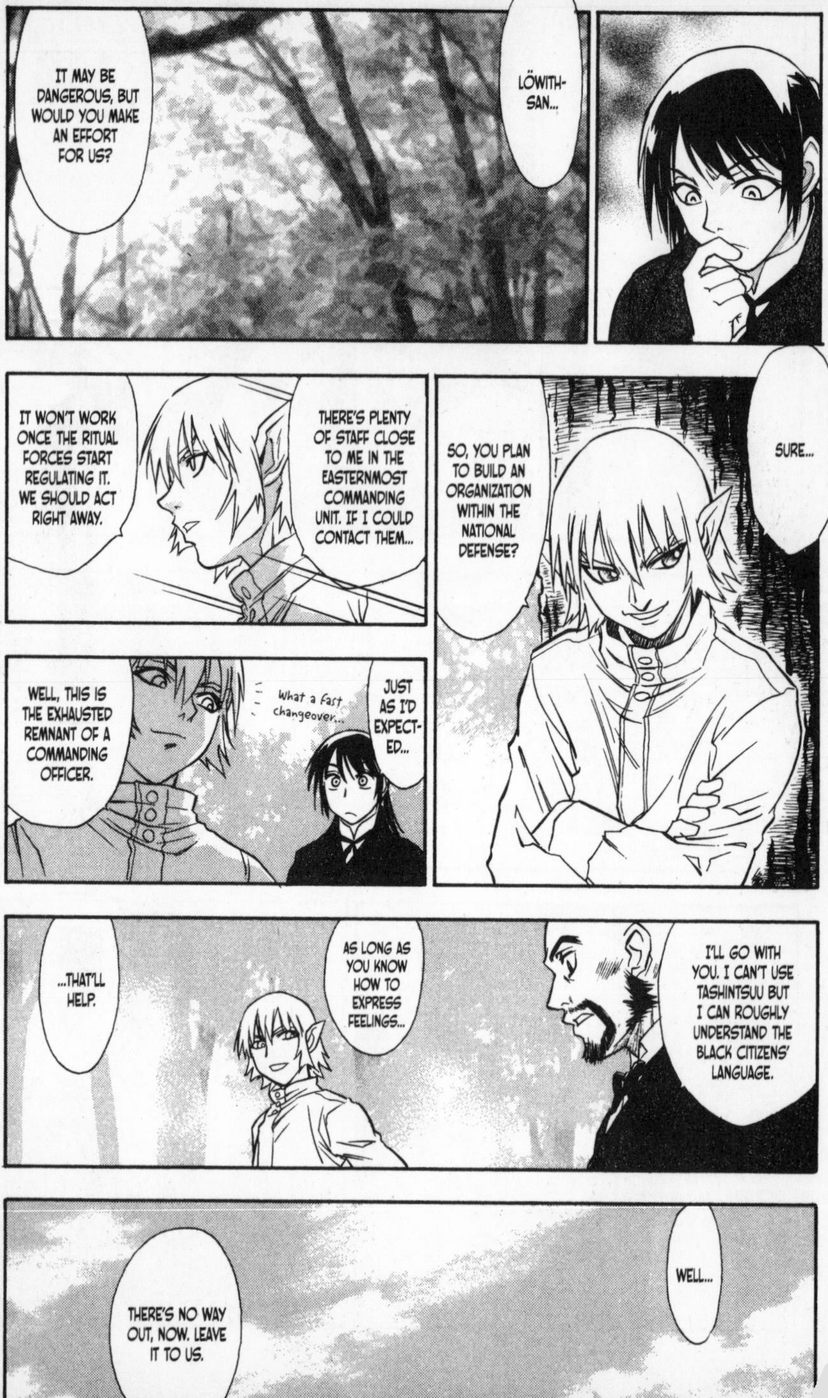
LÖWITH-SAN...
IT MAY BE DANGEROUS, BUT WOULD YOU MAKE AN EFFORT FOR US?
SURE...
SO, YOU PLAN TO BUILD AN ORGANIZATION WITHIN THE NATIONAL DEFENSE?
THERE'S PLENTY OF STAFF CLOSE TO ME IN THE EASTERNMOST COMMANDING UNIT. IF I COULD CONTACT THEM...
IT WON'T WORK ONCE THE RITUAL FORCES START REGULATING IT. WE SHOULD ACT RIGHT AWAY.
JUST AS I'D EXPECTED...
What a fast changeover...
WELL, THIS IS THE EXHAUSTED REMNANT OF A COMMANDING OFFICER.
I'LL GO WITH YOU. I CAN'T USE TASHINTSUU BUT I CAN ROUGHLY UNDERSTAND THE BLACK CITIZENS' LANGUAGE.
AS LONG AS YOU KNOW HOW TO EXPRESS FEELINGS...
...THAT'LL HELP.
WELL...
THERE'S NO WAY OUT, NOW. LEAVE IT TO US.

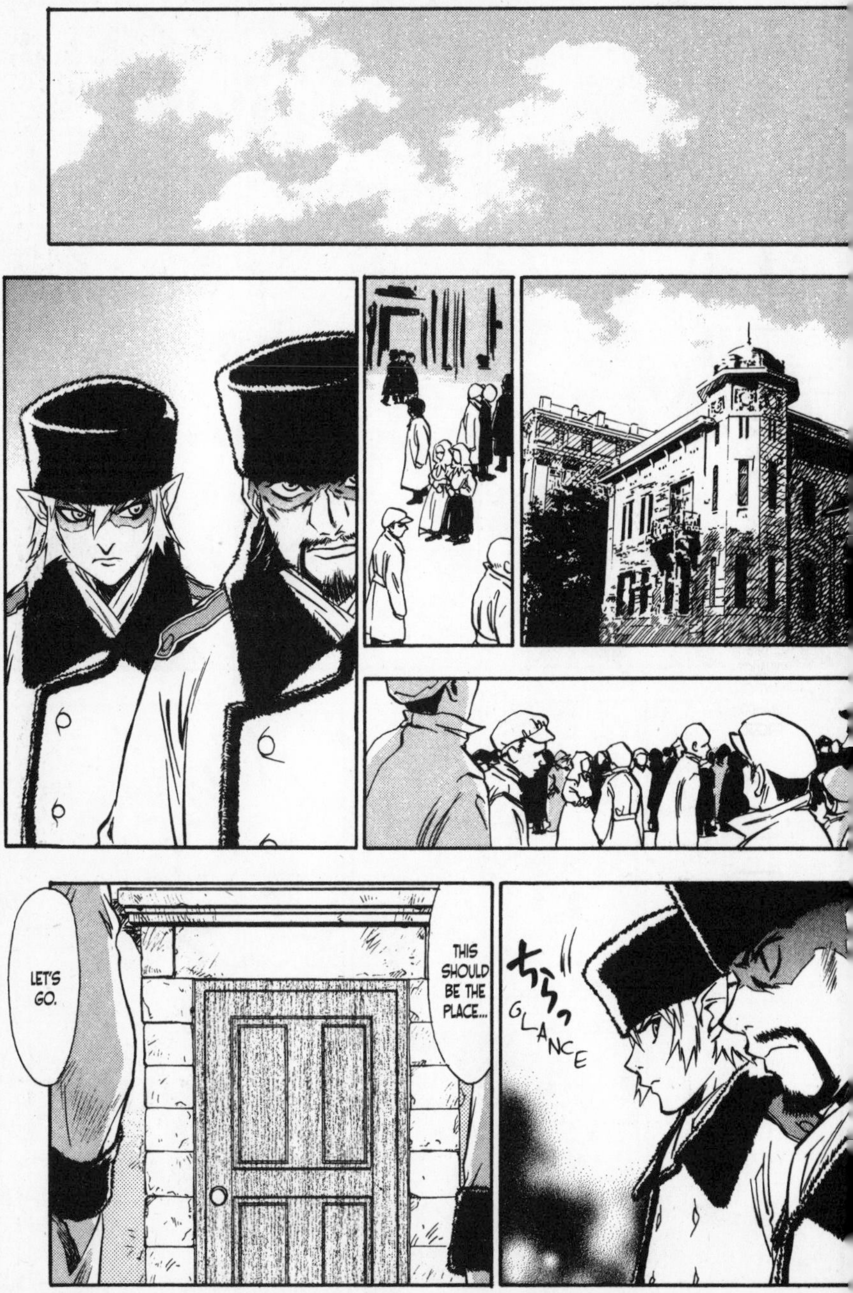
ちらっ
GLANCE
THIS SHOULD BE THE PLACE...
LET'S GO.

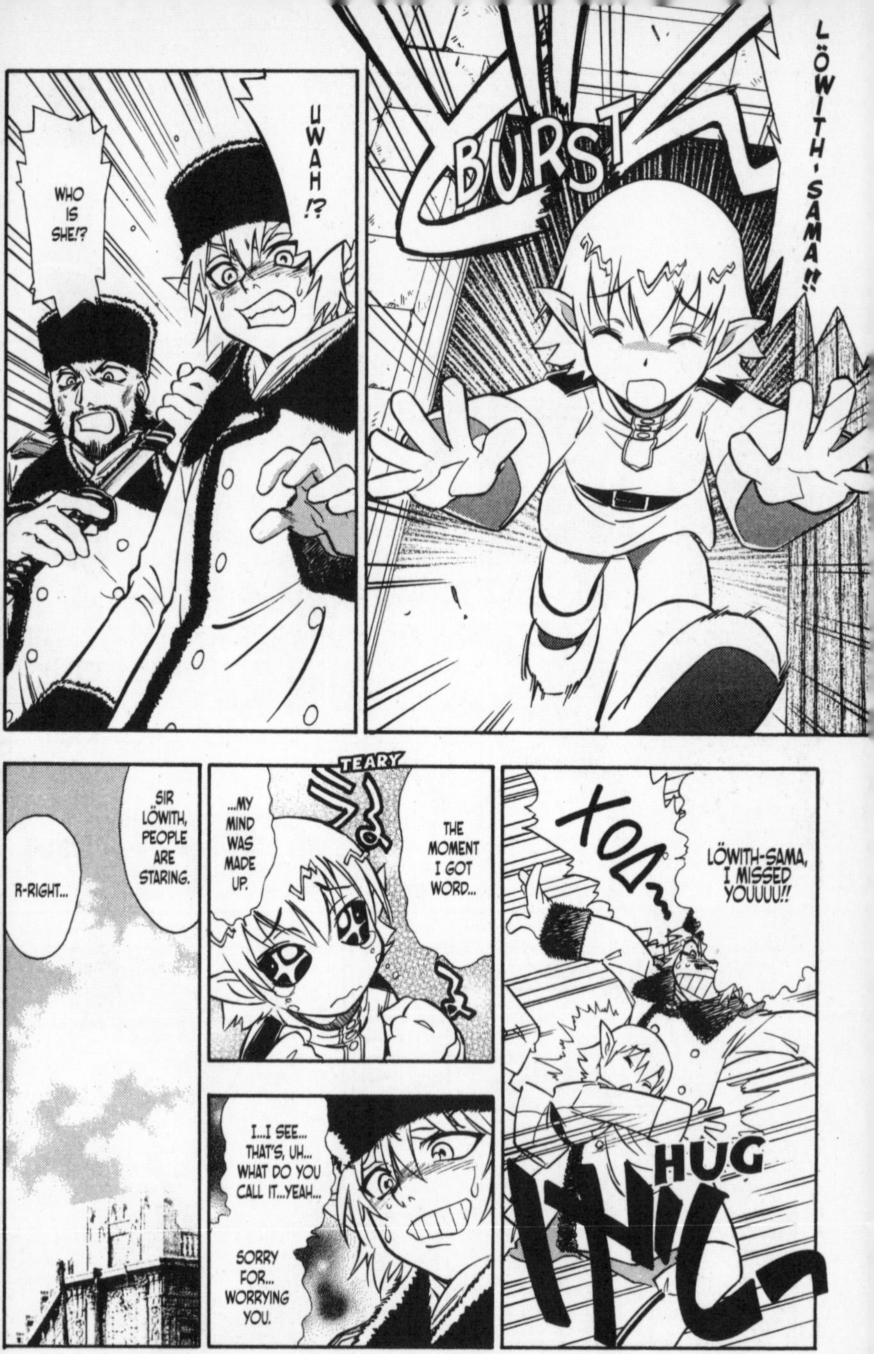
LÖWITH-SAMA!!
BURST
UWAH!?
WHO IS SHE!?
LÖWITH-SAMA, I MISSED YOUUUU!!
HUG
TEARY
THE MOMENT I GOT WORD...
...MY MIND WAS MADE UP.
I...I SEE... THAT'S, UH... WHAT DO YOU CALL IT...YEAH...
SORRY FOR... WORRYING YOU.
SIR LÖWITH, PEOPLE ARE STARING.
R-RIGHT...

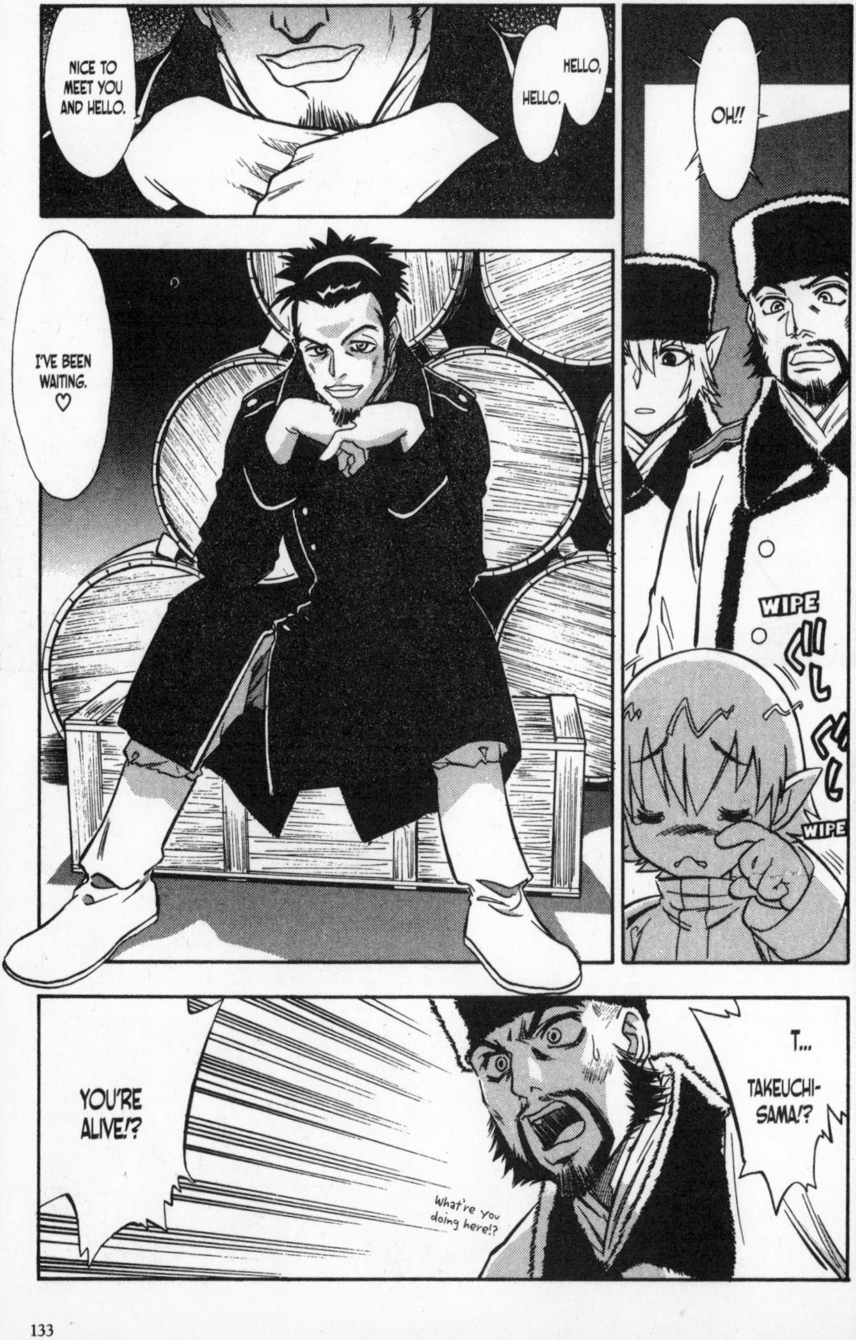
OH!!
WIPE
WIPE
HELLO, HELLO.
NICE TO MEET YOU AND HELLO.
I'VE BEEN WAITING. ♡
T... TAKEUCHI-SAMA!?
YOU'RE ALIVE!?
What're you doing here!?

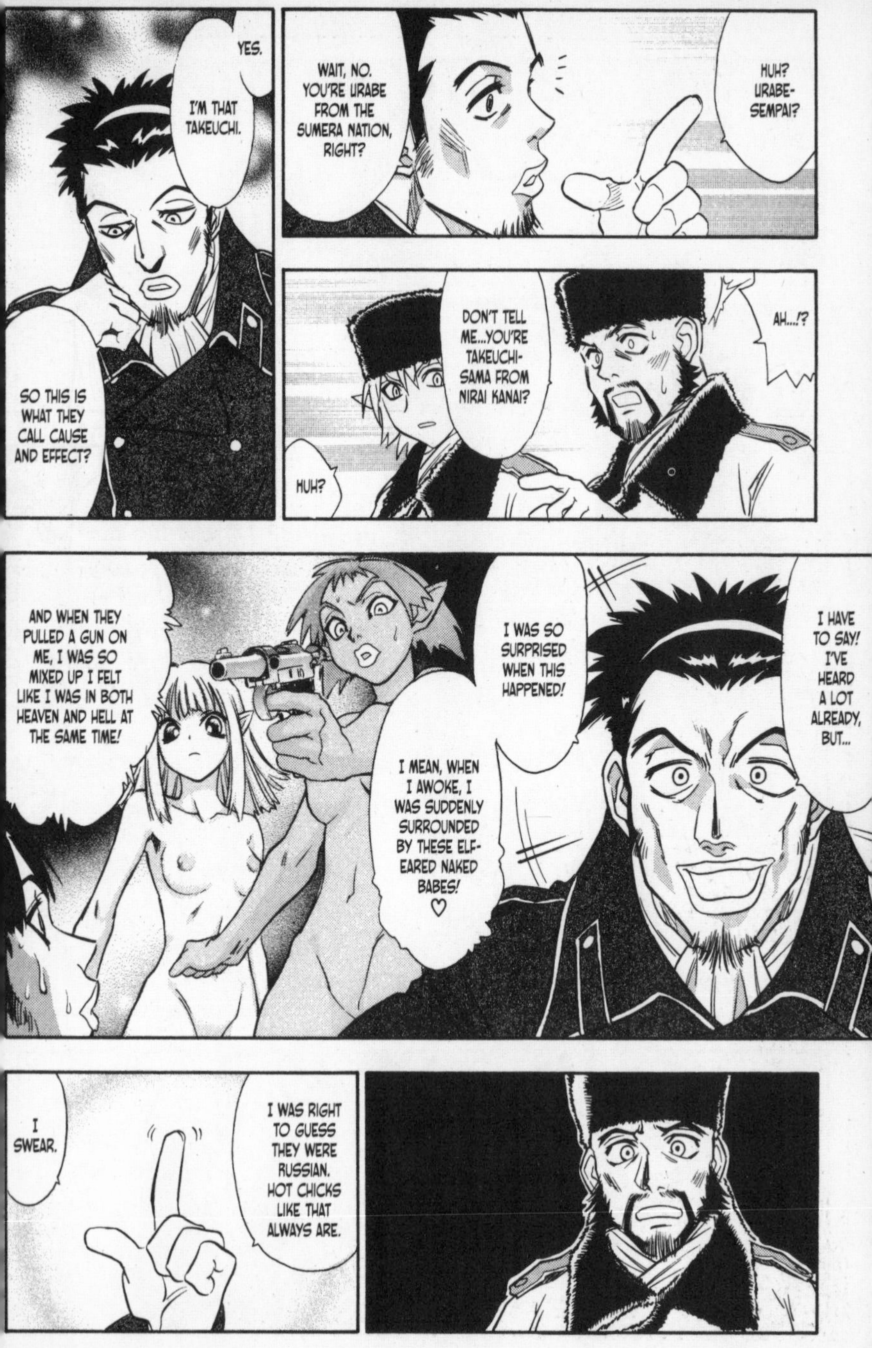
HUH? URABE-SEMPAI?
WAIT, NO. YOU'RE URABE FROM THE SUMERA NATION, RIGHT?
AH...!?
DON'T TELL ME...YOU'RE TAKEUCHI-SAMA FROM NIRAI KANAI?
HUH?
YES.
I'M THAT TAKEUCHI.
SO THIS IS WHAT THEY CALL CAUSE AND EFFECT?
I HAVE TO SAY! I'VE HEARD A LOT ALREADY, BUT...
I WAS SO SURPRISED WHEN THIS HAPPENED!
I MEAN, WHEN I AWOKE, I WAS SUDDENLY SURROUNDED BY THESE ELF-EARED NAKED BABES! ♡
AND WHEN THEY PULLED A GUN ON ME, I WAS SO MIXED UP I FELT LIKE I WAS IN BOTH HEAVEN AND HELL AT THE SAME TIME!
I WAS RIGHT TO GUESS THEY WERE RUSSIAN. HOT CHICKS LIKE THAT ALWAYS ARE.
I SWEAR.

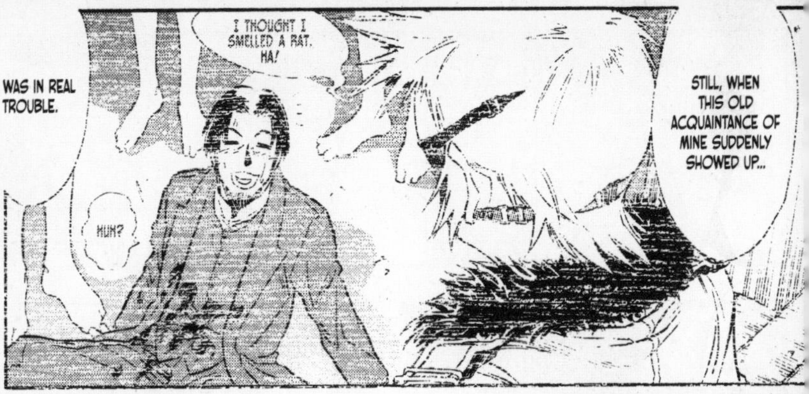
STILL, WHEN THIS OLD ACQUAINTANCE OF MINE SUDDENLY SHOWED UP...
I THOUGHT I SMELLED A RAT. HA!
...I WAS IN REAL TROUBLE.
HUH?

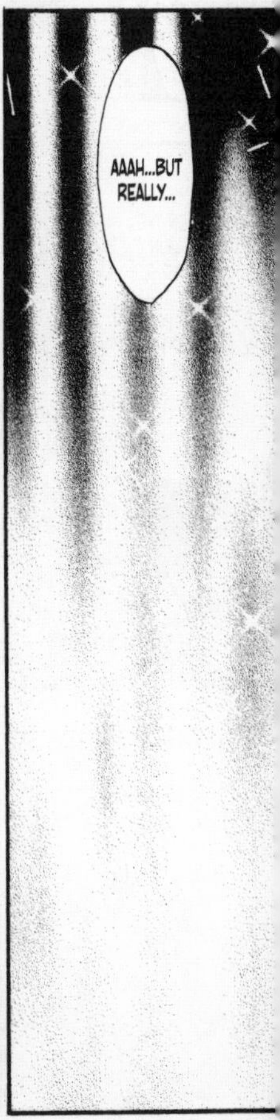
AAAH...BUT REALLY...

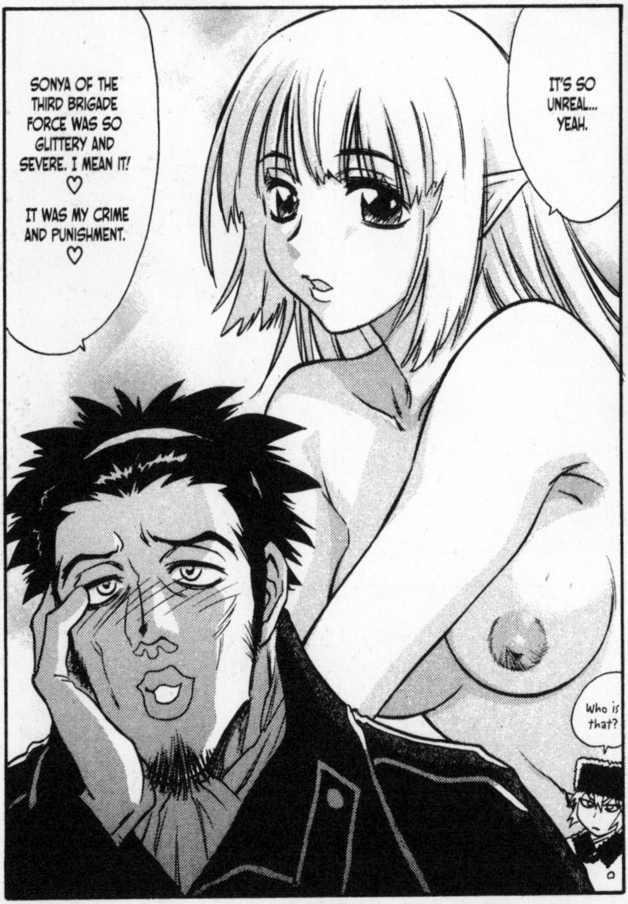
IT'S SO UNREAL... YEAH.
SONYA OF THE THIRD BRIGADE FORCE WAS SO GLITTERY AND SEVERE. I MEAN IT! ♡
IT WAS MY CRIME AND PUNISHMENT. ♡
Who is that?

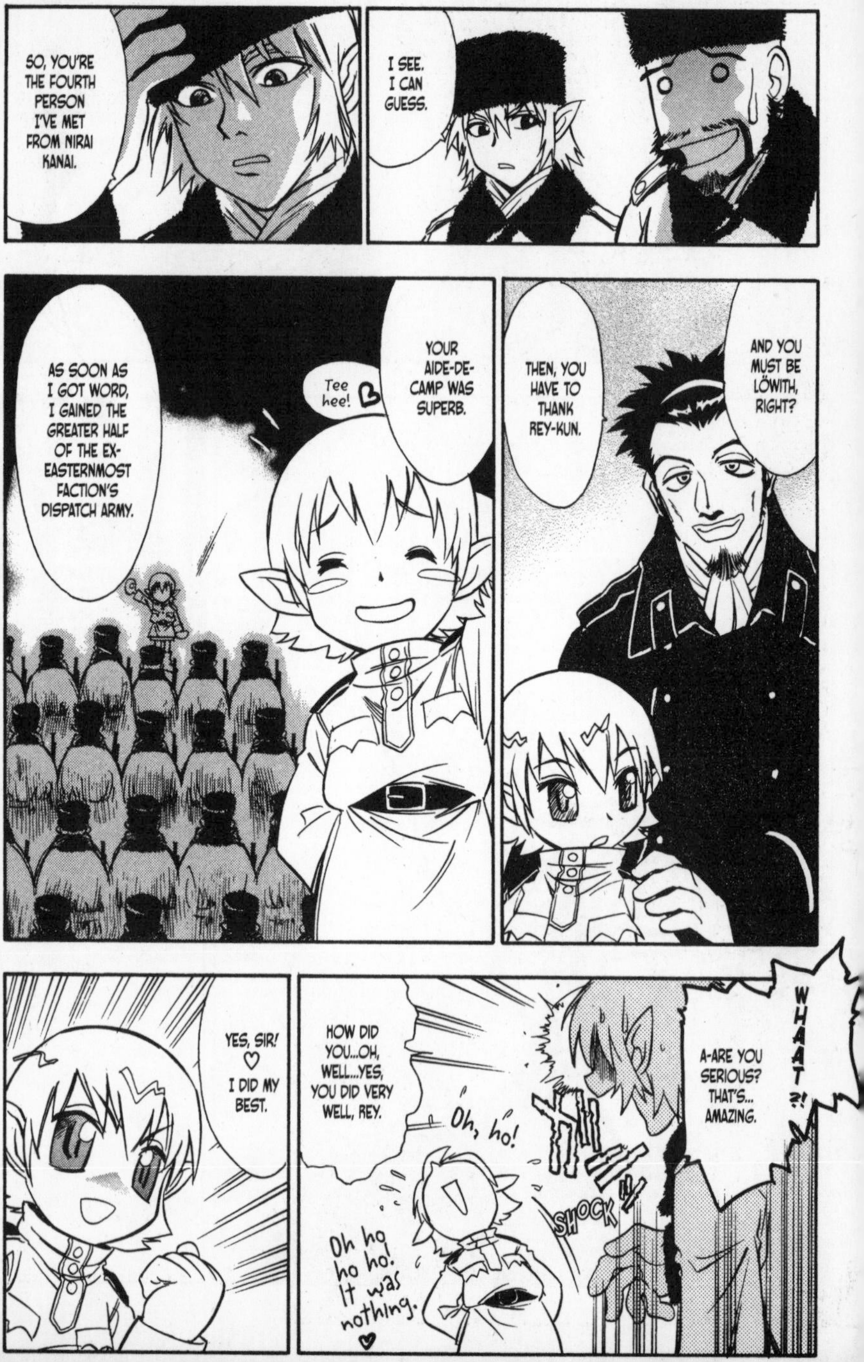
I SEE. I CAN GUESS.
SO, YOU'RE THE FOURTH PERSON I'VE MET FROM NIRAI KANAI.
AND YOU MUST BE LÖWITH, RIGHT?
THEN, YOU HAVE TO THANK REY-KUN.
YOUR AIDE-DE-CAMP WAS SUPERB.
Tee hee! ♡
AS SOON AS I GOT WORD, I GAINED THE GREATER HALF OF THE EX-EASTERNMOST FACTION'S DISPATCH ARMY.
WHAAT?!
A-ARE YOU SERIOUS? THAT'S... AMAZING.
SHOCK
HOW DID YOU...OH, WELL...YES, YOU DID VERY WELL, REY.
Oh, ho!
Oh ho ho ho! It was nothing. ♡
YES, SIR! ♡ I DID MY BEST.

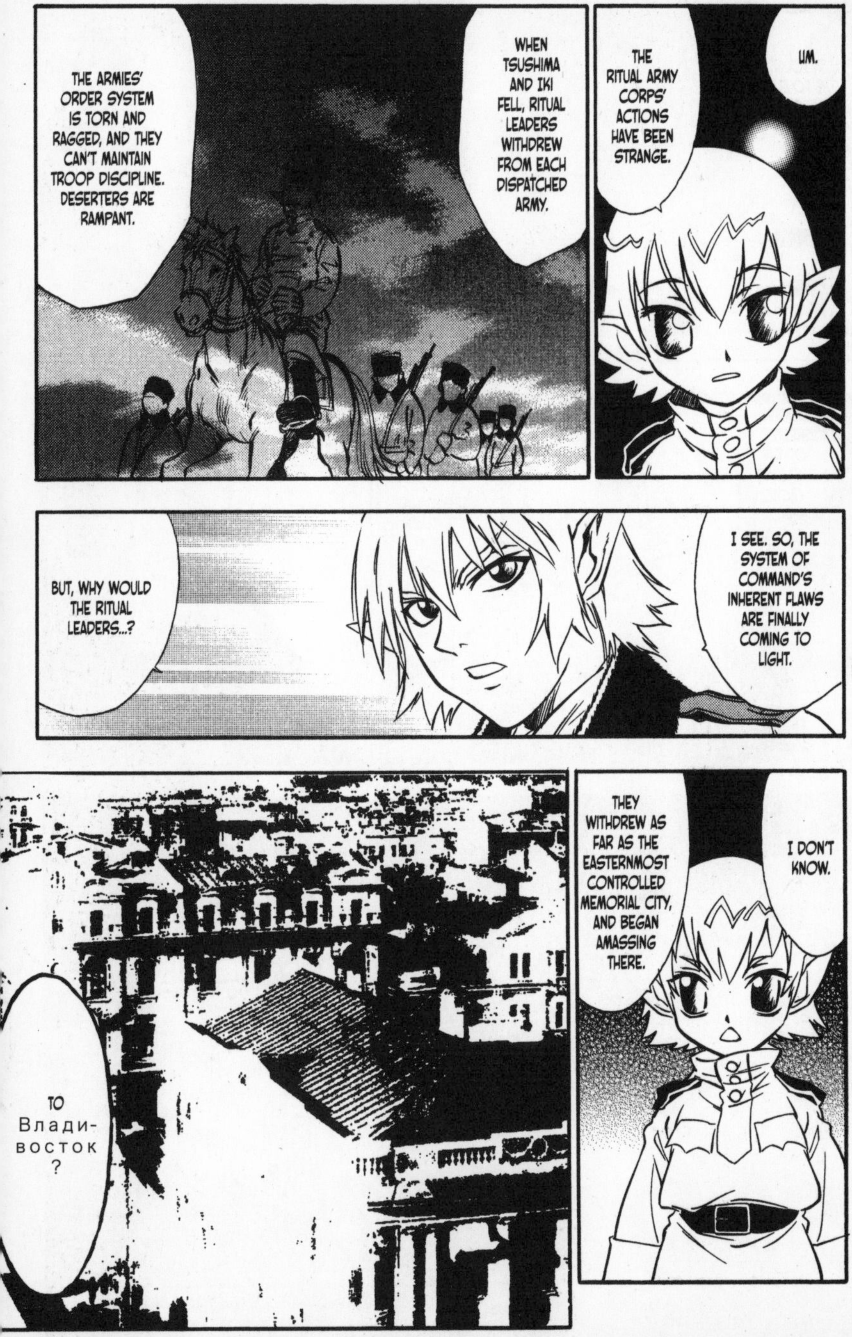
UM.
THE RITUAL ARMY CORPS' ACTIONS HAVE BEEN STRANGE.
WHEN TSUSHIMA AND IKI FELL, RITUAL LEADERS WITHDREW FROM EACH DISPATCHED ARMY.
THE ARMIES' ORDER SYSTEM IS TORN AND RAGGED, AND THEY CAN'T MAINTAIN TROOP DISCIPLINE. DESERTERS ARE RAMPANT.
I SEE. SO, THE SYSTEM OF COMMAND'S INHERENT FLAWS ARE FINALLY COMING TO LIGHT.
BUT, WHY WOULD THE RITUAL LEADERS...?
I DON'T KNOW.
THEY WITHDREW AS FAR AS THE EASTERNMOST CONTROLLED MEMORIAL CITY, AND BEGAN AMASSING THERE.
TO Влади-восток?

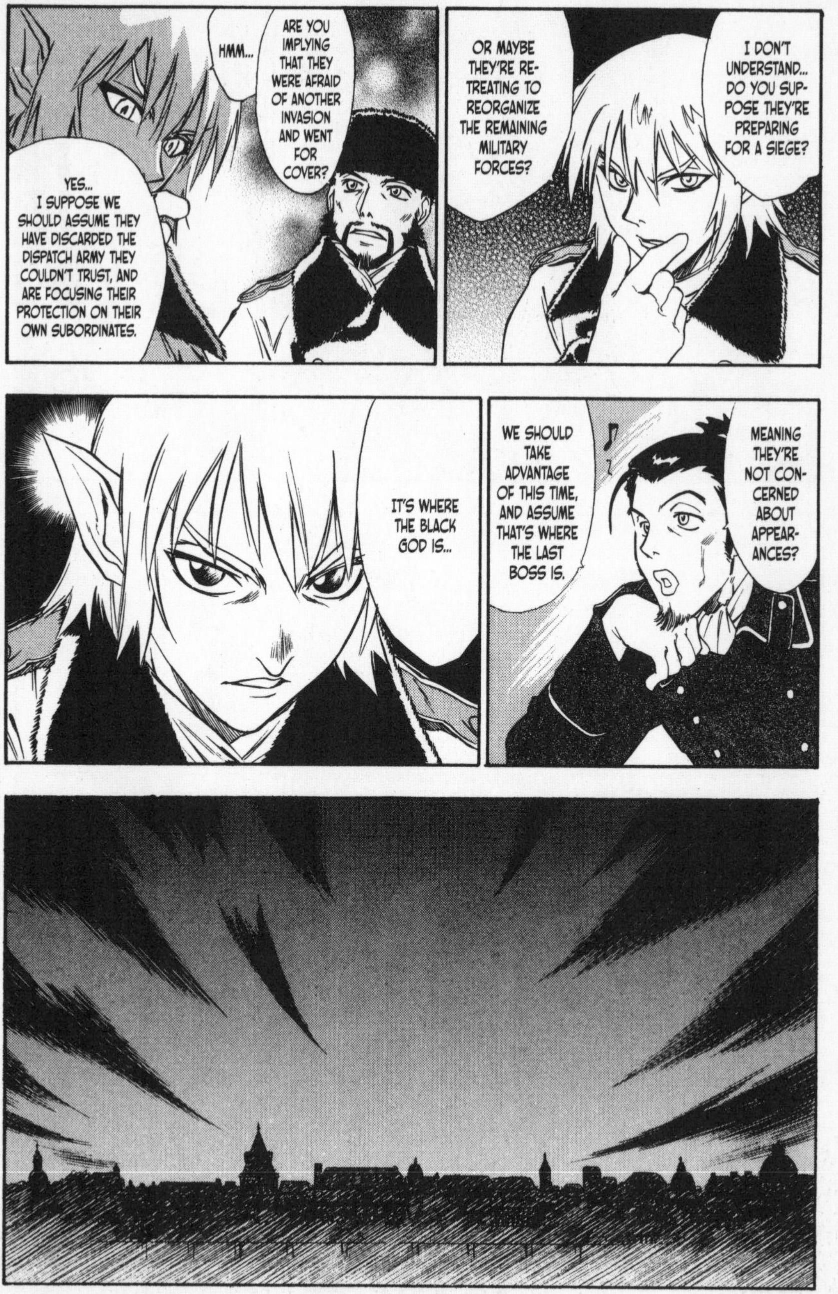
I DON'T UNDERSTAND... DO YOU SUPPOSE THEY'RE PREPARING FOR A SIEGE?
OR MAYBE THEY'RE RETREATING TO REORGANIZE THE REMAINING MILITARY FORCES?
ARE YOU IMPLYING THAT THEY WERE AFRAID OF ANOTHER INVASION AND WENT FOR COVER?
HMM...
YES... I SUPPOSE WE SHOULD ASSUME THEY HAVE DISCARDED THE DISPATCH ARMY THEY COULDN'T TRUST, AND ARE FOCUSING THEIR PROTECTION ON THEIR OWN SUBORDINATES.
MEANING THEY'RE NOT CONCERNED ABOUT APPEARANCES?
WE SHOULD TAKE ADVANTAGE OF THIS TIME, AND ASSUME THAT'S WHERE THE LAST BOSS IS.
IT'S WHERE THE BLACK GOD IS...

Chapter 37 : OVER

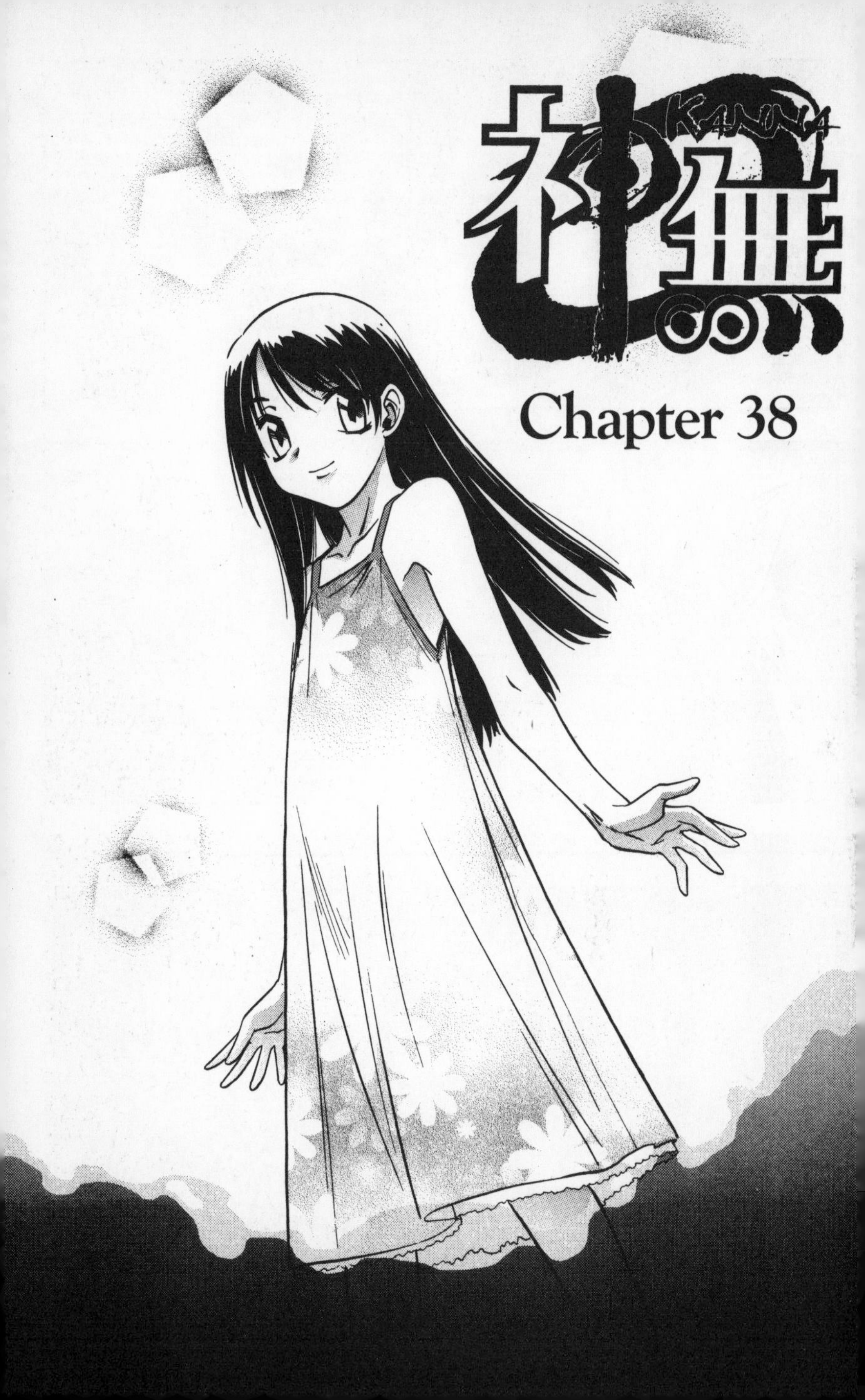
KANNA
神無
Chapter 38

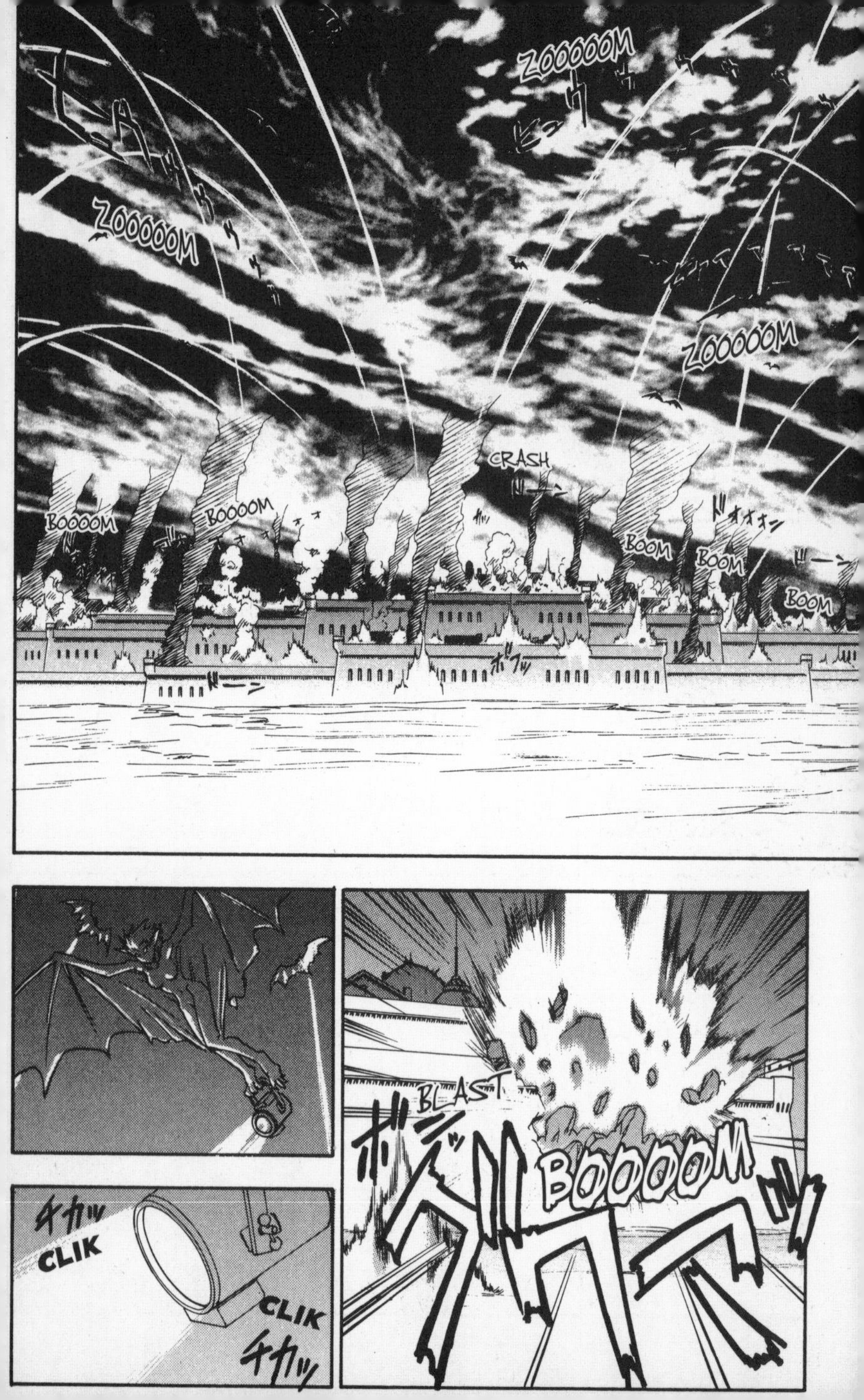
ZOOOOOM
ZOOOOOM
ZOOOOOM
CRASH
BOOM
BOOM
BOOM
BOOOOM
BOOOOM
BLAST
BOOOOM
チカッ
CLIK
CLIK
チカッ

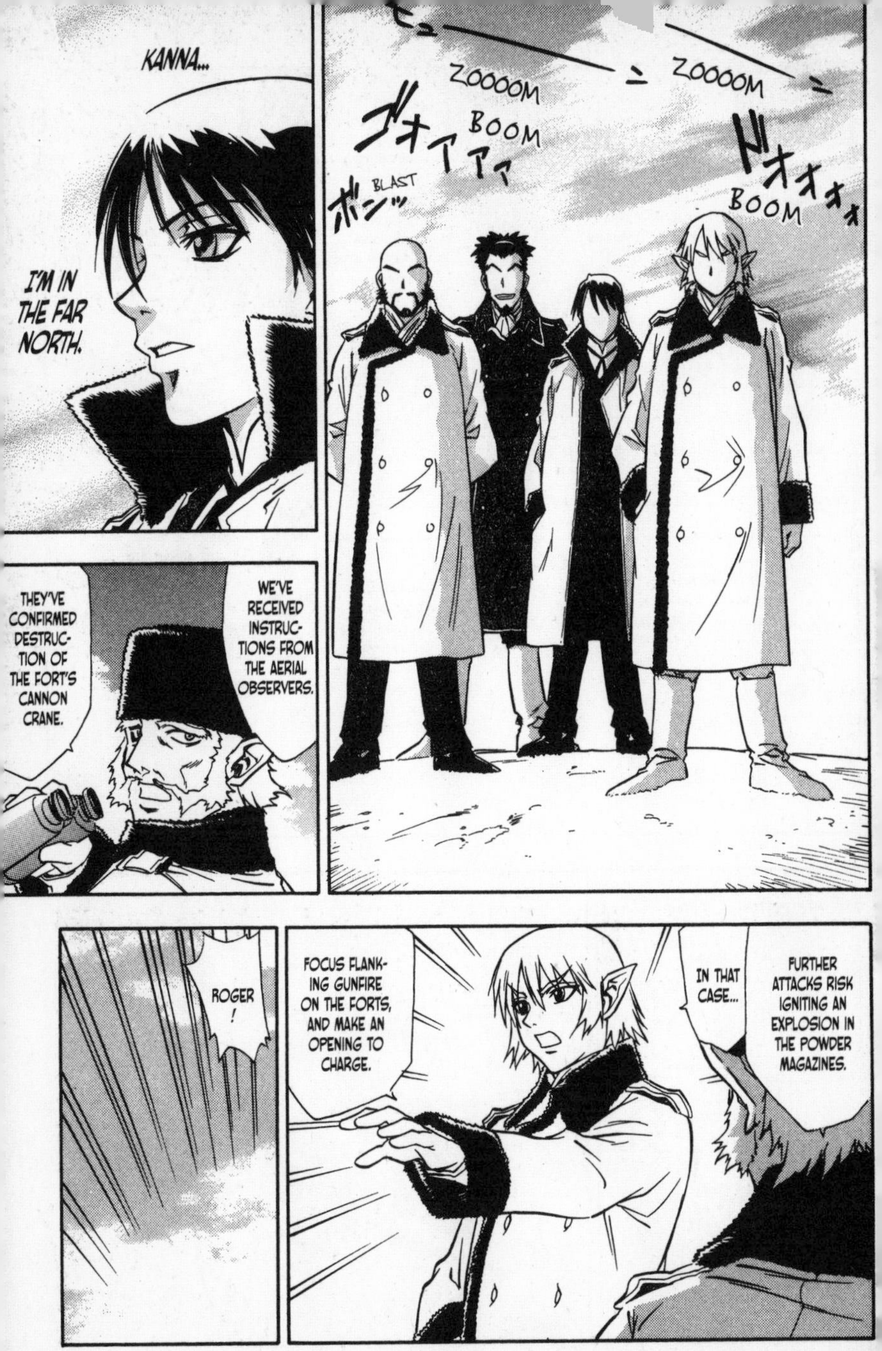
ZOOOOM
ZOOOOM
ドオオオォ
BOOM
ゴオアアァ
BOOM
ボンッ
BLAST
KANNA...
I'M IN THE FAR NORTH.
WE'VE RECEIVED INSTRUCTIONS FROM THE AERIAL OBSERVERS.
THEY'VE CONFIRMED DESTRUCTION OF THE FORT'S CANNON CRANE.
FURTHER ATTACKS RISK IGNITING AN EXPLOSION IN THE POWDER MAGAZINES.
IN THAT CASE...
FOCUS FLANKING GUNFIRE ON THE FORTS, AND MAKE AN OPENING TO CHARGE.
ROGER!

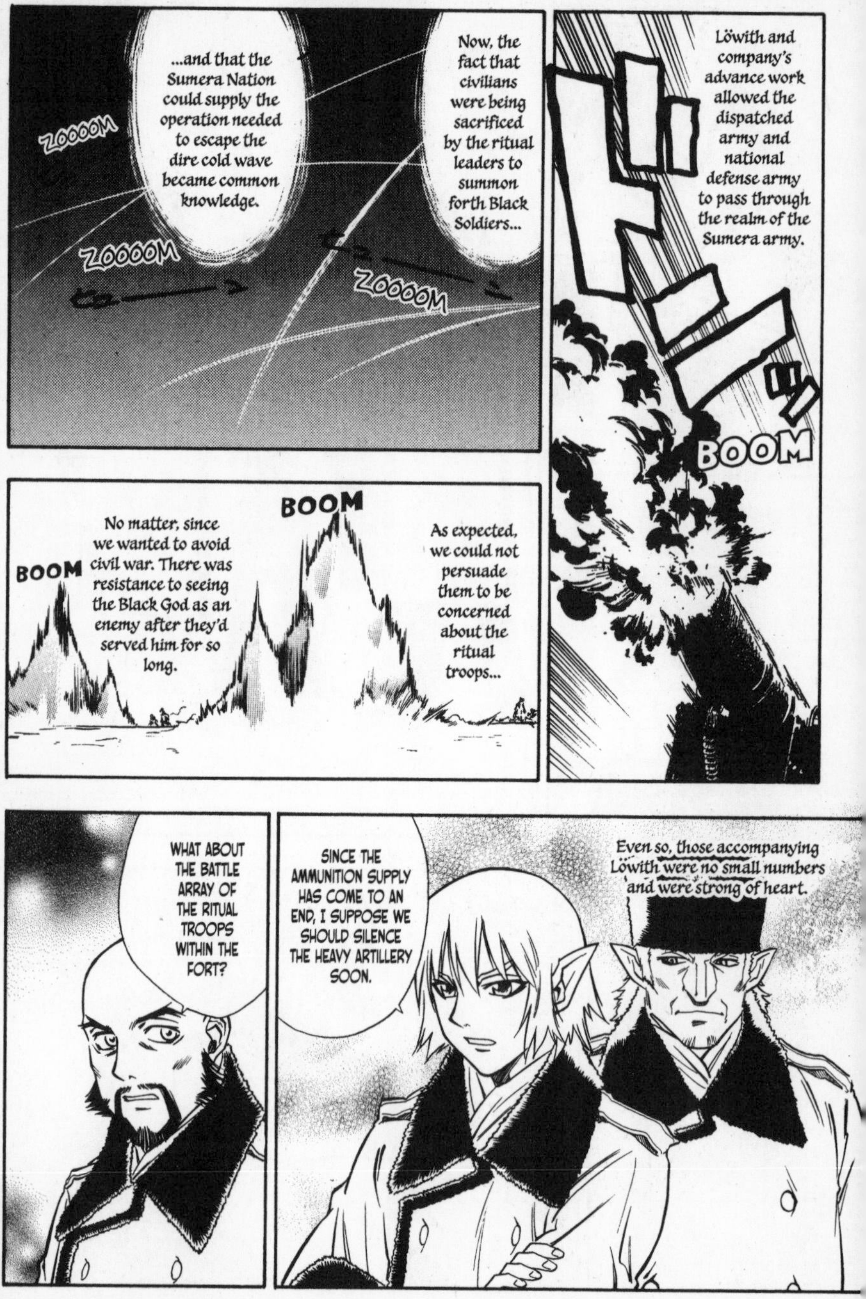
Löwith and company's advance work allowed the dispatched army and national defense army to pass through the realm of the Sumera army.
BOOM
Now, the fact that civilians were being sacrificed by the ritual leaders to summon forth Black Soldiers...
...and that the Sumera Nation could supply the operation needed to escape the dire cold wave became common knowledge.
ZOOOOM
ZOOOOM
ZOOOOM
BOOM
As expected, we could not persuade them to be concerned about the ritual troops...
No matter, since we wanted to avoid civil war. There was resistance to seeing the Black God as an enemy after they'd served him for so long.
BOOM
Even so, those accompanying Löwith were no small numbers and were strong of heart.
SINCE THE AMMUNITION SUPPLY HAS COME TO AN END, I SUPPOSE WE SHOULD SILENCE THE HEAVY ARTILLERY SOON.
WHAT ABOUT THE BATTLE ARRAY OF THE RITUAL TROOPS WITHIN THE FORT?

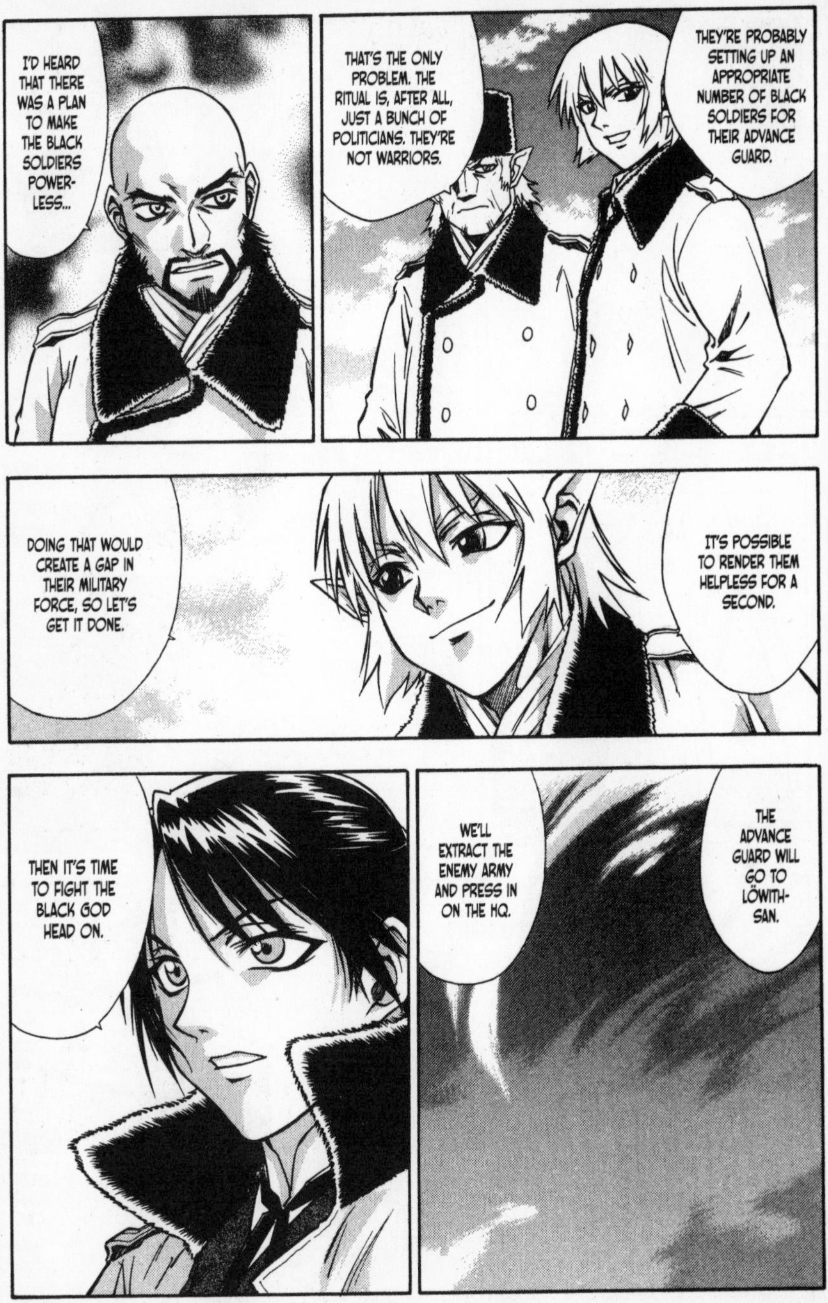
THEY'RE PROBABLY SETTING UP AN APPROPRIATE NUMBER OF BLACK SOLDIERS FOR THEIR ADVANCE GUARD.
THAT'S THE ONLY PROBLEM. THE RITUAL IS, AFTER ALL, JUST A BUNCH OF POLITICIANS. THEY'RE NOT WARRIORS.
I'D HEARD THAT THERE WAS A PLAN TO MAKE THE BLACK SOLDIERS POWER-LESS...
IT'S POSSIBLE TO RENDER THEM HELPLESS FOR A SECOND.
DOING THAT WOULD CREATE A GAP IN THEIR MILITARY FORCE, SO LET'S GET IT DONE.
THE ADVANCE GUARD WILL GO TO LÖWITH-SAN.
WE'LL EXTRACT THE ENEMY ARMY AND PRESS IN ON THE HQ.
THEN IT'S TIME TO FIGHT THE BLACK GOD HEAD ON.

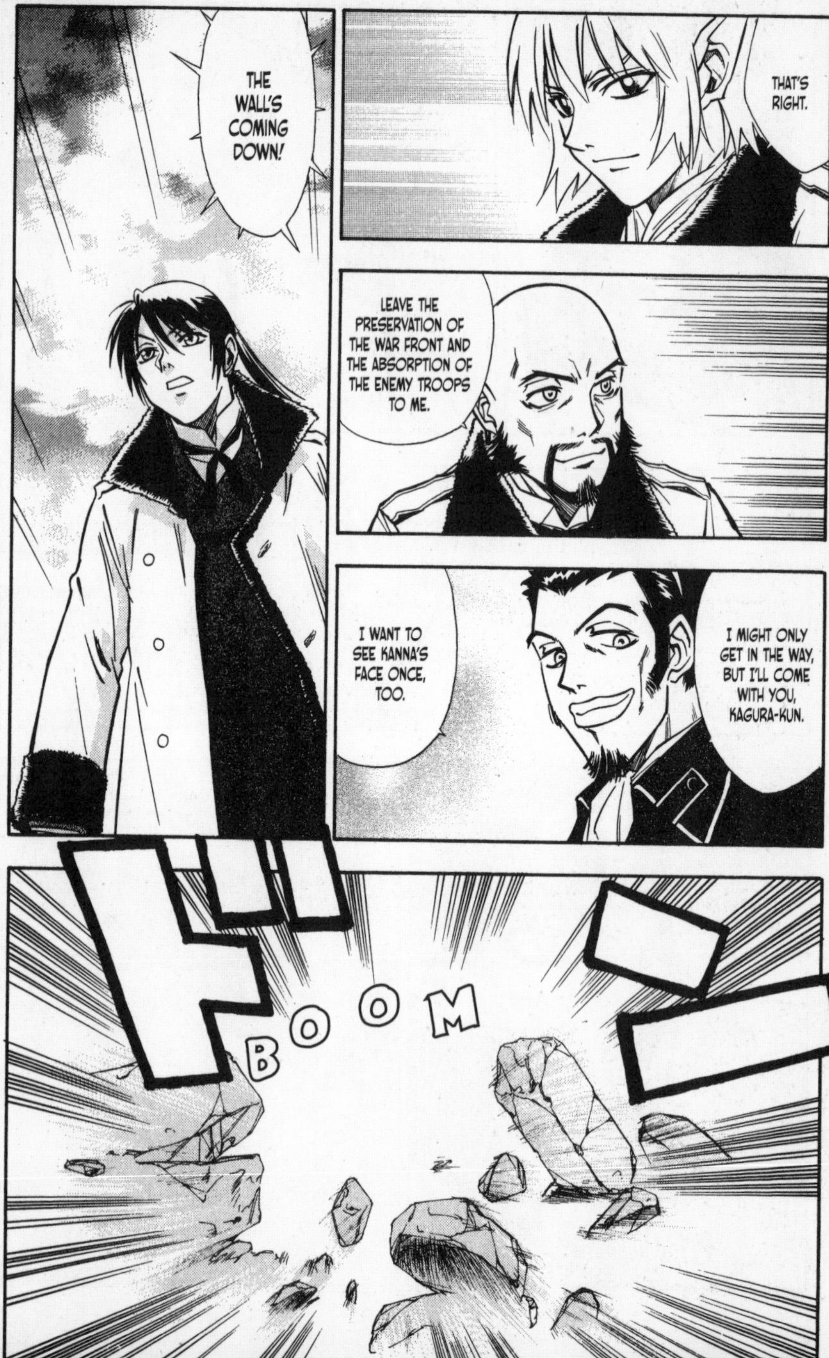
THAT'S RIGHT.
LEAVE THE PRESERVATION OF THE WAR FRONT AND THE ABSORPTION OF THE ENEMY TROOPS TO ME.
I MIGHT ONLY GET IN THE WAY, BUT I'LL COME WITH YOU, KAGURA-KUN.
I WANT TO SEE KANNA'S FACE ONCE, TOO.
THE WALL'S COMING DOWN!
BOOM

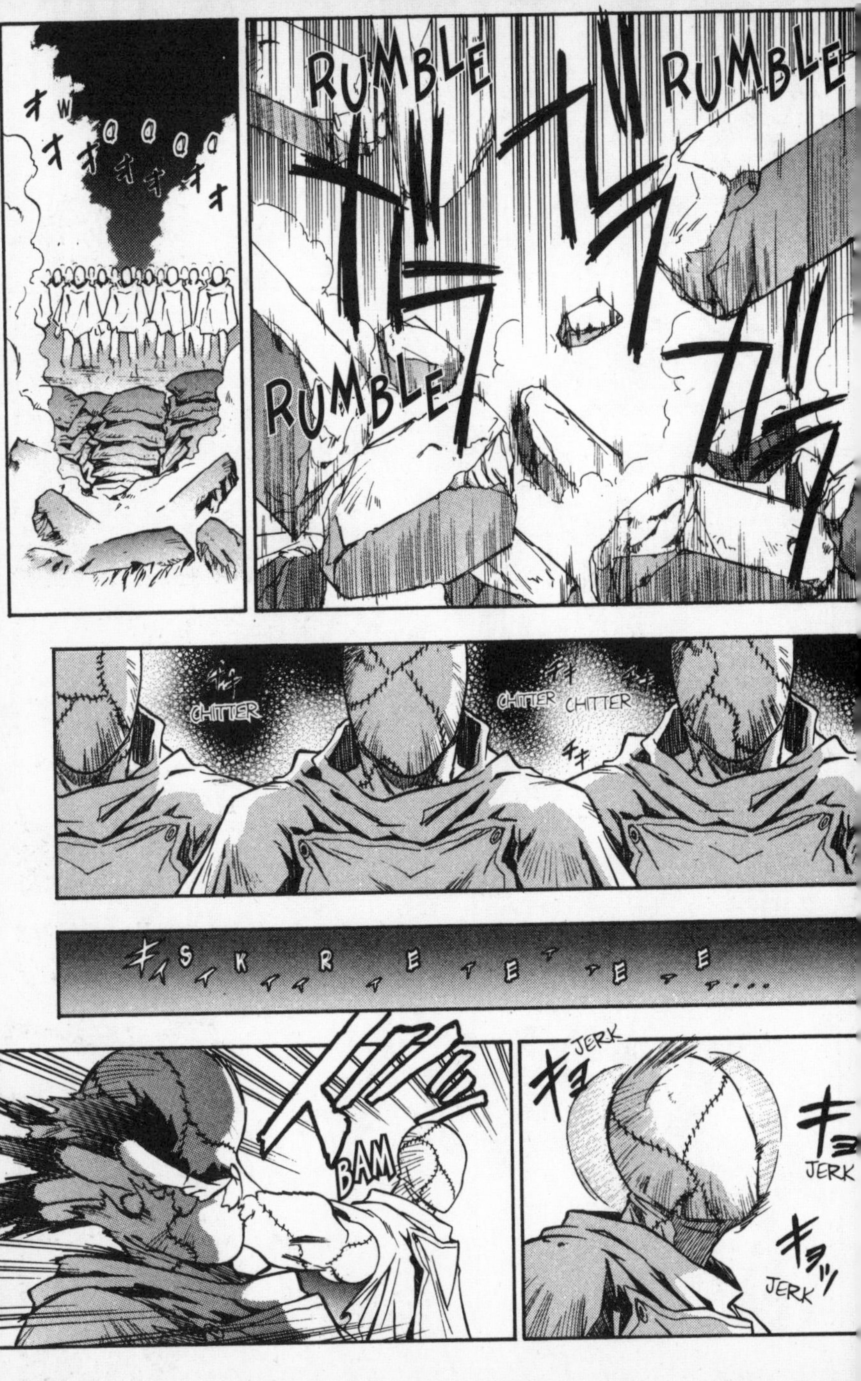
RUMBLE
RUMBLE
RUMBLE
WOOOOO
CHITTER
CHITTER
CHITTER
SKREEEE...
JERK
JERK
JERK
BAM

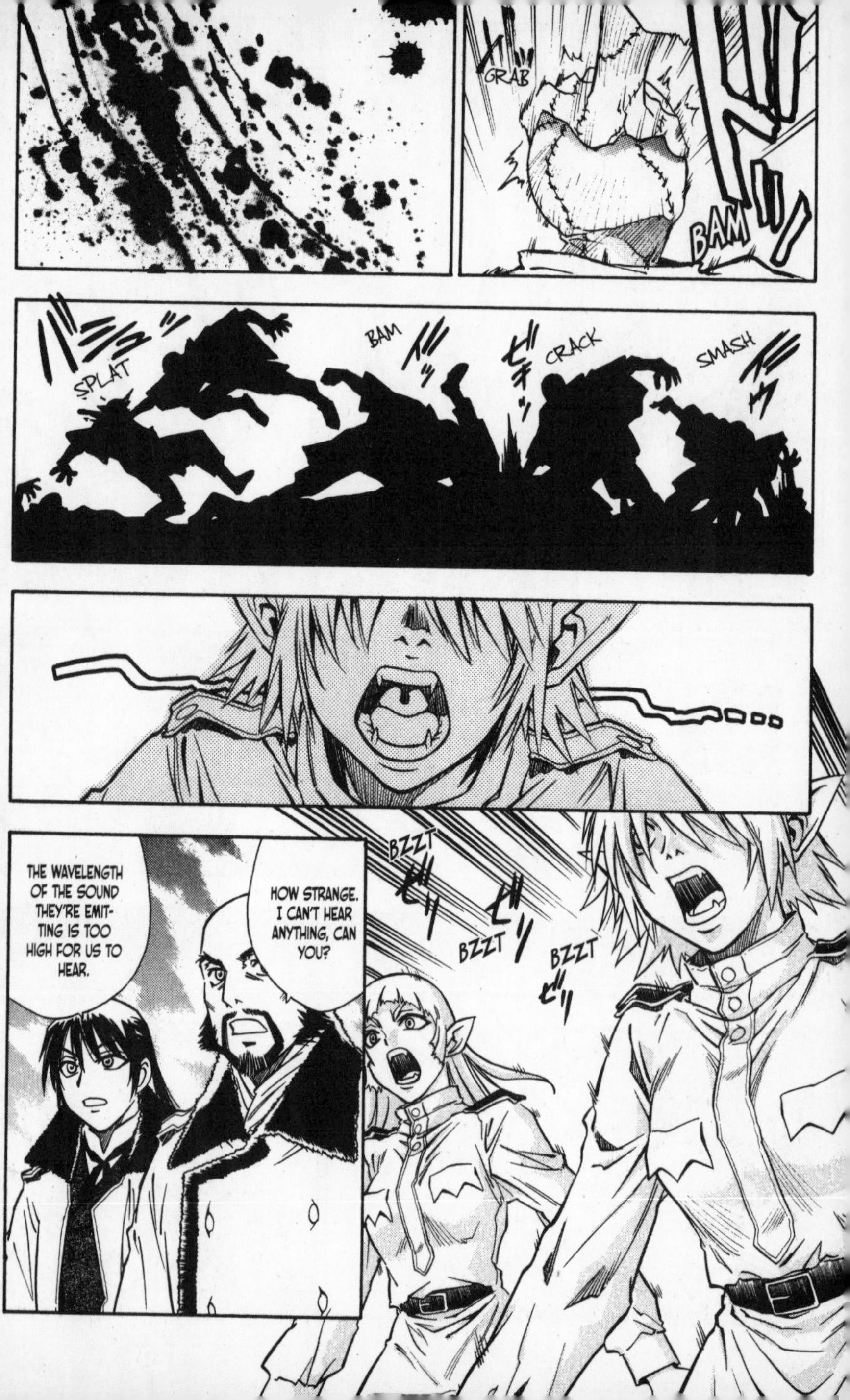
GRAB
BAM
SMASH
CRACK
BAM
SPLAT
BZZT
BZZT
BZZT
HOW STRANGE. I CAN'T HEAR ANYTHING, CAN YOU?
THE WAVELENGTH OF THE SOUND THEY'RE EMITTING IS TOO HIGH FOR US TO HEAR.

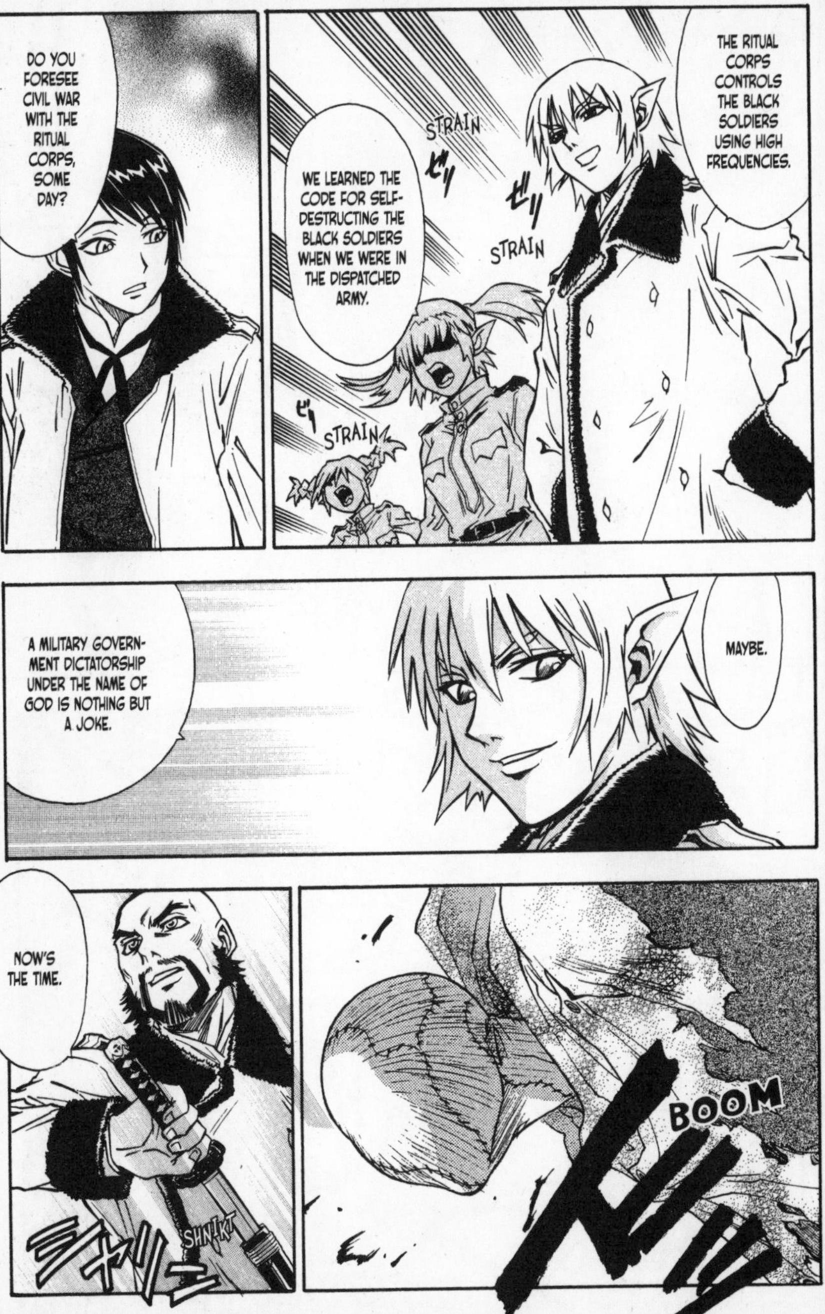
THE RITUAL CORPS CONTROLS THE BLACK SOLDIERS USING HIGH FREQUENCIES.
STRAIN
STRAIN
WE LEARNED THE CODE FOR SELF-DESTRUCTING THE BLACK SOLDIERS WHEN WE WERE IN THE DISPATCHED ARMY.
STRAIN
DO YOU FORESEE CIVIL WAR WITH THE RITUAL CORPS, SOME DAY?
MAYBE.
A MILITARY GOVERNMENT DICTATORSHIP UNDER THE NAME OF GOD IS NOTHING BUT A JOKE.
BOOM
NOW'S THE TIME.
SHNKT

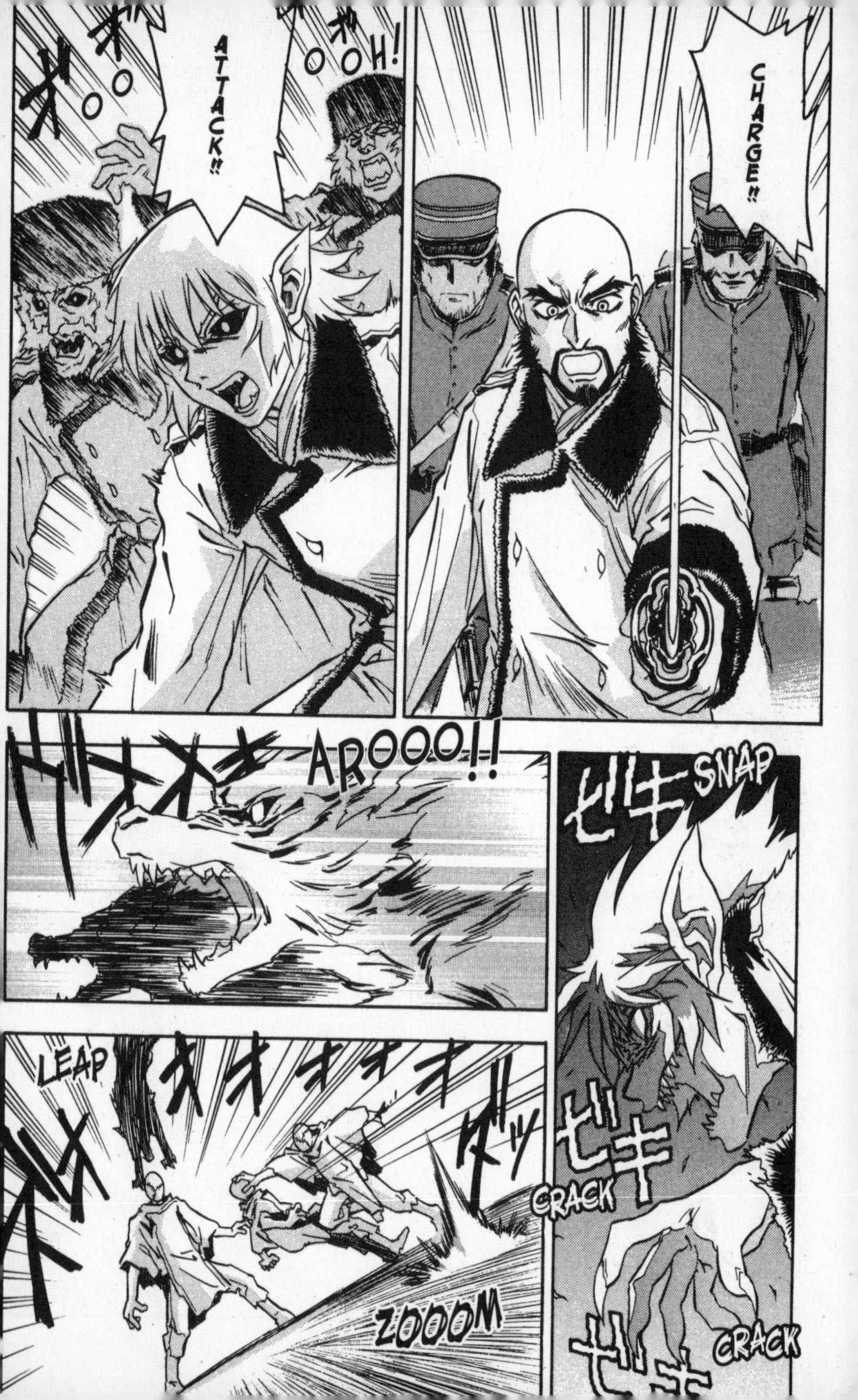
CHARGE!!
OOH!
ATTACK!!
OOO
SNAP
CRACK
CRACK
AROOO!!
LEAP
ZOOOM

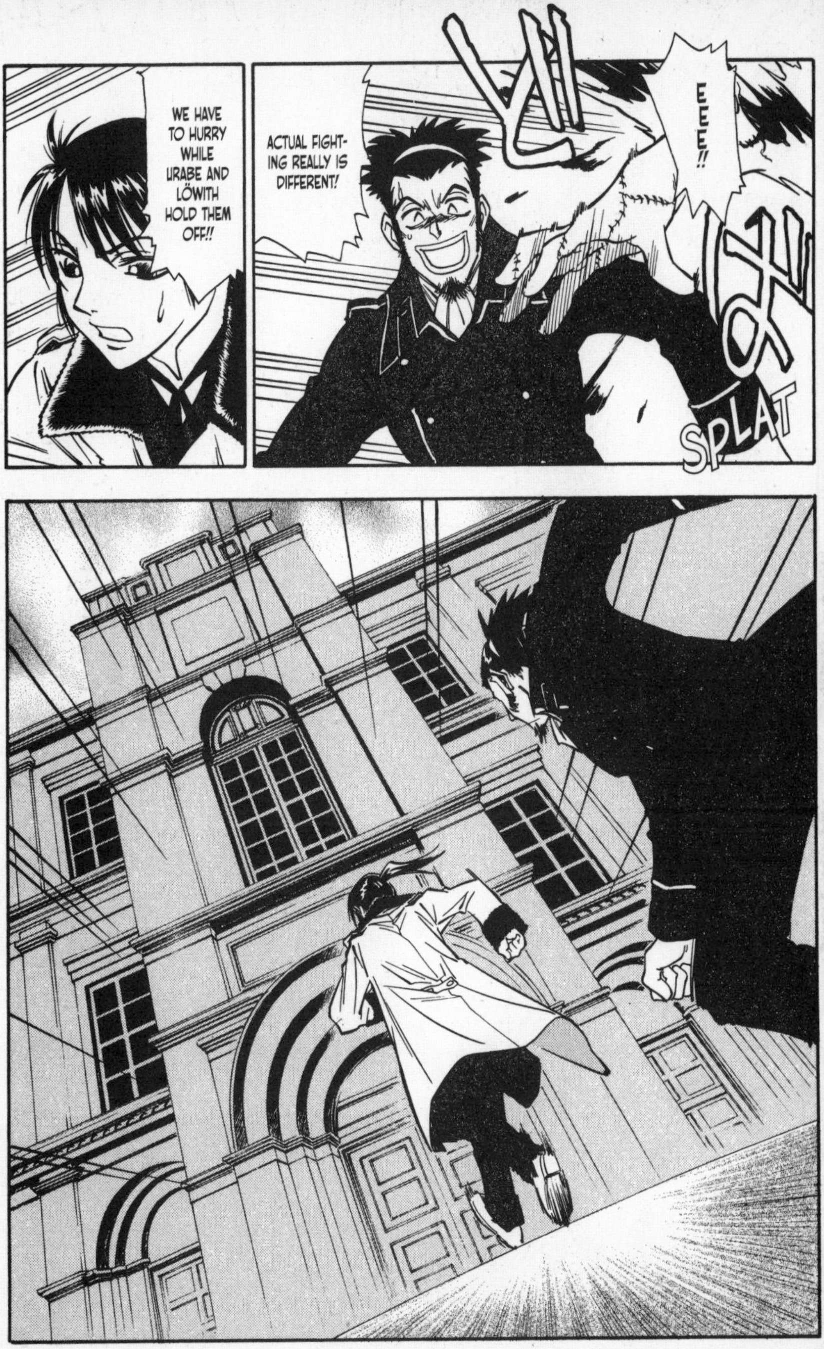
EEE!!
SPLAT
ACTUAL FIGHTING REALLY IS DIFFERENT!
WE HAVE TO HURRY WHILE URABE AND LÖWITH HOLD THEM OFF!!

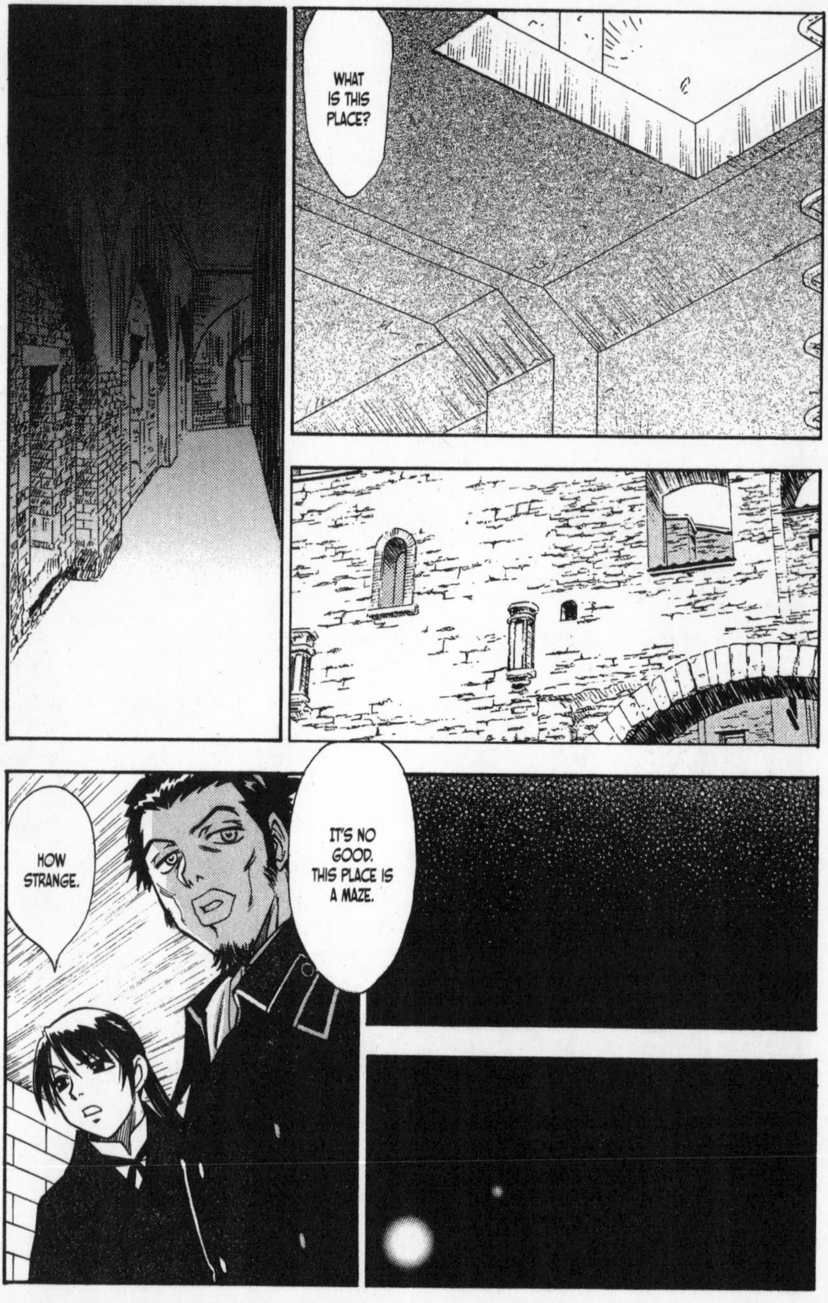
WHAT IS THIS PLACE?
IT'S NO GOOD. THIS PLACE IS A MAZE.
HOW STRANGE.

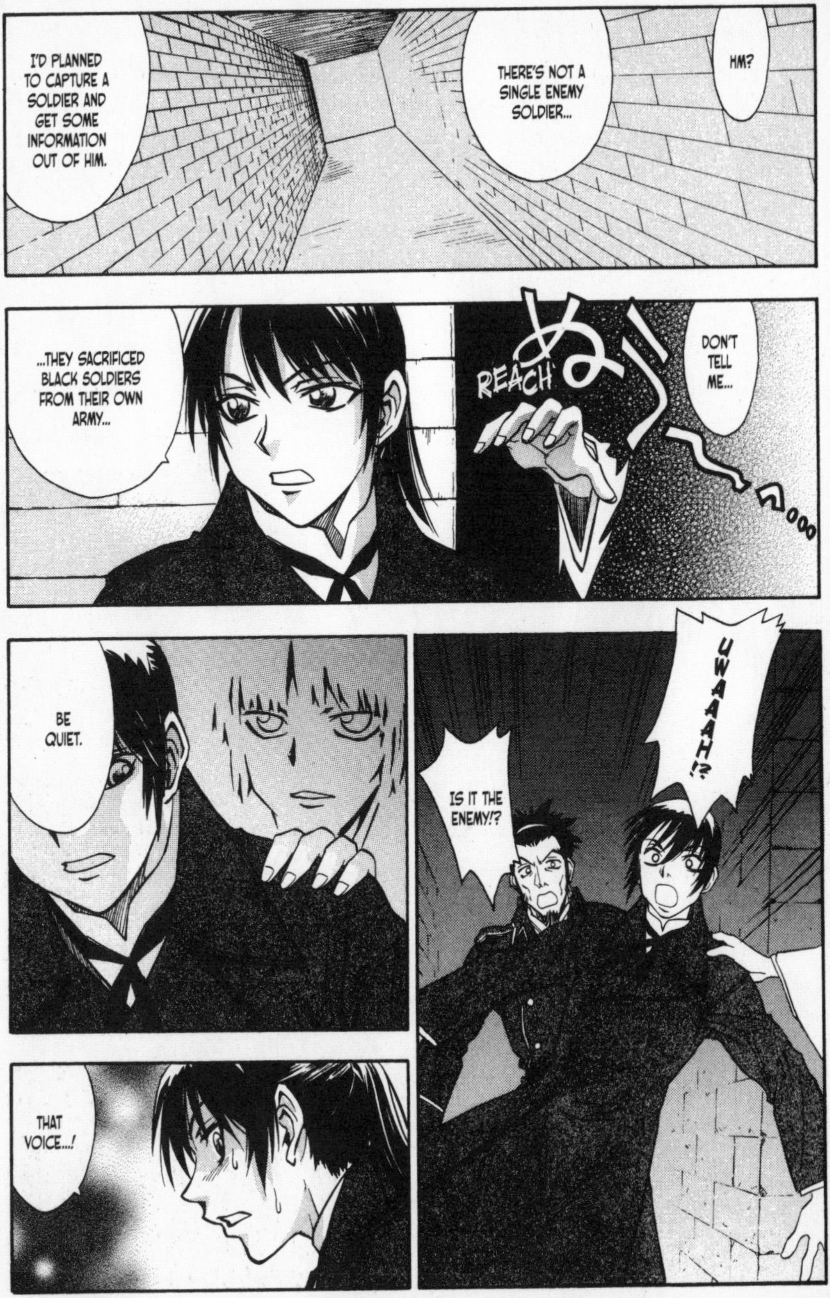
HM?
THERE'S NOT A SINGLE ENEMY SOLDIER...
I'D PLANNED TO CAPTURE A SOLDIER AND GET SOME INFORMATION OUT OF HIM.
DON'T TELL ME...
REACH
...THEY SACRIFICED BLACK SOLDIERS FROM THEIR OWN ARMY...
UWAAAAH!?
IS IT THE ENEMY!?
BE QUIET.
THAT VOICE...!

YAOKI!?

SORRY FOR MAKING YOU WAIT, KAGURA-SAMA.

ALL WE SEIMON* HAVE RUDELY ENTERED UPON THIS LAND.

*See translator's notes

WHY!?

SEIMON!?

WHERE ARE THE OTHERS?

WE HAVE TO END THIS, NOW.

THERE IS ONE THING THAT LIMITS THE CURRENT OF THE BLACK ARMY'S FACTION OF THE ENGAKU* AND WE SEIMON.

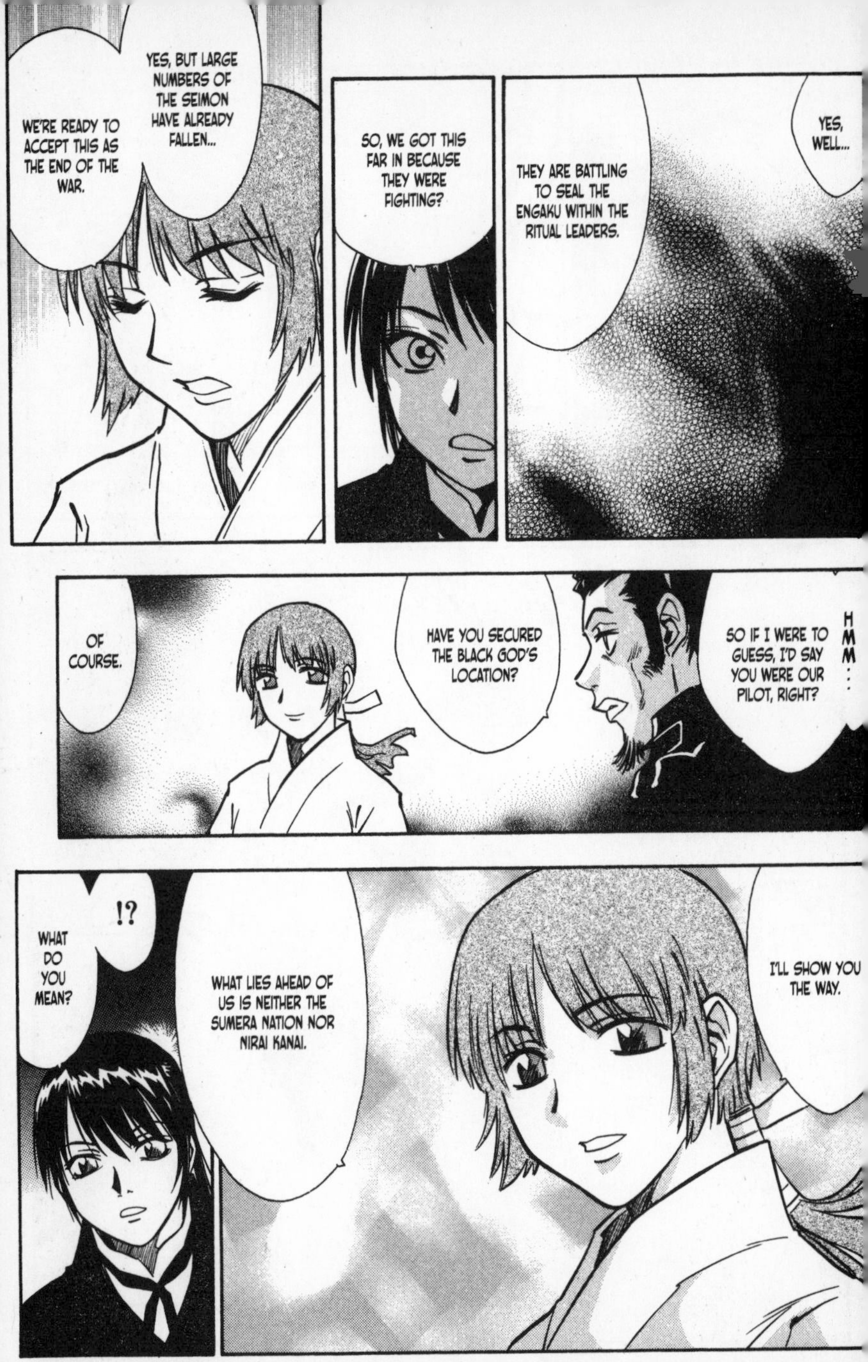
YES, WELL...
THEY ARE BATTLING TO SEAL THE ENGAKU WITHIN THE RITUAL LEADERS.
SO, WE GOT THIS FAR IN BECAUSE THEY WERE FIGHTING?
YES, BUT LARGE NUMBERS OF THE SEIMON HAVE ALREADY FALLEN...
WE'RE READY TO ACCEPT THIS AS THE END OF THE WAR.
HMM...
SO IF I WERE TO GUESS, I'D SAY YOU WERE OUR PILOT, RIGHT?
HAVE YOU SECURED THE BLACK GOD'S LOCATION?
OF COURSE.
I'LL SHOW YOU THE WAY.
WHAT LIES AHEAD OF US IS NEITHER THE SUMERA NATION NOR NIRAI KANAI.
!?
WHAT DO YOU MEAN?

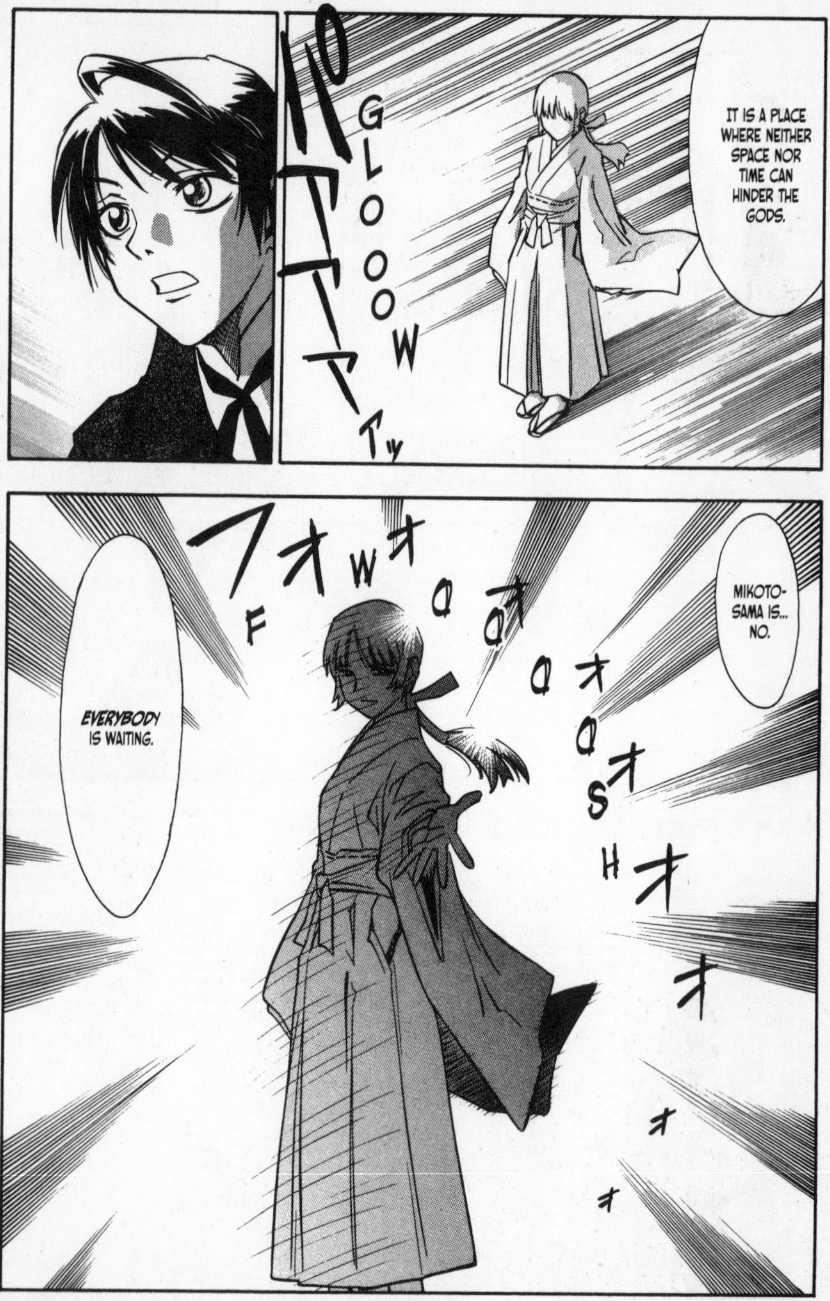
IT IS A PLACE WHERE NEITHER SPACE NOR TIME CAN HINDER THE GODS.
GLOOOW
MIKOTO-SAMA IS... NO.
FWOOOSH
EVERYBODY IS WAITING.

Chapter 38 : OVER

神無 KANNA

Chapter 39

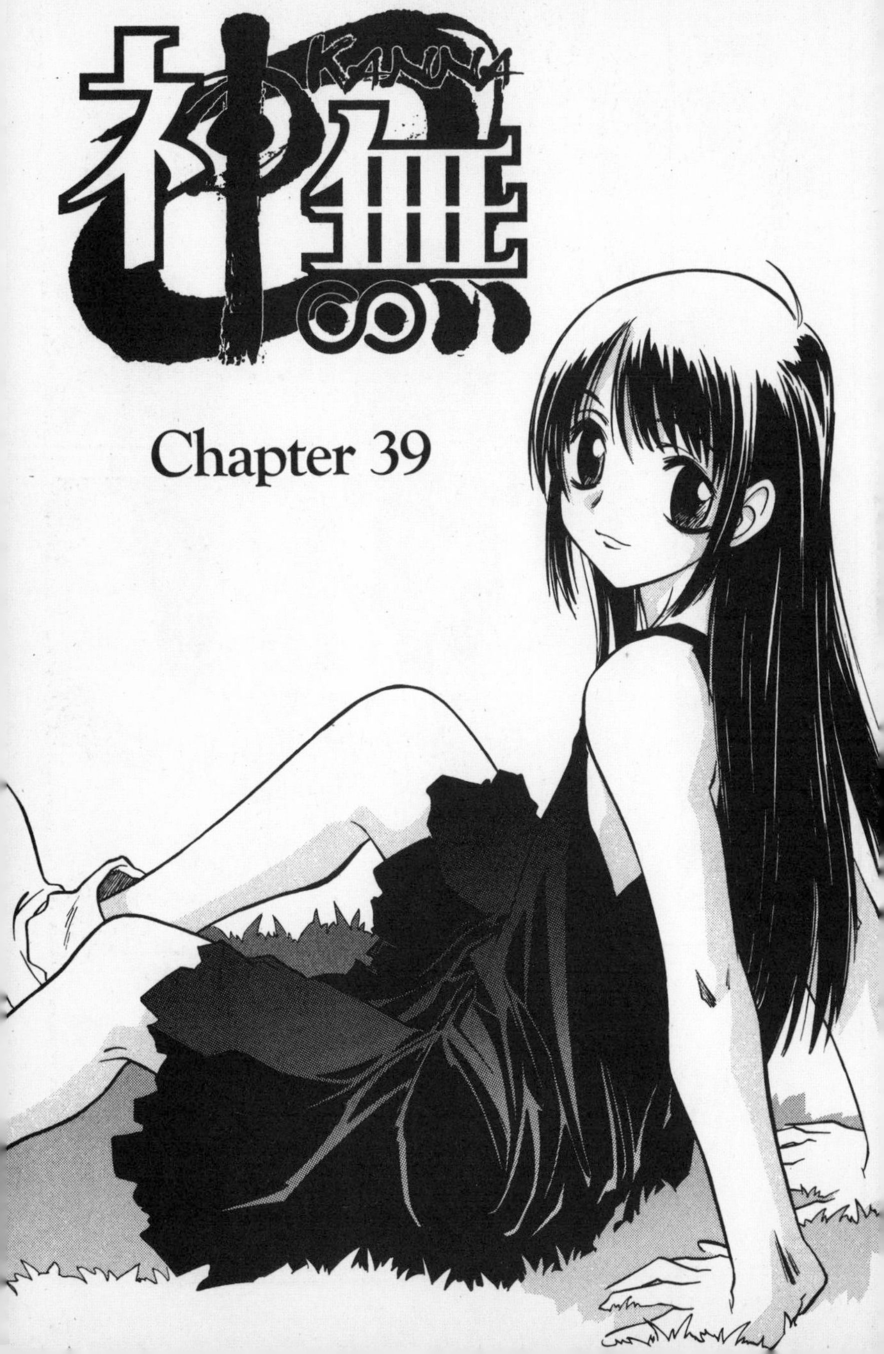

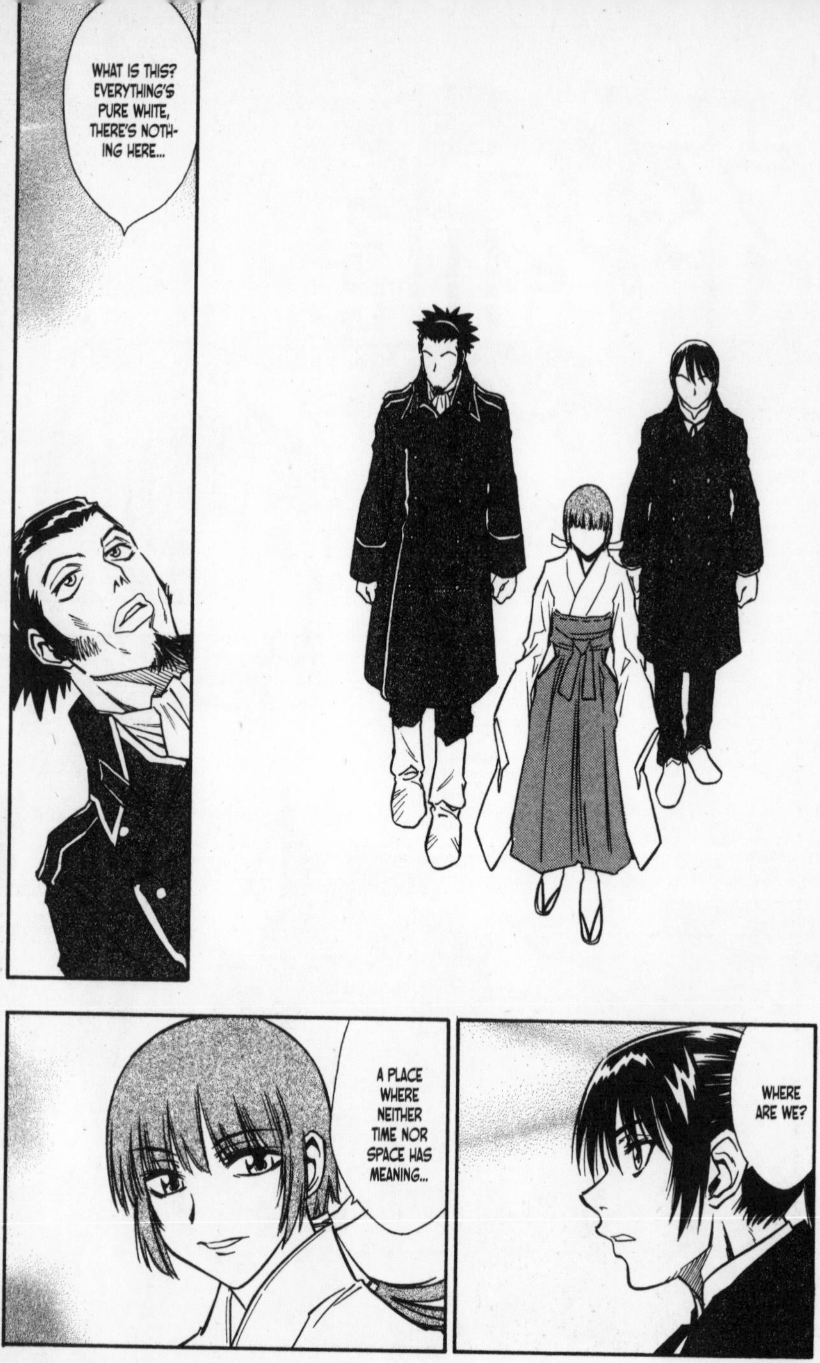
WHAT IS THIS? EVERYTHING'S PURE WHITE, THERE'S NOTH-ING HERE...
WHERE ARE WE?
A PLACE WHERE NEITHER TIME NOR SPACE HAS MEANING...

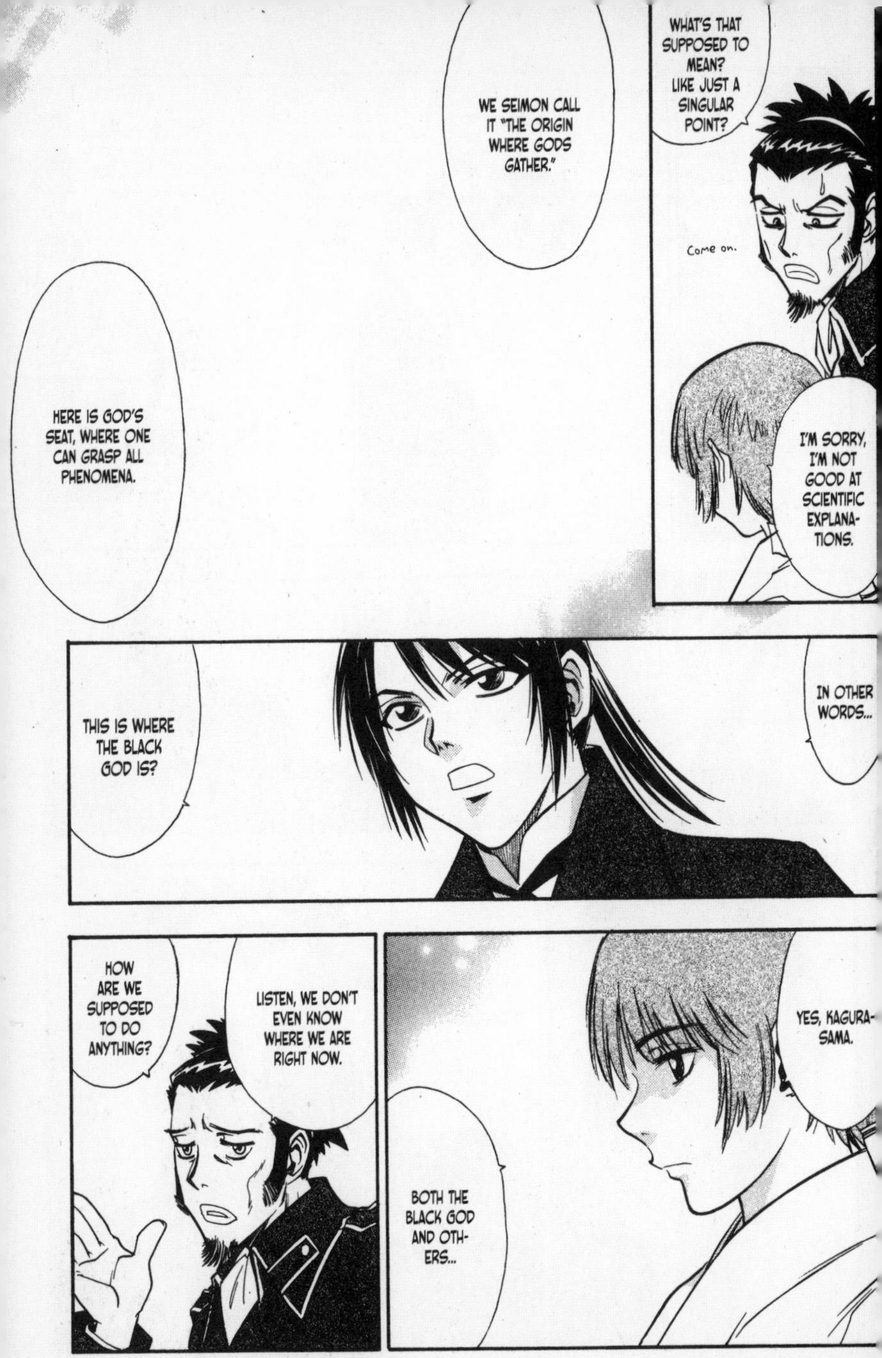
WHAT'S THAT SUPPOSED TO MEAN? LIKE JUST A SINGULAR POINT?
Come on.
I'M SORRY, I'M NOT GOOD AT SCIENTIFIC EXPLANATIONS.
WE SEIMON CALL IT "THE ORIGIN WHERE GODS GATHER."
HERE IS GOD'S SEAT, WHERE ONE CAN GRASP ALL PHENOMENA.
IN OTHER WORDS...
THIS IS WHERE THE BLACK GOD IS?
YES, KAGURA-SAMA.
BOTH THE BLACK GOD AND OTHERS...
LISTEN, WE DON'T EVEN KNOW WHERE WE ARE RIGHT NOW.
HOW ARE WE SUPPOSED TO DO ANYTHING?

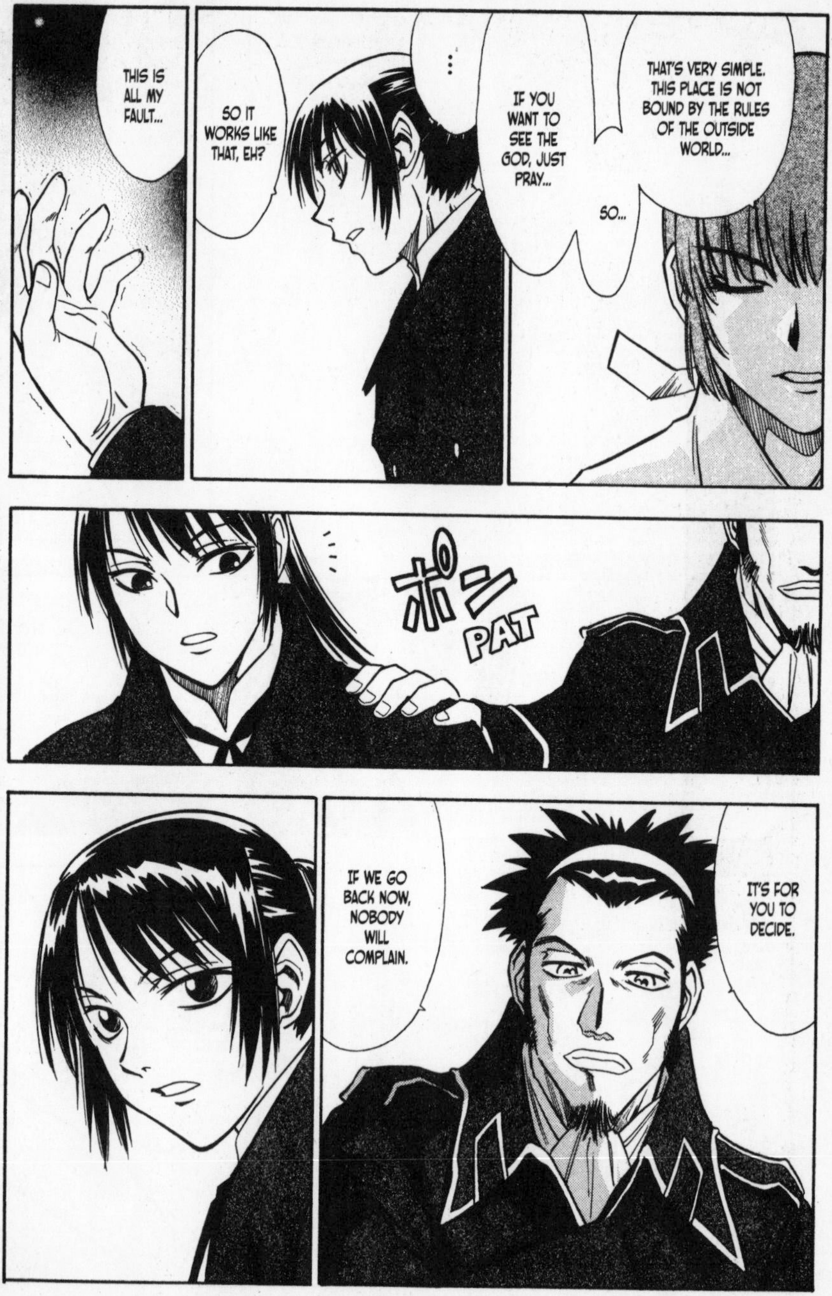
THAT'S VERY SIMPLE. THIS PLACE IS NOT BOUND BY THE RULES OF THE OUTSIDE WORLD...
SO...
IF YOU WANT TO SEE THE GOD, JUST PRAY...
...
SO IT WORKS LIKE THAT, EH?
THIS IS ALL MY FAULT...
ポン
PAT
IT'S FOR YOU TO DECIDE.
IF WE GO BACK NOW, NOBODY WILL COMPLAIN.

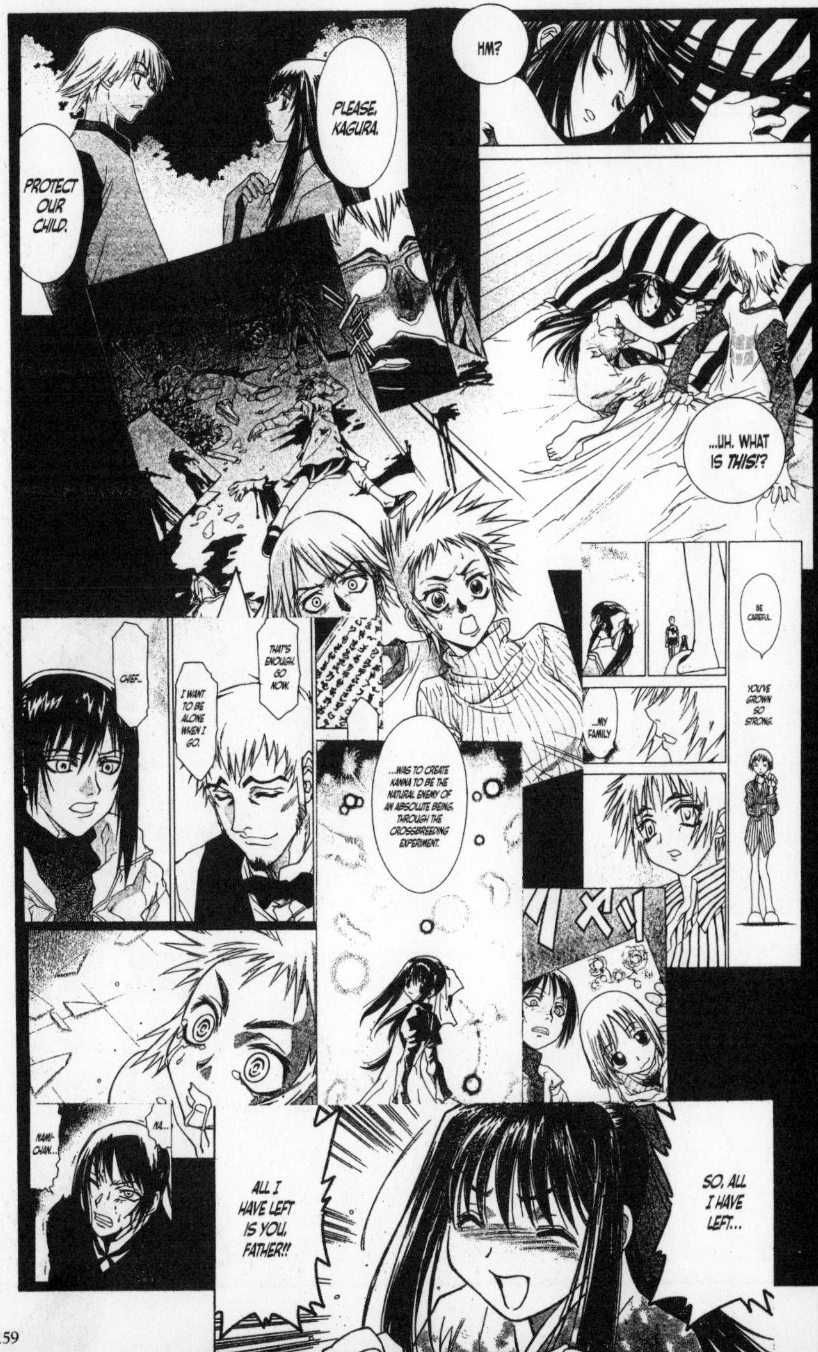
HM?
...UH. WHAT IS THIS!?
PLEASE, KAGURA.
PROTECT OUR CHILD.
BE CAREFUL.
YOU'VE GROWN SO STRONG.
...MY FAMILY
...WAS TO CREATE KANNA TO BE THE NATURAL ENEMY OF AN ABSOLUTE BEING, THROUGH THE CROSSBREEDING EXPERIMENT.
THAT'S ENOUGH. GO NOW.
I WANT TO BE ALONE WHEN I GO.
CHIEF...
SO, ALL I HAVE LEFT...
ALL I HAVE LEFT IS YOU, FATHER!!
NA...
NAMI-CHAN...

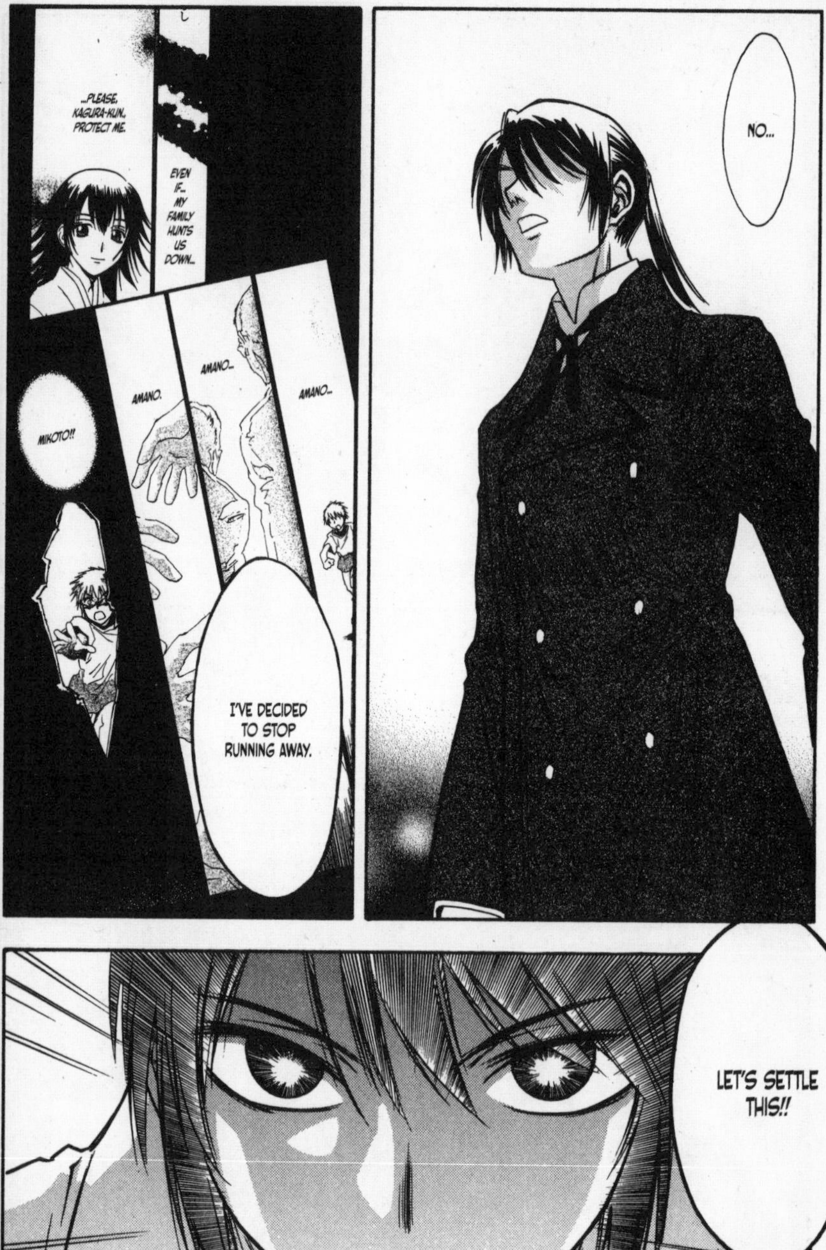
NO...
EVEN IF... MY FAMILY HUNTS US DOWN...
...PLEASE, KAGURA-KUN... PROTECT ME.
AMANO...
AMANO...
AMANO.
MIKOTO!!
I'VE DECIDED TO STOP RUNNING AWAY.
LET'S SETTLE THIS!!

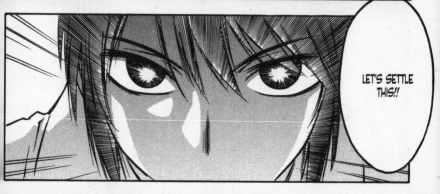

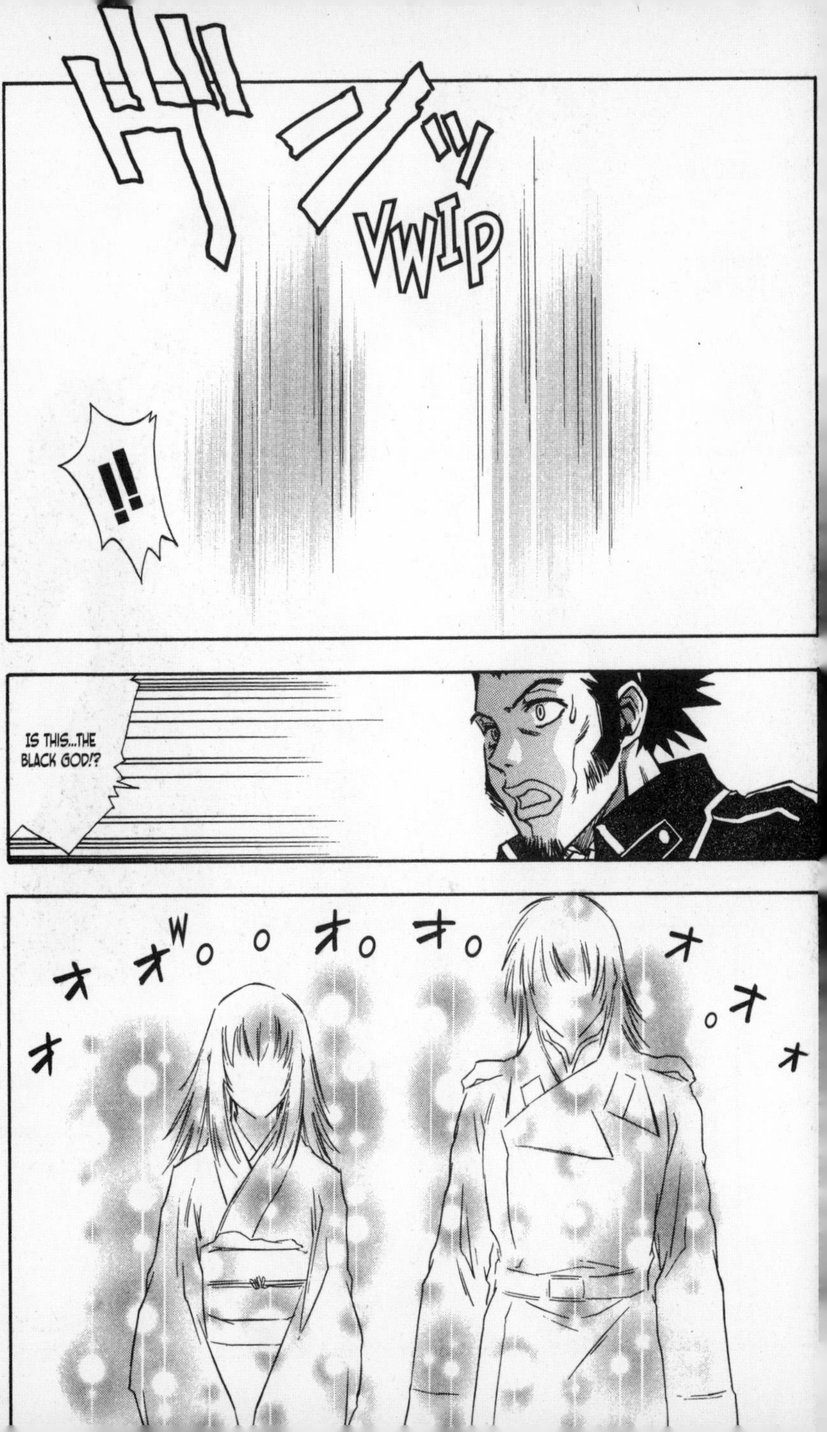
VWIP
!!
IS THIS...THE BLACK GOD!?

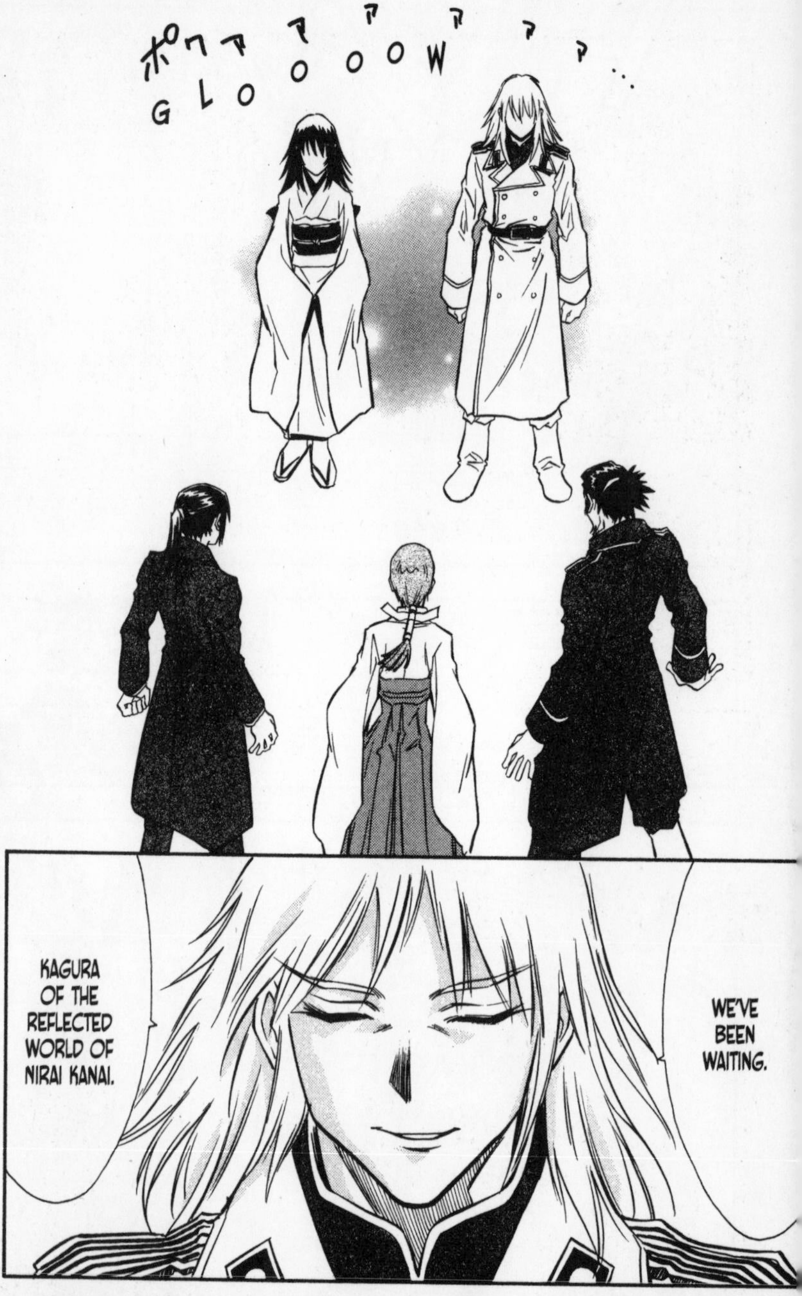
ポワァァァァァ
GLOOOOW...
WE'VE BEEN WAITING.
KAGURA OF THE REFLECTED WORLD OF NIRAI KANAI.

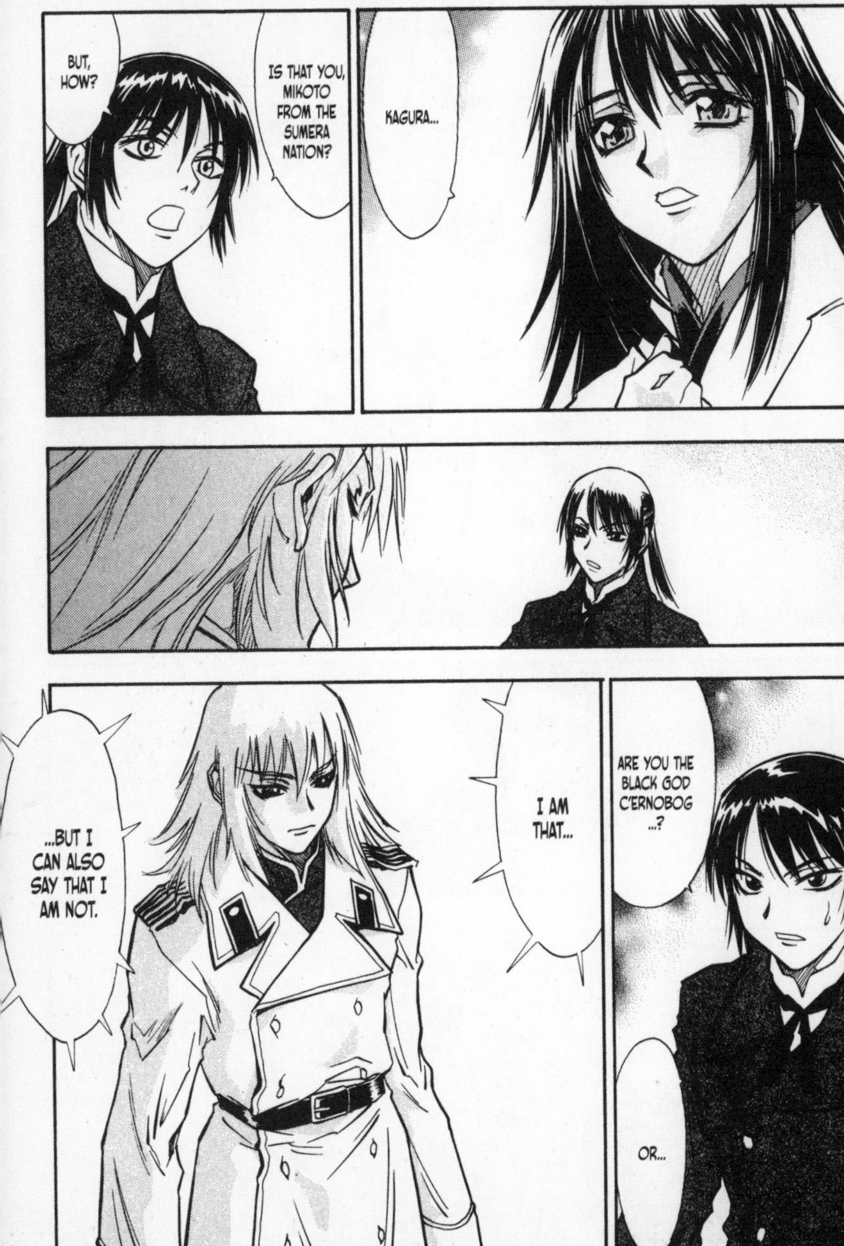
KAGURA...
IS THAT YOU, MIKOTO FROM THE SUMERA NATION?
BUT, HOW?
ARE YOU THE BLACK GOD C'ERNOBOG ...?
OR...
I AM THAT...
...BUT I CAN ALSO SAY THAT I AM NOT.

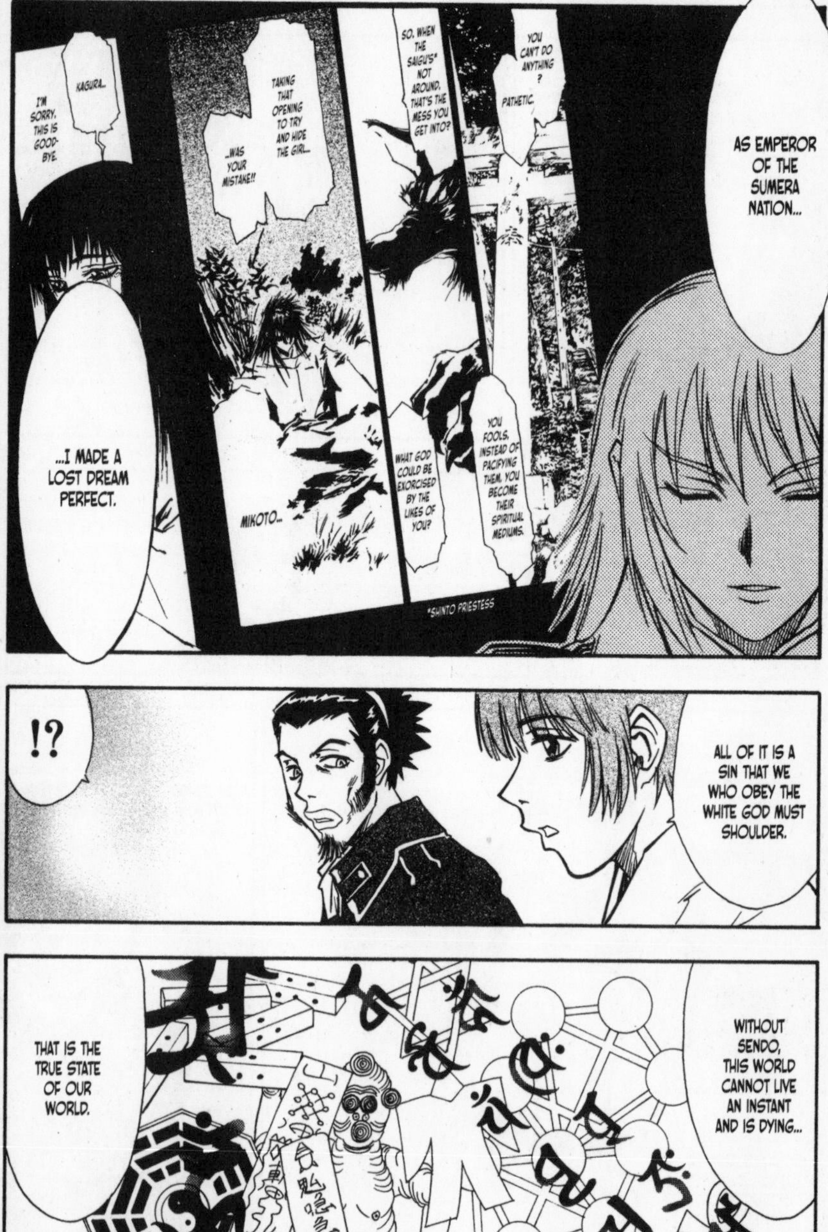
AS EMPEROR OF THE SUMERA NATION...
YOU CAN'T DO ANYTHING?
PATHETIC.
YOU FOOLS, INSTEAD OF PACIFYING THEM, YOU BECOME THEIR SPIRITUAL MEDIUMS.
SO, WHEN THE SAIGU'S* NOT AROUND, THAT'S THE MESS YOU GET INTO?
WHAT GOD COULD BE EXORCISED BY THE LIKES OF YOU?
TAKING THAT OPENING TO TRY AND HIDE THE GIRL...
...WAS YOUR MISTAKE!!
MIKOTO...
KAGURA...
I'M SORRY, THIS IS GOOD-BYE.
...I MADE A LOST DREAM PERFECT.
*SHINTO PRIESTESS
ALL OF IT IS A SIN THAT WE WHO OBEY THE WHITE GOD MUST SHOULDER.
!?
WITHOUT SENDO, THIS WORLD CANNOT LIVE AN INSTANT AND IS DYING...
THAT IS THE TRUE STATE OF OUR WORLD.

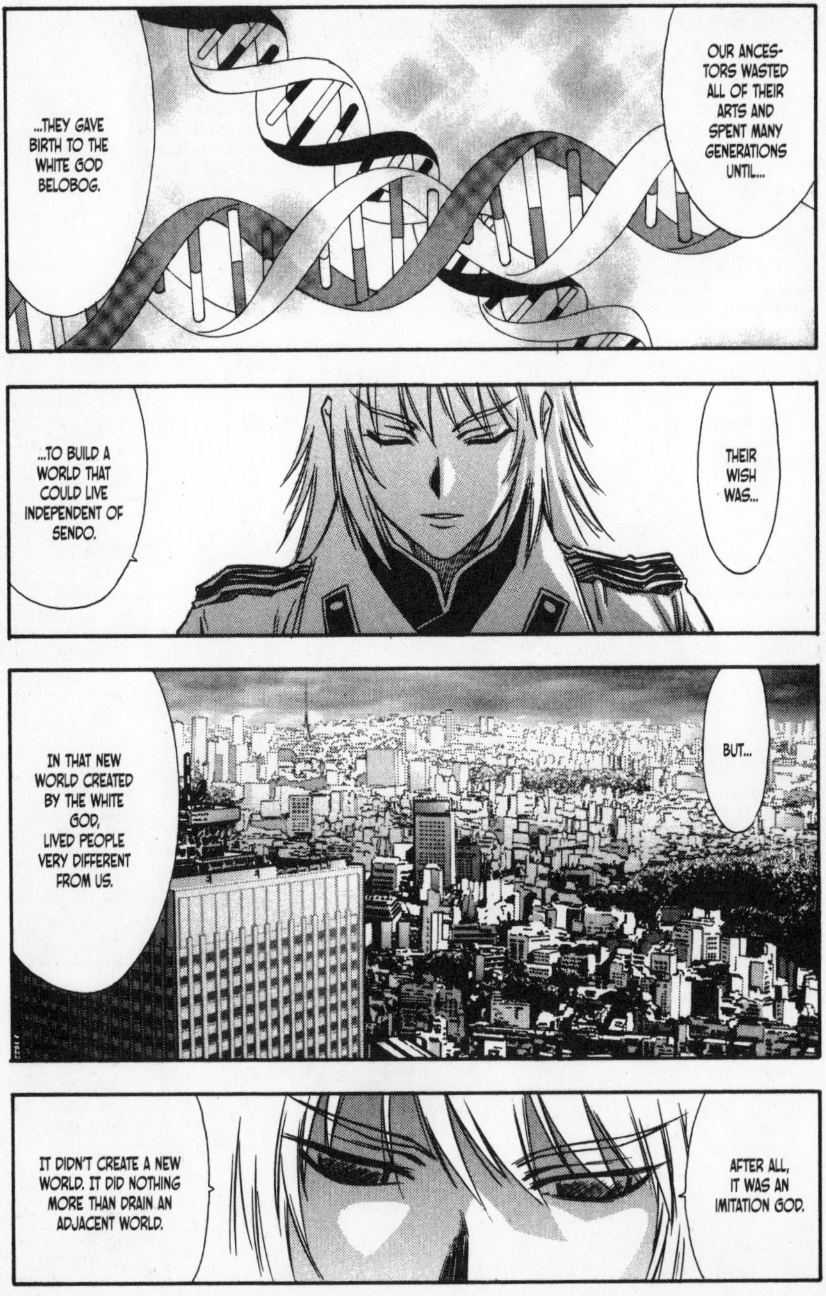
OUR ANCES-TORS WASTED ALL OF THEIR ARTS AND SPENT MANY GENERATIONS UNTIL...
...THEY GAVE BIRTH TO THE WHITE GOD BELOBOG.
THEIR WISH WAS...
...TO BUILD A WORLD THAT COULD LIVE INDEPENDENT OF SENDO.
BUT...
IN THAT NEW WORLD CREATED BY THE WHITE GOD, LIVED PEOPLE VERY DIFFERENT FROM US.
AFTER ALL, IT WAS AN IMITATION GOD.
IT DIDN'T CREATE A NEW WORLD. IT DID NOTHING MORE THAN DRAIN AN ADJACENT WORLD.

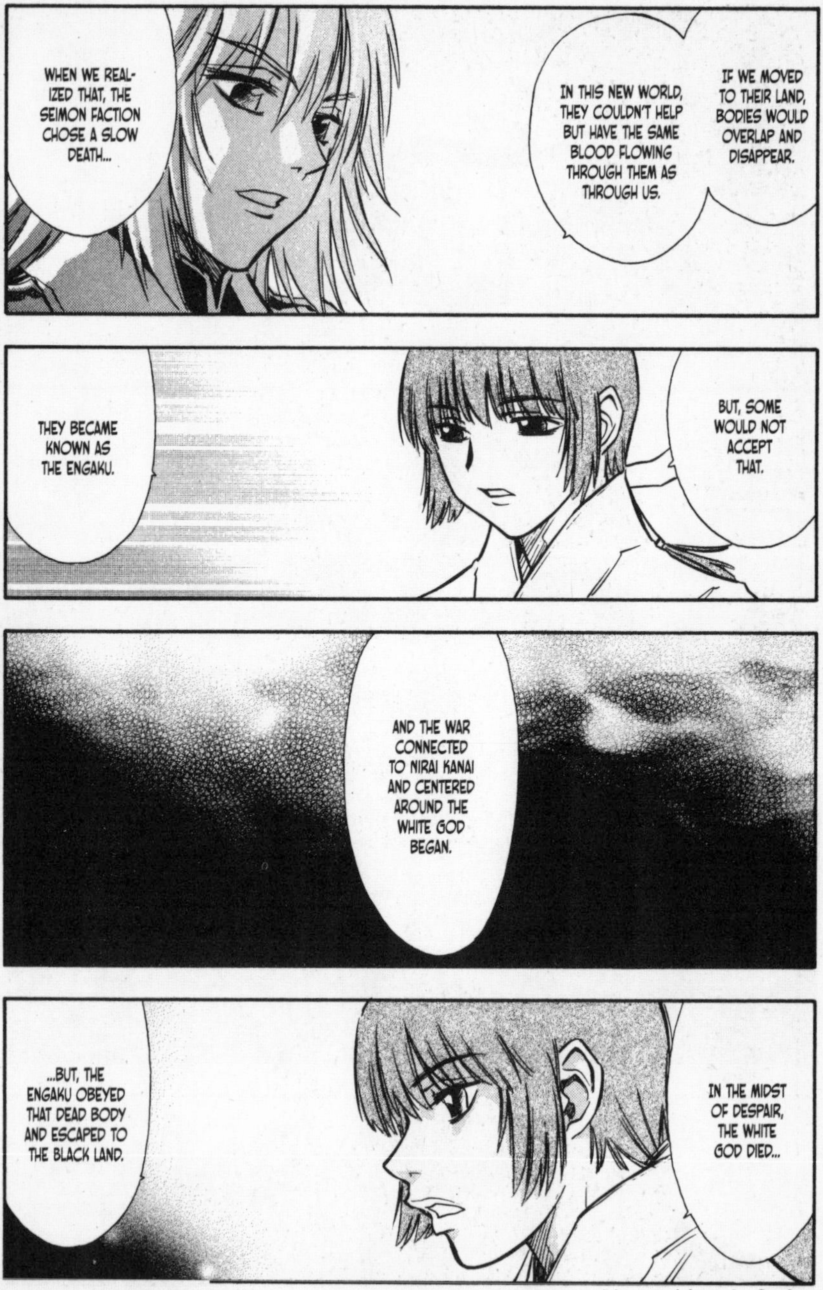
IF WE MOVED TO THEIR LAND, BODIES WOULD OVERLAP AND DISAPPEAR.
IN THIS NEW WORLD, THEY COULDN'T HELP BUT HAVE THE SAME BLOOD FLOWING THROUGH THEM AS THROUGH US.
WHEN WE REAL-IZED THAT, THE SEIMON FACTION CHOSE A SLOW DEATH...
BUT, SOME WOULD NOT ACCEPT THAT.
THEY BECAME KNOWN AS THE ENGAKU.
AND THE WAR CONNECTED TO NIRAI KANAI AND CENTERED AROUND THE WHITE GOD BEGAN.
IN THE MIDST OF DESPAIR, THE WHITE GOD DIED...
...BUT, THE ENGAKU OBEYED THAT DEAD BODY AND ESCAPED TO THE BLACK LAND.

Chapter 39 : OVER

Chapter 40

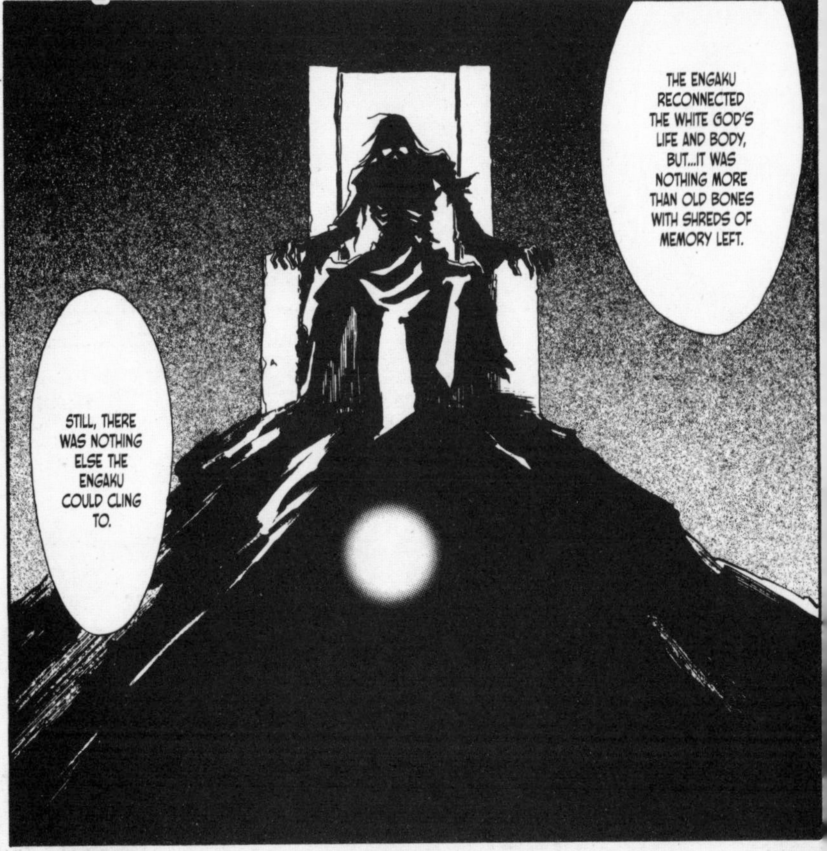
THE ENGAKU RECONNECTED THE WHITE GOD'S LIFE AND BODY, BUT...IT WAS NOTHING MORE THAN OLD BONES WITH SHREDS OF MEMORY LEFT.
STILL, THERE WAS NOTHING ELSE THE ENGAKU COULD CLING TO.

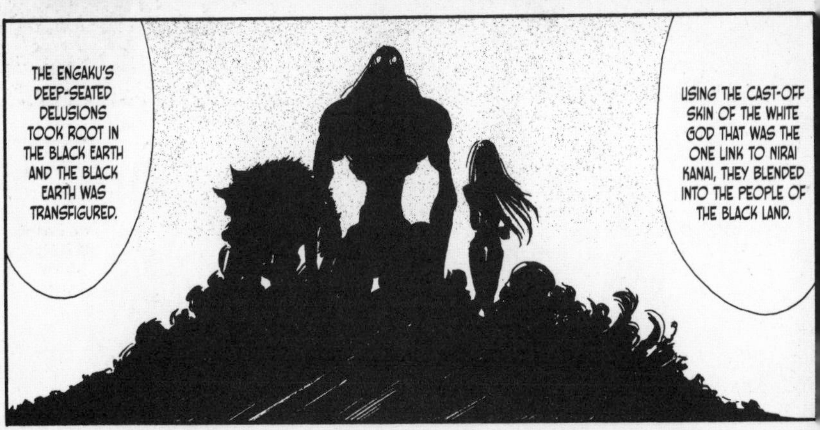
USING THE CAST-OFF SKIN OF THE WHITE GOD THAT WAS THE ONE LINK TO NIRAI KANAI, THEY BLENDED INTO THE PEOPLE OF THE BLACK LAND.
THE ENGAKU'S DEEP-SEATED DELUSIONS TOOK ROOT IN THE BLACK EARTH AND THE BLACK EARTH WAS TRANSFIGURED.

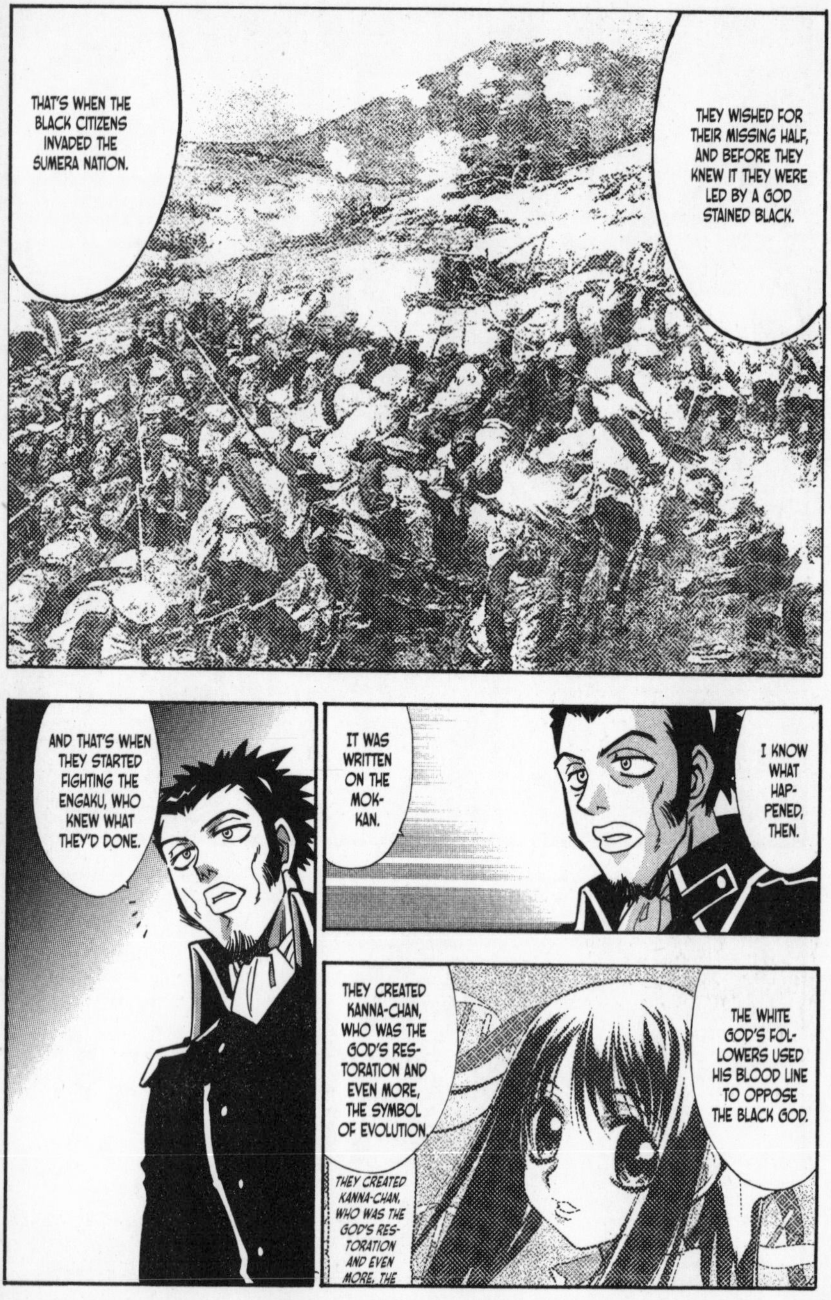
THEY WISHED FOR THEIR MISSING HALF, AND BEFORE THEY KNEW IT THEY WERE LED BY A GOD STAINED BLACK.
THAT'S WHEN THE BLACK CITIZENS INVADED THE SUMERA NATION.
I KNOW WHAT HAPPENED, THEN.
IT WAS WRITTEN ON THE MOKKAN.
THE WHITE GOD'S FOLLOWERS USED HIS BLOOD LINE TO OPPOSE THE BLACK GOD.
THEY CREATED KANNA-CHAN, WHO WAS THE GOD'S RESTORATION AND EVEN MORE, THE SYMBOL OF EVOLUTION.
THEY CREATED KANNA-CHAN, WHO WAS THE GOD'S RESTORATION AND EVEN MORE, THE
AND THAT'S WHEN THEY STARTED FIGHTING THE ENGAKU, WHO KNEW WHAT THEY'D DONE.

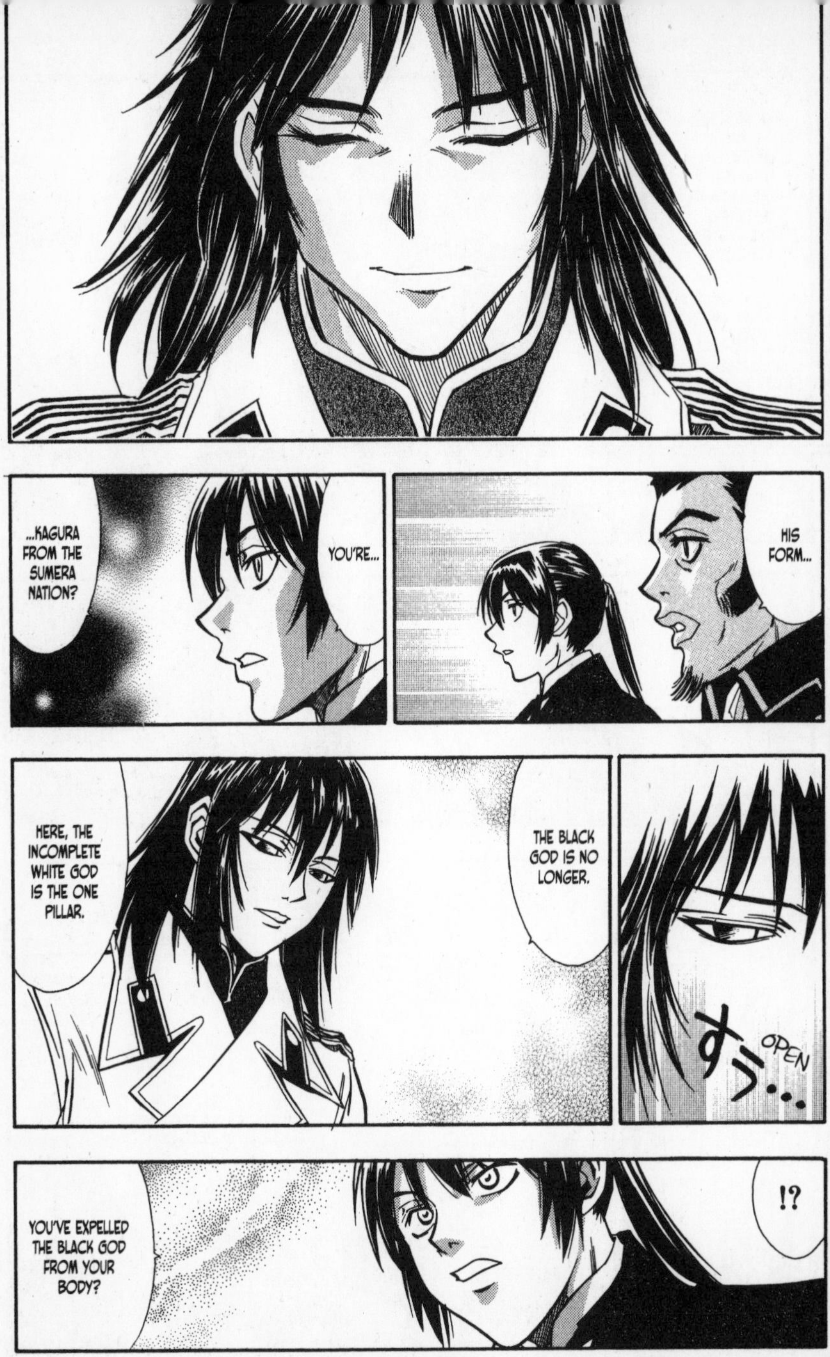
HIS FORM...
YOU'RE...
...KAGURA FROM THE SUMERA NATION?
すう...
OPEN
THE BLACK GOD IS NO LONGER.
HERE, THE INCOMPLETE WHITE GOD IS THE ONE PILLAR.
!?
YOU'VE EXPELLED THE BLACK GOD FROM YOUR BODY?

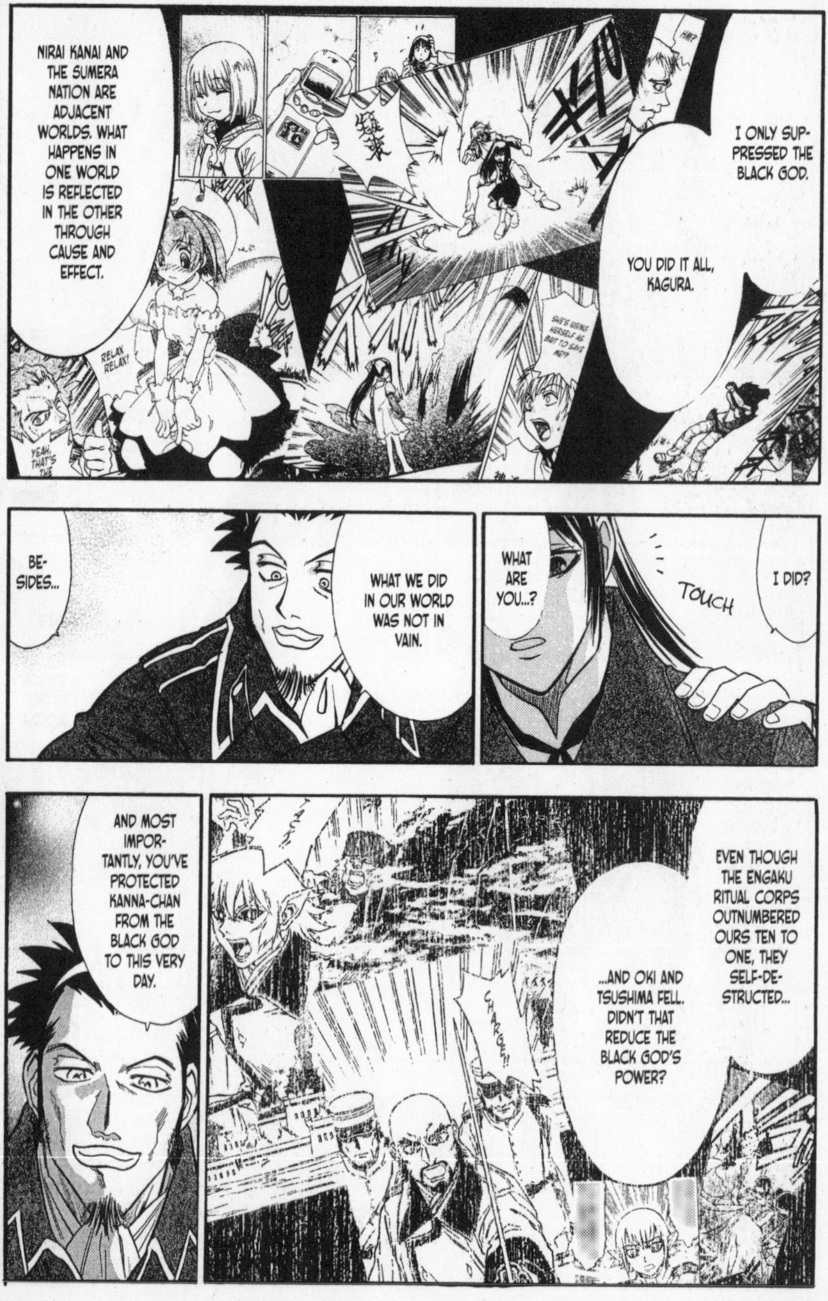
HM?
I ONLY SUPPRESSED THE BLACK GOD.
YOU DID IT ALL, KAGURA.
SHE'S USING HERSELF AS BAIT TO SAVE ME!?
RELAX RELAX!
YEAH, THAT'S THE
NIRAI KANAI AND THE SUMERA NATION ARE ADJACENT WORLDS. WHAT HAPPENS IN ONE WORLD IS REFLECTED IN THE OTHER THROUGH CAUSE AND EFFECT.
I DID?
TOUCH
WHAT ARE YOU...?
WHAT WE DID IN OUR WORLD WAS NOT IN VAIN.
BESIDES...
EVEN THOUGH THE ENGAKU RITUAL CORPS OUTNUMBERED OURS TEN TO ONE, THEY SELF-DESTRUCTED...
...AND OKI AND TSUSHIMA FELL. DIDN'T THAT REDUCE THE BLACK GOD'S POWER?
CHARGE!!
AND MOST IMPORTANTLY, YOU'VE PROTECTED KANNA-CHAN FROM THE BLACK GOD TO THIS VERY DAY.

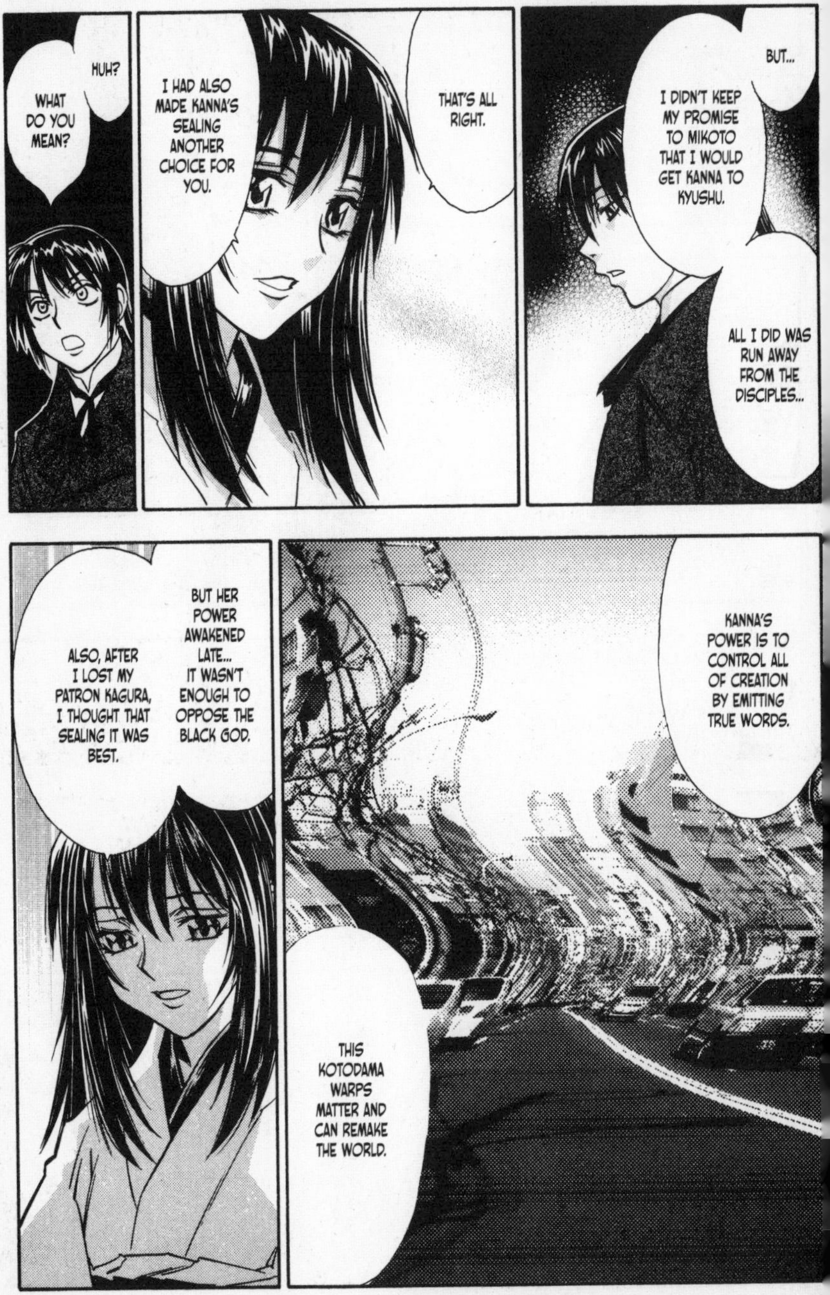
BUT...
I DIDN'T KEEP MY PROMISE TO MIKOTO THAT I WOULD GET KANNA TO KYUSHU.
ALL I DID WAS RUN AWAY FROM THE DISCIPLES...
THAT'S ALL RIGHT.
I HAD ALSO MADE KANNA'S SEALING ANOTHER CHOICE FOR YOU.
HUH?
WHAT DO YOU MEAN?
KANNA'S POWER IS TO CONTROL ALL OF CREATION BY EMITTING TRUE WORDS.
THIS KOTODAMA WARPS MATTER AND CAN REMAKE THE WORLD.
BUT HER POWER AWAKENED LATE... IT WASN'T ENOUGH TO OPPOSE THE BLACK GOD.
ALSO, AFTER I LOST MY PATRON KAGURA, I THOUGHT THAT SEALING IT WAS BEST.

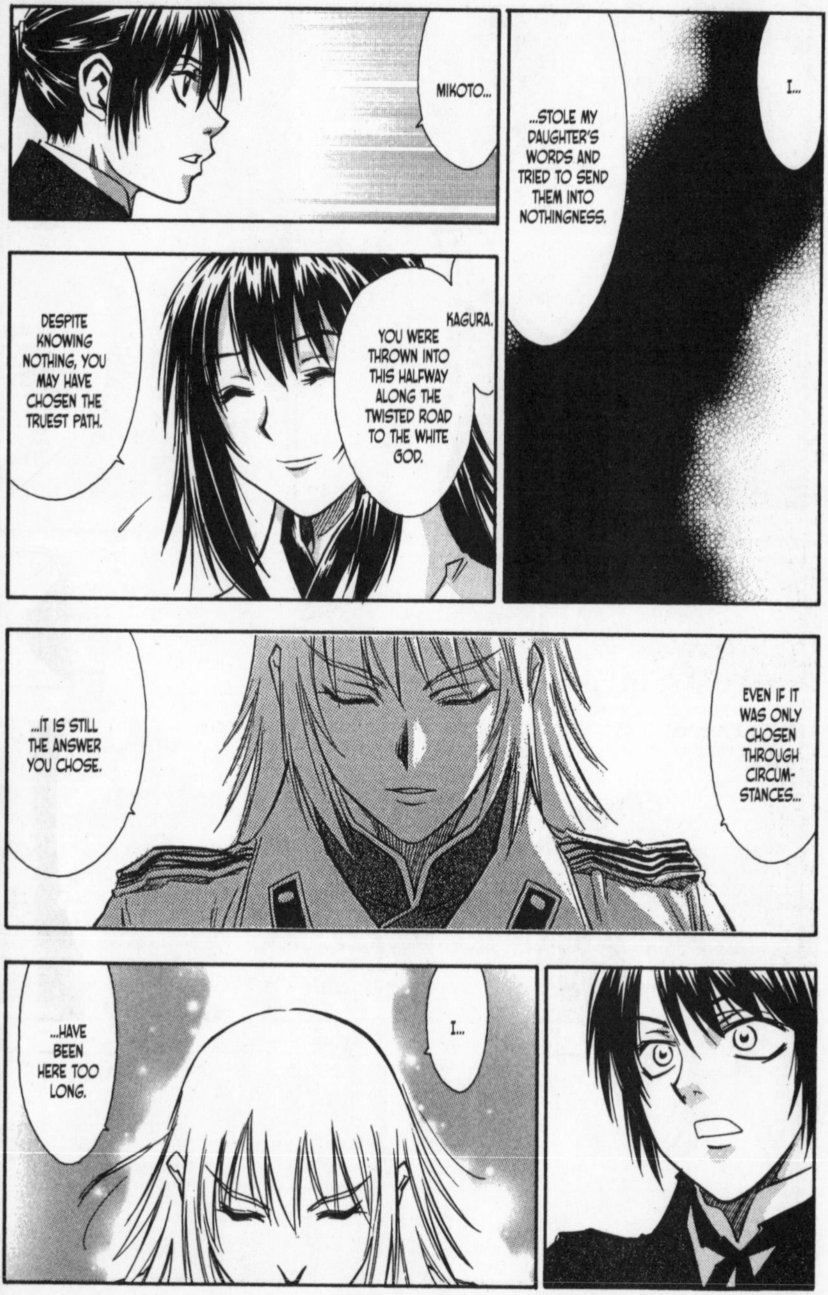
I...
...STOLE MY DAUGHTER'S WORDS AND TRIED TO SEND THEM INTO NOTHINGNESS.
MIKOTO...
KAGURA.
YOU WERE THROWN INTO THIS HALFWAY ALONG THE TWISTED ROAD TO THE WHITE GOD.
DESPITE KNOWING NOTHING, YOU MAY HAVE CHOSEN THE TRUEST PATH.
EVEN IF IT WAS ONLY CHOSEN THROUGH CIRCUM-STANCES...
...IT IS STILL THE ANSWER YOU CHOSE.
I...
...HAVE BEEN HERE TOO LONG.

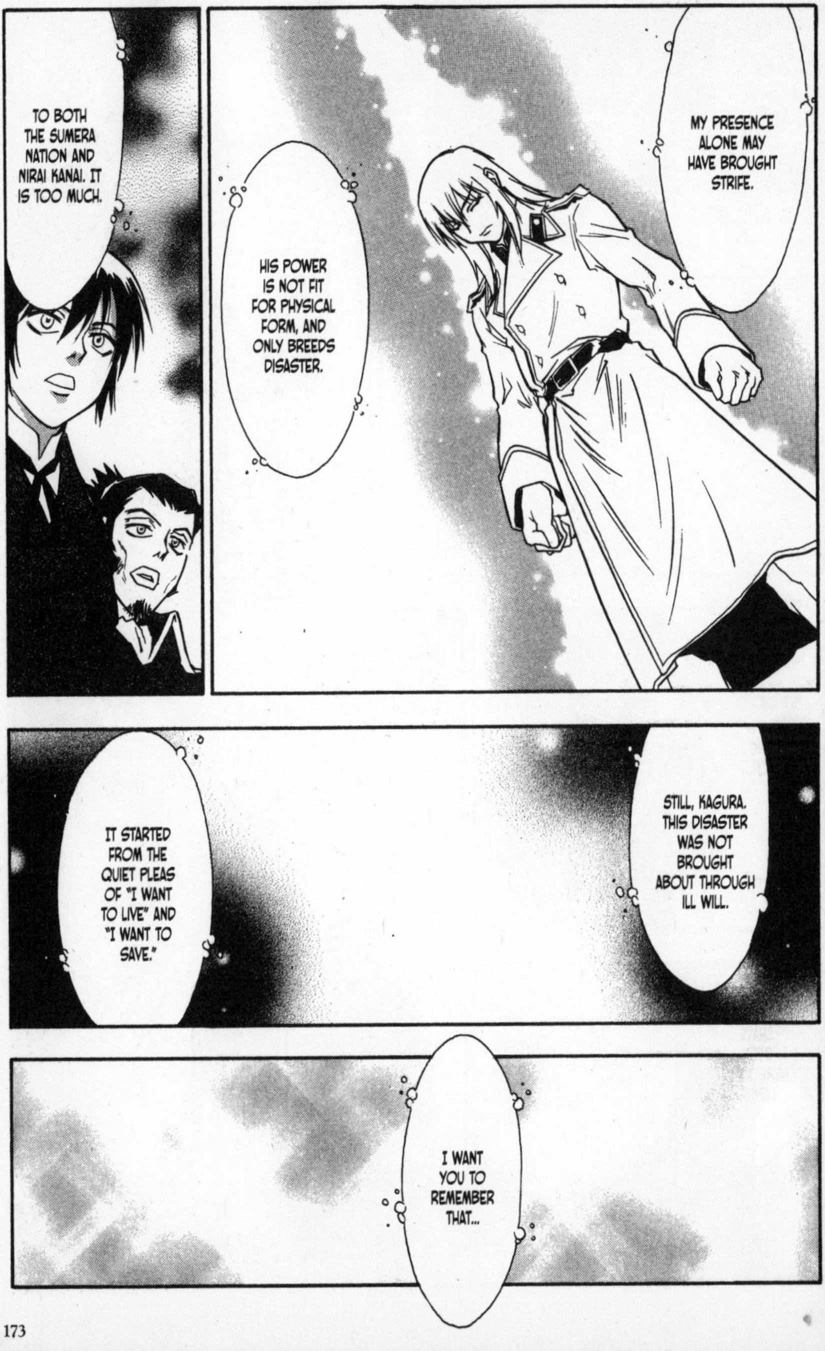
MY PRESENCE ALONE MAY HAVE BROUGHT STRIFE.
HIS POWER IS NOT FIT FOR PHYSICAL FORM, AND ONLY BREEDS DISASTER.
TO BOTH THE SUMERA NATION AND NIRAI KANAI. IT IS TOO MUCH.
STILL, KAGURA. THIS DISASTER WAS NOT BROUGHT ABOUT THROUGH ILL WILL.
IT STARTED FROM THE QUIET PLEAS OF "I WANT TO LIVE" AND "I WANT TO SAVE."
I WANT YOU TO REMEMBER THAT...

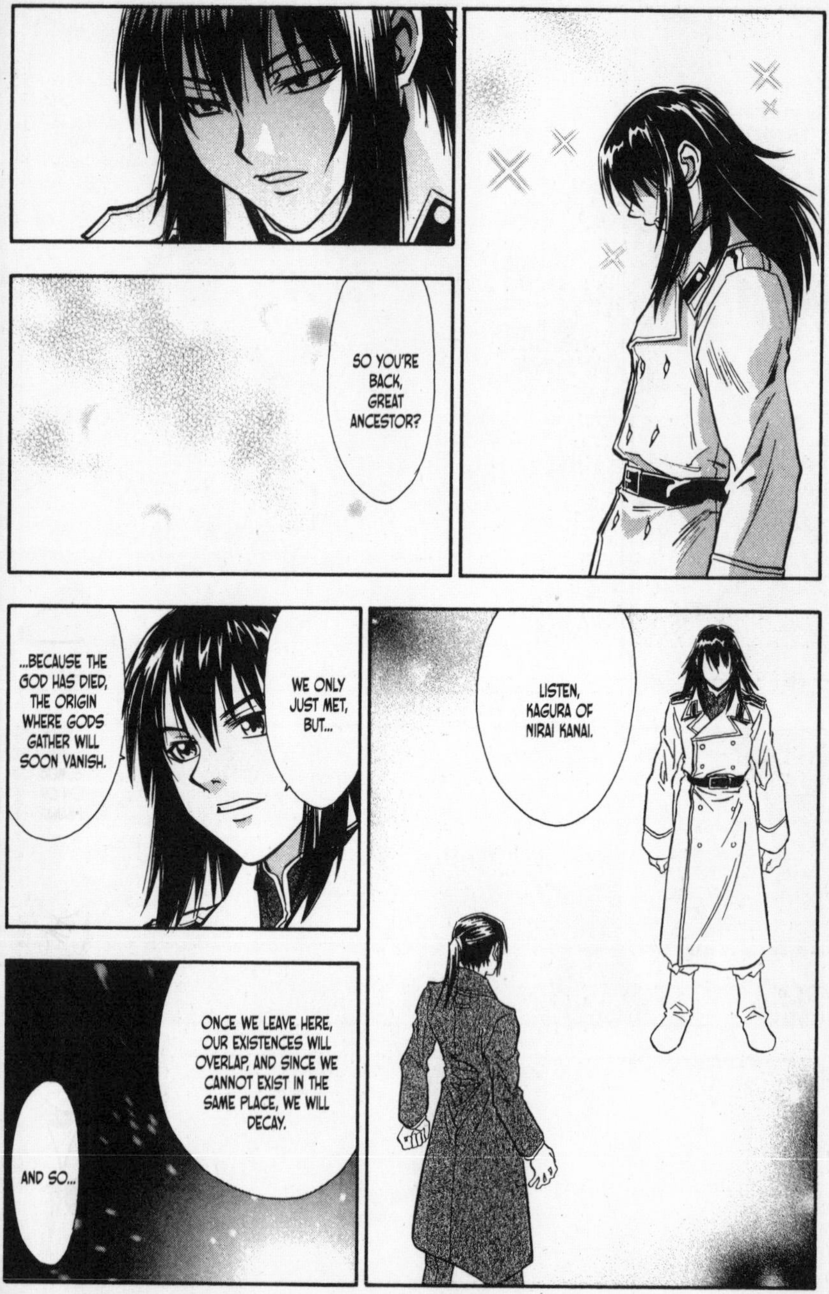
SO YOU'RE BACK, GREAT ANCESTOR?
LISTEN, KAGURA OF NIRAI KANAI.
WE ONLY JUST MET, BUT...
...BECAUSE THE GOD HAS DIED, THE ORIGIN WHERE GODS GATHER WILL SOON VANISH.
ONCE WE LEAVE HERE, OUR EXISTENCES WILL OVERLAP, AND SINCE WE CANNOT EXIST IN THE SAME PLACE, WE WILL DECAY.
AND SO...

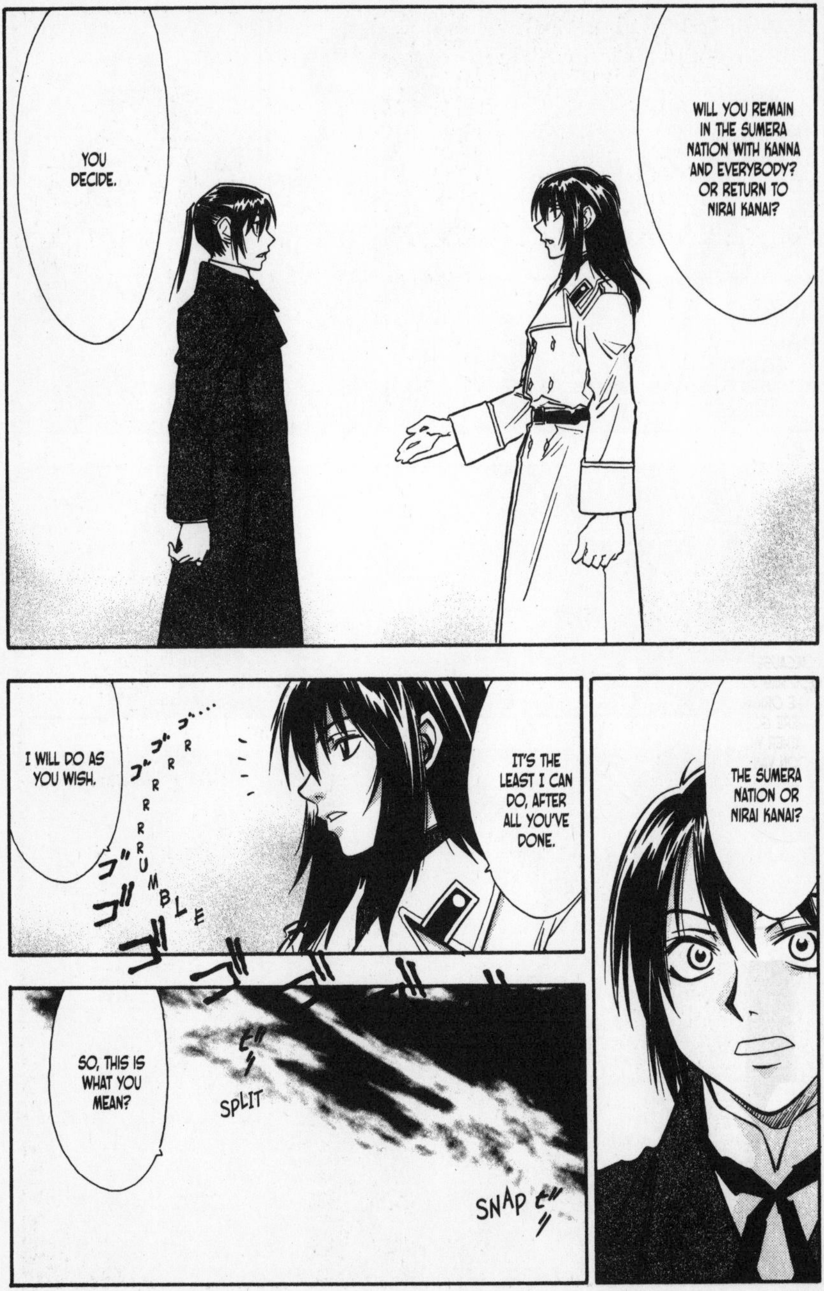

WILL YOU REMAIN IN THE SUMERA NATION WITH KANNA AND EVERYBODY? OR RETURN TO NIRAI KANAI?
YOU DECIDE.
THE SUMERA NATION OR NIRAI KANAI?
IT'S THE LEAST I CAN DO, AFTER ALL YOU'VE DONE.
I WILL DO AS YOU WISH.
RRRRRRUMBLE
SPLIT
SO, THIS IS WHAT YOU MEAN?
SNAP

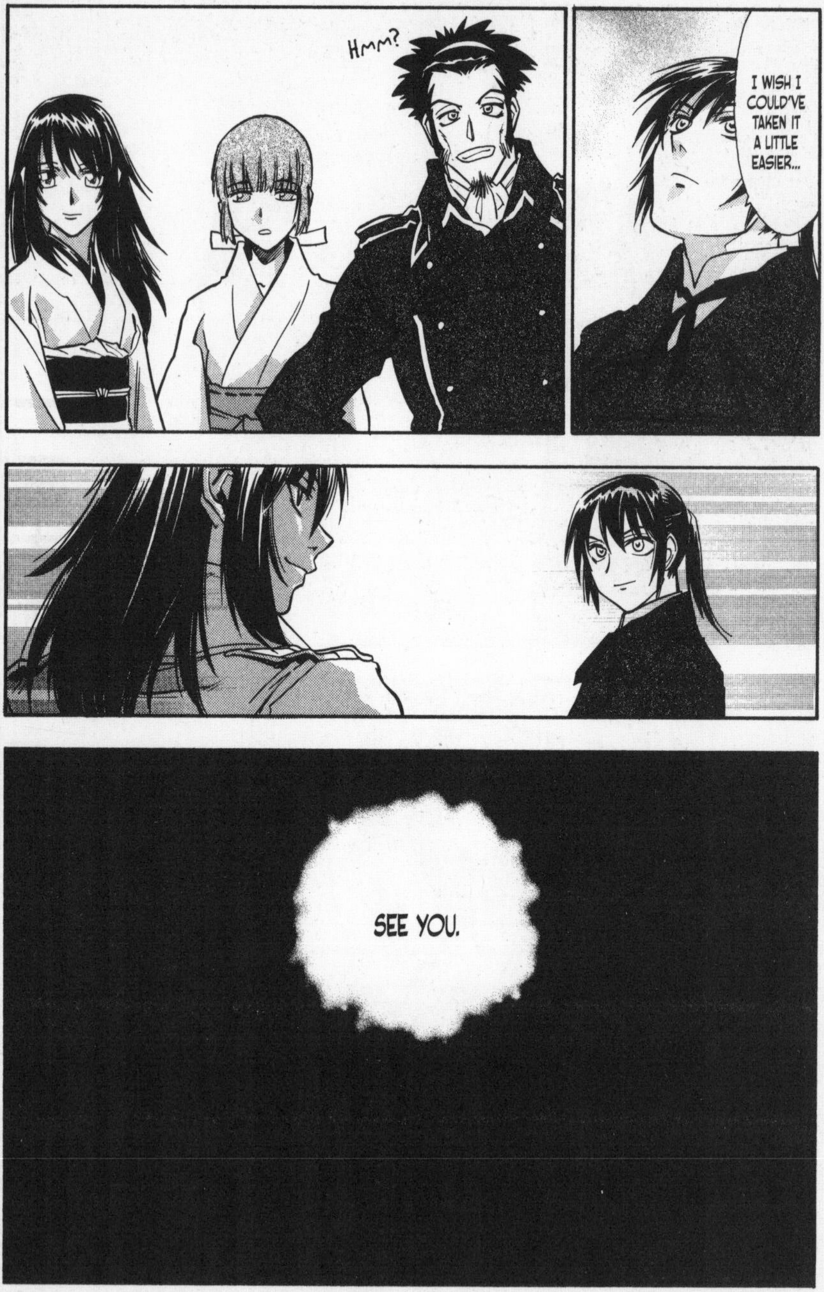
I WISH I COULD'VE TAKEN IT A LITTLE EASIER...
HMM?
SEE YOU.

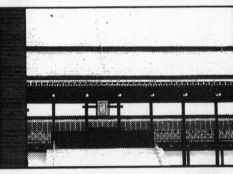

BUT,
REALLY...

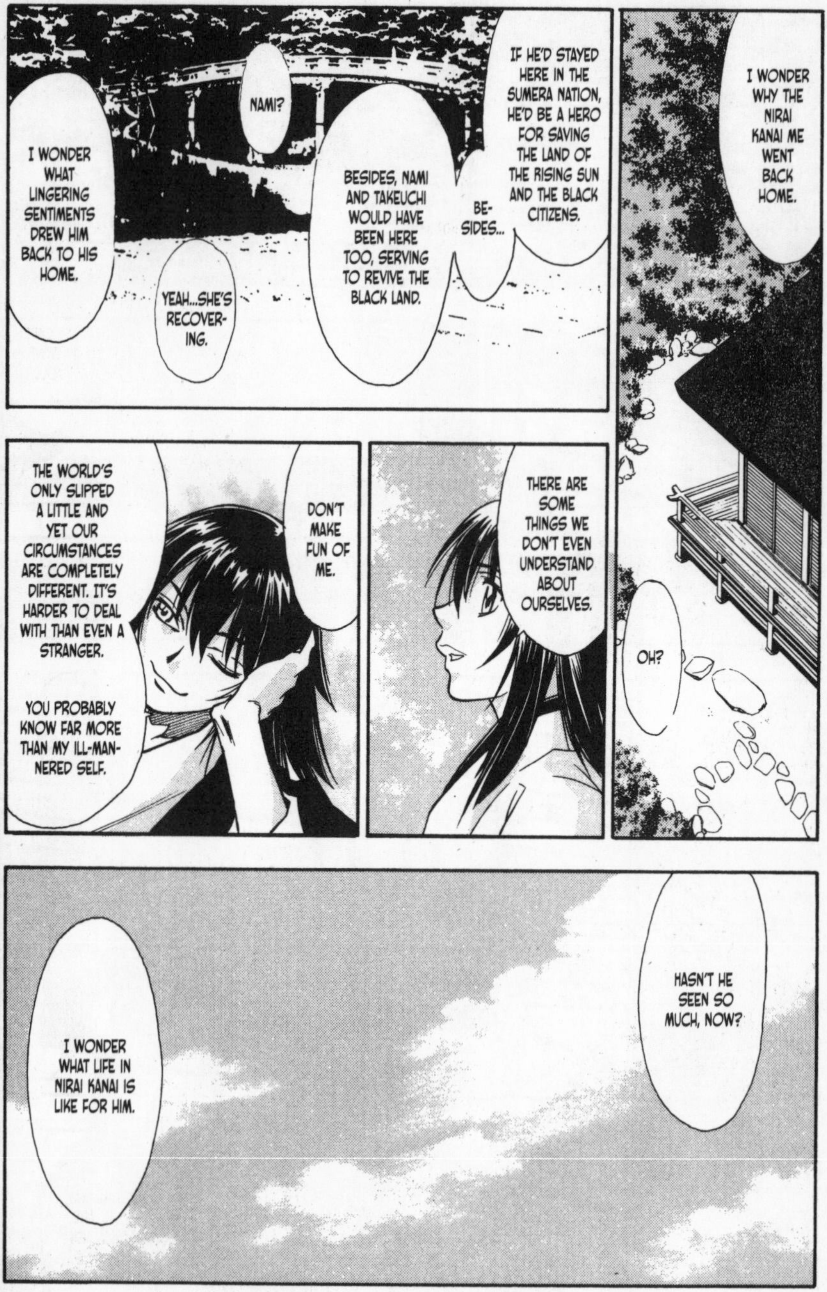
I WONDER WHY THE NIRAI KANAI ME WENT BACK HOME.
OH?
IF HE'D STAYED HERE IN THE SUMERA NATION, HE'D BE A HERO FOR SAVING THE LAND OF THE RISING SUN AND THE BLACK CITIZENS.
BE-SIDES...
BESIDES, NAMI AND TAKEUCHI WOULD HAVE BEEN HERE TOO, SERVING TO REVIVE THE BLACK LAND.
NAMI?
YEAH...SHE'S RECOVER-ING.
I WONDER WHAT LINGERING SENTIMENTS DREW HIM BACK TO HIS HOME.
THERE ARE SOME THINGS WE DON'T EVEN UNDERSTAND ABOUT OURSELVES.
DON'T MAKE FUN OF ME.
THE WORLD'S ONLY SLIPPED A LITTLE AND YET OUR CIRCUMSTANCES ARE COMPLETELY DIFFERENT. IT'S HARDER TO DEAL WITH THAN EVEN A STRANGER.
YOU PROBABLY KNOW FAR MORE THAN MY ILL-MAN-NERED SELF.
HASN'T HE SEEN SO MUCH, NOW?
I WONDER WHAT LIFE IN NIRAI KANAI IS LIKE FOR HIM.

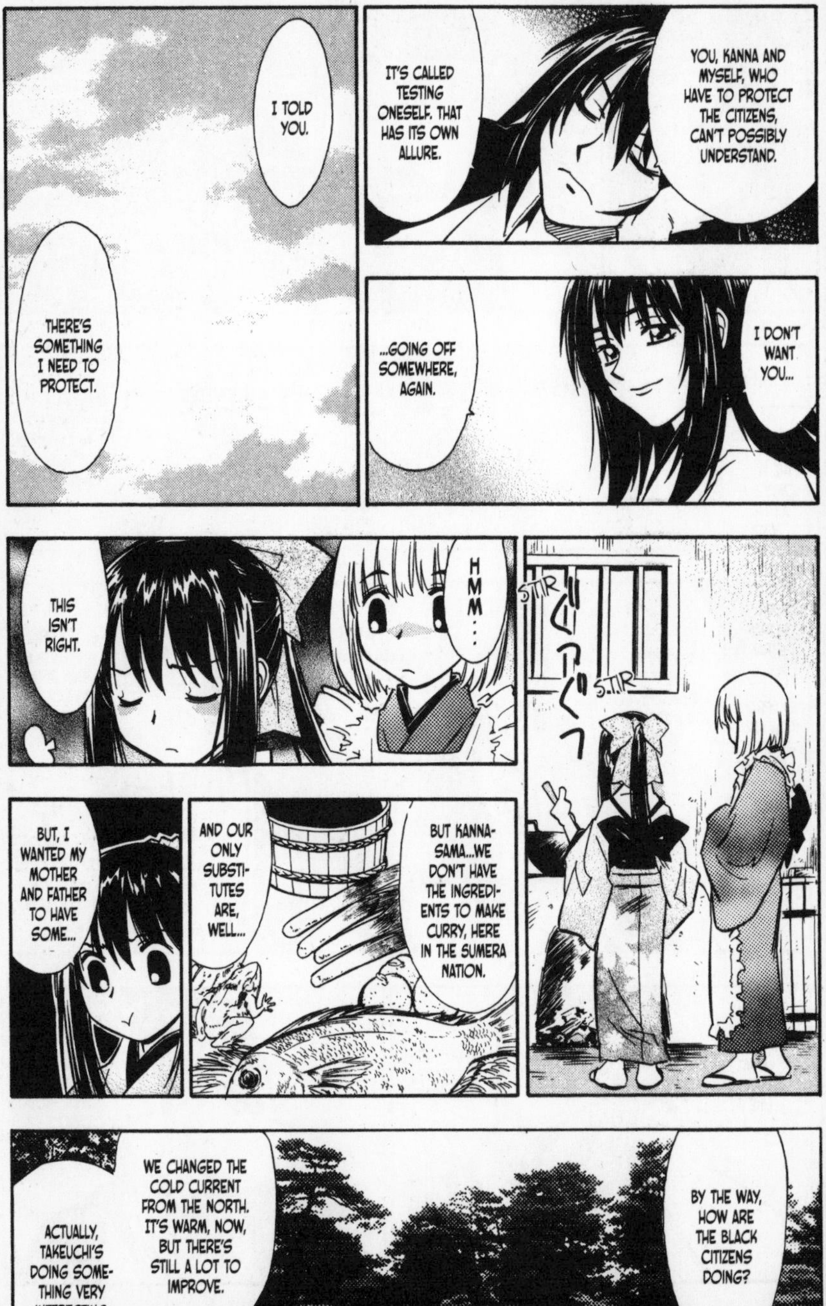
YOU, KANNA AND MYSELF, WHO HAVE TO PROTECT THE CITIZENS, CAN'T POSSIBLY UNDERSTAND.
IT'S CALLED TESTING ONESELF. THAT HAS ITS OWN ALLURE.
I DON'T WANT YOU...
...GOING OFF SOMEWHERE, AGAIN.
I TOLD YOU.
THERE'S SOMETHING I NEED TO PROTECT.
STIR
STIR
HMM...
THIS ISN'T RIGHT.
BUT KANNA-SAMA...WE DON'T HAVE THE INGREDIENTS TO MAKE CURRY, HERE IN THE SUMERA NATION.
AND OUR ONLY SUBSTITUTES ARE, WELL...
BUT, I WANTED MY MOTHER AND FATHER TO HAVE SOME...
BY THE WAY, HOW ARE THE BLACK CITIZENS DOING?
WE CHANGED THE COLD CURRENT FROM THE NORTH. IT'S WARM, NOW, BUT THERE'S STILL A LOT TO IMPROVE.
ACTUALLY, TAKEUCHI'S DOING SOMETHING VERY INTERESTING.

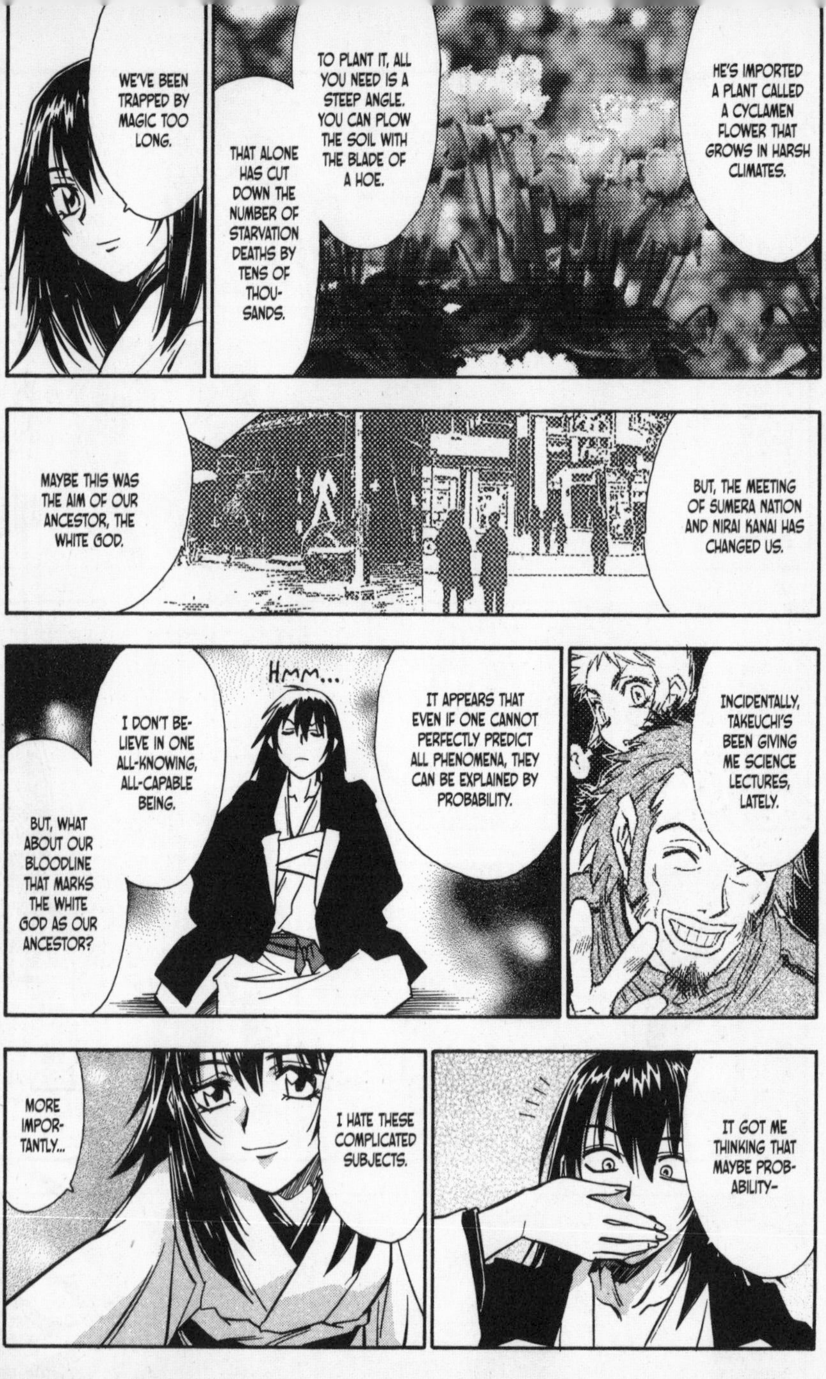
HE'S IMPORTED A PLANT CALLED A CYCLAMEN FLOWER THAT GROWS IN HARSH CLIMATES.
TO PLANT IT, ALL YOU NEED IS A STEEP ANGLE. YOU CAN PLOW THE SOIL WITH THE BLADE OF A HOE.
THAT ALONE HAS CUT DOWN THE NUMBER OF STARVATION DEATHS BY TENS OF THOU-SANDS.
WE'VE BEEN TRAPPED BY MAGIC TOO LONG.
BUT, THE MEETING OF SUMERA NATION AND NIRAI KANAI HAS CHANGED US.
MAYBE THIS WAS THE AIM OF OUR ANCESTOR, THE WHITE GOD.
INCIDENTALLY, TAKEUCHI'S BEEN GIVING ME SCIENCE LECTURES, LATELY.
IT APPEARS THAT EVEN IF ONE CANNOT PERFECTLY PREDICT ALL PHENOMENA, THEY CAN BE EXPLAINED BY PROBABILITY.
HMM...
I DON'T BE-LIEVE IN ONE ALL-KNOWING, ALL-CAPABLE BEING.
BUT, WHAT ABOUT OUR BLOODLINE THAT MARKS THE WHITE GOD AS OUR ANCESTOR?
IT GOT ME THINKING THAT MAYBE PROB-ABILITY-
I HATE THESE COMPLICATED SUBJECTS.
MORE IMPOR-TANTLY...

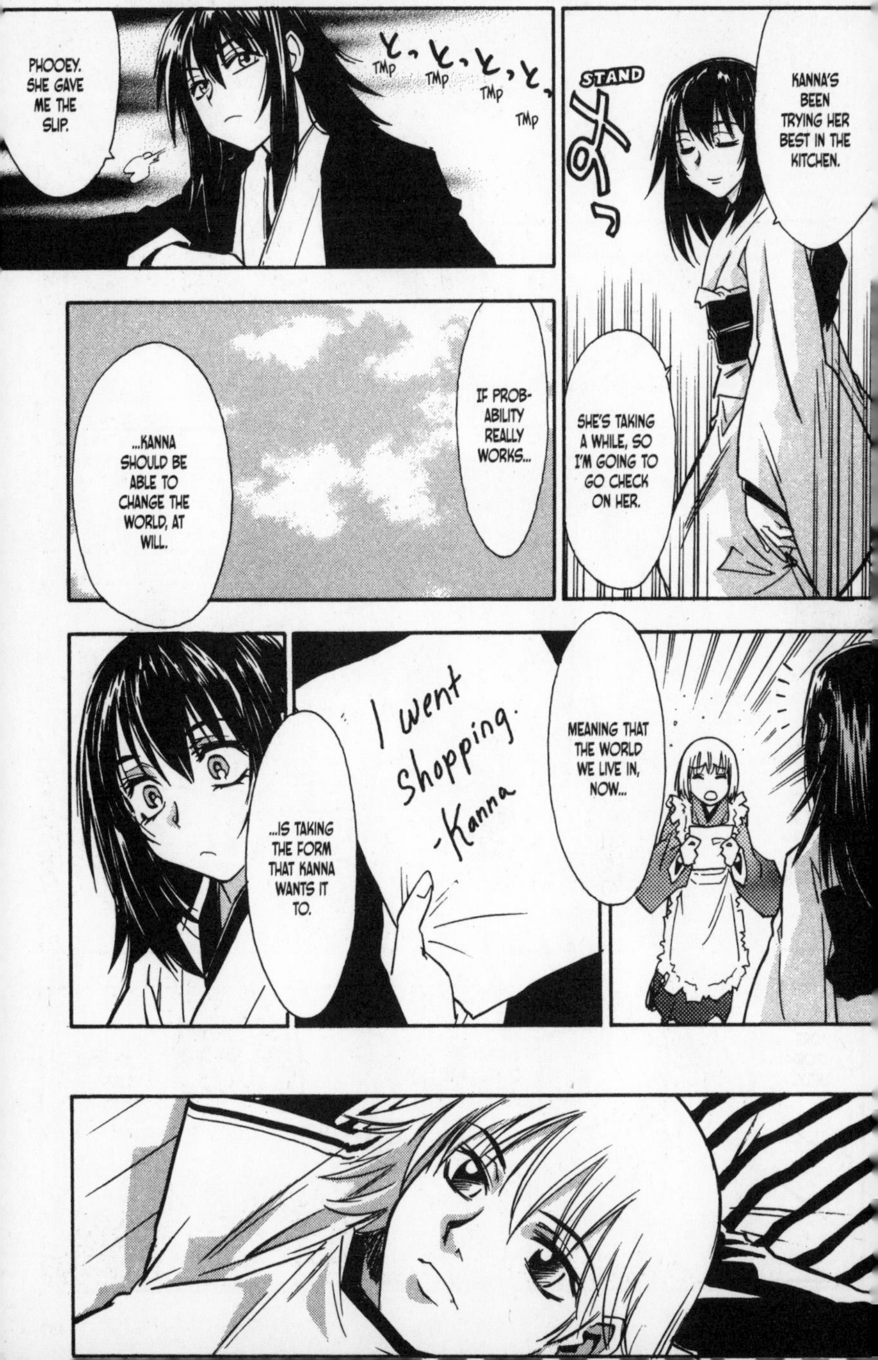
KANNA'S BEEN TRYING HER BEST IN THE KITCHEN.
STAND
SHE'S TAKING A WHILE, SO I'M GOING TO GO CHECK ON HER.
PHOOEY. SHE GAVE ME THE SLIP.
TMp TMp TMp TMp
IF PROB-ABILITY REALLY WORKS...
...KANNA SHOULD BE ABLE TO CHANGE THE WORLD, AT WILL.
MEANING THAT THE WORLD WE LIVE IN, NOW...
I went shopping. -Kanna
...IS TAKING THE FORM THAT KANNA WANTS IT TO.

WHAT WAS THE WORLD THAT THE WHITE GOD WANTED?
COSPLAY STORE HAS NEW OWNER
HOW IS MISS NAMI'S YOUNGER SISTER DOING? AS FOR MYSELF, THIS IS WHAT'S BEEN GOING ON IN MY LIFE.
ANIMEZOO
TAKEUCHI AND TAKEUCHI
OH, WELL...
I DON'T KNOW, BUT AT SOME POINT...
...I SUP-POSE IT SHOULD BE STARTING SOON.
ALL THE THINGS I LEFT BEHIND...
TMP
TMP

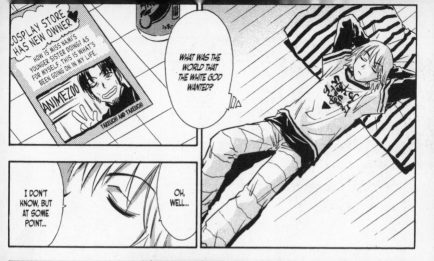

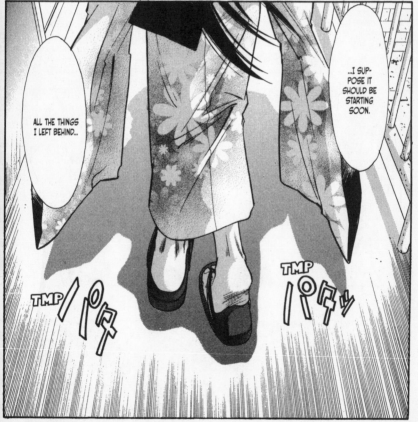

Chapter 40 : OVER

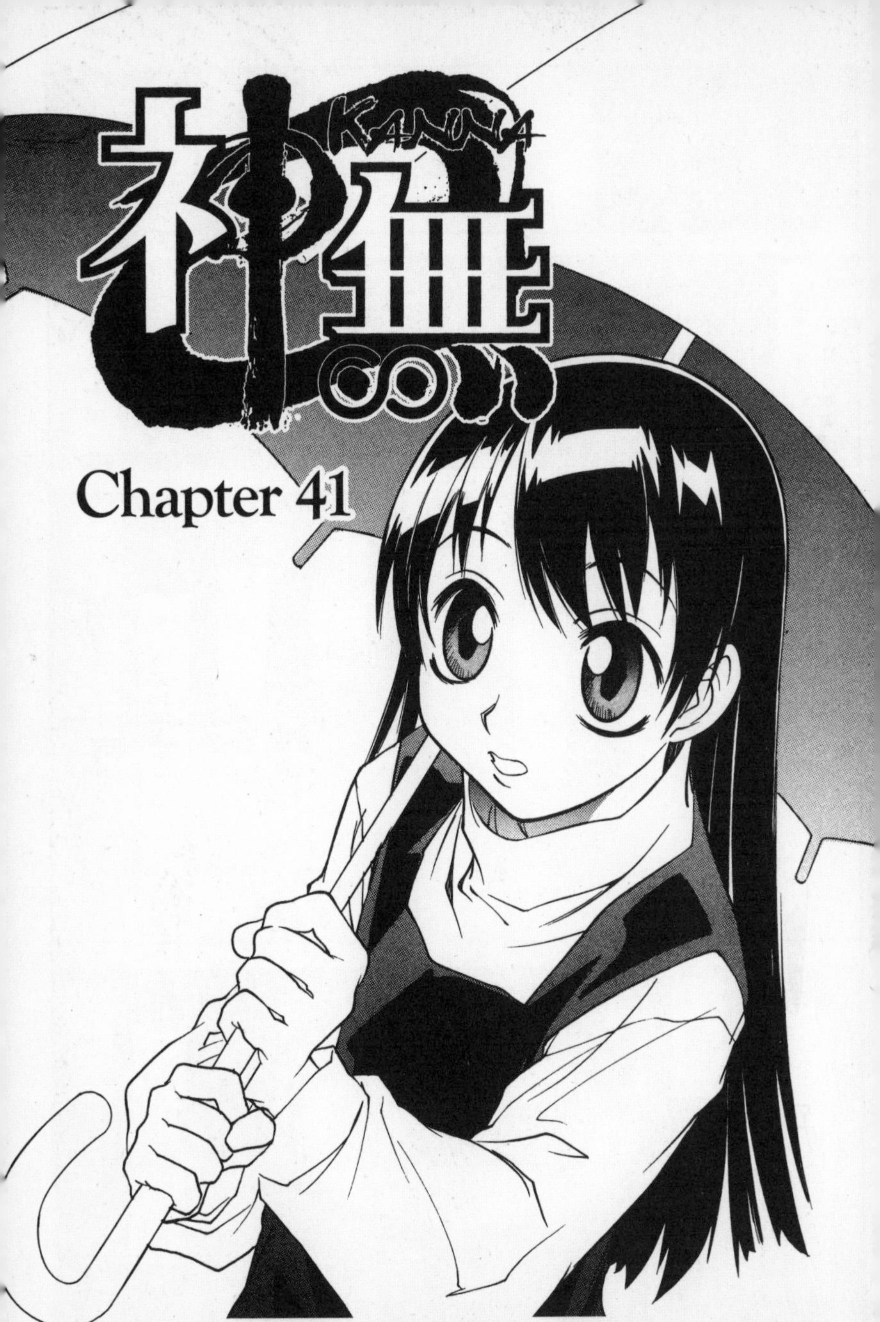
神無
KANNA

Chapter 41

This story is the last chapter written before the end of the main story. When it was serialized in the magazine, it was arranged as Kagura's dream, and so in the compilation of the bound comic, it was corrected to fit its original form.

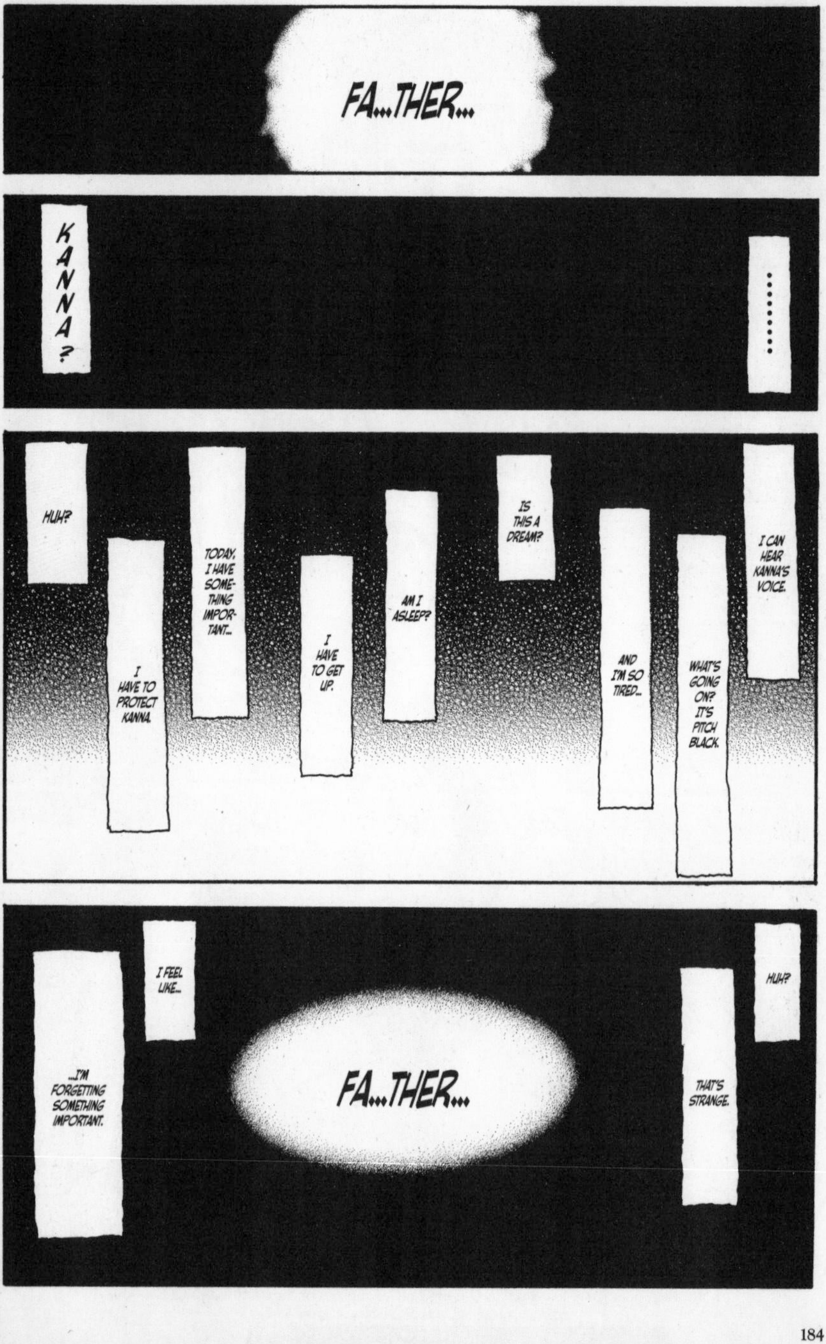
FA...THER...
....
KANNA?
I CAN HEAR KANNA'S VOICE.
WHAT'S GOING ON? IT'S PITCH BLACK.
AND I'M SO TIRED...
IS THIS A DREAM?
AM I ASLEEP?
I HAVE TO GET UP.
TODAY, I HAVE SOME-THING IMPOR-TANT...
I HAVE TO PROTECT KANNA.
HUH?
HUH?
THAT'S STRANGE.
FA...THER...
I FEEL LIKE...
...I'M FORGETTING SOMETHING IMPORTANT.

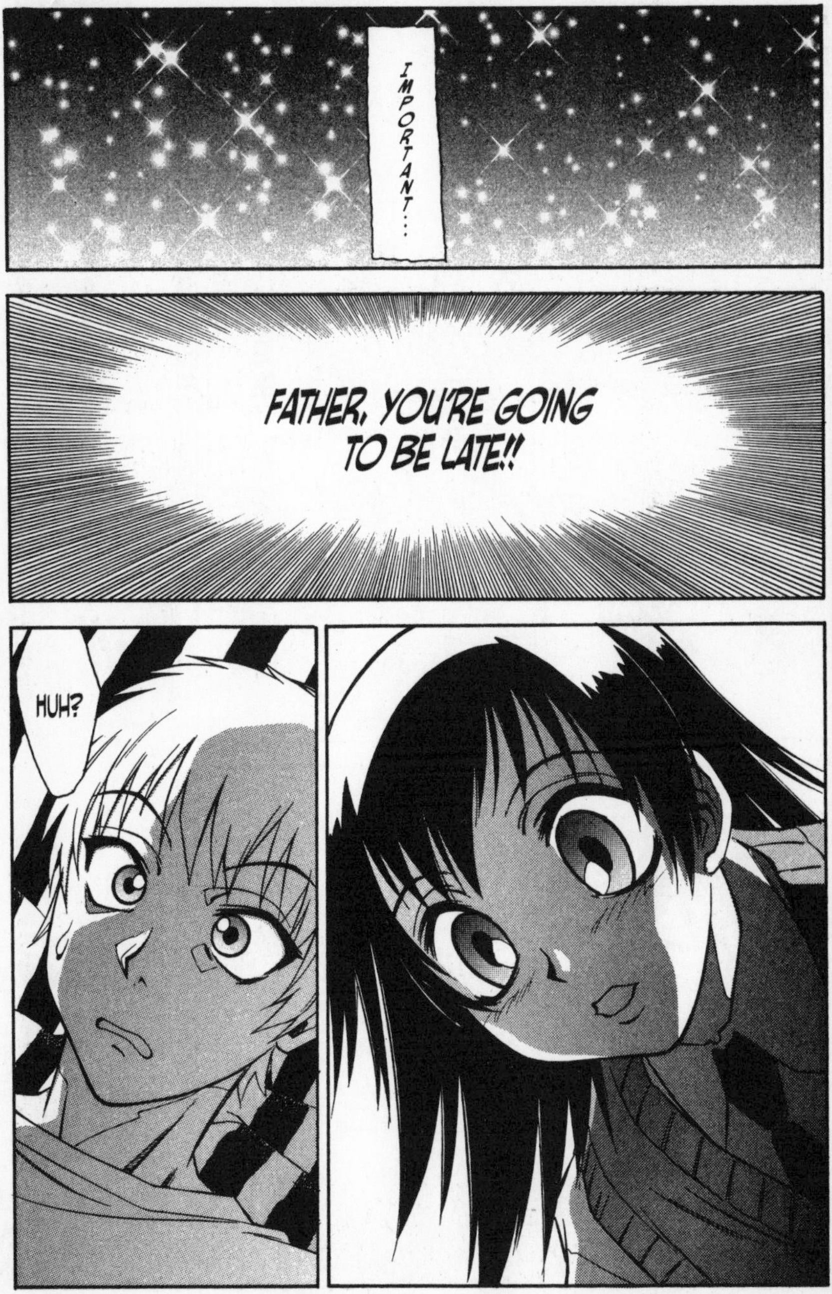
IMPORTANT...
FATHER, YOU'RE GOING TO BE LATE!!
HUH?

SMECK

UWAAAAH!!

!!!

CRMBL

FUNK IS BACK

SHOVE

EEK!!

WAH!

SPEAK-ING OF WHICH, SHE LOOKS LIKE MIKOTO.

I FEEL LIKE I KNOW HER...

WH... WHO IS THIS GIRL?

WHAT'S SHE DOING IN MY ROOM?

HUH??

HMM?

AH!♡

BUT...YOU SUDDENLY...

I'M SORRY.

FATHER.

HUH...?

KANNA?

KANNA?

WHAAAT!?

FATHER!

YEAH?

?

IS SOME-THING WRONG?

WAIT... HOLD ON A MINUTE.

IS THIS SOME KIND OF SPELL? IT WAS SO BLACK BEFORE...LET'S SEE...

THAT'S SO WEIRD... I COULD'VE SWORN SHE WAS STILL TINY...

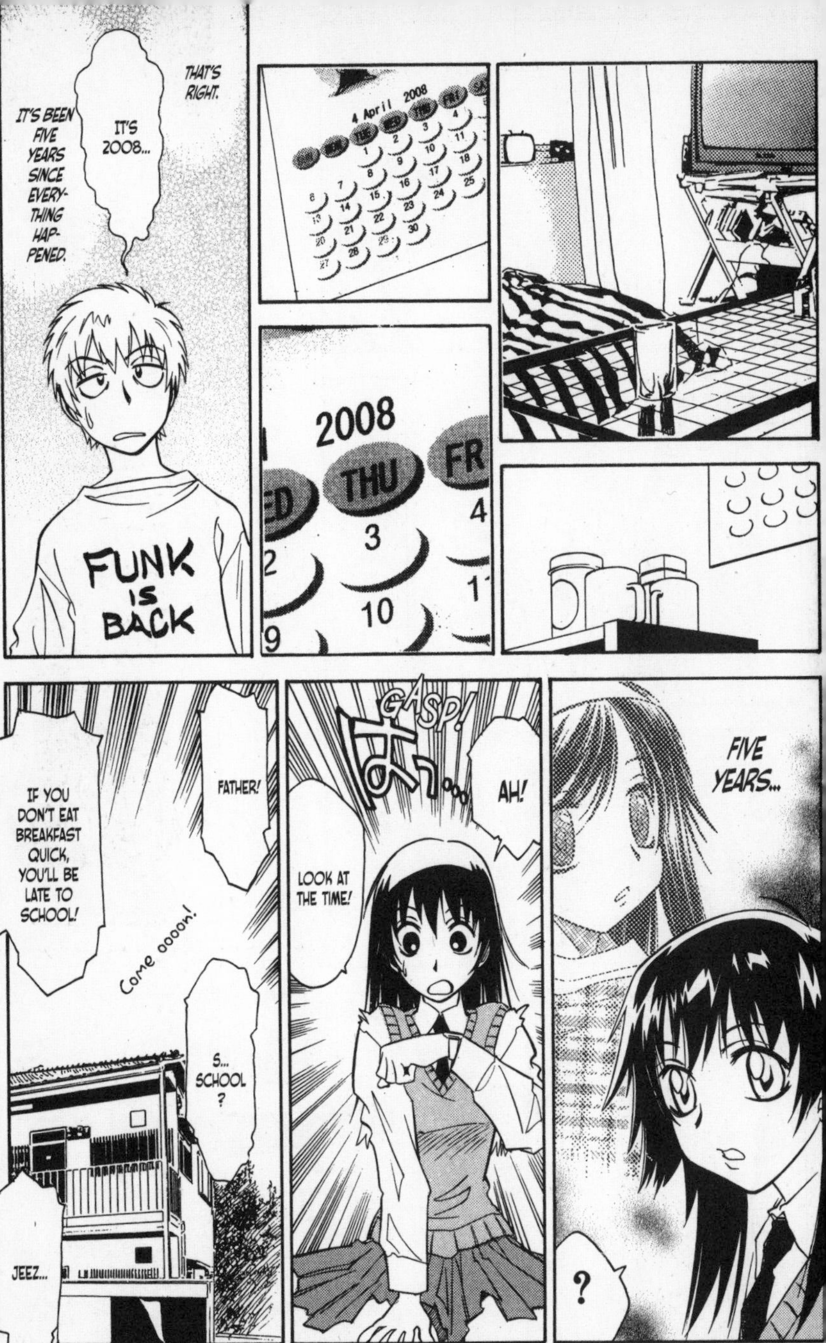
4 April 2008
2008
THU
THAT'S RIGHT.
IT'S 2008...
IT'S BEEN FIVE YEARS SINCE EVERYTHING HAPPENED.
FUNK IS BACK
FIVE YEARS...
?
GASP!
AH!
LOOK AT THE TIME!
FATHER!
IF YOU DON'T EAT BREAKFAST QUICK, YOU'LL BE LATE TO SCHOOL!
Come oooon!
S... SCHOOL?
JEEZ...

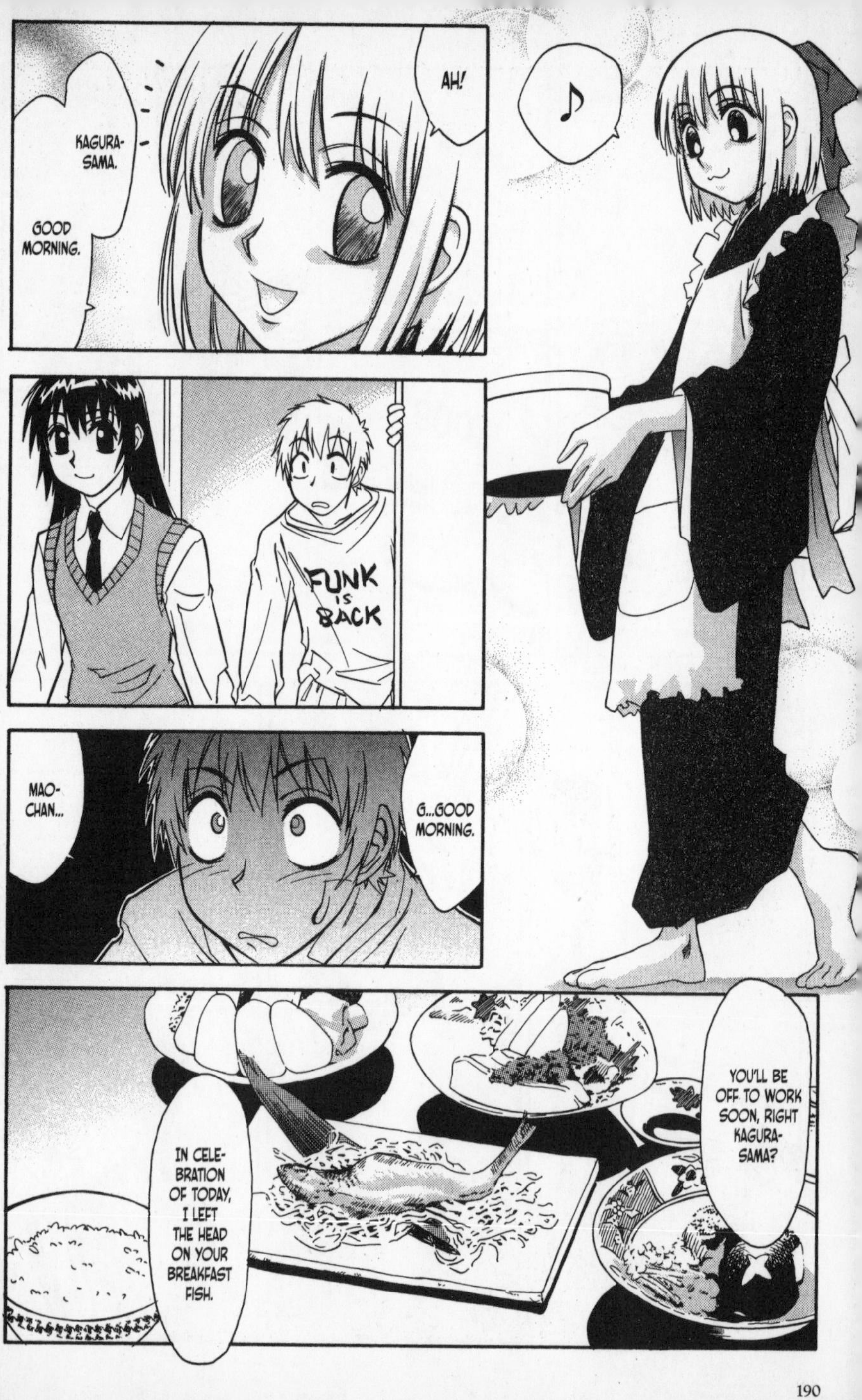
♪
AH!
KAGURA-SAMA.
GOOD MORNING.
G...GOOD MORNING.
MAO-CHAN...
YOU'LL BE OFF TO WORK SOON, RIGHT KAGURA-SAMA?
IN CELEBRATION OF TODAY, I LEFT THE HEAD ON YOUR BREAKFAST FISH.

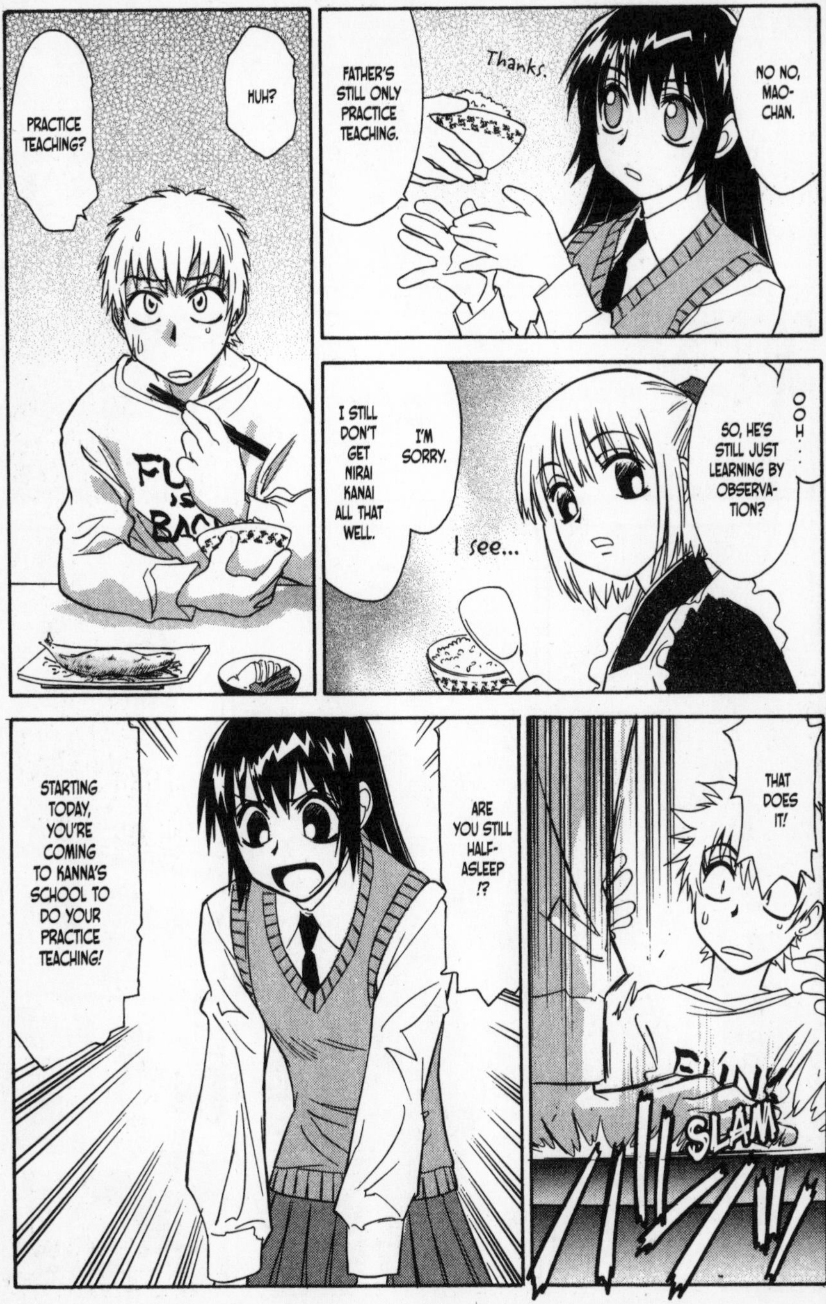
NO NO, MAO-CHAN.
Thanks.
FATHER'S STILL ONLY PRACTICE TEACHING.
OOH...
SO, HE'S STILL JUST LEARNING BY OBSERVATION?
I see...
I'M SORRY.
I STILL DON'T GET NIRAI KANAI ALL THAT WELL.
HUH?
PRACTICE TEACHING?
THAT DOES IT!
SLAM
ARE YOU STILL HALF-ASLEEP!?
STARTING TODAY, YOU'RE COMING TO KANNA'S SCHOOL TO DO YOUR PRACTICE TEACHING!

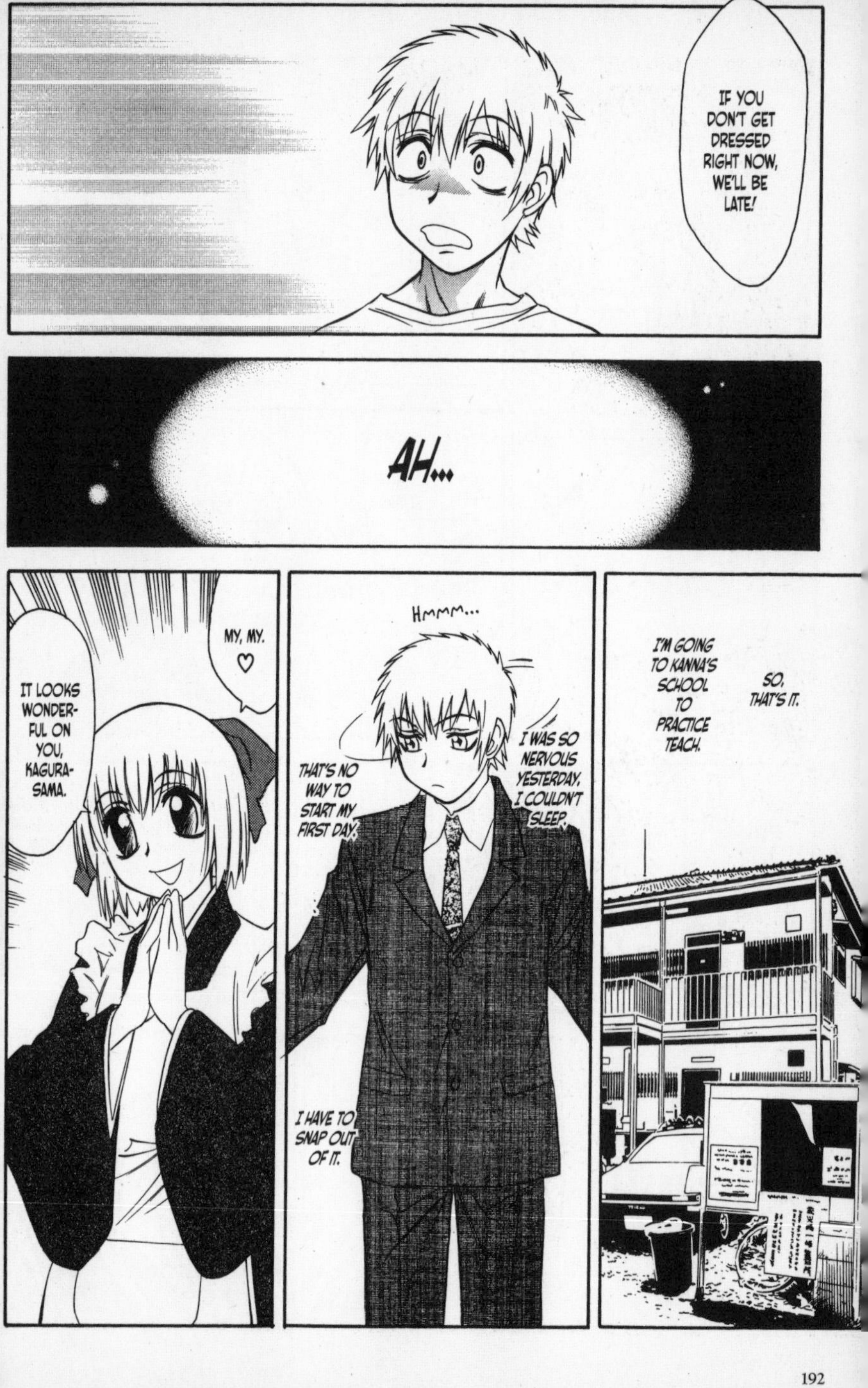
IF YOU DON'T GET DRESSED RIGHT NOW, WE'LL BE LATE!
AH...
SO, THAT'S IT.
I'M GOING TO KANNA'S SCHOOL TO PRACTICE TEACH.
HMMM...
I WAS SO NERVOUS YESTERDAY, I COULDN'T SLEEP.
THAT'S NO WAY TO START MY FIRST DAY.
I HAVE TO SNAP OUT OF IT.
MY, MY. ♡
IT LOOKS WONDER-FUL ON YOU, KAGURA-SAMA.

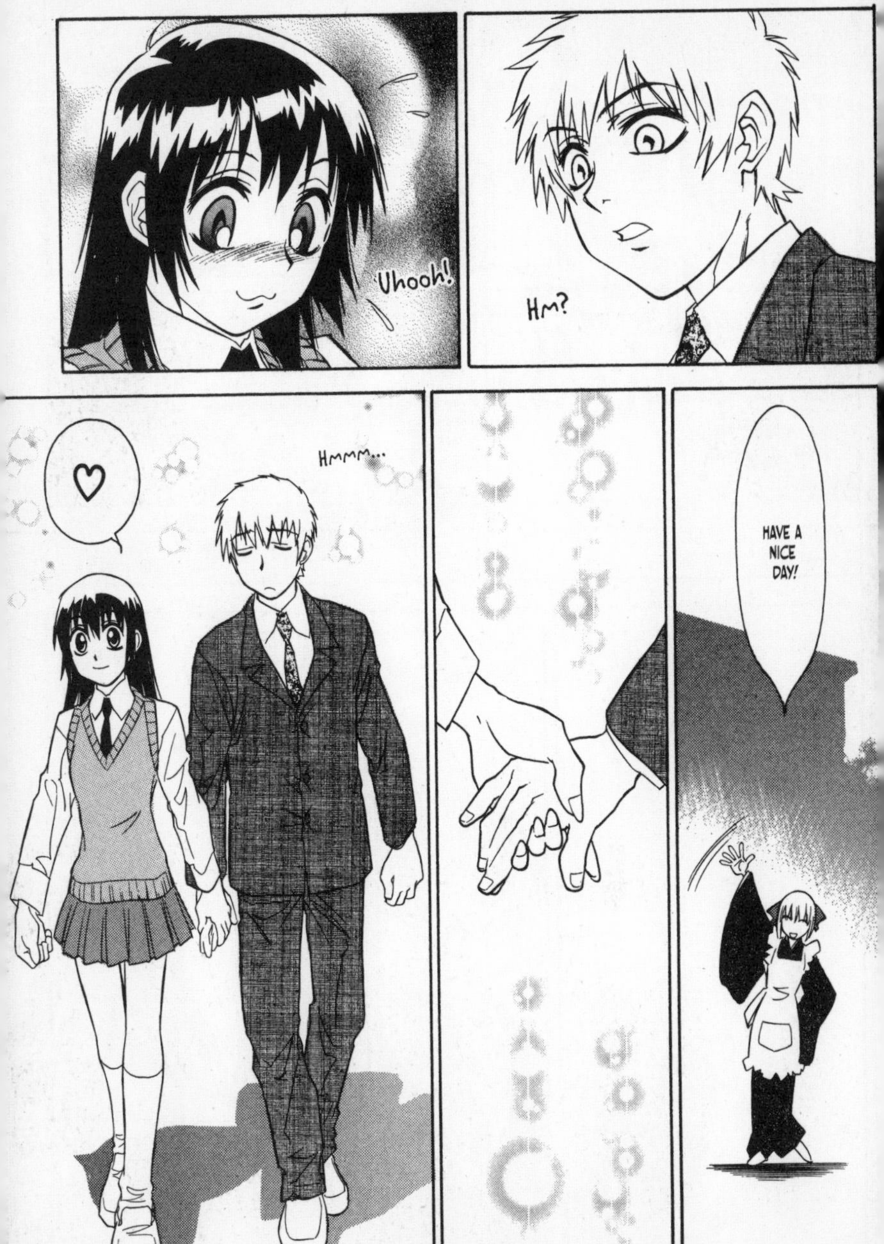
Hm?
Uhooh!
HAVE A NICE DAY!
Hmmm...
Empty-handed

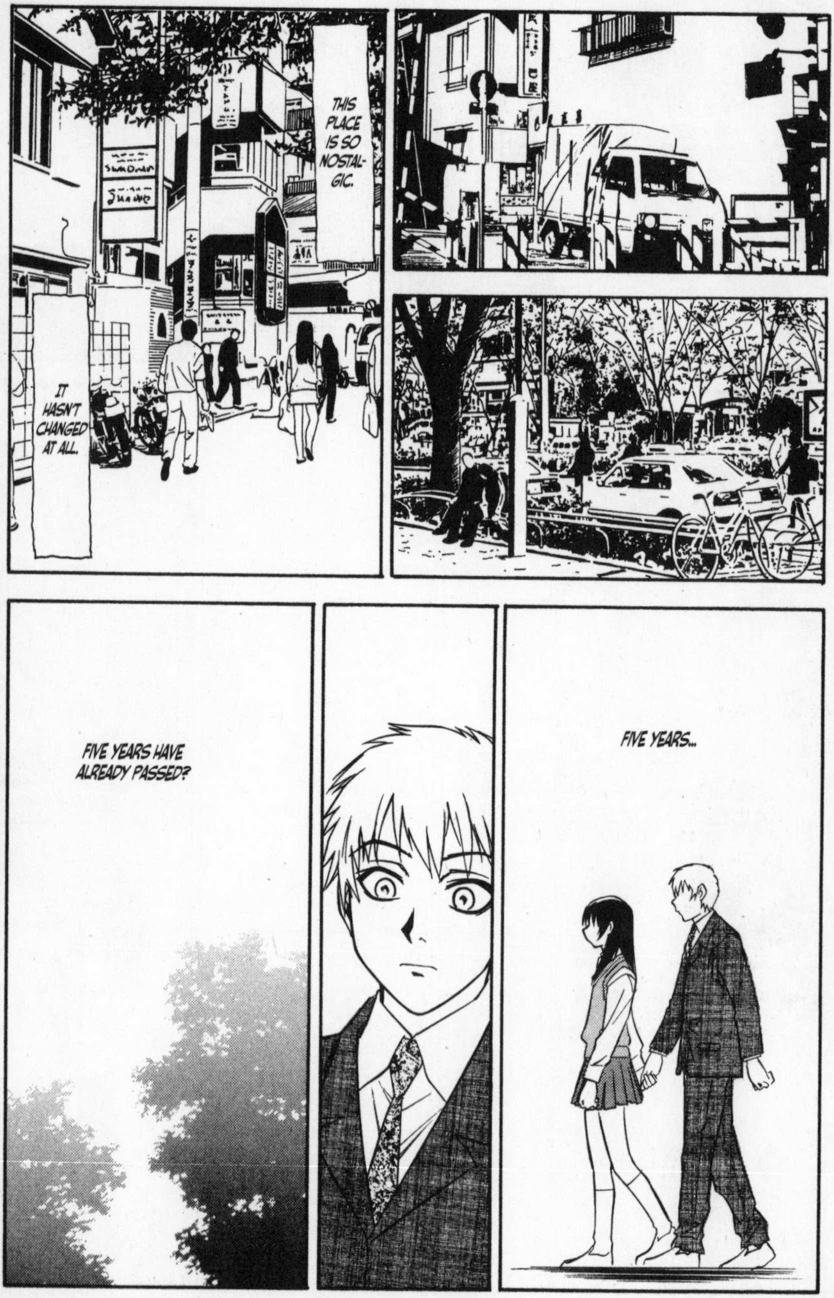
THIS PLACE IS SO NOSTAL-GIC.
IT HASN'T CHANGED AT ALL.
FIVE YEARS...
FIVE YEARS HAVE ALREADY PASSED?

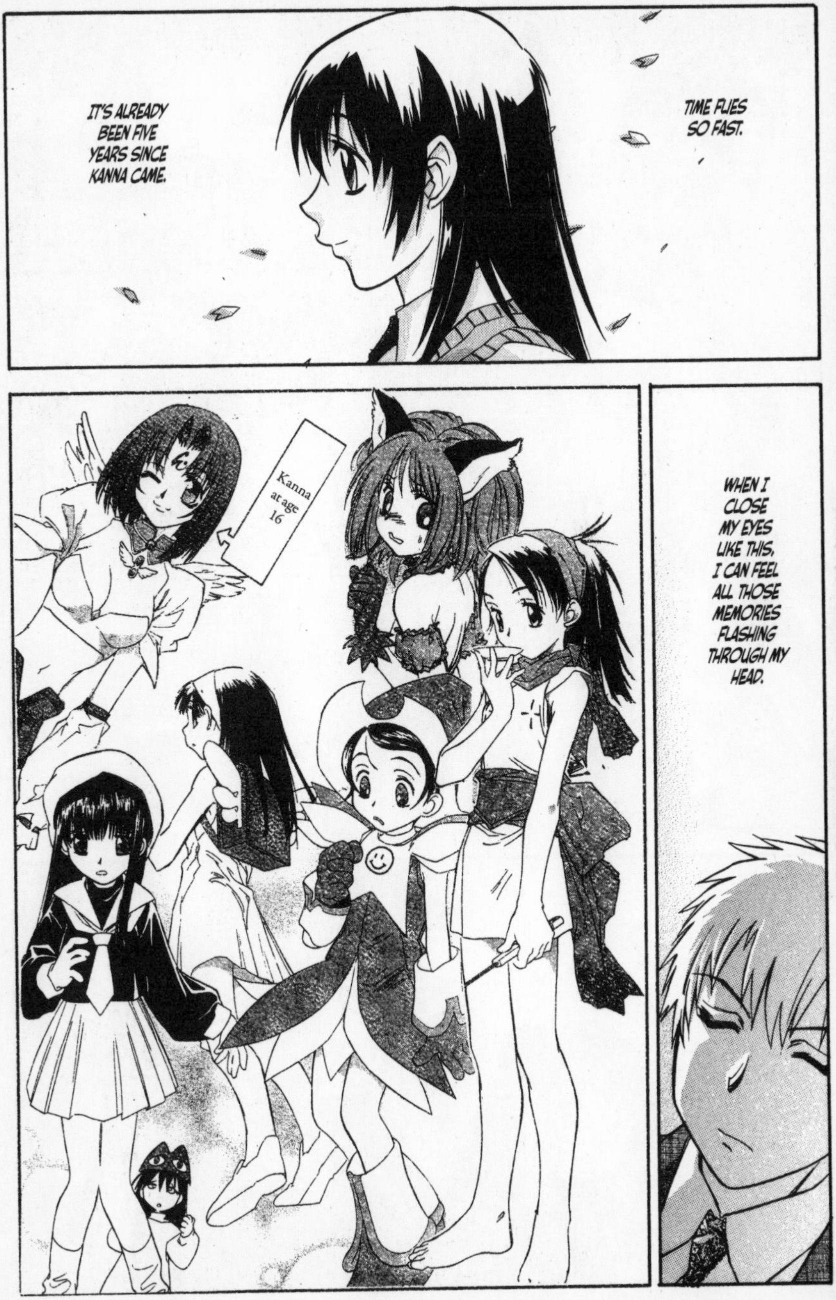
TIME FLIES SO FAST.
IT'S ALREADY BEEN FIVE YEARS SINCE KANNA CAME.
WHEN I CLOSE MY EYES LIKE THIS, I CAN FEEL ALL THOSE MEMORIES FLASHING THROUGH MY HEAD.
Kanna at age 16

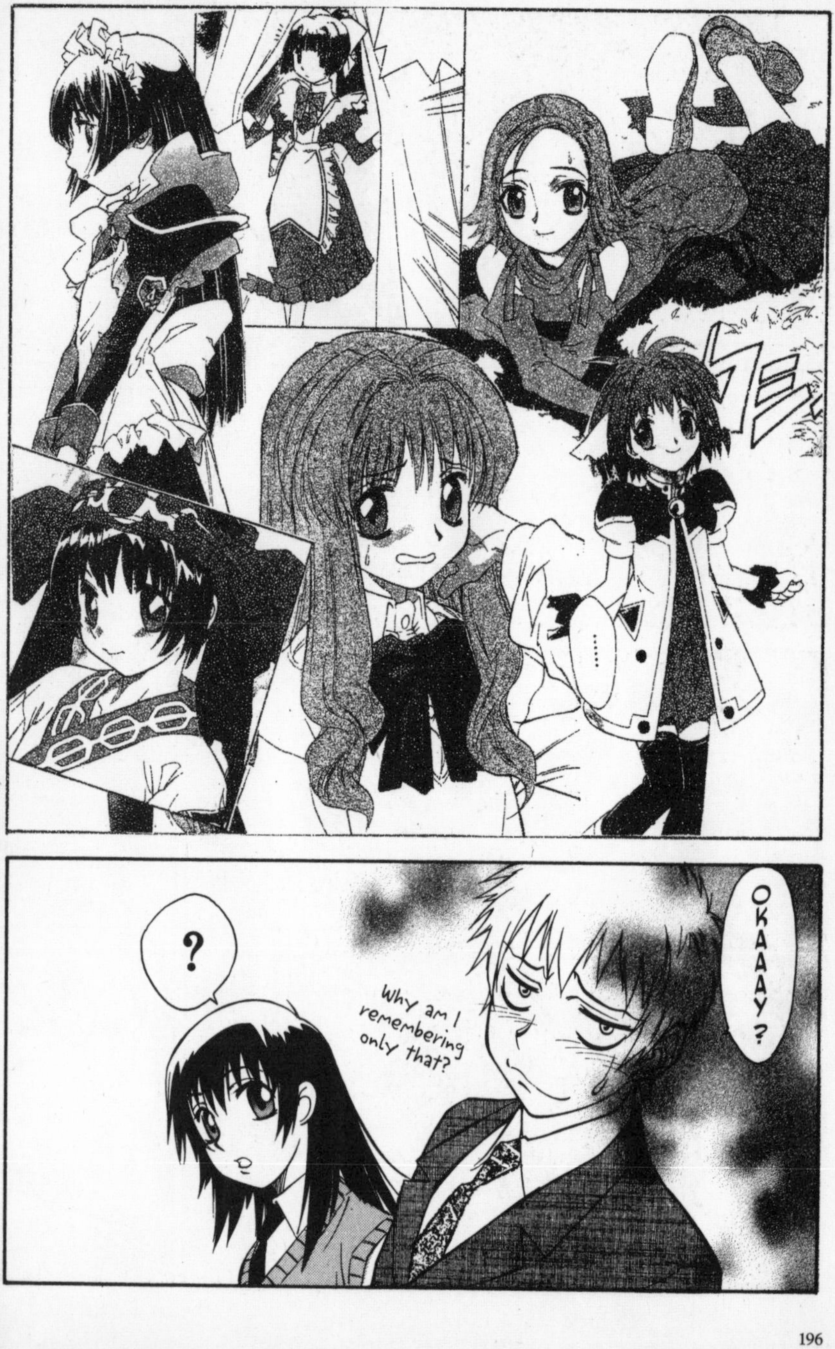
......
OKAAAY?
Why am I remembering only that?
?

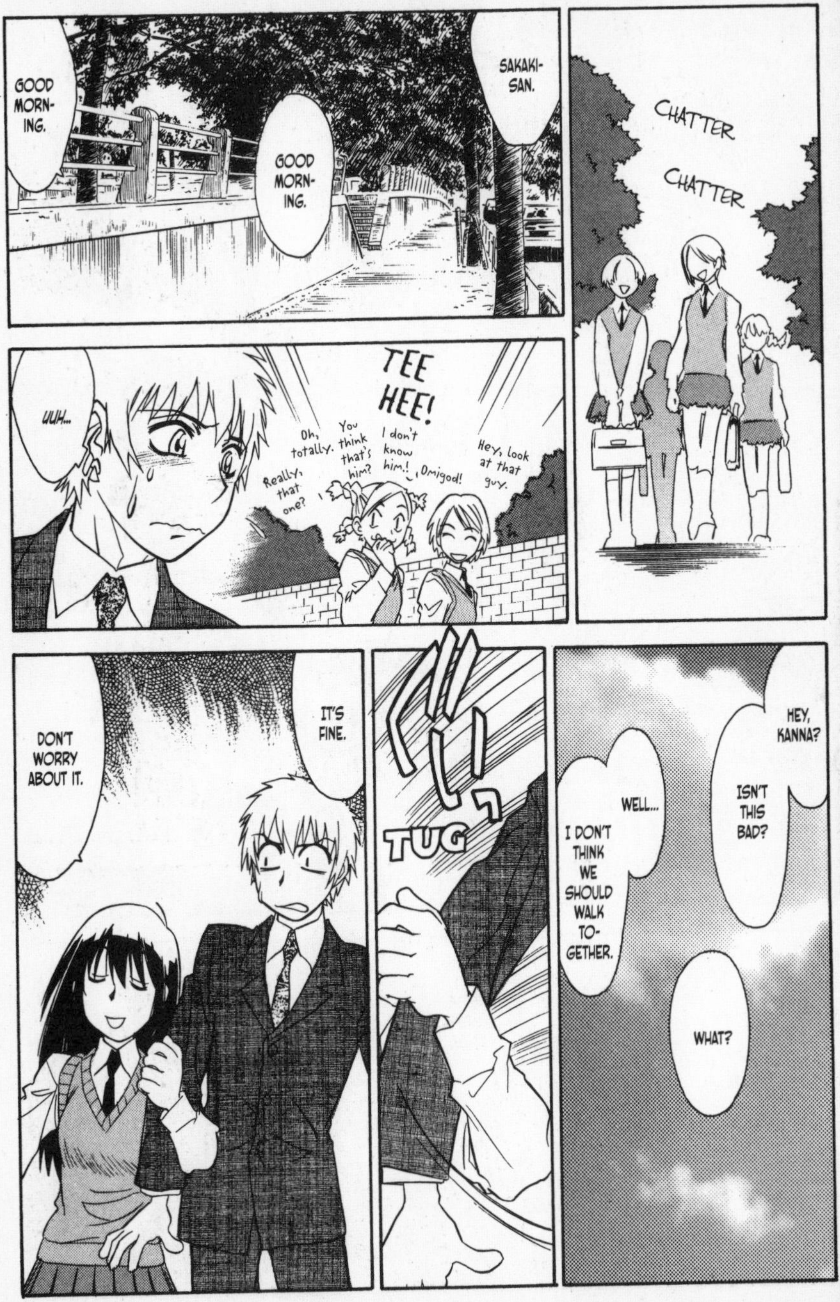
CHATTER
CHATTER
SAKAKI-SAN.
GOOD MORNING.
GOOD MORNING.
TEE HEE!
Hey, look at that guy.
I don't know him!
Omigod!
You think that's him?
Oh, totally.
Really, that one?
UUH...
HEY, KANNA?
ISN'T THIS BAD?
WELL...
I DON'T THINK WE SHOULD WALK TOGETHER.
WHAT?
TUG
IT'S FINE.
DON'T WORRY ABOUT IT.

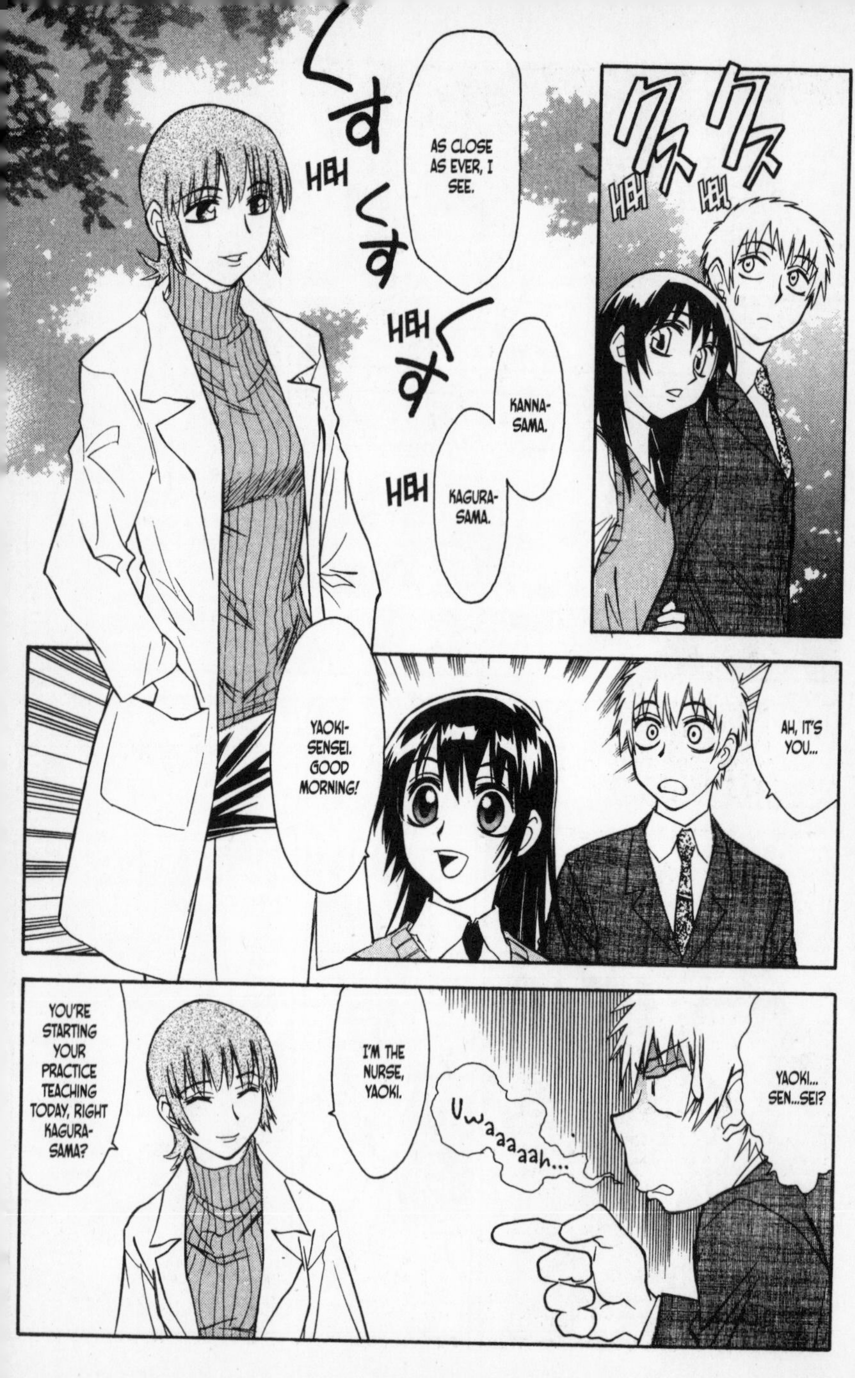

クスクス
HEH HEH
HEH
くすくす
HEH
AS CLOSE AS EVER, I SEE.
くすくす
HEH
KANNA-SAMA.
HEH
KAGURA-SAMA.
AH, IT'S YOU...
YAOKI-SENSEI. GOOD MORNING!
YAOKI... SEN...SEI?
Uwaaaaah...
I'M THE NURSE, YAOKI.
YOU'RE STARTING YOUR PRACTICE TEACHING TODAY, RIGHT KAGURA-SAMA?

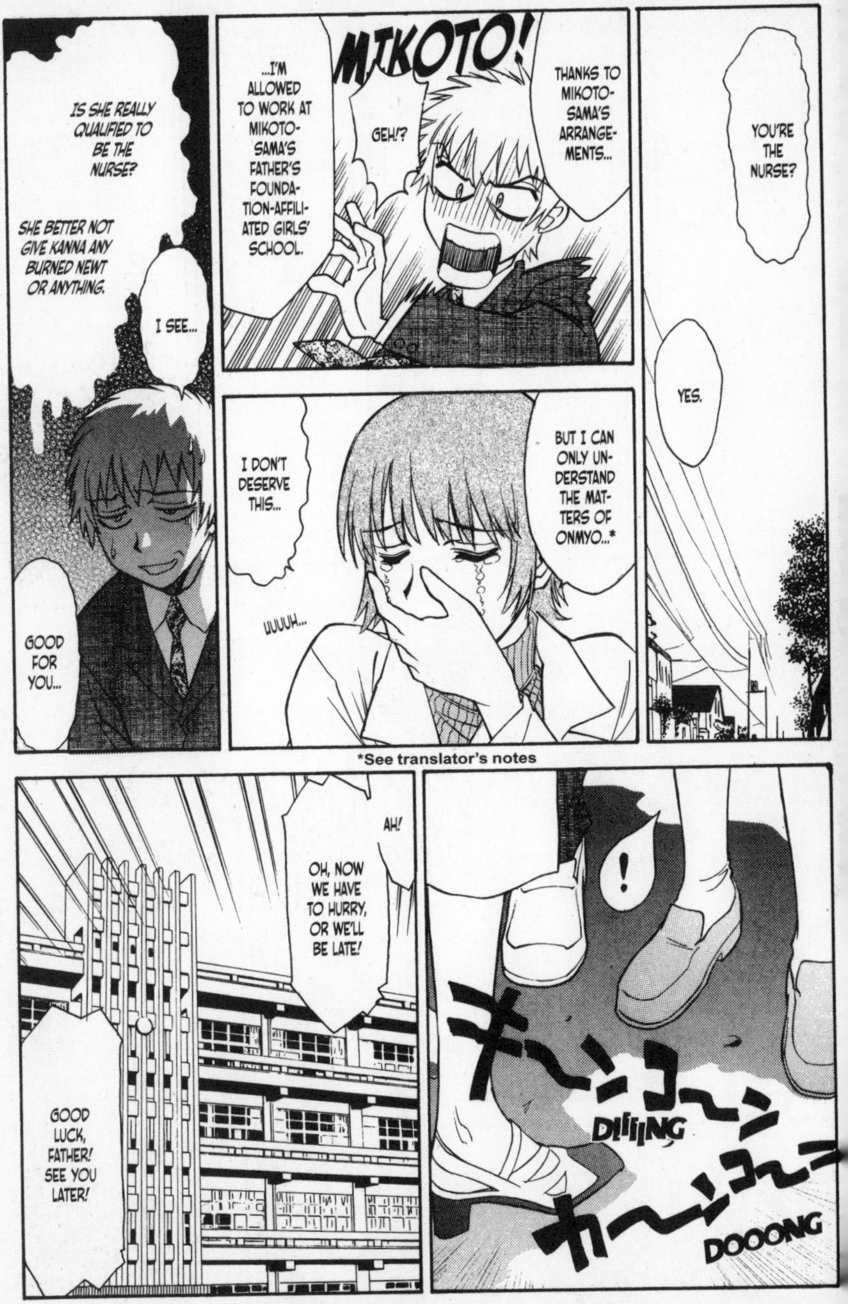
YOU'RE THE NURSE?
YES.
THANKS TO MIKOTO-SAMA'S ARRANGEMENTS...
MIKOTO!
GEH!?
...I'M ALLOWED TO WORK AT MIKOTO-SAMA'S FATHER'S FOUNDATION-AFFILIATED GIRLS' SCHOOL.
BUT I CAN ONLY UNDERSTAND THE MATTERS OF ONMYO...*
I DON'T DESERVE THIS...
UUUUH...
IS SHE REALLY QUALIFIED TO BE THE NURSE?
SHE BETTER NOT GIVE KANNA ANY BURNED NEWT OR ANYTHING.
I SEE...
GOOD FOR YOU...
!
DIIIING
DOOONG
AH!
OH, NOW WE HAVE TO HURRY, OR WE'LL BE LATE!
GOOD LUCK, FATHER! SEE YOU LATER!

*See translator's notes

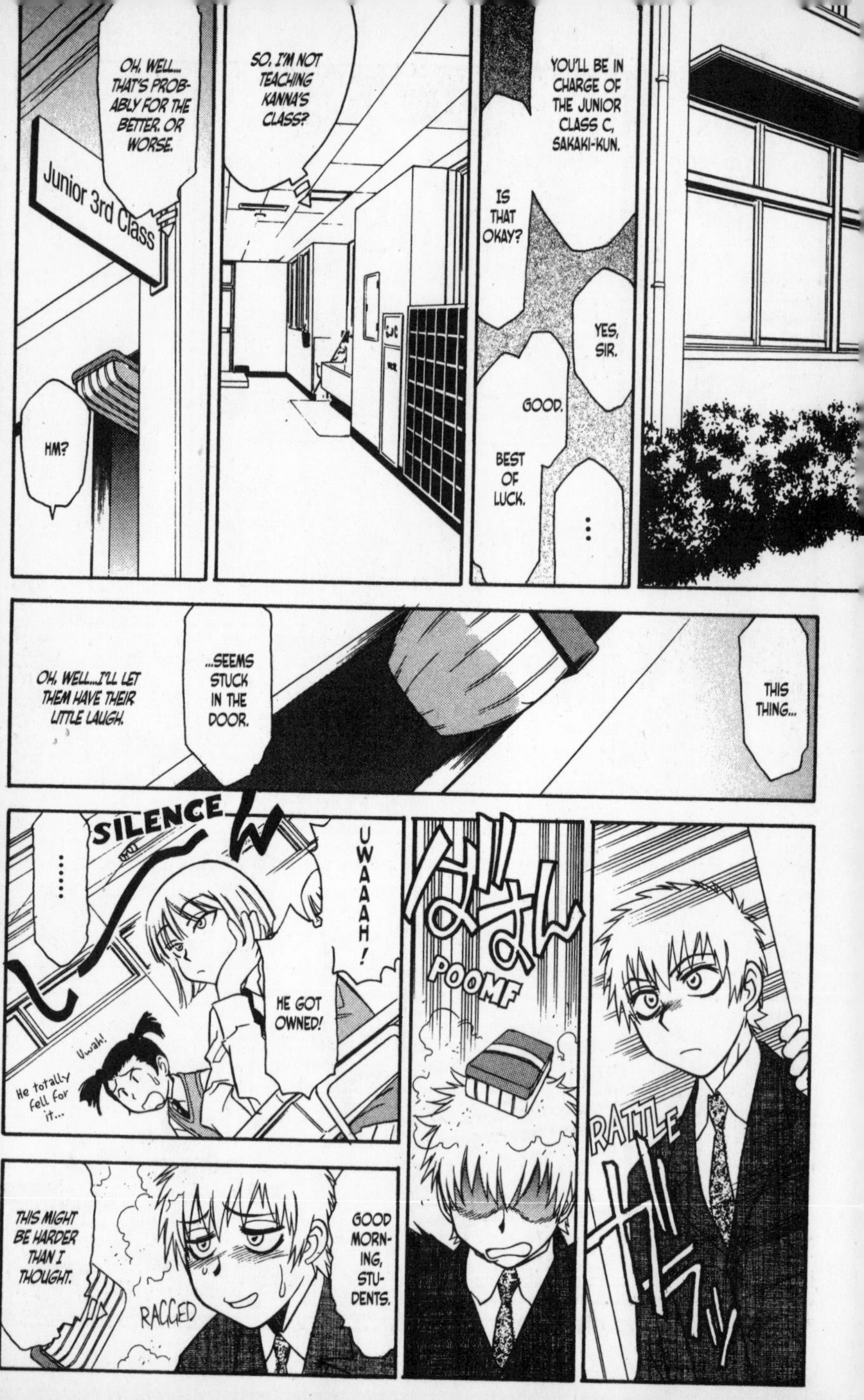
YOU'LL BE IN CHARGE OF THE JUNIOR CLASS C, SAKAKI-KUN.
IS THAT OKAY?
YES, SIR.
GOOD.
BEST OF LUCK.
...
SO, I'M NOT TEACHING KANNA'S CLASS?
OH, WELL... THAT'S PROB-ABLY FOR THE BETTER. OR WORSE.
Junior 3rd Class
HM?
THIS THING...
...SEEMS STUCK IN THE DOOR.
OH, WELL...I'LL LET THEM HAVE THEIR LITTLE LAUGH.
RATTLE
POOMF
SILENCE
......
UWAAAAH!
HE GOT OWNED!
Uwah!
He totally fell for it...
GOOD MORN-ING, STU-DENTS.
THIS MIGHT BE HARDER THAN I THOUGHT.
RAGGED

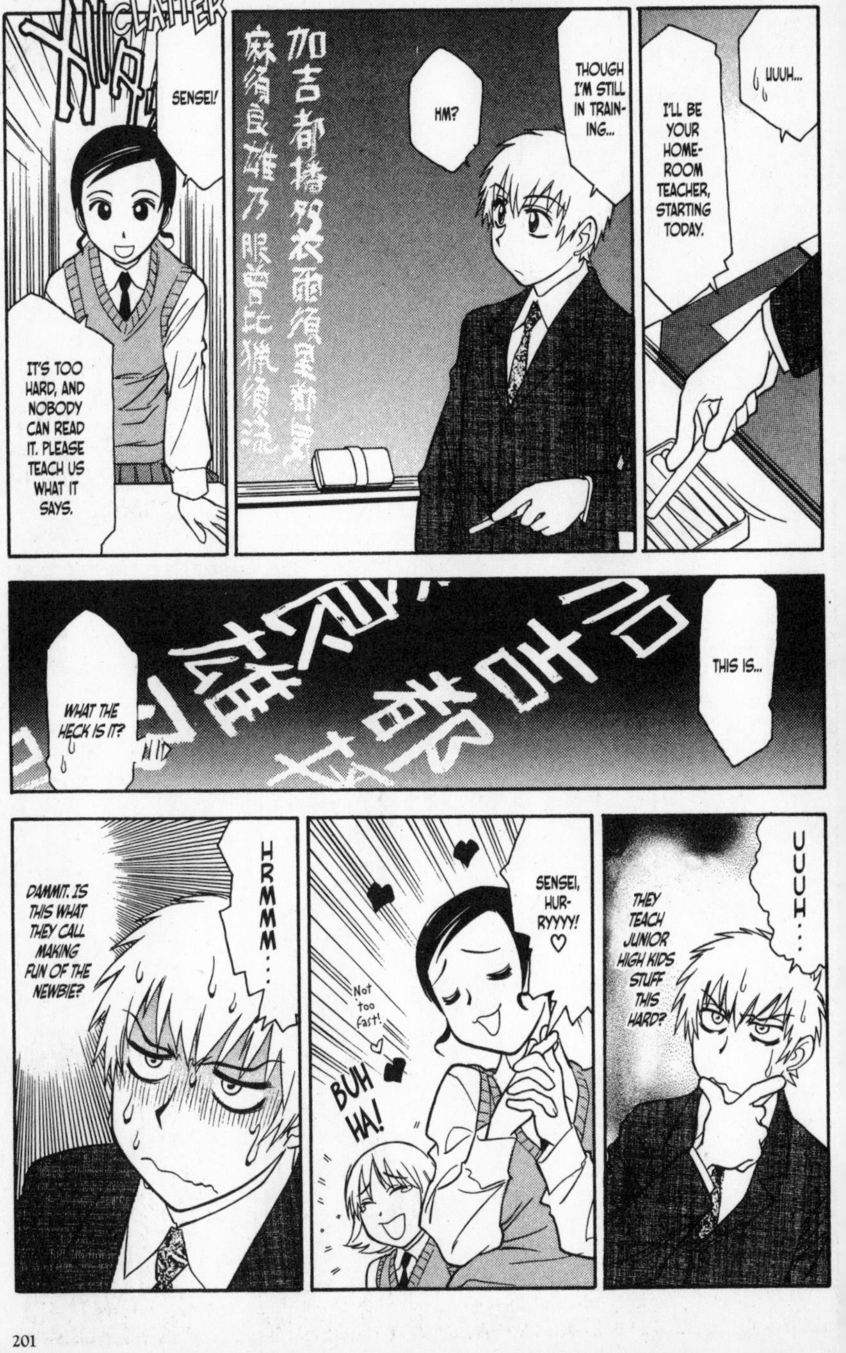
UUUH...
I'LL BE YOUR HOME-ROOM TEACHER, STARTING TODAY.
THOUGH I'M STILL IN TRAIN-ING...
HM?
CLATTER
SENSEI!
IT'S TOO HARD, AND NOBODY CAN READ IT. PLEASE TEACH US WHAT IT SAYS.
THIS IS...
WHAT THE HECK IS IT?
UUUH...
THEY TEACH JUNIOR HIGH KIDS STUFF THIS HARD?
SENSEI, HUR-RYYYY! ♡
Not too fast! ♡
BUH HA!
HRMMM...
DAMMIT. IS THIS WHAT THEY CALL MAKING FUN OF THE NEWBIE?

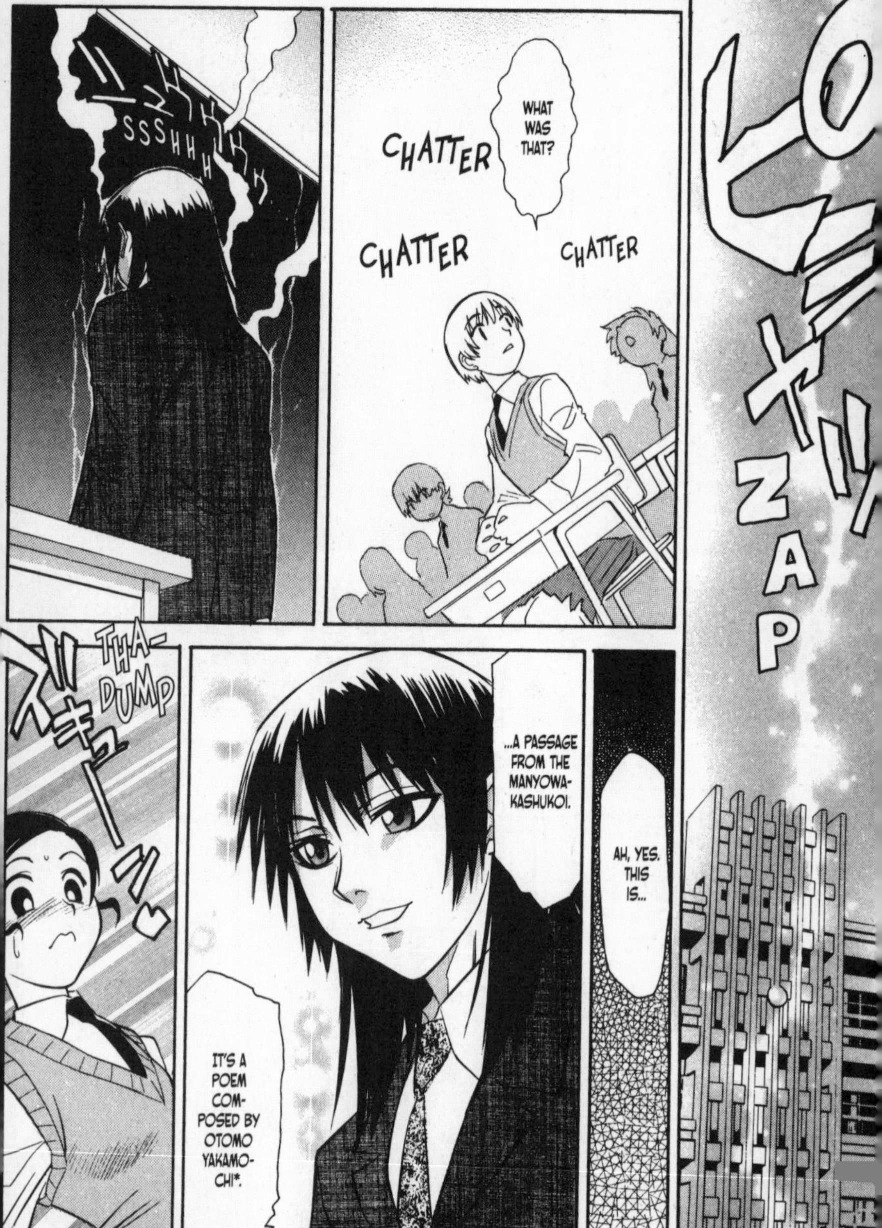
ZAP
CHATTER
WHAT WAS THAT?
CHATTER
CHATTER
SSSHHHH
AH, YES. THIS IS...
...A PASSAGE FROM THE MANYOWA-KASHUKOI.
IT'S A POEM COM-POSED BY OTOMO YAKAMO-CHI*.
THA-DUMP

*See translator's notes

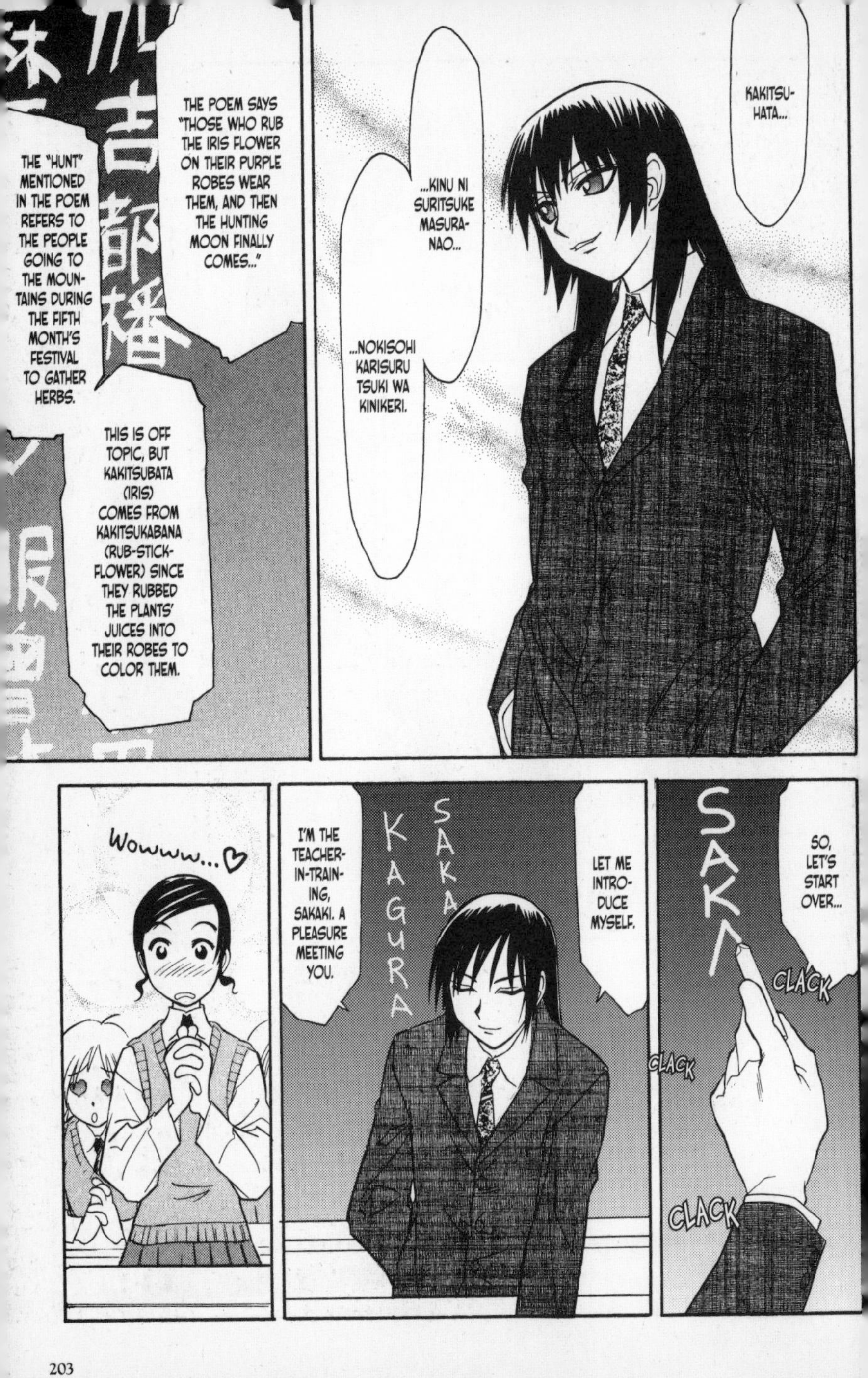
KAKITSU-HATA...
...KINU NI SURITSUKE MASURA-NAO...
...NOKISOHI KARISURU TSUKI WA KINIKERI.
THE POEM SAYS "THOSE WHO RUB THE IRIS FLOWER ON THEIR PURPLE ROBES WEAR THEM, AND THEN THE HUNTING MOON FINALLY COMES..."
THE "HUNT" MENTIONED IN THE POEM REFERS TO THE PEOPLE GOING TO THE MOUN-TAINS DURING THE FIFTH MONTH'S FESTIVAL TO GATHER HERBS.
THIS IS OFF TOPIC, BUT KAKITSUBATA (IRIS) COMES FROM KAKITSUKABANA (RUB-STICK-FLOWER) SINCE THEY RUBBED THE PLANTS' JUICES INTO THEIR ROBES TO COLOR THEM.
SAKA
SO, LET'S START OVER...
CLACK
CLACK
CLACK
LET ME INTRO-DUCE MYSELF.
SAKA
KAGURA
I'M THE TEACHER-IN-TRAIN-ING, SAKAKI. A PLEASURE MEETING YOU.
Wowww...♥

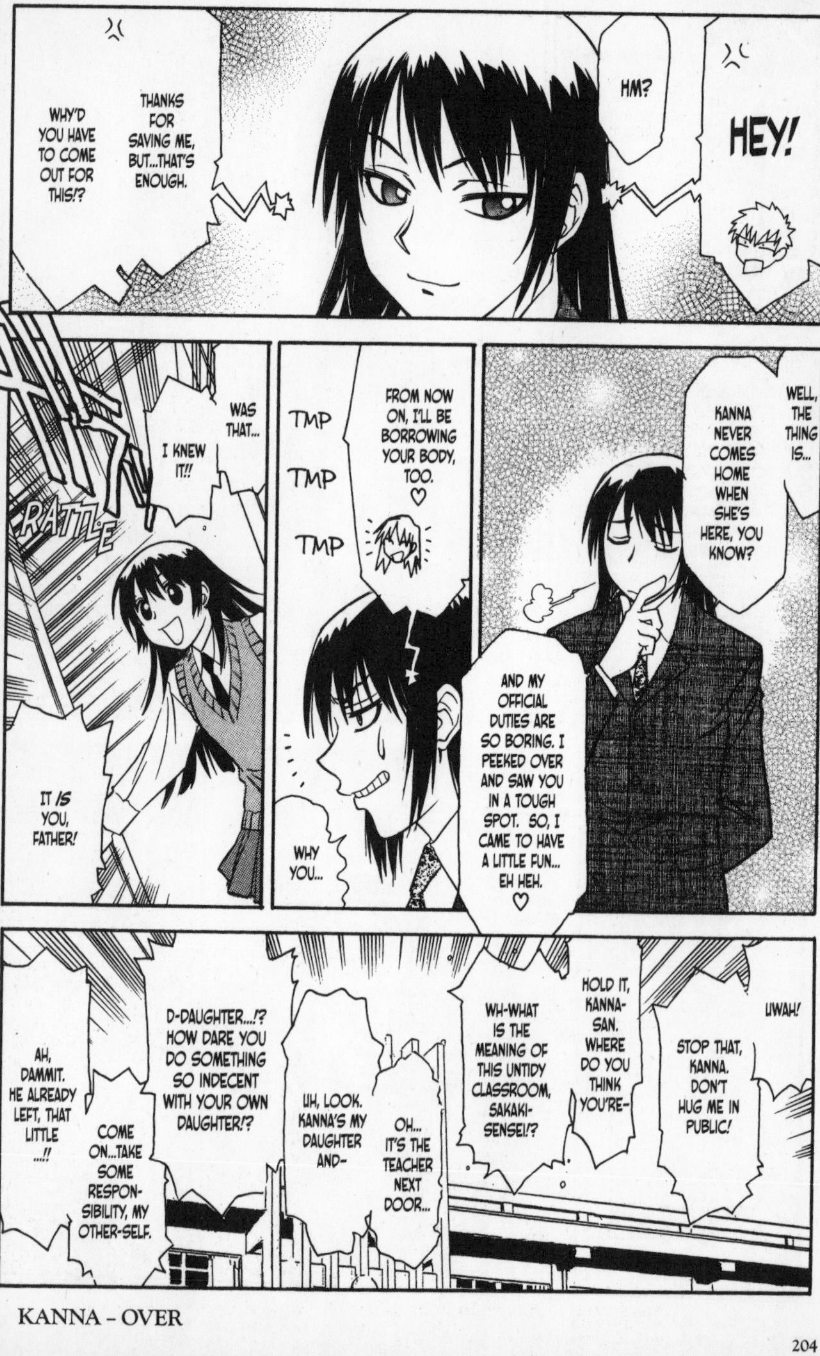
HEY!
HM?
THANKS FOR SAVING ME, BUT...THAT'S ENOUGH.
WHY'D YOU HAVE TO COME OUT FOR THIS!?
WELL, THE THING IS...
KANNA NEVER COMES HOME WHEN SHE'S HERE, YOU KNOW?
AND MY OFFICIAL DUTIES ARE SO BORING. I PEEKED OVER AND SAW YOU IN A TOUGH SPOT. SO, I CAME TO HAVE A LITTLE FUN... EH HEH. ♡
FROM NOW ON, I'LL BE BORROWING YOUR BODY, TOO. ♡
TMP
TMP
TMP
WHY YOU...
WAS THAT...
I KNEW IT!!
RATTLE
IT *IS* YOU, FATHER!
UWAH!
STOP THAT, KANNA. DON'T HUG ME IN PUBLIC!
HOLD IT, KANNA-SAN. WHERE DO YOU THINK YOU'RE-
WH-WHAT IS THE MEANING OF THIS UNTIDY CLASSROOM, SAKAKI-SENSEI!?
OH... IT'S THE TEACHER NEXT DOOR...
UH, LOOK. KANNA'S MY DAUGHTER AND-
D-DAUGHTER...!? HOW DARE YOU DO SOMETHING SO INDECENT WITH YOUR OWN DAUGHTER!?
COME ON...TAKE SOME RESPONSIBILITY, MY OTHER-SELF.
AH, DAMMIT. HE ALREADY LEFT, THAT LITTLE ...!!

KANNA - OVER

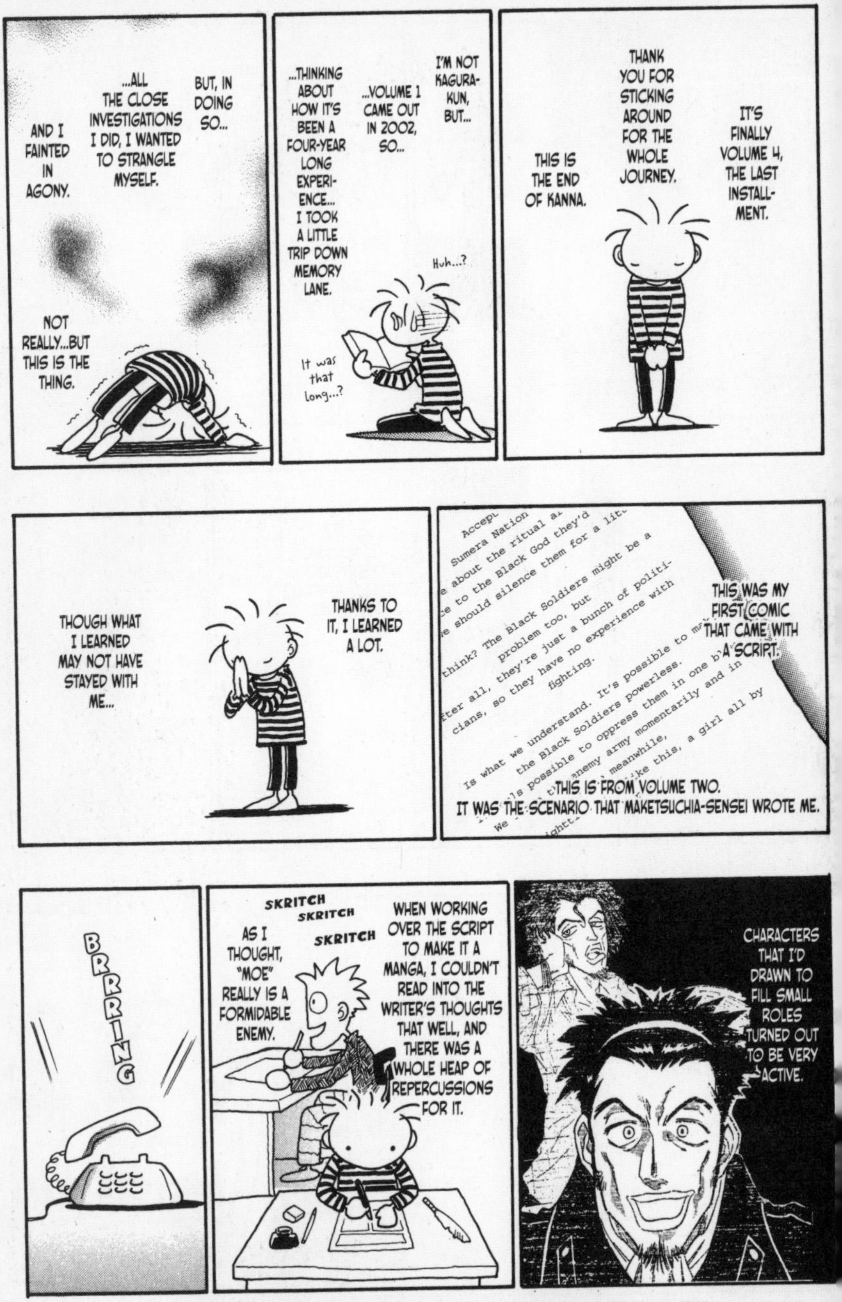
IT'S FINALLY VOLUME 4, THE LAST INSTALL-MENT.
THANK YOU FOR STICKING AROUND FOR THE WHOLE JOURNEY.
THIS IS THE END OF KANNA.
I'M NOT KAGURA-KUN, BUT...
...VOLUME 1 CAME OUT IN 2002, SO...
...THINKING ABOUT HOW IT'S BEEN A FOUR-YEAR LONG EXPERI-ENCE... I TOOK A LITTLE TRIP DOWN MEMORY LANE.
Huh...?
It was that long...?
BUT, IN DOING SO...
...ALL THE CLOSE INVESTIGATIONS I DID, I WANTED TO STRANGLE MYSELF.
AND I FAINTED IN AGONY.
NOT REALLY...BUT THIS IS THE THING.
THIS WAS MY FIRST COMIC THAT CAME WITH A SCRIPT.
Sumera Nation
problem too, but
fighting.
the Black Soldiers powerless.
THIS IS FROM VOLUME TWO.
IT WAS THE SCENARIO THAT MAKETSUCHIA-SENSEI WROTE ME.
THANKS TO IT, I LEARNED A LOT.
THOUGH WHAT I LEARNED MAY NOT HAVE STAYED WITH ME...
CHARACTERS THAT I'D DRAWN TO FILL SMALL ROLES TURNED OUT TO BE VERY ACTIVE.
WHEN WORKING OVER THE SCRIPT TO MAKE IT A MANGA, I COULDN'T READ INTO THE WRITER'S THOUGHTS THAT WELL, AND THERE WAS A WHOLE HEAP OF REPERCUSSIONS FOR IT.
SKRITCH
SKRITCH
SKRITCH
AS I THOUGHT, "MOE" REALLY IS A FORMIDABLE ENEMY.
BRRRING

* SINCE IT'S DIFFICULT TO ADAPT SUCH A THING INTO MANGA STRAIGHT-ON, I HAD TO REARRANGE IT AND SUPPLEMENT IT AND WHATNOT.

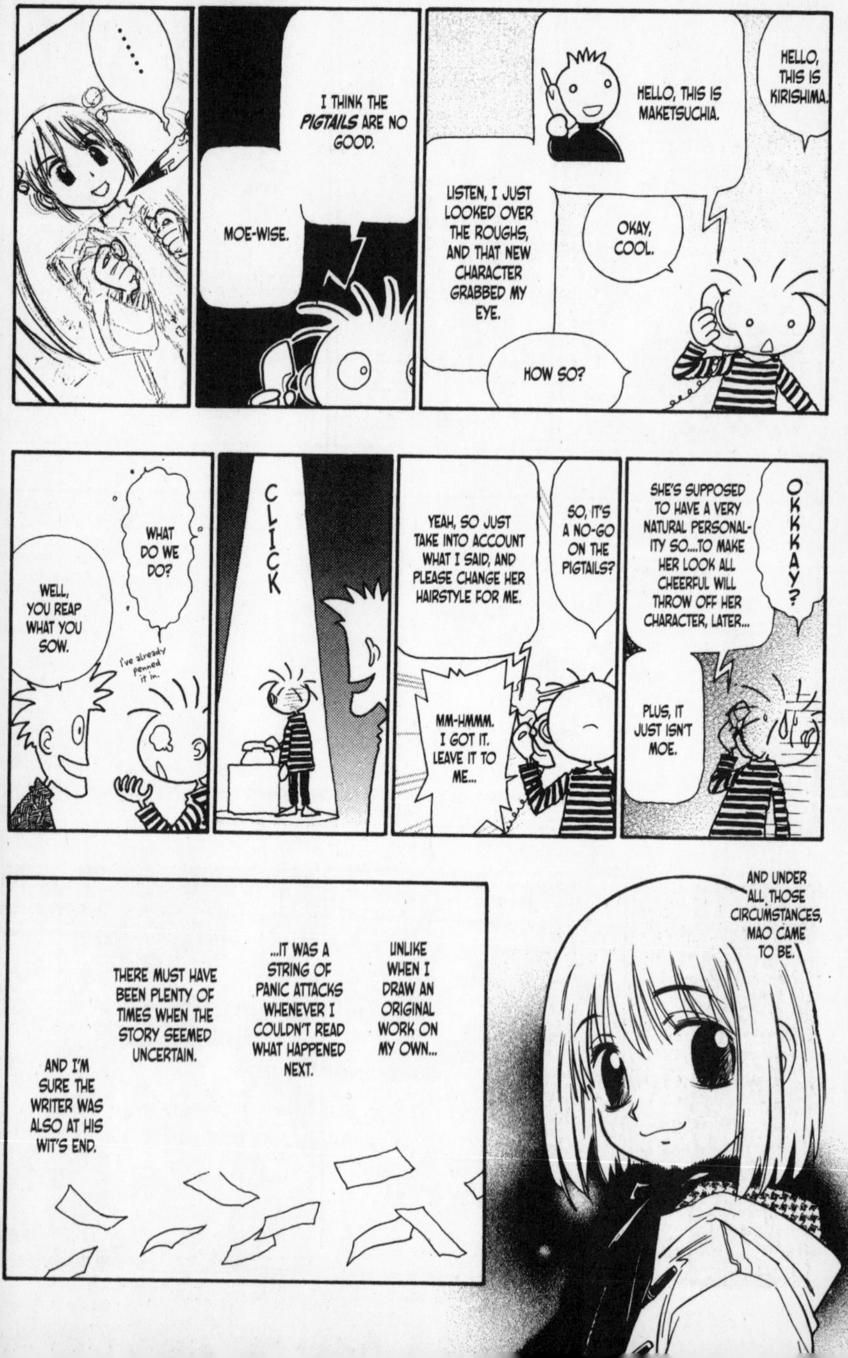
HELLO, THIS IS KIRISHIMA.
HELLO, THIS IS MAKETSUCHIA.
OKAY, COOL.
LISTEN, I JUST LOOKED OVER THE ROUGHS, AND THAT NEW CHARACTER GRABBED MY EYE.
HOW SO?
I THINK THE *PIGTAILS* ARE NO GOOD.
MOE-WISE.
......
OKKKAY?
SHE'S SUPPOSED TO HAVE A VERY NATURAL PERSONAL-ITY SO....TO MAKE HER LOOK ALL CHEERFUL WILL THROW OFF HER CHARACTER, LATER...
PLUS, IT JUST ISN'T MOE.
SO, IT'S A NO-GO ON THE PIGTAILS?
YEAH, SO JUST TAKE INTO ACCOUNT WHAT I SAID, AND PLEASE CHANGE HER HAIRSTYLE FOR ME.
MM-HMMM. I GOT IT. LEAVE IT TO ME...
CLICK
WHAT DO WE DO?
WELL, YOU REAP WHAT YOU SOW.
I've already penned it in.
AND UNDER ALL THOSE CIRCUMSTANCES, MAO CAME TO BE.
UNLIKE WHEN I DRAW AN ORIGINAL WORK ON MY OWN...
...IT WAS A STRING OF PANIC ATTACKS WHENEVER I COULDN'T READ WHAT HAPPENED NEXT.
THERE MUST HAVE BEEN PLENTY OF TIMES WHEN THE STORY SEEMED UNCERTAIN.
AND I'M SURE THE WRITER WAS ALSO AT HIS WIT'S END.

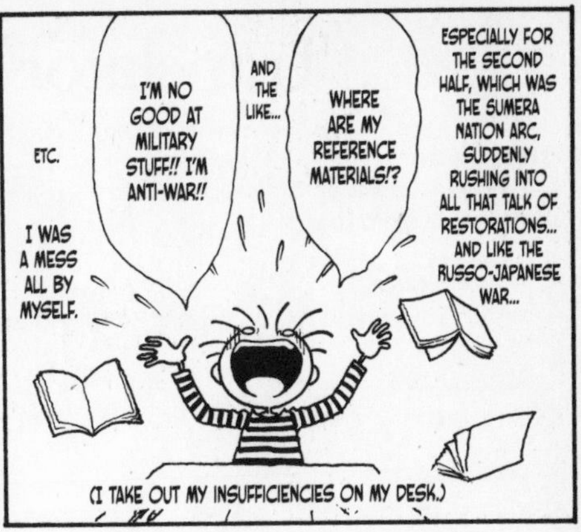
ESPECIALLY FOR THE SECOND HALF, WHICH WAS THE SUMERA NATION ARC, SUDDENLY RUSHING INTO ALL THAT TALK OF RESTORATIONS... AND LIKE THE RUSSO-JAPANESE WAR...
WHERE ARE MY REFERENCE MATERIALS!?
AND THE LIKE...
I'M NO GOOD AT MILITARY STUFF!! I'M ANTI-WAR!!
ETC.
I WAS A MESS ALL BY MYSELF.
(I TAKE OUT MY INSUFFICIENCIES ON MY DESK.)

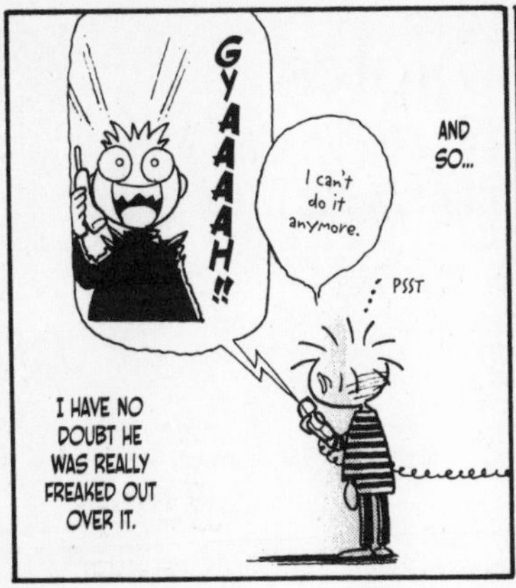
AND SO...
I can't do it anymore.
PSST
GYAAAAH!!
I HAVE NO DOUBT HE WAS REALLY FREAKED OUT OVER IT.

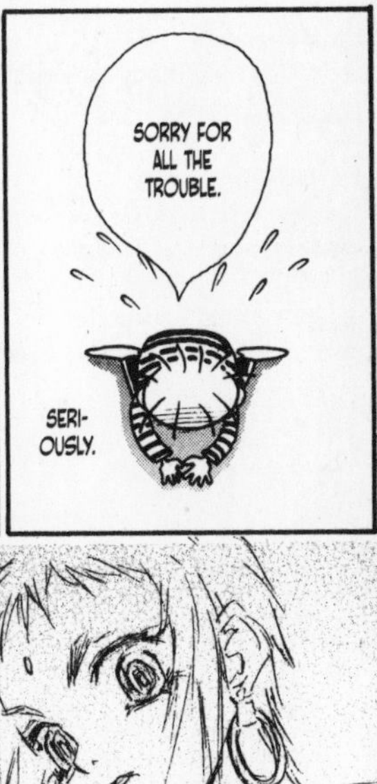
SORRY FOR ALL THE TROUBLE.
SERI-OUSLY.

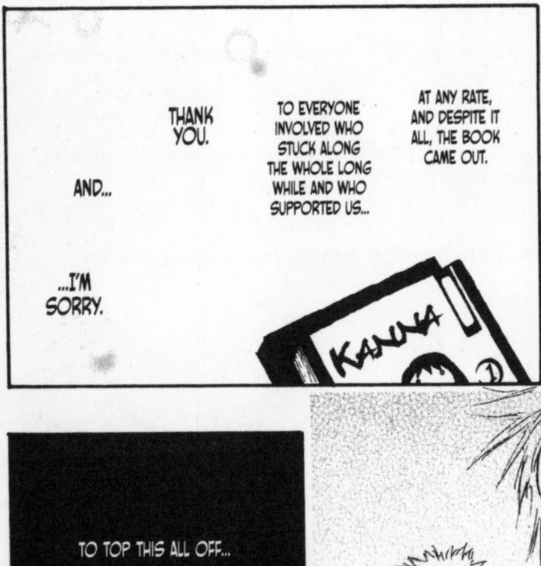
AT ANY RATE, AND DESPITE IT ALL, THE BOOK CAME OUT.
TO EVERYONE INVOLVED WHO STUCK ALONG THE WHOLE LONG WHILE AND WHO SUPPORTED US...
THANK YOU.
AND...
...I'M SORRY.
KANNA
1

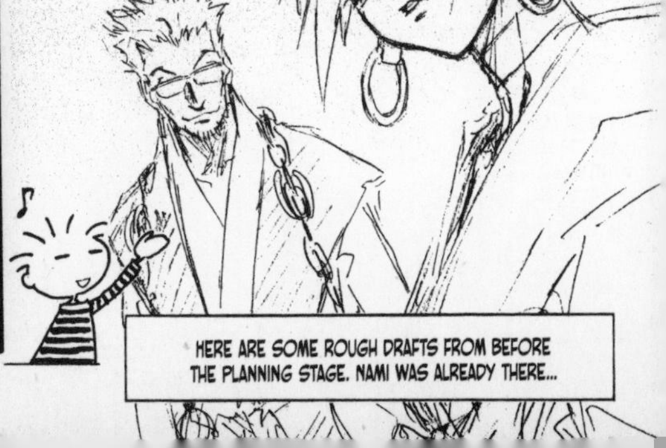
HERE ARE SOME ROUGH DRAFTS FROM BEFORE THE PLANNING STAGE. NAMI WAS ALREADY THERE...

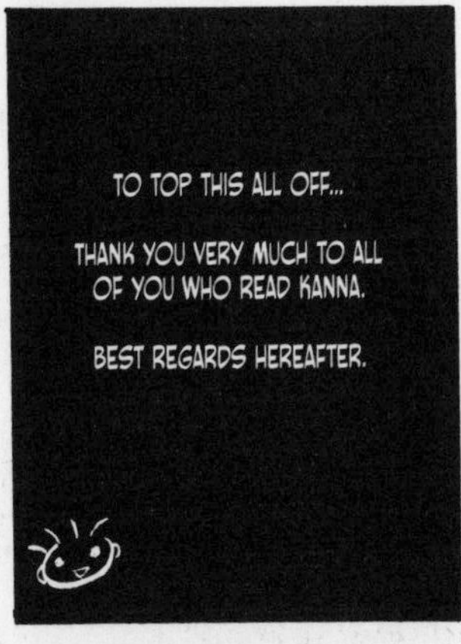
TO TOP THIS ALL OFF...
THANK YOU VERY MUCH TO ALL OF YOU WHO READ KANNA.
BEST REGARDS HEREAFTER.

THE END

Translator's Notes

Pg. 31 – *longmai*
Written as 龍脈 , this means "dragon pulse". It refers to the flow of *chi* in the earth and is considered similar to blood vessels in the human body.

Pg. 77 – *jinosukutsuu*
One of the Six Superhuman powers – the ability to transport yourself.

Pg. 92 – *tashintsuu*
The ability to read another person's heart. Similar to telepathy, but in a much more spiritual sense.

Pg. 152 – *seimon*
Broken down, this means "voice" and "gate." In modern usage, the word literally means "glottis," but context here suggests the more fantastic meaning of "voice gateway" or something similar.

Pg. 152 – *engaku*
A Buddhist term. In original Sanskrit it is "*pratyekabuddha*" which means "a world where one can feel fate and enjoy Enlightenment."

Pg. 199 – *onmyo*
This probably refers to *Onmyo-Do*, which was a science thousands of years ago. It was based on oriental astrology, the almanac, various methods of fortune-telling, and the mystical Tao religion.

Pg. 202– Otomo Yakamochi
Born circa 718, he was a Japanese statesman and poet, and a member of the Thirty-six Poetry Immortals.

They finally
built a better
boyfriend.

A.I. REVOLUTION

by Yuu Asami

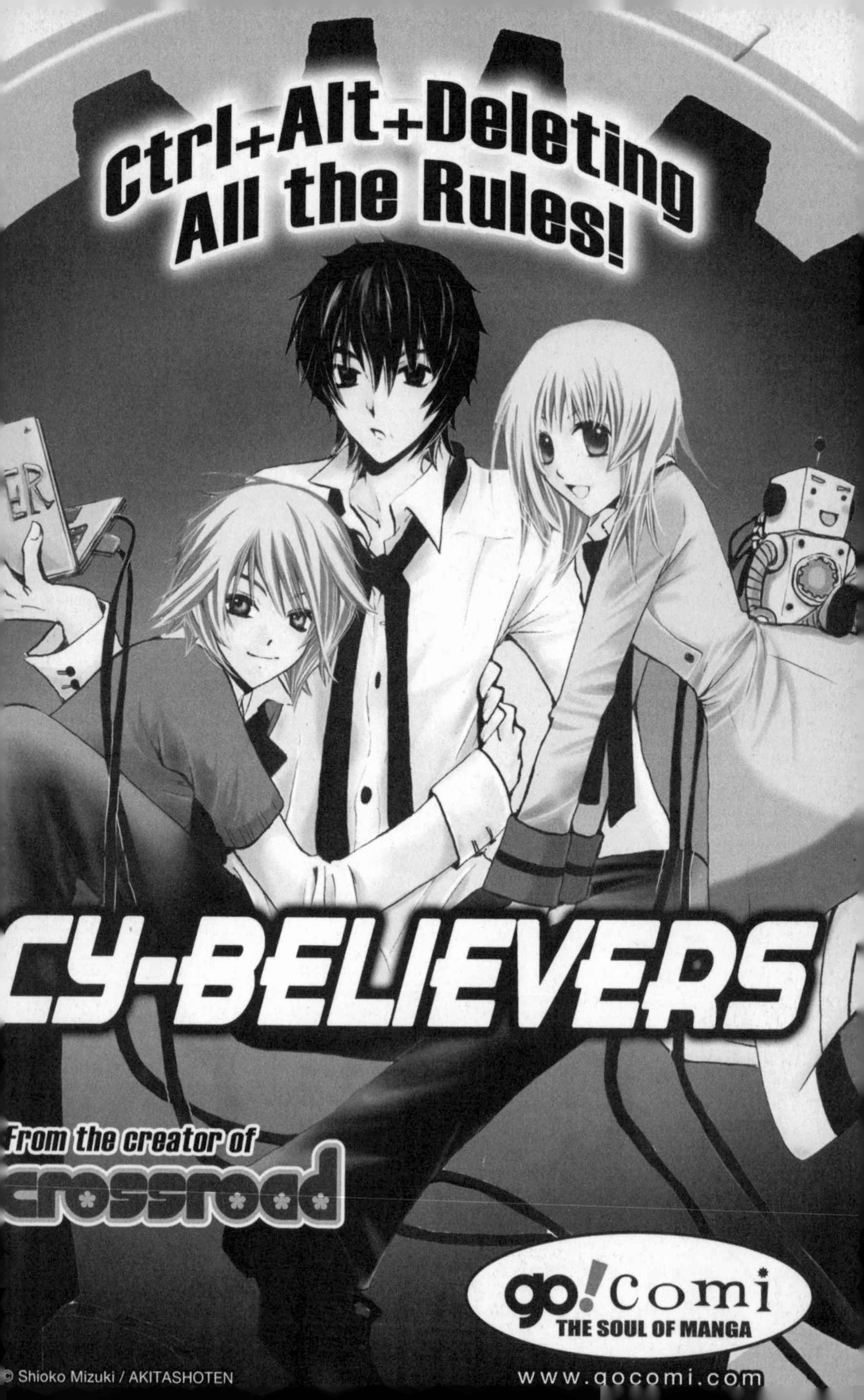
Ctrl+Alt+Deleting
All the Rules!
CY-BELIEVERS
From the creator of
crossroad
go!comi
THE SOUL OF MANGA
© Shioko Mizuki / AKITASHOTEN
www.gocomi.com

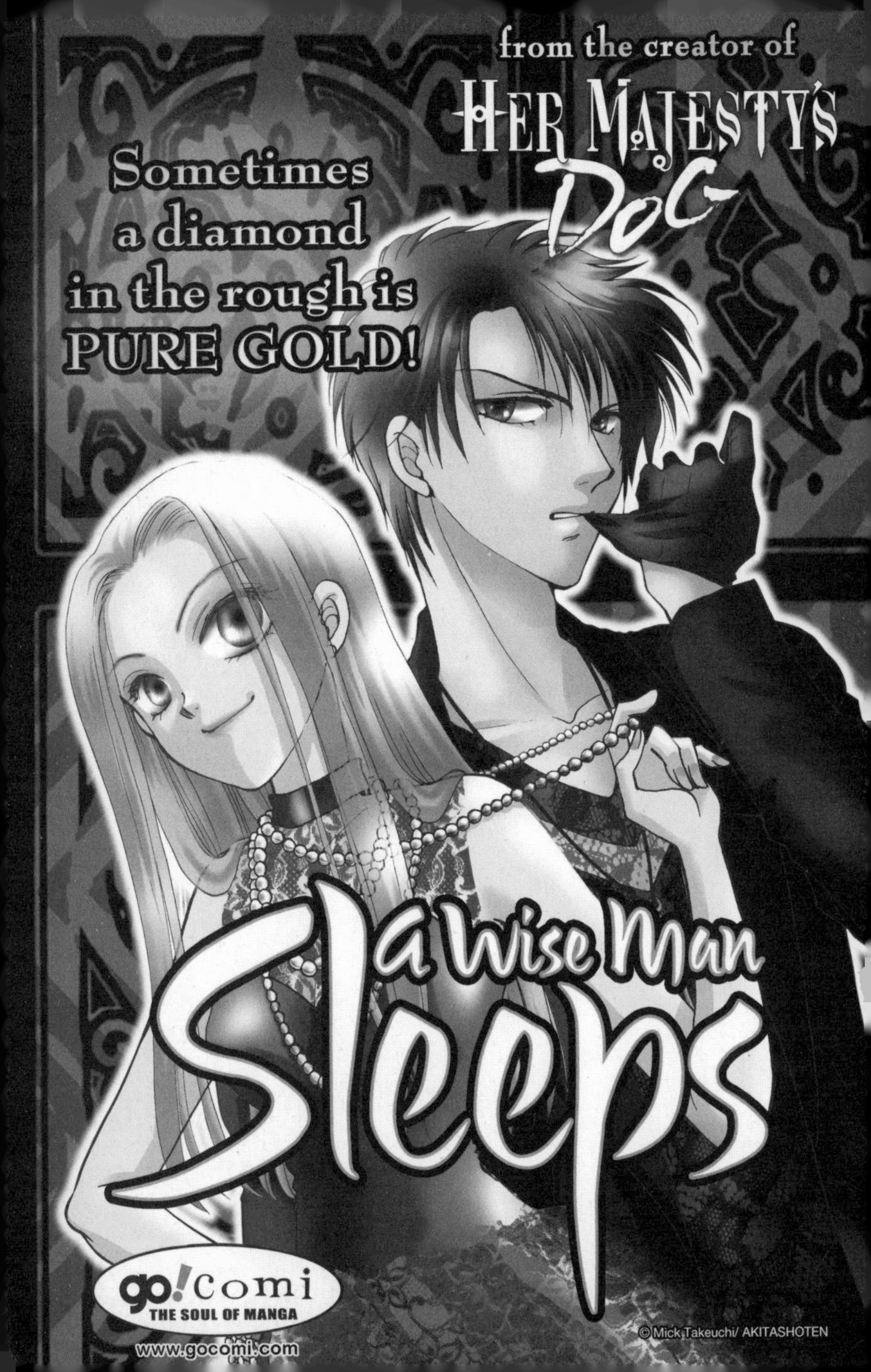

from the creator of
HER MAJESTY'S DOG
Sometimes a diamond in the rough is PURE GOLD!
A Wise Man Sleeps
go!comi
THE SOUL OF MANGA
www.gocomi.com
© Mick Takeuchi/ AKITASHOTEN

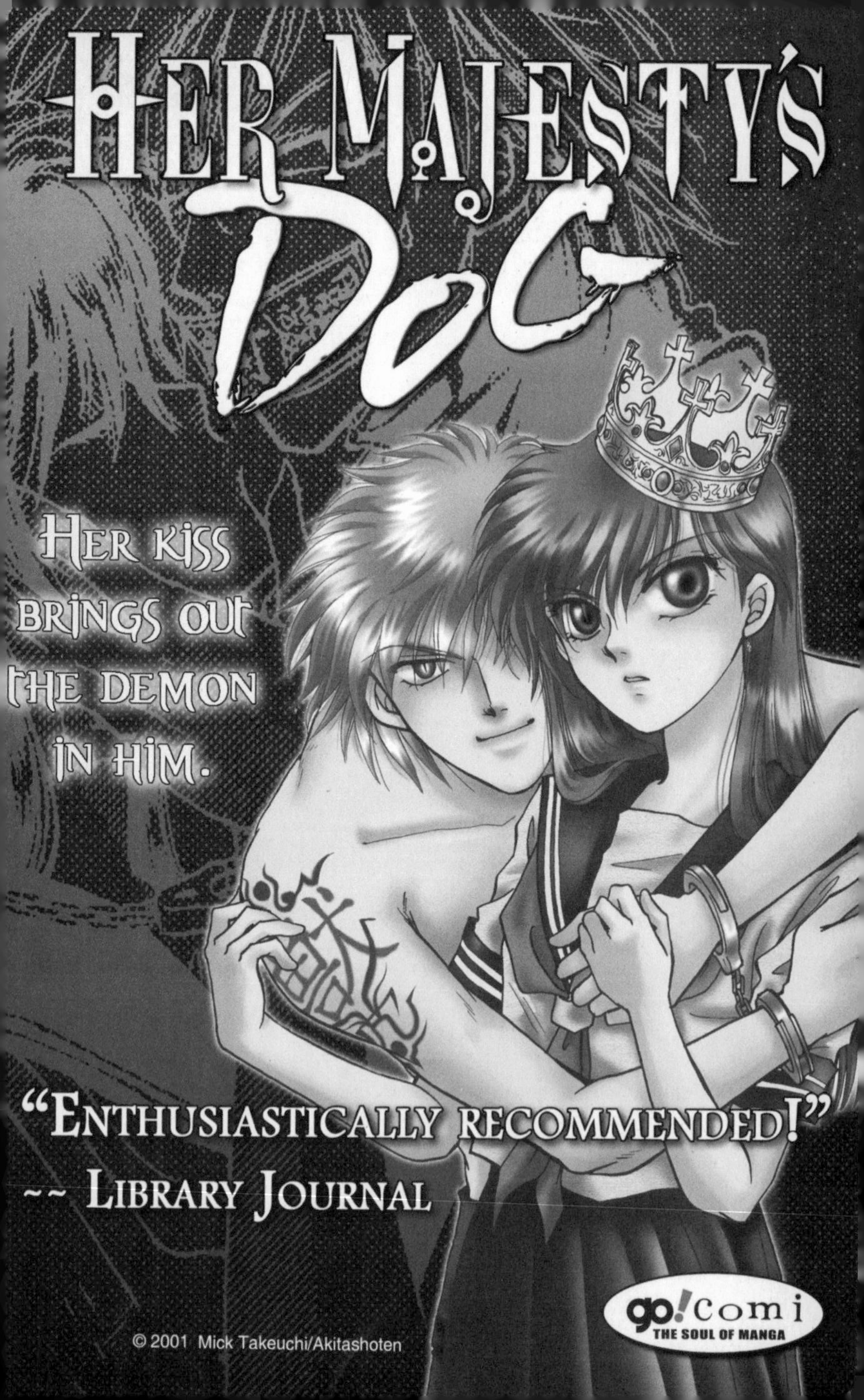
HER MAJESTY'S DOG
HER KISS BRINGS OUT THE DEMON IN HIM.
"ENTHUSIASTICALLY RECOMMENDED!"
-- LIBRARY JOURNAL
go!comi
THE SOUL OF MANGA
© 2001 Mick Takeuchi/Akitashoten

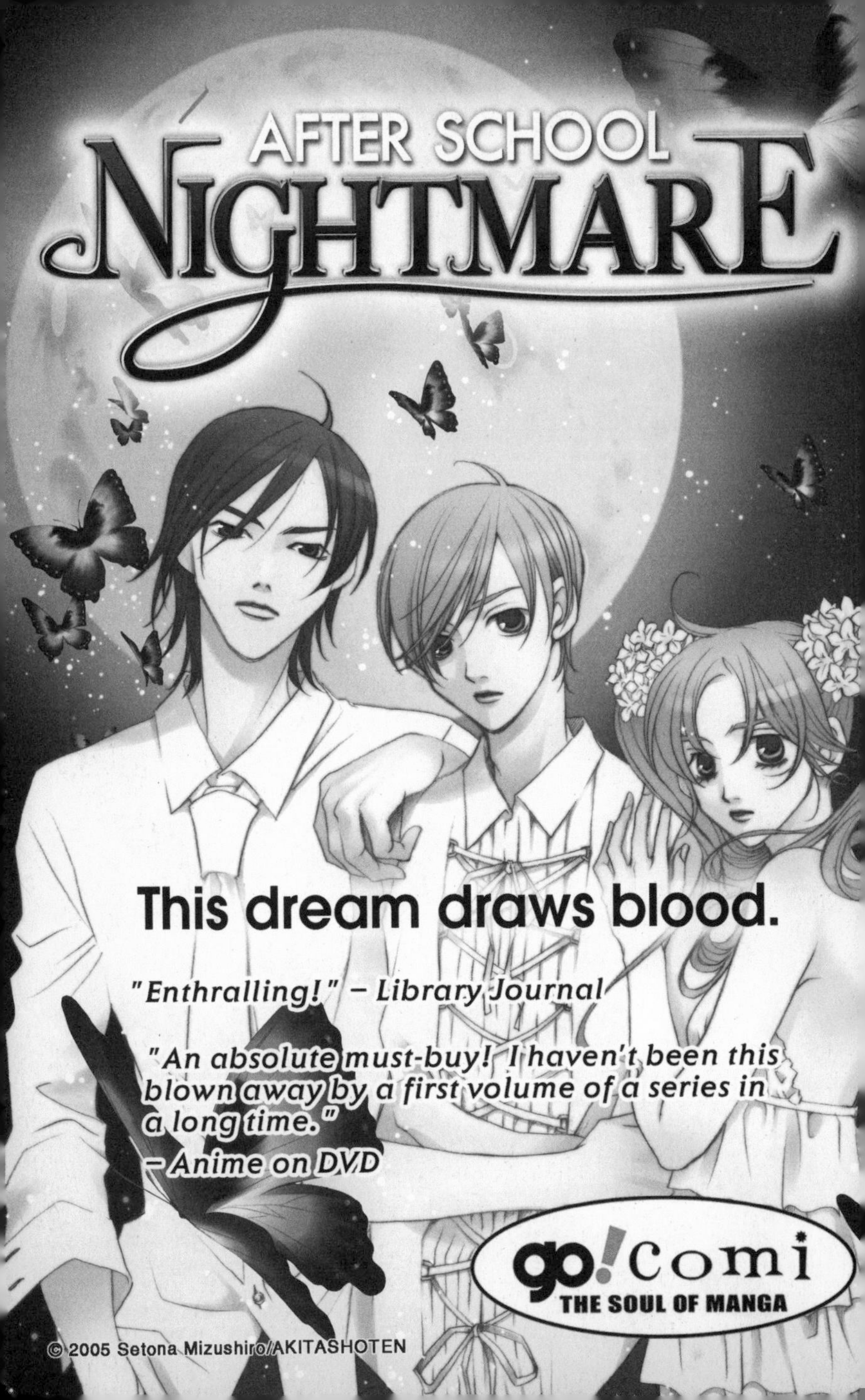
AFTER SCHOOL
NIGHTMARE
This dream draws blood.
"Enthralling!" – Library Journal
"An absolute must-buy! I haven't been this blown away by a first volume of a series in a long time."
– Anime on DVD
go!comi
THE SOUL OF MANGA
© 2005 Setona Mizushiro/AKITASHOTEN

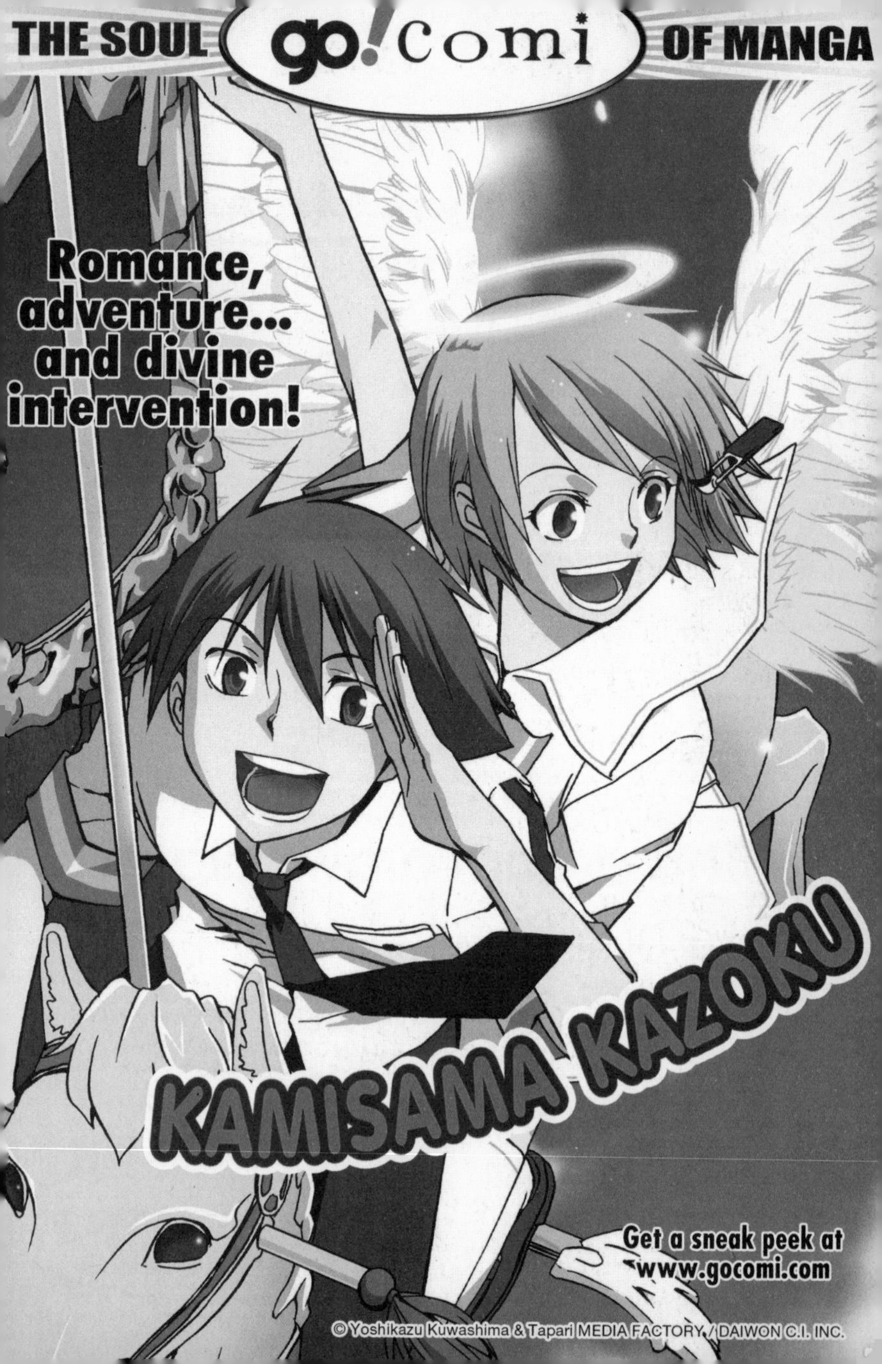
THE SOUL go!comi OF MANGA
Romance, adventure... and divine intervention!
KAMISAMA KAZOKU
Get a sneak peek at www.gocomi.com
© Yoshikazu Kuwashima & Tapari MEDIA FACTORY / DAIWON C.I. INC.

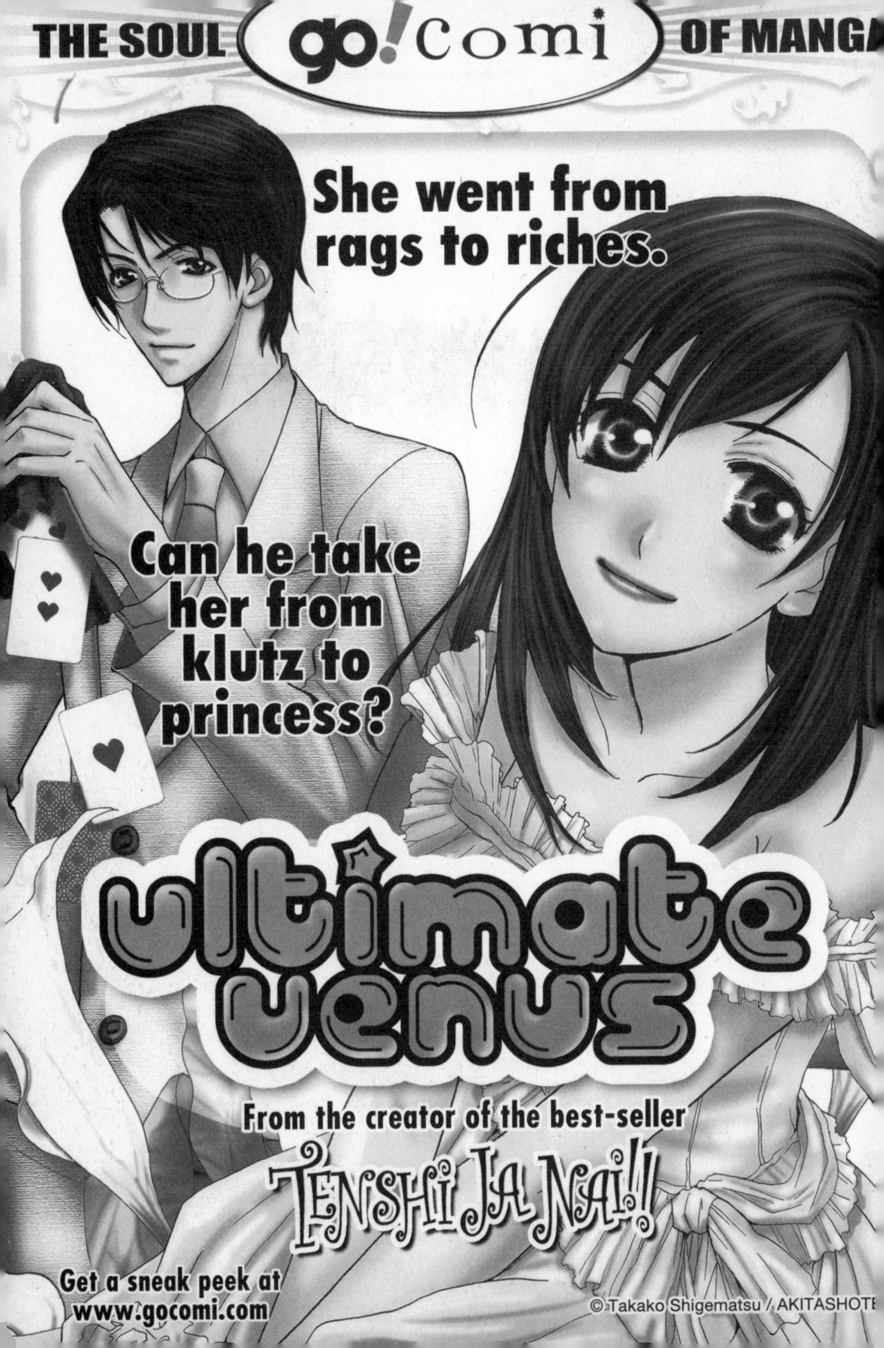
THE SOUL go!comi OF MANGA
She went from rags to riches.
Can he take her from klutz to princess?
ultimate venus
From the creator of the best-seller
TENSHI JA NAI!!
Get a sneak peek at www.gocomi.com
© Takako Shigematsu / AKITASHOTE

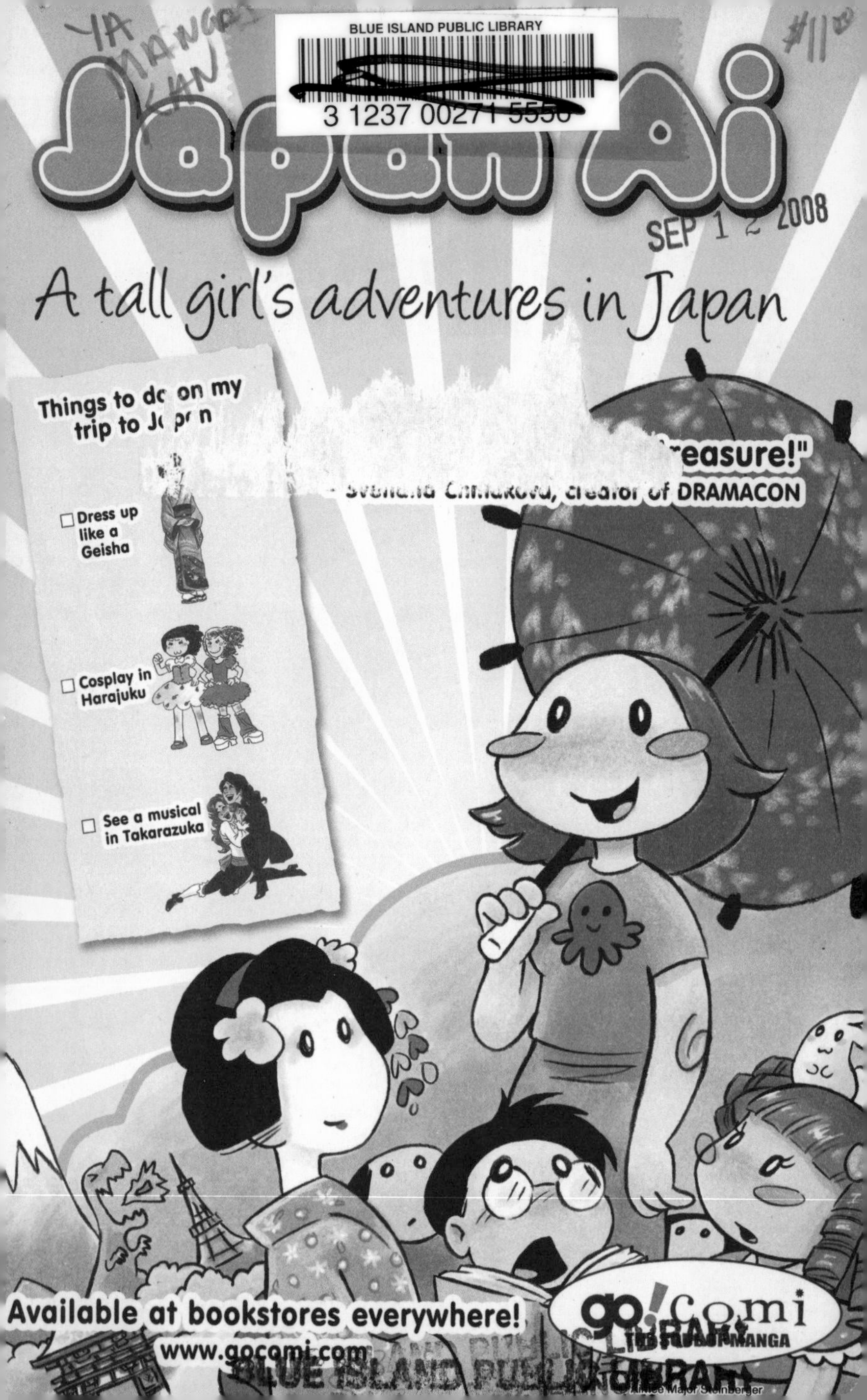
BLUE ISLAND PUBLIC LIBRARY
Japan Ai
SEP 12 2008
A tall girl's adventures in Japan
Things to on my
trip to
Dress up like a Geisha
Cosplay in Harajuku
See a musical in Takarazuka
creator of DRAMACON
Available at bookstores everywhere!
www.gocomi.com
go!comi
BLUE ISLAND PUBLIC LIBRARY
© Aimee Major Steinberger